Also by the Author

100 Questions Every First-Time Home Buyer Should Ask

100 Questions Every Home Seller Should Ask

100 Questions Every Home Seller Should Ask

with Answers from Top Brokers from Around the Country

ILYCE R. GLINK

THREE RIVERS PRESS
NEW YORK

Published by Three Rivers Press, New York, New York.
Member of the Crown Publishing Group.

Random House, Inc. New York, Toronto, London, Sydney, Auckland
www.randomhouse.com

Originally published by Times Books in 1995.

Printed in the United States of America

Library of Congress Cataloging-in-Publication Data

Glink, Ilyce R.
100 questions every home seller should ask : with answers from top brokers from around the country / Ilyce R. Glink.—1st ed.
p. cm.
Includes index.
ISBN 0-8129-2406-1
1. House selling. 2. House selling—United States. I. Title.
II. Title: One hundred questions every home seller should ask.
HD1379.G582 1995
333.33'83—dc20 94-44004

9 8 7

For my husband, Sam.

And for home sellers everywhere:
May you have wind in your sales.

Contents

Preface

As the title implies, this is a book for people who would like to sell their home. I've been asked if homeowners really need a book that will walk them through the process of selling their property. They wonder if it isn't enough to simply stick a "for sale" sign in the front yard and cash the check at the closing. Yes, if you're the kind of person lucky enough to win the lottery. For those who are unlucky, sellers throughout history have developed an arsenal of tactics to improve the salability of their property that begins with prayer and includes regularly burning incense. And there's a whole group of sellers who believe if you bury certain religious icon (I've been told it's a statue of Saint Joseph) upside down in your backyard, you'll sell your home within a matter of weeks. They say it works no matter what religion you practice.

But the majority of home sellers shouldn't rely on luck,

prayer, or what's buried in the garden when it comes to selling their biggest asset. The most successful sellers plan and prepare for the sale of their home. They know that spending a few dollars in the right places will help their home stand out from the competition; they know that this investment might even reap hundreds or thousands of dollars of instant profit. They know choosing the right broker—or choosing not to use a broker—can make all the difference. And they recognize that when you're trying to sell in a buyer's market, you need all the help you can get.

I wrote this book as a companion to my first book, *100 Questions Every First-Time Home Buyer Should Ask.* The idea came from a conversation I had with a homeowner who was transferred by her employer a short time after she had bought and moved into her first home. Still shocked by the thought of moving so soon, she asked what she should do next. As I tried to help her find an answer, I discovered that sellers all over the country ask the same basic questions about this complicated, emotional process. Once again, it became clear that not every seller remembers to ask every question. And when it comes to selling your home, those unanswered questions can take a bite out of your profits, and make the entire process less pleasant than it could be.

That's because the path that leads to the successful sale of your home is often filled with difficult twists and turns, plus plenty of potholes. I hope that *100 Questions Every Home Seller Should Ask* will help you find your bearing. I've tried to organize this book so that it will mirror your own experiences, and phrased the questions in the way I thought you'd ask them yourself. There are two ways to read this book: You can start with the introduction and read straight through Question 100. Or you can pick it up when you have a specific question that requires immediate attention. I recommend you do both.

One final thought: As I was writing this book, my husband, Sam, and I sold our second home. Needless to say, I wish I had written the end before we had even begun to think about our sale. I hope you learn as much from our mistakes as we did from making them.

Good luck!

Ilyce R. Glink
January 1995

P.S. If you have a question that wasn't answered in the book, or if you'd like to share your home-selling experiences, you may write to me at the following address: Ilyce R. Glink, Real Estate Matters Syndicate, P.O. Box 366, Glencoe, Illinois 60022. My internet address is IlyceGlink@aol.com.

100 Questions Every Home Seller Should Ask

Introduction

There are few moments as confusing as the moment you realize the time has come to sell your home.

In that singular moment, most sellers are awash with emotions ranging from near hysteria to giddy acceptance. Your home has been your castle, your safe haven, the center of your family's universe. You have lived there happily with your spouse or partner, and perhaps with children, an aged parent, a beloved pet. You have planted gardens, raked leaves, painted walls, added rooms, cleaned gutters, and replaced windows, roofs, hot water heaters, and who knows what else. You have spent a fortune on mortgage payments, real estate taxes, and water and sewer bills, and you have invested an enormous effort to make it the best home it could be.

And yet the time has come to say good-bye to this houseful of memories and take a step forward. Some *four million* families—nearly eight each minute—will sell their homes this year. Some will sell because the head of the household has been offered a big promotion requiring an out-of-state transfer. Some will sell because they have begun to have families and have run out of space for the children and their toys and pets and mess. Some will sell so their children can go to better schools, or so they will be closer to work or to their houses of worship. Some will sell because they have had a reversal of fortune, lost their jobs, become disabled, gotten divorced, or experienced some other calamity too emotionally, physically, or financially difficult to deal with. Some will sell because their aging parents need to move in with them but require separate, special quarters. Some will sell because their children have grown and started lives of their own and the house suddenly seems much too big, or because their home is located in a city that suddenly seems too cold in winter. Some will sell because their parents, who spent a lifetime in that house, have died and they, the next generation, have already bought homes of their own in a different part of the state or country.

There are dozens of reasons you might want to—or have to—sell your home. In retrospect, making the decision may seem to have been the easy part. Once the decision is made, the chaos and confusion that go hand in hand with selling your home begin. You must decide how much you want to fix up your home before you put it on the market, then choose a broker, negotiate the commission, and determine a listing price. You must keep your house clean and be ready to show it on a moment's notice. You must host brokers' lunches and weekend open houses. And that's just the beginning. Meanwhile, you're juggling the move you must now make. You're wondering if you should make an offer on another home before you sell. You're trying to calculate how much money you'll get from the sale of your home. You're concerned about whether your prospective buyer will find problems with your home.

Most sellers have an unending stream of questions—as well they should. Whether you've never sold a home before or you've sold several, selling your home today can be complex, confusing, and frustrating. Why? The answer is simple: The residential real estate game has changed.

Today's sellers face a myriad of incredibly intricate issues, compounded in recent years by a plethora of sophisticated changes in the laws of agency and brokerage. Seller disclosure—where the seller must disclose everything he or she knows about a home that might materially and adversely affect its value—and buyer brokerage—where the agent or "buyer's" broker takes on the fiduciary duty to the buyer instead of the seller—have come up on the horizon, and state laws that address the responsibility of the seller are changing. Plus, in our litigious society, more buyers are apt to sue the seller, along with the seller's broker, if something goes wrong with the home after closing. All of these changes have made it more important than ever for home sellers to educate themselves: Instead of *caveat emptor* ("buyer beware"), real estate professionals now say "seller be warned."

Another significant factor affecting sellers is that the residential real estate market has shifted again. Once the super-high interest rates (15 to 18 percent) of the early 1980s faded away, sellers controlled the market, which meant there was more demand for homes than housing stock to satisfy it. Prices escalated grandly, sometimes as much as 15 or 20 percent in a single year. Many markets became overpriced, and folks who purchased homes in 1988 or 1989 bought at the peak. As we moved into the 1990s, and into one of the worst recessions since the 1930s, buyers stopped buying. Those homeowners who bought high and needed to sell suffered. That buyer's market made it especially difficult for sellers who needed to sell their homes fast and get out. Those sellers, particularly in southern California and New England, took huge losses. In San Francisco, Los Angeles, New York, and New Jersey some properties fell more than 50 percent in value.

Only now, in the mid-1990s, are we beginning to see the marketplace restored to some sort of equilibrium. Much of this is due to the drop in interest rates to their lowest levels in thirty years. Sellers who refinanced their big homes are staying in them. Fewer homes are being put on the market, but buyers—buoyed by a stronger national economy—are out in force. There is more demand for fewer houses. It seems, finally, homeowners are beginning to enjoy the first real sellers' market in nearly a decade.

Another factor at work is that buyers today are a lot more sophisticated and knowledgeable about the home-buying process. They know that the dollar is power and that it rests in their hands. They have come to embrace buyer brokerage, and demand seller disclosure and home warranties. They try to renegotiate after inspections, and understand that in a tight buyer's market you'll be happy that they're interested at all. Yet that sophistication also means today's buyers recognize a house that's priced fairly. After my husband, Sam, and I sold our home in Chicago, we wanted to move to one of Chicago's older suburbs. This was 1994, and houses that were priced right would literally sell overnight. For a few months in the early part of the year, some homes were receiving multiple offers on the day they were listed. In fact, I remember calling our broker to ask about one house only to be told that the house had come on the market on Tuesday and the seller had received four offers by Thursday.

These subtle shifts in the marketplace have troubling implications for sellers: Your home might sit on the market for a lot longer today than in the early to mid-1980s, and you may have difficulties even in getting an offer for it. Or, if it sells quickly, you may well wonder if you underpriced your home. (Your broker will never say that. She'll reassure you that your home was priced "just right" or "at the market.")

In some respects, sellers who choose to forge ahead alone have the toughest time of all. FSBO (pronounced "fizz-bo") is the common acronym for homes that are "for sale by owner." But the connotations run much deeper. Until now, when technology has begun to open up marketing avenues to FSBO properties that were formerly the domain of real estate agents, sellers who chose to sell their own property found it difficult to adequately advertise and market the availability of their homes. Brokers, who until the early 1990s primarily worked for the sellers, didn't risk showing FSBO property to their buyers for fear they wouldn't receive a commission. Today, sophisticated sellers in hot markets understand that if they play their cards right, they can sell their home without a broker. Or they cooperate with a buyer's broker and pay only 2.5 to 3.5 percent of the sales price as a commission instead of a full 5 to 7 percent. On a $100,000 house, that extra $3,000 might mean the difference between profit and loss, especially in areas hard-hit by the recession of the early 1990s.

In a slow sellers' market, you must either get lucky—and have the right buyer walk through your front door—or utilize every resource available. That may mean hiring a broker, increasing the commission to the selling broker, and offering incentives. Even in a balanced market, where the number of buyers roughly equals the number of sellers, selling property can be a very tricky business.

Redlining, Steering, and the Signage War

Today's sellers must confront the issues of the 1990s (like buyer brokerage, seller disclosure, agency disclosure, and new state laws that seem to pop up like tulips in spring), but there are old issues to deal with as well. One of the more heinous is known as *redlining*, so named because lenders used to take a red pencil and outline areas of a city or its suburbs where they would not make loans to prospective buyers. Essentially, they excluded certain kinds of people from purchasing property in certain kinds of neighborhoods, cutting down the numbers of available buyers.

The practice of *steering*, where a broker attempts to steer buyers to, or away from, a particular suburb, also continues. But it has become a subtle art, practiced at an almost subconscious level in order to stay one step ahead of increasingly sophisticated buyers and sellers. As a knowledgeable seller, you shouldn't care who purchases your house as long as they have the financial wherewithal to do so. But for some reason, in some areas, a few brokers continue to care. African Americans, Hispanics, and Asians who strive to move out of immigrant neighborhoods often face the more horrific forms of this hateful type of prejudice. But it happens to minority Caucasian groups as well. One couple, who happen to be Jewish, asked their broker if she thought they would like living in a particular exclusive community on the north shore of Chicago known as much for its lack of ethnic diversity as its beautiful homes. "We were told we'd probably be happier living elsewhere," the wife said.

As sellers, one of your greatest issues may concern the "for sale" sign you or your broker puts up in your front yard. That is, if you're allowed by law to place a "for sale" sign at all. Signage wars have become the last resort for many municipalities trying to protect against the scourge of *white flight*. White flight occurs when the Caucasian residents of a community panic at the thought of minorities moving into their community. It starts with a few homeowners who put their homes up for sale and sell to minority families. Then other homeowners in the neighborhood fear that the community is going to pot. They, too, put their homes up for sale. Prices drop, and pretty soon the community has changed. Officials of these cities and villages say prohibiting "for sale" signs is also a way of deflecting *panic peddling*, an illegal and unethical practice in which brokers will try to get business by telling homeowners that they'd better sell before the "undesirables" move in and destroy their property values. Community activists and housing authorities often take the municipal government's side in the signage wars because they, too, believe that homeowners can be spooked by too many "for sale" signs in a neighborhood at once. On the other hand, prohibiting "for sale" signs has been construed by some courts as a violation of your First Amendment rights to free speech. You have a constitutional right to say what you want to say, and that includes the right to say your home is for sale. And, fair rights activists argue, folks got used to seeing plenty of "for sale" signs during the most recent recession, when so many people were losing their jobs and needed to sell their homes.

The bottom line, of course, is that white flight and panic peddling are some of real estate's evil by-products of racism and prejudice. And they must be fought by homeowners of goodwill everywhere. Remember, the color of your home buyer's skin doesn't matter. What matters is that the buyer's money is the same shade of green as yours.

Diversity and Questions of Race

That said, how you handle questions about the racial and ethnic diversity of your neighborhood is important. If you're in the enviable position of having several potential buyers to choose from, you have the right to choose which contract you'll accept. If you base that decision on race or religion instead of, say, the amount of money being offered, that's your choice. But it is against the law to discriminate in advertising. You cannot, for example, tell your broker to bring only white people or black people to showings in your home. If your broker is a member of the local *multiple listing service* (MLS), she must list your property, and any qualified buyer may tour it with a member broker.

Brokers are also obligated by law not to discriminate against potential buyers. They may not steer a home buyer away from one neighborhood toward another. They are also prohibited from disclosing the racial, religious, or ethnic makeup of a community. They are discouraged from revealing crime statistics. (But brokers should tell buyers where they can go to get that information.)

As a seller, you should be equally sensitive when discussing the ethnic, racial, or religious particulars of your community. Your job as a seller is to encourage *everyone* to consider buying your house. You will never know what hot spots or hidden prejudices a potential home buyer may have. If, for example, you stress that your suburb has a "nice working-class white community," you may not know that the buyer wants to live only in an upscale "professional" community;

your seemingly innocent comment may forever turn him or her off from looking to buy in your neighborhood, let alone your house. If the garden-variety person on the street is extremely sensitive today, home buyers are even more so, since they're about to make the most important and expensive financial decision of their lives. They want that choice to be smart and well-informed, and they will listen closely to anything they perceive to be remotely bad about a potential neighborhood.

Before you are asked, think about how you will answer questions about your home and your neighborhood. Take a potential "bad" situation and try to turn it into something positive that will counteract or neutralize potential prejudices.

One of your primary responsibilities as a seller should be to stress the high points about your home and the neighborhood. You want people to like your home and like the location. You want buyers to feel comfortable and relaxed about investing a good chunk of their savings there. You want to be honest in as positive a way as possible. That's one of your primary responsibilities as a seller.

Disclosure

You have other responsibilities, as well. Today, nearly every state requires sellers to disclose problems or conditions that can't readily be seen or detected but that could materially affect the value of the house. For example, if you know your roof leaks in a thunderstorm but you've had the dark brown water stain on your ceiling repaired and painted so the ceiling looks fine, you must disclose the fact that your roof leaks—or has leaked in the past—to a potential buyer. The law differs from state to state, with some states requiring the disclosure in writing while others may let you make it verbally. Many states have written *seller disclosure* forms into their real estate laws. And even if disclosure isn't mandated by the state, many large real estate companies have seller disclosure forms they ask every seller to fill out and sign. These questionnaires are detailed and may seem invasive to sellers who haven't thought much about their home's flaws and peccadillos. But they are a fact of life for sellers, and by the year 2000 every state will likely mandate written seller disclosure.

Pressure

Cleaning your home, setting a listing price, waiting out the offer, and seller disclosure are all pieces of the puzzle. Selling your home may be both the most frustrating and the most rewarding experience of your life. If you sell your home easily, you may wonder why folks shed so many tears over the process. But if you don't have that kind of luck—and luck does, in fact, play a large part in the successful sale of a home—you may find yourself in a pressured situation, particularly if you've gone out and bought another home or if you have to move on a tight timetable. Generally, selling your home *will* be a stressful experience. That is true even for homes that sell quickly, because even if you get an offer the first week your home is on the market, it won't seem fast enough. In fact, offers never come fast enough. And the longer your home is listed, the more agonizing the wait.

I am often asked what sellers can do to relieve the anxiety. Selling your home is a very complex process and takes planning and a lot of hard work to pull off successfully. There are few quick fixes here. If you want to give away your property for less than it's worth, you can probably do it in a few hours. But depending on how hot the market is in your area, selling your home will require time and energy and flexibility. Your kids will resent the constant intrusions, unfamiliar faces tromping through their playground; you will resent sweeping up after them, washing their shoe grime off your kitchen tile floor again and again. You can relieve some of the anxiety by making your home look as good as possible on as little money as possible, choosing a good broker, and pricing the home correctly for the market you're in today. Then all that's left to do is to wait out the storm.

PART I

Am I Ready to Sell?

QUESTION 1

Am I ready to sell?

The decision to sell is psychologically and emotionally complicated. You must decide if, and when, you should leave the protected environment you've called home for the past however many years of your life. The longer you live in your home, the more dramatic and difficult the decision to leave will usually be. A home of one to five years is more easily sold and replaced than a home of thirty years or more, one in which you raised your family and set down roots. It can be heartbreaking to sell a generational home, one in which, perhaps, you were raised yourself.

When the decision to move is made for you, it's as if the rug has been pulled out from underneath your feet. If an employer transfers you or your spouse to another city or state, you may have to sell your home quickly—unless you can afford to rent it. If you get divorced or lose your job, you may find yourself unable to afford the monthly mortgage payments. On the other hand, if you're trading up because you've gotten married, started a family, or received a promotion at work, your time frame for selling may be more flexible. More important, because you've made the decision your emotions are more in check. In these situations, you'll feel better about moving because you're more in control of your house-selling destiny.

Here are some reasons people choose to sell their home:

- *Marriage*. Suddenly, the one-bedroom condo you purchased several years ago doesn't seem quite big enough for the two of you, your spouse's "stuff," and your wedding gifts. You figure it's time to trade up to a two- or three-bedroom house that will accommodate your future family.
- *Children*. A growing family is one of the most frequent reasons people sell their homes. As children grow, they seem to spread out all over the house. With more rooms, you reason, there's a greater chance of containing the spread. You may also want them to benefit from a better school system.
- *Job Promotion*. As families become more affluent, there is a desire to acquire some of the trappings of success, including a bigger and better home. Of course, most families, no matter how well they're doing, will need to sell their current home first and use the equity as a down payment on a larger home. A job

change may also change the distance of the commute to work. Many families sell their home to move to a new area that is close to the spouse's new job.

- *Job Loss.* Losing a job is difficult enough emotionally. When a new job is not easily found, or if the replacement job pays less money with fewer benefits, there can be a devastating domino effect that includes selling the house.
- *Divorce.* If you are counting on two paychecks to pay the mortgage, and one of them disappears, monthly mortgage payments can be devastating financially. Additionally, in most divorce cases, the familial home's equity becomes the primary asset. Either one spouse must buy out the other's share in the home or the home is sold and the equity is split.
- *Aging Parent.* As our parents and grandparents age, they sometimes require specialized living arrangements. If a parent can no longer care for himself or herself, let alone a house, that home may need to be sold. If the parent is going to move in with his or her adult children, separate quarters may need to be built to accommodate special needs, such as a wheelchair, or to add a first-floor bedroom. Or both the parents and the children may need to sell their homes to purchase something large enough and specialized enough to accommodate all their needs.
- *Inheritance.* You may receive a windfall from a family member or friend that includes property. You may not want to live in that home, however, and are considering putting it up for sale.

But whether you choose the timing of your sale, or it is chosen for you, selling and moving are an emotional burden, one that gets heavier as you move further into the process.

One thing you can do to counteract these feelings is to distance yourself emotionally from your home. Brokers say that the moment a homeowner turns into a seller the process goes much more smoothly. What do they mean by that? Well, homeowners tend to be territorial about their homes. That's understandable. After all, a home is where the heart and hearth are. You've filled your home with the possessions of a lifetime, raised your family in it, and put down roots into the community around it. Having potential buyers walk through your personal space is intrusive, to say the least. When they start to poke through your linen cabinets and closets, open every door, get on their hands and knees and inspect your attic or crawl space, and track mud and grime onto your spotless floors—well, it's like having someone tromp through a flower bed with heavy work boots. Homeowners are easily crushed by a potential buyer's negative comments about their home and neighborhood. Their emotional armor, protecting home turf, isn't usually very strong.

Homeowners also tend to be unrealistic about the actual value of their home. They want, and expect, it to be the most valuable house in the community and will overlook the obvious in order to justify those feelings. It doesn't matter that the Smiths' house has an extra bedroom, or that the Bells have an additional half bath, or that the O'Gradys' house sits on a double lot.

Sellers, however, are an entirely different breed. Homeowners become sellers when they detach themselves emotionally from the house. Some brokers say it's when sellers emotionally move out of their home. They no longer look at their property as "their" home. Instead, it becomes a commodity for sale. Nothing more, and nothing less.

And sellers are very interested in what kinds of amenities are contained within the Smiths', Bells', and O'Gradys' homes. They want to know the exact sales price of each recently sold home in the neighborhood, and how many bedrooms, bathrooms, and square feet it has. Suddenly, it may not pay to be the biggest house on the block, because true sellers know that sophisticated buyers don't want to purchase the showpiece home of a neighborhood—there's a better chance for appreciation with a smaller home on a better block.

Sellers welcome prospective buyers with steaming vats of cider and freshly baked cookies or bread. Buyers are invited to treat the house as if it were their own home. They may blacken clean carpets and floors with their muddy boots in winter. They are invited to scrutinize every closet, open the mirrored medicine cabinet, and poke around the basement's nooks and crannies. And should a potential buyer offer a critical comment about the house, a seller will look for ways, if possible, to improve the situation, rather than harbor hurt feelings.

A home seller is realistic about the actual value of his or her home. Sellers look carefully at the broker-prepared *comparative marketing analysis* (CMA) and choose the price that most closely meets the market; they want to price their home where it will sell quickly but not underprice or overprice it. They understand the broker's maxim about selling real estate—"Your first offer is your best offer"—and take it to heart. They want to encourage buyers, not discourage them. It's a completely different stance from a homeowner's territorial urges.

So a homeowner, you see, is a far cry from a home seller. Are you ready to be a home seller? Being a home seller means giving up a certain autonomy; you become dependent, to a greater or lesser extent, on the wills and desires of buyers. But in the end, once you've sold your home, that emotional pre-separation lessens the anxiety of the actual move. You've already distanced yourself from your old home and are looking forward to moving into your new home.

Let's get going.

QUESTION 2

How quickly do I want to move? How quickly do I have to move?

Timing is everything in real estate. In my first book, *100 Questions Every First-Time Home Buyer Should Ask*, I spent a lot of ink discussing the timing issue. I asked readers, How long are you planning to live in your new house? The question is important, because how long you plan to live in your new house should affect each part of the process, including what you buy, when you buy, and how you plan to pay for it. By knowing how long you plan to live in a home, you can make a successful choice.

Timing is important to sellers, too. In some respects, sellers have more important timing issues than buyers. While buyers at least control their involvement in the process (they usually can freely choose when to buy a home), sellers often find themselves in a time crunch. There are external factors at work in the selling process that buyers never face. For example, if your company decides to transfer you across the country, you're not going to have unlimited time to sell your home. Or, if you or your spouse loses a job, and paying the mortgage is dependent upon that income, you might find yourself in a position where you'd have to quickly put up your home for sale. Or, if you've already bought another house and paying two mortgages is quickly depleting your bank account, you probably should sell or rent your original home as quickly as possible.

Of course some sellers have the luxury of time, at least initially. If you want to move your family across town to a bigger house in a better neighborhood, but haven't yet bought that new home, you have some time to play the market. Then there are sellers who simply want to test the market. They say to themselves, "I'll move only if I get my price," and then they put their homes up for sale well above the market price.

How do you figure out what your true motives are for selling? Start by asking yourself these two questions: How quickly do I want to move? How quickly do I have to move? The answers will form the basis for your seller's wish list and reality check. How quickly you *want* to move is the timing situation you hope for, whereas how quickly you *have* to move is the timing situation you, unfortunately, must live with.

Use the following checklist to help you think about where you're going and how quickly you want to, or have to, be there:

- Why am I selling my home?
- What is the ideal month for me to sell my home?
- Ideally, when would I want to move from my home?
- Do I have a definitive date by which I must be out of my home?
- How quickly do I have to sell my home?
- What is the most amount of time I have to sell my home?

Knowing how quickly you want to, or have to, sell your home directly affects the amount of money you're ultimately going to ask for it. In other words, how close to its market price you list your home—also known as listing your home "close to the bone"—will depend on how quickly you want to sell the home and get out. (For more information on pricing your home, see Questions 26 and 27.) There is generally an inverse relationship at work in this situation: The lower the list price, the more quickly you'll get an offer. If you price your house as close to the market price as possible, in a normal, balanced market you should get a good offer relatively quickly. How quickly? Perhaps within a few days, or perhaps within a few weeks. Certainly, there should be some real interest within the first three or four weeks after the home has been listed.

Conversely, the higher your initial list price, the further away it may be from your home's true market price. A higher list price means you'll receive less interest from serious buyers and, perhaps, fewer offers. For the most part, today's home buyers are a savvy bunch: After looking at twenty or thirty homes, they know when one is overpriced, and generally by how much. If your home is overpriced, you'll know because there will be few buyers who come through your door. At the same time, you may hear of other comparable homes that sell, while yours gets stale on the market.

Again, it all comes back to timing. If you want to, or have to, sell your home quickly, you're going to list your home at a lower price. If you want to sell your home in a week—guaranteed!—you can always price it less than its market value. If you want to sell your home in a day, you can price it 10 to 20 percent below market value and take out a huge newspaper ad advertising that fact. That kind of aggressive pricing and marketing will surely bring some offers in a hurry.

Of course, if you have all the time in the world, you have the right to take a flier and list your house above its market value. There may just be a buyer out there who falls in love with your house and *has* to have it, no matter what the price. It happens every day of the year. A New York City homeowner recently named her price for a 3,000-square-foot, three-bedroom pre-World War II vintage residence overlooking the east side of Central Park. The house was priced well above what her broker thought was the market for that home, and yet someone came and fell in love with the views and terrace. And made an offer right on the spot. The condo owner walked away with an extra $300,000 (the original list price was $1.8 million), and the buyer bought himself a terrace overlooking Central Park. And a new market price was set for apartments in that building.

Just remember to start the process of selling your home by knowing when you want to move—and when you have to move.

QUESTION 3

When is the best time to sell my home? What are selling seasons?

Real estate professionals are notorious optimists. If you ask when you should sell your home, almost all will say, "Now is the best time to sell your home." If you ask them when you should buy a home, they'll give you much the same answer. Real estate is an industry of immediacy. If you're smart about the process of buying and selling, you'll do well even in a deflated seller's market like the one we saw during the recession in the early 1990s.

Still, we've all been conditioned to think about buying and selling in terms of seasons. Why is that? Originally, the seasons were summer and fall, corresponding loosely to our basic educational system of semesters. Kids go off to school in September, and parents generally like their kids to be settled by the beginning of the school year; or, if a mid-year move is necessary, then at the beginning of the second semester, in January. The other popular time to move is just after school lets out, in June. As you may remember from your rental days, many apartment rentals begin on either May 1 or October 1. That corresponds roughly to spring and fall, but is a month off our school semester system. According to a *Chicago Tribune* article, one explanation for why the months are slightly off is that landlords figured parents would be highly motivated to keep their kids in school until the end of the semester, if not the year. To keep families renting, some ingenious landlord reset the rental clock so that families, averse to interrupting the school year, would sign another lease.

So what's this all got to do with picking the best seasons for buying and selling a home? When those families finally outgrew their apartments and decided to purchase something, they still wanted to accommodate the school schedule. And they wanted to wait until the end of their leases, so they weren't paying rent and making mortgage payments at the same time. But home buyers know that it often takes a while to find the right house. They figured they'd better start looking for a house sometime in the early spring, say February or March, if they wanted to move in June, after graduation, or over the summer. Similarly, home buyers who wanted to get the kids acclimated to the new house before the start of the second semester, figured they should start looking for a house sometime during the early fall, perhaps in September or October. And because sellers wanted to attract the most interest possible, they waited to put their homes up for sale until the spring or the fall selling seasons began, typically in February and March and September and October.

Although no one knows for sure, it's likely that the spring and fall home-selling seasons grew out of these notions. And for the most part, up until the late 1980s, you could depend on them. Spring was traditionally the busiest time of year for real estate, a time when sellers put their homes up en masse and buyers went out in full force. Business would die down in July and August, as buyers who had bought moved into their new homes and became homeowners, and sellers who had sold cashed their checks and moved on. Once the kids went back to school, the real estate market started picking up steam again. The fall was traditionally busy through Thanksgiving weekend, when everything died down until after Super Bowl Sunday, in late January. Then the cycle would begin again.

Since the beginning of the 1990s, the predictable cycle of spring and fall selling seasons has begun to shift. Real estate today is a year-round business. And agents say they do nearly as much business in December as in June—there are fewer home buyers working the market but those who are there are serious about what they're looking for. How do you figure out which is the best time to list your home for sale? Each of the seasons—spring, summer, fall, and winter—has its own characteristics. Let's take a look:

- *Spring.* Still the busiest time of the year for buyers and sellers, spring offers sellers the opportunity to showcase their home at its best. With the winter melt-off (for those of you living in cold-weather climates), spring sellers can thoroughly inspect the exterior of their home and create some fantastic curb appeal. There's also something nice about listing your home when it's not too hot or too cold out and the air is fresh. If your house doesn't have central air-conditioning, you might prefer to have buyers come through during the spring or fall rather than in the heat of summer, when your window units might be blasting.

Downside: None, except those problems that are weather related. For buyers, spring is the start of the new year. What's left of Christmas bonuses becomes a down payment, as buyers develop a "new year, new house" mentality.

- *Summer.* If you're living in a house with a garden, summer might prove to be the best time to show off your green thumb. Home buyers come through houses looking for such amenities as a well-cared-for garden, something they can maintain, rather than starting one from scratch. Also, if your kids are away for the summer, you might be able to keep their rooms clean from showing to showing. If you have central air, this season is a great time to show it off. If you have easy access to summer recreational activities such as a beach, a lake, or community tennis courts or swimming pools, buyers will be especially eager to hear it.

  Downside: Most times, kids are home for the summer, and you'll have double duty making sure their rooms are clean enough for buyers to get through them. A lot of folks take their vacation during the summer, so the market is often reduced to folks who are serious about buying and selling.

- *Fall.* If you're going to list your home during the fall, you'll have the change of seasons to contend with. Depending on where you are in the country, autumn colors and falling leaves might make extra work. With children back at school, however, daytime showings might be easier to accommodate. Because of the tax benefits of homeownership, there is also a push for home buyers to get into their new homes by December 31 (buyers may deduct any mortgage interest they've paid in the year plus any points they paid to get the loan if they close by year end).

  Downside: Depending on how quickly or slowly your home sells, you may still have it on the market during the beginning of the winter holiday season. Because fall sellers generally pull their homes off the market during the holidays, fall becomes a shorter selling season. Also, homes that don't sell in fall can be stigmatized by being held over on the market until the new year. An old listing number in the MLS can give buyers the misleading impression that your home has been on the market for a long time and you might be willing to accept a lower offer.
- *Winter.* There are several big pluses to listing your home by mid-November. Brokers say that while the numbers of people they work with and the numbers of sellers decline, the total number of sales barely drops below the monthly average set during the rest of the year. The winter holiday sales phenomenon, as it has come to be known, shows that only the most motivated buyers and sellers are active in the market during this time.

Downside: If you're going to list during this part of the year, you have to expect the unexpected: buyers who want showings at odd hours or during your family holiday parties. You may have to herd your family out into the garden while the prospective buyer takes a look around. In cold-weather climates, expect potential buyers to track mud, snow, and salt through your home. Keep your holiday decorations low-key, as not everyone who walks through the door will be of your religion or enjoy the holidays with your fervor. On the other hand, the smells of holiday baking may soften even the toughest buyer's heart. Successful winter holiday sellers are those who are realistic. Inflated prices won't attract any attention.

Now that you've had a look at the seasons, how do you decide which is the best season to sell? While sellers often get to choose when they list their home (unless they are being transferred immediately), it's not necessary to wait nearly a year just to catch "the perfect season." It's always a good time to sell your home if you're smart about what you're doing. Price is the great equalizer—a well-priced home should sell easily in any season.

The point is, every season offers some pluses and minuses. If you want to list your home in the spring, you might want to list in mid-January, rather than waiting for February or March. That way, you'll get the jump on your neighbors who are also selling. On the other hand, if you wait until mid-March, when many of the spring houses have already come on the market and buyers are hungry for something new, you might get even more attention. If you're planning to use a real estate agent or broker, talk to that person and ask about the various selling seasons in your area.

Successful Home Seller Tip: Here's the secret to selling, and I'll repeat it throughout this book: If you price your home correctly—that means close to its market value—you should have an offer within a reasonable amount of time (perhaps one week to three months). If you price your home under the market price, you should have an offer almost immediately (within three to four weeks). If you overprice your property, it will sit on the market until a prospective buyer walks through the door, falls in love with your home, and either doesn't know or doesn't care what the true market value of the property is. But don't sit around waiting for that unsophisticated buyer. You might just wait a long, long time.

PART II

Putting My House in Order

OBJECTIVITY: LOOKING THROUGH A BUYER'S EYES

QUESTION 4

How can I make my home more salable?

Mike and Betty had just gotten married when they decided that Betty's two-bedroom condo wasn't going to work for the two of them. While the condo had 1,400 square feet and was within walking distance of Betty's job, Mike's commute was more than an hour each way in heavy traffic. They sat in the living room about three weeks after returning from their honeymoon and surveyed the situation. "We looked around and noticed that what had been a clean, organized, and spacious apartment had turned into a cluttered mess, with my stuff and his stuff and our wedding presents stacked in boxes all over the place," Betty said.

As homeowners, we often find ourselves posing as collectors. We collect clothes, toys, children, mementos, tools, broken appliances, rusted pipes, books, papers, filing cabinets, and boxes of such inherited treasures as someone else's clothes, books, papers, and broken dishes. We keep these things partly out of laziness, partly out of the belief that one day these things—like Barbie dolls in their original wrappings—will be worth a fortune, and partly because they help us establish a sense of history and identity.

What many sellers fail to understand, however, is that the concept of being a seller clashes directly with the concept of being a collector. If you want to sell your home, you're going to have to clear out and clean out your home, from top to bottom, and that means parting with some of your collectible treasures. If the thought of parting with your Aunt Sallie's flabby twin mattresses that you've stored in your basement since 1956 is overwhelming, you will need to become an excellent organizer to shield your "stuff" from the buyer's view. How you can do this effectively will be the subject of the next few questions.

All of this boils down to knowing what buyers want to see when they walk through your front door, and, more important, what you want them to see when they come through your home for a showing. Buyers want to see a clean, open, spacious home that will allow them to live in the style they envision within their mind's eye. Since that's wholly intangible, sellers must ready their home as if preparing a blank canvas upon which any buyer could paint the house of his or her dreams. That dovetails nicely into what you, the seller, want the buyer to see during a showing. You want your home to be as clean and as bare as possible (while still looking lived in), so that the buyer can see the structure or the "bones" of the home. Instead of wasting valuable minutes of a showing examining your collection of antique figurines, you want buyers to be looking at the floors, walls, room sizes, and other major features of the home. You want them to be struck by the spaciousness and graciousness of your home.

There are several ways in which you can create this sense of spaciousness and graciousness. The following suggestions elaborate on these ideas:

1. *Unclutter your home*. The idea is to remove almost everything from all tables, countertops, and bookshelves. Pack away all but one of those family photos on the piano. Take the stacked videos off the top of your VCR and TV, and gather up the CDs that are strewn on the floor. Leave only a few nicely spaced coats in the closet. Pack away most of your sweaters so that the bedroom closets seem bigger. The subtle effects of these changes can't be overstated (for more ideas on uncluttering your home, see Question 7).
2. *Make it neutral.* When researching a newspaper article on sellers several years ago, I toured a house on the north side of Chicago that had a lovely cream-colored dining room, living room, and entry hallway. This is what brokers call a "neutral" decor; again, it gets back to the blank canvas mentality, which basically says that buyers are more able to visualize the house of their dreams if your house is decorated in such neutral shades as white, eggshell, pale gray, or beige. Unfortunately, this same Chicago house also had a wood floor in the kitchen that had been painted

fire engine red, and a child's bedroom that had been painted an unappealing shade of lime green. If it is not economically feasible to repaint the entire interior of your home before selling it, consider painting over any loud or obtrusive colors that may take away from a buyer's ability to see the bones of your home. (See Question 8 for more information.)

3. *Throw out or give away.* It's no use uncluttering your kitchen countertops or bookshelves if all you're going to do is stack these items or boxes in closets, the basement, or the attic. Do yourself a favor (and save yourself hundreds or thousands of dollars when you move) and either throw out or give away anything you haven't used or thought about in the past five years. If you're really ambitious, throw out or give away anything you haven't used in the past three years. If you want to raise some money, try hosting a garage sale. What is left can be donated to charity. Current tax laws permit the donor to deduct a percentage of the item's original value from his or her income taxes. (Check with your tax adviser for more details.) Of course, don't throw away things that are valuable (comic books from the 1960s or your grandmother's sterling service set) or things you might need in your new home. My mother-in-law once held a garage sale and sold all of her hangers. Of course, when she moved to her new condo, she realized she had nothing to hang her clothes on and ended up buying new hangers.
4. *If it's broke, fix it.* The door that creaks when you open it, then doesn't really shut properly. The torn living room window screen. The broken window in the second bedroom, courtesy of your neighbor's son's first

home run. The icemaker that doesn't make ice. Buyers are easily distracted, and they're looking for every reason *not* to buy your house. If you've got an obvious problem, it's important to fix it before you put your house up for sale—even before you show your home to the brokers who will provide you with a comparative marketing analysis. Why? Because savvy buyers nitpick the small stuff, even if they love the house. It's part of their strategy to bargain down your price and to justify offering you a lower price. And brokers sometimes have a tough time seeing past the obvious flaws. You want to make the very best impression. So make sure everything works properly, shuts firmly, and looks as neat and presentable as possible. (Whether or not you should undertake major renovations—and which renovations those should be—before you sell is discussed in Questions 8 and 9.)

If you unclutter your home, make the color scheme as neutral as possible, give or throw away most of your unused or old clothing and broken household appliances, and fix the small things that are broken around your home, you'll have taken a very large step toward making your home more salable. Your home will look much more spacious and will begin to shine. In fact, if you do these things, you'll probably take a good look around and wonder briefly why you're moving from such a wonderful place. That's how Sam and I felt as we were packing things away in preparation for selling our last home. We turned to each other and said, "Hey, this is a really great place."

In the rest of this section, we'll talk about the different things you need to do to put your house in order before listing it for sale.

QUESTION 5

How can I look at my home through a buyer's eyes? How can I become more objective when looking at my home?

Why does the grass always seem greener in your neighbor's yard? If you don't see your neighbor seeding, weeding, fertilizing, watering, and cutting his lawn, it's easy to fool yourself into thinking that the lawn has grown and maintained itself. If you think about it, the "grass is always greener" cliché is all about perspective. From where you sit, struggling with daily life, someone else's life—and lawn—always looks better and easier.

Home sellers fall into this psychological trap, too. Someone else's house is bound to sell faster, look better, and attract more interest than your house. But one of the secrets to selling successfully is to gain some perspective about your home. It's important to relearn how to step back and view your home as a house with four walls, a ceiling, and a floor, sitting on a piece of earth in a particular location in a particular neighborhood. It's important to put yourself back into your home-buyer shoes. They're bound to feel uncomfortable at first. After all, you haven't worn them in a long time.

The first thing you need to do is think about what attracted you to the house in the first place. Patrick, a book author, recalled that price and space were the prime reasons he and his wife, Sue, bought their house in Chicago. "It was a nice big brick building, and we liked brick because we thought about heating the place and maintenance and things like that. Inside, it was a terrible sight, with ugly wall-to-wall carpeting, and nearly every room had paneling. But it had good space and good light. It looked like a good street, though it wasn't as good as we thought. And it has improved a lot since then. But I remember there were children playing and not a lot of graffiti. And we could afford it." Ling, a homeowner in San Francisco, said he chose his home because it had the right numbers and was situated correctly on the block. "The concept of *Feng Shui* is very important to the Chinese. This house had very positive numbers. It was also the right size for my family, and in a nice neighborhood." Ling remembered he passed up a bigger home for the same money because the numbers spelled "death" in Chinese. When Sam and I found our second home, we were attracted to the large, sunny rooms and the view. We also liked the proximity to downtown Chicago, the twenty-four-hour security, and the fact that the bus stopped right in front of the building.

Remembering why you initially liked a house is important because future buyers may be attracted to the same amenities. It's up to you to point them out. For example, Pat and Sue were attracted to the brick exterior of the home, the size of the home, and the block it was on. Since they've lived there, they've extensively remodeled the home, replastering walls and replacing outdated plumbing. The agent who markets their home should concentrate on the brick exterior, the extensive renovation, and how nice and family-oriented their block has become. These are basic home values that will be important to most buyers; they should be pointed out by the agent and featured in the promotional literature used to sell the home.

Ling was attracted to the house's numbers and the way it was situated. Because Ling's home is in a neighborhood that has many Chinese residents, Ling would be wise to point out these attributes to prospective buyers if they are Chinese. I liked the sunny south view, the generous room sizes, and the twenty-four-hour security of our home. When we sold that home, we stressed these qualities to potential buyers. Since that building doesn't have an attached garage, we stressed how convenient it would be to live there without a car.

Remembering what originally attracted you to your home is one way you can step back and become objective about it. But it is also important to remember what you disliked about the home and what you've done during the time you've lived in the house to change some of those negatives into positives. For example, Patrick and Sue realized parts of their home needed work, but they also realized their home had far more positives than negatives. Over the years, they've worked on the negatives, and should certainly boast about the excellent shape their home is in now. If over the years you've replaced the plumbing, roof, furnace, or electrical wiring, replastered the walls, recarpeted, repainted, rehabbed bathrooms or the kitchen, bought new appliances, or built a new garage, you should feel free to list these items in great detail for the buyer.

Another way to gain perspective about your home is to visit other homes in the neighborhood that are for sale. Try to find some that are similar in size to yours and are listed for a little more money than you'd ideally like to get for your home. Many of the owners or brokers will host an open house from time to time. Take advantage of the opportunity to see what your competition looks like. Compare room sizes, amenities, number of bathrooms, garages, kitchens, gardens, and even the type of siding and architectural styles of the homes. When buyers come to your door, they're going to carry with them mental images of all the other homes they've seen in your neighborhood in your price range. By comparing your home to the others on the market, and then compensating for missing amenities by either adding them or lowering your price, you're sure to get the best price for your property.

QUESTION 6
What is curb appeal?

Curb appeal is the term brokers use to describe how homes look from the curb or sidewalk in front of the home. It's important that your house (curb appeal applies mainly to single-family homes and town houses rather than condos, since most condo associations care for the exterior and common areas of the property) has an excellent street presence and curb appeal. Your home's curb appeal must impress a prospective buyer. If buyers like what they see from the street—or their car window—they will be more likely to go up and take a closer look. Perhaps they'll even walk through your home.

When you've lived in a home for years, you sometimes take your home's curb appeal for granted. Stepping back from the stoop often allows you to gain additional perspective about your home. Several years ago, one Detroit seller failed to realize her foundation had cracked and the house had settled. From the curb, it appeared that her house was aiming to be the city's answer to the Tower of Pisa, in Italy. Needless to say, her listing price didn't reflect the work that needed to be done to bring the house up to shape, and she was left wondering why she hadn't received an offer while other homes on the block were selling.

Carefully reviewing your curb appeal is important, since homes often take on the personalities of their owners. It can happen through landscaping, through the interior decor, and sometimes through artwork or the little knickknacks we all seem to collect through the years. Distinctive personalities are fine, but they can narrow the appeal of your home. On Plum Island, in Massachusetts, a small green house had miniature leprechauns and knickknacks sitting in each pane of the front windows. The owner, a merry soul in ill health, invited the buyer and her family to admire his "friendly" house, not realizing how difficult to show his decorating had made the home. It was dark, cluttered, foul-smelling, and entirely unappealing.

Although you probably go in and out of your home several times on a given day, allow yourself to walk to the street curb, turn around, and give your home a fresh look. What do you see? The house should have a neat, trim appearance that is open and inviting. The exterior should be freshly painted or cleaned with soap and water (try a power washer to clean heavy-duty dirt off vinyl siding). If your home looks dark, drab, or dreary, consider repainting it white. (Brokers say white homes sell more quickly than homes of other colors.) To add a little lively flavor, you might want to paint the trim and window frames in color, perhaps black, red, or green.

Next, take a look at your roof. It should be in good condition, without any peeling or torn shingles. Gutters and downspouts should be in good repair, and cleaned out. If you live in a warm-weather climate, or are selling during spring, summer, or autumn, consider putting out a couple of wicker rocking chairs, some potted plants, and perhaps a hanging basket or two. If your mailbox is run down or nondescript, consider repainting it red or getting an oversized, cast-iron English post box. Dress up the porch so that prospective buyers can easily envision themselves sitting there enjoying a lazy Sunday afternoon.

Maintaining and enhancing the landscape is incredibly important to the curb appeal of your home. Lawns should be cut regularly and manicured. Bushes should be trimmed and flowers should be planted. During winter, your walk and driveway should be shoveled immediately after every snowfall to make sure that prospective buyers and their brokers don't slip and fall. If you have a walk that's not much more than broken pieces of cement, consider repaving it.

When Wayne and Suzanne were trying to sell their home in Indianapolis, they invited friends over for a Tom Sawyer-like afternoon of painting the tall wood fence that surrounded the house and backyard. Suzanne then planted brightly colored flowers against the white fence and hung flower boxes. Wayne cut and trimmed the hedges. Suzanne stood back to take a look. Not bad, she thought, but that house should be a different color. Although they had aluminum siding on their farmhouse-style home, she and Wayne opted to repaint it a charming combination of mauve and gray with barn-red trim. When they finally listed the home, it sold quickly.

Of course, cultivating a charming exterior won't sell your home if the interior is a mess. But it should help get prospective buyers across the threshold.

Successful Home Seller Tip: If you'd like an expert opinion on what you should do to improve the curb appeal of your home, ask the three brokers you invite over to present their comparative marketing analysis (CMA). Each broker should be happy to discuss the changes he or she feels would improve your chances of selling your home quickly, and for more money. (For more information on CMAs and choosing a broker, see Question 18.)

QUESTION 7
How do I unclutter my home?

About six months before we decided to sell our home, we had some guests stay with us for the July Fourth weekend. They were going to stay in our second bedroom, which I had been using as my office. Since I had a work deadline that weekend, Sam moved his fold-out table from the dining room—where it usually stood against the wall with all kinds of stuff on it—into our bedroom. When I walked back into the dining room, I was struck by how large it suddenly seemed. The room looked like it had grown a full two feet wider in the space of a few minutes. Meanwhile, our bedroom looked tiny and cluttered. I realized then that moving a piece of furniture—even a modest piece—can make a huge difference in the way a room looks and feels.

This lesson really hit home a few months later, when we were about to list our home for sale. The dining room had become Sam's at-home office, complete with two huge gray metal filing cabinets we had attempted to blend into the surroundings by covering with a large blue tablecloth. (No one ever mistook those mismatched filing cabinets for a nice side table.) The cabinets and desk were littered with books and papers and receipts and a computer. It was a mess. In fact, the whole house was a mess. For a couple married only five years, our home looked like we had lived there for thirty years.

As we discussed earlier, as homeowners we often find ourselves masquerading as collectors. While many of these items remind us of places we've been or things we've done, to buyers they simply look like fodder for a garage sale. Again, what many homeowners fail to remember is that the concept of being a seller clashes directly with the concept of being a collector.

If you truly want to sell your home, you're going to have to clear out and clean out your home, from top to bottom, and that may mean parting with some of your collectibles or putting them in storage. I can't say this often enough. When buyers walk through your front door, they want to see a clean, open, spacious home that will allow them to live in the style they envision within their mind's eye. Since that's wholly intangible—you can't possibly know what each buyer imagines his or her dream home to be—you must ready your home as if preparing a blank canvas upon which any buyer could paint the house of his or her dreams.

As a seller, you want your home to be as clean and neutral as possible (while still looking lived-in), so that the buyer can see the structure or "bones" of the home. (The "bones" of your home includes windows, arches, doorways, walls, floors, moldings, ceilings, fireplaces, and built-ins.) Most buyers have a difficult time visualizing what a home will look like with their furniture in it. Your furniture, artwork, and knickknacks become distractions that many buyers' imaginations will have to work overtime to surmount. Buyers who have to work that hard trying to picture how they'll live in your home won't buy it. They'll move on to the next house.

There are two basic things you must do to unclutter your home:

1. *Remove almost everything from all tables, countertops, and bookshelves*. Pack extra family photos and gather up loose sheet music stacked on the piano. Take the

videos off your VCR and TV, and gather up the CDs that are strewn on the floor. Leave only a few nicely spaced coats in the closet. In fact, pack away half of your clothes so that your closets seem bigger. Give away most of your plants, or rearrange them unobtrusively in one corner of your home. Gather up your children's toys, books, art projects, and homework and stack them neatly in their bedrooms. Remove all magnets, papers, your child's first drawings, and the invitation to your cousin's baby shower from the refrigerator door. Take everything off the bathroom sink; remove all but one razor from the shower. Do the laundry as frequently as necessary to avoid having huge piles of dirty clothes spilling out of the hamper. Clean out your basement and attic, neatly stacking any boxes you have stored there. The subtle, positive effects of these changes can't be overstated. The more you unclutter your home, the more finely attuned your eye will become to areas that have yet to be tackled.

2. *Throw out, store, or give away much of the furniture, knickknacks, or personal items in your home.* It's no use uncluttering your kitchen countertops or bookshelves if all you're going to do is stack these items or boxes in closets, the basement, or the attic. Let's start with the interior. Store all excess furniture, including sofas, end tables, stools, and chairs. Make simple arrangements with your furniture, so that each room has a clean, well-defined look that highlights the best feature. For example, if you have a spectacular view of the city or garden from your living room, your furniture should be arranged in such a way that a buyer can walk in a straight line from the door to the window. (Make sure that window is so clean it sparkles!)

> If your bedroom has a cozy sitting area by a fireplace, make sure the fireplace can be seen from the doorway. If your family room has French doors leading to a patio, make sure the path is clear and open. Have you reclaimed some long-lost space?

Now let's look at the exterior of your home. In addition to the seasonal maintenance, it's important to keep children's toys and gardening equipment neatly stored in your garage or a tool shed. Buyers will want to inspect the garage, so it's best to keep it neat and tidy. Tools, gardening equipment, bicycles, and strollers should be neatly stored—off the garage floor, if possible.

As we discussed earlier, do yourself a favor—and save hundreds of dollars when you move—and either throw out or give away anything you haven't used or thought about in the past three to five years. Once you've uncluttered your home, it will be easier for you to see which repairs, renovations, and improvements you should make before you try to sell your home.

CHOOSING THE IMPORTANT REPAIRS AND RENOVATIONS

QUESTION 8

What are the most important repairs, renovations, and improvements I should make to my home before I sell?

When it comes to selling their home, homeowners generally fall into one of two categories: those who want to fix and rehab everything before they sell, and those who don't want to do anything. As is usually true, neither extreme is the right choice.

The first thing you should do is decide whether you're going to sell your home in "mint" condition or in "as is" condition, or somewhere in between. Scott, a top real estate broker in Wilmington, Delaware, describes "mint" (also known as "move-in") condition like this: "What we expect to see are carpet and walls in neutral colors, and there is rarely wallpaper. Electricity, plumbing, and fixtures have been upgraded or replaced. Everything is fresh, clean, and immaculate." "As is" condition runs the gamut from dirty ("With dust balls the size of tumbleweeds," says Scott) to broken down and in need of repair. You'll often see homes that need a lot of work and are referred to as "handyman's specials" or "needs loving care."

Homes that are in mint condition sell for more money than homes that need fixing up. The reason is simple: Most buyers don't want to do the work, or they don't have the time, or they don't have the extra cash needed to finance a major renovation. Though it's not possible or necessary for you to completely renovate your home before selling it to reap the most money possible, most sellers have some things they can do to their home to improve it before selling it. Once you get the clutter out of the way, you'll begin to see the bare bones of your home and can assess what kind of renovation it will take to sell quickly.

Choosing Wisely

Before you run out to your local Wal-Mart or Sears and begin pricing new kitchen cabinets, let's talk about what kinds of renovations are appropriate to do when you're preparing your home for sale. There are exterior renovations and interior renovations, and it is not necessary to essentially rebuild your home to sell it quickly and for a good price. In fact, many renovations—like a brand-new kitchen or bath—are expensive and time-consuming. They also may not return 100 percent of your investment if you try to sell your home within a year of completing a major renovation project.

Exterior renovations you should consider include things like repainting your siding, replacing the roof, fixing gutters, repairing broken steps, and replacing broken windows and screens. Interior renovations include cosmetic changes (like repainting and replacing worn-out carpeting), household repairs (like tightening doorknobs and oiling squeaking hinges), and replacing old or broken kitchen appliances and the mechanicals of the home. Since Question 6 (What is curb appeal?) deals with things you can do to improve the exterior of your home, let's talk about what you can do to fix up the interior of your house for sale.

Let's start with what you shouldn't do. Completely remodeling a kitchen or gutting a bathroom or putting in a fireplace is exactly the wrong kind of renovation to attempt before you sell your home. While it's true that studies have shown that homeowners or sellers who remodel their bathrooms or kitchens generally recoup most or all of their money and sometimes turn a profit, it's not the kind of major project you want to attempt just before trying to sell your home. First, you may not get your money out of the job and second, you certainly won't benefit from using the new amenities. Besides, remodeling your kitchen can take months, including one month when your kitchen might be completely unusable. And that's if your contractors show up every day.

When you think about getting your home ready for sale, you should think about doing things to your home that will cost relatively little but will dramatically increase the value and salability of your home. To identify potential fix-up projects, ask yourself the following questions:

1. What color are my walls and carpet? What condition are they in? Are there any signs of damage or past leaks?
2. Does everything work in my house? Does every light turn on? Do all the electrical sockets work? Are there any faucets that leak? Do all the appliances work?
3. What is the state of the kitchen? Do the kitchen cabinets look fresh and in good shape? Is the floor in good shape? Do the refrigerator and freezer work properly? What about the oven, range, and disposal?
4. What are the states of the bathrooms? Are the floors in good shape? Is the grout in good repair? Is anything damaged? Do the tub and shower drain properly? Does the toilet flush properly? Are there any drips or leaks? Are the tiles firmly attached to the walls and floors?
5. Are the curtains or window treatments in good shape? Are the shower curtains in good shape?

Walls and Carpets

Let's start at the top of the list. The best money you can spend is to replace colorful or worn-out carpeting and patterned wallpaper with new carpeting or paint in white or neutral shades (neutral includes eggshells, whites, creams, light beiges, and pale grays). The general rule is, the lighter the better. Dark walls and floors tend to make rooms look smaller and darker. That isn't good. You want your home to look as large and bright as possible. Besides being more attracted to bright and sunny homes, home buyers can more easily imagine their own furnishings fitting into your home if the palette is white or neutral. While you may think forest green wallpaper and plaid carpeting look chic in your family room, that kind of decor can be distracting. A buyer may be unable to see past the decor to the "bones" or structure of the room.

I once toured a home in which each room was painted a different, obtrusive, dark color. What had once been a nice hardwood floor had been painted in a black-and-white checkerboard pattern. The children's bedrooms were covered with stickers and magazine pin-ups. I asked the homeowner if she planned to remove the stickers and repaint the rooms before listing her house. "I really feel that the process of selling our home is intrusive enough. I didn't want our children to feel as if their identities had been stripped away," she said. You'll have to make the decision about how much to infringe on your children's identities, but a house that's uniformly neutral in color will sell faster and with less aggravation than one that features every color of the psychedelic rainbow.

Of course, not every home is going to need a fresh coat of paint and a change of carpet. If you've recently installed expensive colored carpet throughout the house and it is in good shape, by all means keep it. You may want to have it cleaned—consider renting a carpet shampooer at your local hardware store—and then complement the clean rug with a fresh coat of white paint on the walls. Or, if you've recently repainted your home, you may just need to touch up a few areas that are showing wear and tear.

Make Sure Everything Works

Once you've made decisions about painting and changing the carpet, it's time to address other problems. It's important to make sure everything works in the house. Some small repairs can help a lot. Every lock should turn easily, door-knobs should be tight. Stairs shouldn't creak, hinges shouldn't squeak, and doors should open and close easily. Prospective buyers shouldn't have to worry that the closet door is off the track or that a closet shelf might collapse and fall on them. These kinds of small problems cause buyers to worry that other things in the house might not be in the best working order. Check faucets to make sure they don't drip. Toilets shouldn't run. Test every electrical socket to be sure it's working (you can do this by taking a night-light or radio and plugging it into each socket), and make sure every light fixture has working light bulbs—brokers love to turn on the lights when showing a home. Test your washer, dryer, dishwasher, disposal, air-conditioning, heating, fans, trash compactor, and microwave before listing your house for sale. Fix any appliance that doesn't work.

The Kitchen and Bathrooms

Everyone wants to buy a home with a new kitchen and bathrooms. Of course, you don't want to invest that kind of money in a house you'll be selling. If you're going to strip your kitchen bare and renovate it before selling there should be a bona fide reason, such as devastation caused by fire, earthquake, or flood. If your kitchen or bathrooms were damaged by a catastrophe, you will be able to choose to redo your kitchen with the insurance money or sell the home in "as is" condition.

There are things, however, that you can do to your kitchen and bathrooms to give them a fresh feeling without going to the time, trouble, and expense of completely gutting them. For example, consider painting your kitchen cabinets white and replacing the hardware with something new, bright, and shiny. Paint the insides of the cabinets and then line them with bright, attractive (but neutral) shelf paper. But don't glue it to the shelves. Instead, tape it down so it is easily removable. If your kitchen floor has seen better days, consider putting down an inexpensive, attractive, wax-free floor. Or, if you have wood floors, consider sanding them or polishing them for a fresh look. Another attractive, yet relatively inexpensive, renovation is to replace the kitchen faucet.

Approach your bathrooms in the same way. Regrout and reseal the tub. (To lighten grout and get rid of mildew, try mixing a little bleach with water and dab onto tile grout with a sponge.) If you have tile floors, you can regrout them or apply a sealant. It is inexpensive to reglaze the bathtub, which will give it a shiny, like-new glow. You can then paint and add new hardware, a new bathmat, some new towels, and a new shower curtain.

Never underestimate the importance of cosmetic, decorative improvements. If you've done it right, buyers may not even notice. But they may react strongly if you haven't.

Curtains and Window Treatments

While we're on the subject of curtains, take a critical look at your window treatments. Buyers like homes that are bright, with lots of windows and sun coming in. When Sam and I bought our second home, the sellers had heavy gold-and-olive velvet draperies in the living room that completely blocked out the sun. (They perfectly matched the gold-and-olive velvet chairs and gold-and-olive flocked-velvet wallpaper, however.) In the second bedroom, the wooden shutters were always closed. The bathroom had a blackout shade to which they had glued a sheet of red-and-black plaid wallpaper.

As long as you're neutralizing your home, consider replacing heavy draperies with inexpensive, neutral, vinyl mini-blinds or curtains. And nothing helps upgrade the feel of a bedroom more than a crisp bedspread or comforter with matching pillows. Consider purchasing a matching shower curtain for the bathroom.

How much should you spend on renovations? The quick answer is as little as possible to make your home look as good as possible. Each home is different and each home seller has a different budget. If you have to replace a hot water tank just before selling, that could add $500 or more to your budget. If all you need to do is paint, consider doing it yourself for the cost of materials. If you plan to hire a professional, the cost will go up. It isn't necessary to buy the best quality carpeting, but don't buy something that will wear through before the sale closes. If you spend $1,000 on painting and new carpeting, you may be able to increase the price of your home by that much or more. Talk to your broker about what kinds of amenities are considered standard for homes in your neighborhood and in your price category.

Successful Home Seller Tip: Your job as a seller is to make your home completely available to potential buyers. Buying neutral carpet and white paint may be the best investment you can make. Make sure everything works in your house and that doorjambs are well oiled and don't squeak. Nail down that loose stair so it doesn't creak when buyers walk on it. Make sure moldings aren't cracked or chipped, that your deck is newly varnished or painted. But don't spend tons of money "gutting your home" before you sell. That's just like flushing money down the drain. And don't make the mistake of overimproving your house for the neighborhood. If you do put in that new kitchen, you may find that you can't get the price you want for the house, and you'll lose money on the sale.

Successful Home Seller Tip: Top brokers often advise sellers not to do "everything" to their home. Even if your home is totally done, the new buyer will want to put his or her stamp on your home, whether that means repainting your white house pink with black shutters or gutting the master bathroom. If you leave something obvious (such as an unfinished basement), feel free to point it out to prospective buyers. It will give them the feeling that there is potential to improve the house and increase its value.

QUESTION 9

Is it more difficult to sell a vacant home than one that is being lived in?

Walking into a vacant house is like looking into an empty jewelry box: Either you can imagine how wonderful it would be if it were all filled up or you can't. Unfortunately, most home buyers fall into the latter category. It's tough for them to imagine what their furniture and household belongings will look like in someone else's vacant home. Unless the home is configured similarly to the home they're coming from, they may have trouble relating to the space.

That's why most brokers say it is more difficult to sell a vacant home. Still, some buyers like vacant homes. They can take the time to slowly scrutinize the home and not run the risk of meeting the seller. But while an empty home might seem brighter and more spacious than one filled with your furniture, proportions might seem out of whack. For example, buyers may not be able to judge if the living room will accommodate their sofa and chairs, *and* Grandma's armoire.

This translates into another of the real estate industry's accepted theorems: Homes that are lived in sell faster than homes that are vacant. While your furniture and decor might be completely different from a prospective buyer's, furniture helps to define space in a room. Carpets, rugs, and artwork help absorb sounds like footsteps, which would otherwise reverberate in an empty home. The smells of dinner cooking in the oven, perfume in the bedroom, and soap in the bathroom give a home an extra-inviting dimension that says, "Real people live here and so could you."

Of course, not everyone can live in their home while they're trying to sell it. Homeowners get transferred or buy new homes and need their belongings. In a bitter divorce, both homeowners may move out of the marital residence, splitting up their belongings at that time.

If you are planning to sell your home and must vacate it before or during the sales process, you should know that a vacant home often takes longer to sell than a furnished house, and sometimes brings the owners less money. "You're not talking about a great deal less money, but vacant homes may take longer to get the [seller's] price," notes Larry, a broker in Wilmington, Delaware.

They also require more work for the seller's sales agent. "The agent should regularly check on the property and make sure that there are plenty of listing sheets, seller disclosure forms, and property condition reports for prospective buyers," says Larry.

Managing the sale of your home once you've moved out can be more difficult, though less intrusive, than for an on-premises seller. Consider following these suggestions:

- *Clean up*. Empty houses have a way of attracting dust balls the size of hockey pucks, so make sure your home is as clean as possible. That may mean hiring a cleaning service from time to time, particularly if your home has sat on the market for more than three months. Consider shampooing rugs and wall-to-wall carpeting, polishing hardwood floors, and waxing vinyl kitchen and bathroom floors. "Your furniture may have left dirt marks on the carpeting. Besides removing stains, shampooing should help freshen up the odor of the place," Larry says.
- *Keep utilities on*. It's important that the electricity, water, and heat work when your home is being shown to a prospective buyer. Buyers will want to see homes in the light and test appliances to make sure they are working. During cold weather, home buyers will appreciate walking into a warm room. While paying utility bills may seem like throwing salt on the wound, you'll appreciate not having to deal with the mess and expense when water pipes burst.
- *Maintain the exterior*. Mow the lawn, trim the hedges, and pick up any debris or garbage that has accumulated. Your listing agent should check the property regularly to make sure its curb appeal hasn't dwindled

with time. He or she should also replenish listing sheets, property inspection reports, and seller disclosure forms and check for any garbage or business cards left by visiting agents, as well as for property damage or acts of vandalism.

- *Maintain the interior.* Make sure all installed light fixtures have fresh bulbs with as high a wattage as possible. Provide floor lamps for rooms that don't have ceiling lights. If agents bring prospective buyers after dark, being able to shed a little light on the house will be vital to getting it sold.

Should you rent furniture to make your house look more homey? Real estate agents debate the merits of this strategy, which, if you rent a whole houseful of furniture, can be costly. Even if you have the money to spare, this plan can backfire by making your living room look more like a warehouse than a place in which a buyer would want to spend some time. On the other hand, some brokers say it's helpful to have a couch in the living room or a dinette set in the dining room to help buyers see the room's proportions. I think neither plan is particularly helpful. If you're not living in the house, having a few pieces of furniture isn't going to fool prospective buyers into thinking you're really there. All they'd have to do is open up a closet and wonder why you don't have any clothes. Also, the additional cost of renting the furniture may not be recovered. If the rental furniture is of a low quality, it may give prospective buyers the wrong impression of your home.

The most important thing you can do when trying to sell a vacant home is to price it competitively. It isn't worth taking a flier and pricing the home for more than the market will bear. The reason is mostly psychological. A vacant home says that you've already moved to your new home and are probably paying two mortgages (your vacant home and the new home), two house insurance premiums, and two property taxes. Walking into your vacant home, a buyer will infer that you are extremely motivated to sell. That fact alone may cause the buyer to take a closer look at your home. If you inflate the listing price of your vacant home, you run the risk of confusing the buyer with mixed messages. The buyer might wonder if you're really interested in selling your home at all.

QUESTION 10
What is a prelisting inspection? And should I have one?

A house inspection is a house inspection, whether it is called a prelisting inspection or a seller's inspection. House inspectors poke around looking for things that are broken, out-of-date, or not in compliance with local housing codes. Buyers and sellers hire professional house inspectors or structural engineers for slightly different reasons. Buyers want a professional house inspection before or just after the contract has been signed so they know what potential problems they've signed on for. Sellers hire inspectors to tell them about the condition of their property so they can either fix the problems before listing or rethink the list price of the home.

Prelisting or seller inspections are becoming more popular as more states require sellers to disclose problems with their homes' condition to the buyer before closing. Many states require that sellers disclose specific information about the condition of the roof, mechanicals, plumbing, electrical service, and even the neighborhood and school districts in writing to buyers. (For more information on seller disclosure, see Question 31.) While this kind of detailed information might make you nervous as a seller, buyers are aware that they can ask for this information (if it isn't already required in your state) and get it. A prelisting inspection helps take some of the "should have known but didn't" worry out of selling your home.

Another excellent reason to pay for a prelisting inspection is if you inherit a house or are the executor of an estate that is attempting to liquidate assets. If you've actually lived in a house, you're more likely to be familiar with the physical state of the property than if you've never spent a night under the roof.

Leverage is another good reason to have a prelisting inspection. Savvy buyers will often try to renegotiate the price of the contract after their inspector turns up problems with the house. If the inspector says the hot water heater may have to be replaced within six months, the buyer may ask you to pay for a new one. Knowing in advance the condition of the home's mechanical systems, roof, foundation, and appliances can help nip this negotiation technique in the bud. After all, you'll know in advance the potential problems of the property and can advertise that the list price reflects the "as is" condition. (Another strategy to counteract the buyer's negotiation strategies is to offer a home warranty. For more information, see Question 29.)

"If you correct those things that you know are wrong with the house before you list it, you can be fairly certain the buyer's inspector is going to give your home a clean bill of health," notes Robert, a professional home inspector in Chicago. If you're in a neighborhood that is popular with

FHA or VA buyers (ask your broker if you're not sure about whether yours is or isn't), you'll need to bring the house up to code before FHA or VA will fund the mortgage. For example, if your house has only 60-amp electrical service, you'll have to bring it up to 100-amp service. If your home has peeling paint, you may be required to fix it before closing. (For more information on what your obligations are to an FHA or VA buyer, see Question 65.)

What are you likely to find in a prelisting inspection? The results might surprise you. In any home built before 1980, you're likely to find asbestos, either in ceiling tiles or, more commonly, wrapped around pipes in the basement. Even really old houses aren't asbestos-proof. When we purchased an 1880s farmhouse in a Chicago suburb a few years ago, the seller, who had lived in the house for nineteen years, was surprised to learn from our house inspector that someone had dumped an asbestos wrapping material in the crawl space under the front porch. Removing the asbestos cost him $1,400.

Inspectors may also find evidence of pests (termites or carpenter ants for example), lead pipes or lead paint, or a long-forgotten underground storage tank. One Cincinnati seller was happy he'd had a prelisting inspection before putting his century-old home on the market. It turned out his home had a plethora of problems, including termites, sewer problems, and layer after layer of amateur repair. The seller was able to disclose the true condition of the property and then priced the property to reflect the condition. When he sold less than a year later, the buyers had far less anxiety about what kind of money pit they were actually purchasing. Privately, the buyers often wondered how the seller could have lived blissfully for so many years in a house that needed so many repairs.

Should you have a prelisting inspection? If you're worried about the condition of the home, and what a buyer's inspector might find, then the answer is yes. Find a good professional home inspector and pay the fee for your own piece of mind. (See Question 11 for more information on how to find a good house inspector.) On the other hand, if you know your property inside and out, or if it is a relatively new home, or if you live in a condominium or co-op, you most likely can skip the prelisting inspection and save yourself the $300 fee.

QUESTION 11
How do I find a good home inspector?

Once you've decided to have a prelisting inspection, you have to find a reputable house inspector or structural engineer. If you look in your telephone book, you'll find dozens of people calling themselves "professional house inspectors." Some of them are, some of them aren't. Some of the most qualified home inspectors are members of the American Society of Home Inspectors (ASHI), a nationwide, nonprofit professional trade association founded in 1976. ASHI admits as members only those home inspectors who have performed at least 750 home inspections according to the ASHI Standards of Practice, or 250 inspections in addition to other licenses and experiences. Applicants must also pass a written exam, receive approval on at least three sample inspection reports, and perform a satisfactory home inspection before a peer review committee.

A problem with all house inspections, however, is that almost none of the states licenses house inspectors (Texas being a notable exception). Structural engineers are licensed by every state, and many will also perform house inspections for the same fee as a professional house inspector. I often recommend that buyers and sellers use a structural engineer instead of a professional house inspector if the home they are purchasing or are living in has been in an earthquake, fire, flood, or suffered some other major calamity.

The process of finding a good inspector (and for the rest of this question, I'll just refer to anyone who inspects your house as an "inspector") is similar to the process you'll go through to find a good broker or a good real estate attorney. Ask your neighbors, friends, doctor, lawyer, or broker which inspectors they've liked. When you call these inspectors:

- Compare fees (they should range from $150 to $500, depending on the size or price of the home).
- Ask what's included in the fee and how long the inspection should take (generally around two hours for a thorough inspection of a moderately sized property).
- Compare telephone manner (the inspector should be courteous and knowledgeable).
- Ask if the inspector is bonded, licensed, and insured.
- Ask if the inspector is a member of ASHI or another professional inspection association.
- Ask what kind of written documentation you will receive from the inspector after the inspection is completed.
- Ask for references—and then call them. It's particularly good to ask for the last three people the inspector has done inspections for. That way, the inspector can't stack the deck with favorable references.

At the end of the inspection, or perhaps the next day, the inspector should give you a written report of what's wrong with the house. If you're smart, you'll have tagged along with the inspector during the inspection. If the inspector does find something wrong, ask him or her to ballpark how much it would cost to have the problem corrected. Replacing an old, inefficient hot water tank with a new one might cost only $500. On the other hand, a new boiler might cost several thousand dollars. You'll want to fix some problems and perhaps offer a cash credit at closing to the buyer for the others.

Successful Home Seller Tip: Be on the lookout for unscrupulous home inspectors who don't provide quality service. Some inspectors schedule as many as four or five inspections in a single day. That's too tight for most inspectors to do the kind of thorough job you're paying for. (It's also a sign of greed, which is never a good business practice.) Depending on the size and shape of your home, your inspection should take between two and three hours, after which you'll want your inspector to sit down and explain to you in detail about the condition of your property. Also, some ASHI-certified inspectors are hiring non-ASHI employees to do inspections. Be certain that the person you hire has the credentials and experience to do the job properly.

Successful Home Seller Tip: Everyone knows that life can be unfair. In that vein, not every home inspection (or home inspector, for that matter) is going to be perfect. No matter how thorough your inspection, the inspector is bound to miss something. But when an unqualified inspector gives your house the okay, you could end up paying plenty for his or her mistakes. Today home inspectors often limit their liability to the amount you paid them as a fee. If you paid them $300, and they missed something on the inspection that winds up costing you $2,000, you may be able to get back only $300 from them. Before you hire a professional house inspector, make sure you find out what their liability policy is, and ask if they have insurance to cover their mistakes.

QUESTION 12

What are environmental toxins? Should I have my home inspected for them before I list it?

As home buyers become more savvy about the environment, they're going to be more concerned about potential environmental problems with your house. Tests for radon, lead paint, leaded water, and asbestos have become a regular part of many real estate contracts. Most professional house inspectors are not qualified to do special tests for toxic substances, though there are separate inspectors who specialize in these areas.

Here are the major toxic substances for which home buyers are inspecting:

Radon. A study in 1989 by the Environmental Protection Agency stated that 22,000 deaths a year are attributed to radon, an invisible, naturally occurring, odorless gas that seeps through cracks in the house or its foundation from the earth. According to an EPA pamphlet, "Radon is the second leading cause of lung cancer in the U.S. after cigarette smoking. As you breathe it in, its decay products become trapped inside your lungs. As these products continue to decay, they release small bursts of energy that can damage lung tissue and lead to lung cancer. It's like exposing your family to hundreds of chest X-rays each year." Of the home buyers and homeowners who actually check for radon, the EPA estimates that around 20 percent will find an unacceptable level.

Should every home seller test his or her home for radon? Absolutely not. First, condo and co-op owners, whose homes are in high rise buildings, don't have to worry about radon. Second, there are areas of the country that are more prone to radon than others. Ask your broker or real estate attorney if your home is located in an area known to have radon problems (remember that radon levels can vary widely from one neighborhood to the next even within these areas). If you are in an area where homes have been found to have unacceptable levels of radon, you can purchase an EPA-listed radon gas test kit in your local hardware store. If that test indicates you have may have a radon problem, you can have a professional radon inspector perform a radon test, *which requires two to four days' exposure in the home.*

The good news is that a radon problem is easily fixable. Emissions can be fixed either by sealing cracks in the basement or by installing an air system that sucks out the gas from beneath the home. For more information on radon, call the EPA's hot line at (800) SOS-RADO.

Asbestos. If your home was built after 1980, you needn't worry about asbestos. If you're selling an older home, it's likely that there is some asbestos in the house.

Asbestos is a microscopic fiber that can become airborne easily and is ingested through the nose or mouth; it lodges in the lung and can cause lung cancer. If the asbestos source is not disturbed, the threat from asbestos is minimal, if any. If you have a prelisting inspection, it's likely the inspector will point out materials that might have asbestos in them. Or you can have an asbestos specialist come out and tell you if you have asbestos in the home and how much it will cost to have it wrapped or removed (the two ways to abate the threat).

Buyers may want you to remove any asbestos before they agree to close on your property, depending on their sophistication and their perception of the probably harm this asbestos could cause. For more information on asbestos, contact your local OSHA (Occupational Safety and Health Administration) office of the federal government, or your local office of the federal Consumer Product Safety Commission.

Lead. High levels of lead in paint and water have been connected with mental and physical development problems, especially in children. Lead is a problem when eaten or inhaled. Lead paint is most often found in older homes (its use in paint has been banned since the 1970s) and can simply be covered up. In HUD homes, or those financed with an FHA mortgage, lead paint must be removed or covered over, or the agency will not fund the purchase of the home. A test by an outside agency can run between $100 and $300, depending on the number of samples tested. An easy way to solve the problem is to simply repaint the interior of your home, especially any areas that are cracking and chipping.

High levels of lead in water are another serious problem, particularly in old homes and apartment buildings. If pipes were soldered together with lead (plumbers today use nickel as a solder), lead particles can be released into your water supply. If the water is contaminated at the source (from your local city or municipal water supply), there isn't much you can do beyond purchasing a water-filtering system. If the problem is lead-soldered pipes, there isn't much you can do unless you replace all the plumbing pipes in your house. That isn't a practical or an economical solution for home sellers. If you know your water is contaminated, you may need to disclose it to prospective buyers.

For more information, call your local office of the federal Consumer Product Safety Commission.

PART III

Putting My Home Up for Sale

DO I NEED A BROKER?

QUESTION 13

Do I need a real estate broker or agent to sell my home? What is a FSBO?

The short answer to the first part of this question is no. You do not need a real estate broker or agent to sell your home. There is no law that requires you to engage the services of a real estate professional before advertising your property for sale. You are entirely free to sell your own property and represent yourself in the negotiations.

Of course, that isn't the answer you'll get from most real estate agents. They will usually tell you professional representation is the only way to go. They will say your property will sell more quickly (often true), for more money (probably true), and with a lot less hassle (possibly true).

But the reality is that many homeowners successfully sell their properties without using the services of their local real estate agent or paying a hefty commission. These resourceful sellers usually have copious amounts of patience and time. Within the industry, homeowners who sell their own homes are usually referred to as *FSBOs* (pronounced "fizz-bos"). The acronym is composed from the first letters of the following phrase: "for sale by owner."

Why would you want to sell your home without a broker? It usually comes down to money. The brokerage commission is far and away the seller's largest cost of sale. The average brokerage commission ranges between 5 and 7 percent of the sales price of the home. If your home sells for $100,000, your broker's commission is $5,000 to $7,000 right off the top of your profits. If your home sells for $300,000, you'll pay the broker between $15,000 and $21,000. (For a more detailed discussion of brokerage commissions, see Question 14.)

That's a lot of cash. FSBOs are generally home sellers who do not want to pay a full broker's commission—though they might be willing to pay a half or partial commission to a buyer's broker. Often, and this is especially true if you haven't owned your home very long, the brokerage commission can eat up most or all of your profit. Sometimes, paying a commission will mean you'll lose money on the sale of your home.

Let's say you bought your home for $190,000 in 1989 in Boston. The year after you bought your home, the bottom dropped out of the market and your home lost 20 or 30 percent of its value overnight. Although the market slowly came back, when you decide to sell in 1995, houses similar to yours are selling for only around $200,000. If you sell your home using the services of a real estate agent, you'll end up paying between $10,000 and $14,000 in commission, not to mention that your home's appreciation failed to keep pace with inflation. In the worst-case scenario, you may have to bring your checkbook to the closing, because you won't have built up enough equity in your home to cover the brokerage commission, loan, and closing costs. You'd sell that Boston home at a loss after paying the brokerage commission.

It's fine to try to save the brokerage commission when you're selling in a hot seller's market. A seller's market implies that there are more buyers than properties available for sale. A buyer's market means there is too much inventory, that there are more homes for sale than buyers to purchase them. If you try to sell on your own in a buyer's market, you may run into trouble. Homes in buyer's markets need all the exposure you can give them, and the best exposure you can buy (with your commission dollars) is being listed in the local Realtor multiple listing service (MLS). (For more information on MLSs, see Question 24.)

FSBO Responsibilities

Selling on your own means more than simply cashing your check at the closing. FSBOs must also take over the responsibilities of the listing agent in addition to the responsibilities of a seller. A FSBO must advertise and market the property, attend all the showings, follow up with the buyers or buyers' brokers, and thoroughly check out any buyer who makes an offer to purchase the home. Those of you who choose to sell on your own must take care of the mechanics and paperwork of selling in addition to keeping your home neat and clean, doing any major or minor repairs, and maintaining the exterior of the home.

FSBOs say saving the 5 to 7 percent commission is worth all the extra work. But it takes a savvy seller to consummate a FSBO deal. Matt and Sally sold their San Francisco Bay Area condo themselves for around $500,000. "We knew the condo was in excellent shape, was in a superhot neighborhood in a very desirable building with good views," Matt recalls. "Condos that went on the market were selling within a few days for nearly full price." Matt and Sally put up a notice in the laundry room about selling their condo. They also advertised in the local newspapers. Within a few days, they had several prospective buyers come through their home. One made an offer, which Matt and Sally accepted. "If we'd used a broker, we would have had to pay a 6 percent commission, which would have cost us $30,000 right off the top," says Sally. "We didn't think a few days of work was worth that much money."

Matt and Sally did several things right in trying to sell their own home: They knew what the competition was and how much it was selling for, and they knew how to correctly advertise the property. Matt and Sally were also selling in what turned out to be the first hot seller's market San Francisco had seen since the recession in the early 1990s. Their experience shows how easy it is to be a FSBO in a hot market. When everyone wants your property, and is willing to pay nearly top dollar for it, it is less necessary for you to use a broker to sell your home. In a hot market, home buyers become predatory, and they will seek out your house. All you have to do is bait the hook: Get your house into selling shape and price it correctly.

Real estate experts, however, estimate that between 85 to 95 percent of all existing homes (this doesn't include new construction) are sold with a broker's help. While some industry observers say the number of FSBOs is rising, I believe the majority of homes will always be sold by the real estate brokerage community. There are solid reasons for that assumption. First, most sellers don't have the time or energy to manage the sale of their home themselves. They're too busy working, raising their families, or caring for aging parents to be on call for every buyer who wants to see their home. And in a slow or dead seller's market, similar to the one experienced by much of the country in the first few years of the 1990s, most sellers will want to take advantage of the broker's resources, professional network, and contacts. Another reason sellers often turn to brokers after trying unsuccessfully to sell the house themselves is price. Most sellers, at least initially, overestimate how much their home is worth and underestimate a home buyer's ability to recognize its true value. A good broker should help you set a listing price that is close to market value by providing you with *comps* (the sales prices of homes similar to yours that have recently sold in your neighborhood).

Do you need a broker to sell your home? If your neighborhood has only a few homes for sale but a lot of buyers who want them, then you may not need to hire a broker to handle your sale. On the other hand, if you don't have the time, organization, patience, or talents necessary to turn a looker into a buyer, or if your neighborhood has too few buyers for all the homes on the market, then you may want to start investigating various real estate agents and the brokers they work for.

QUESTION 14

What is the broker's commission? Is it negotiable?

When Julia, a St. Louis, Missouri, homeowner, decided to sell her home, she asked her neighbors about the commissions they had paid to brokerage firms. "I discovered that the commissions ran the gamut from 4 percent to 8 percent, which really surprised me," she recalled. "I had always thought that commissions were set at 6 percent."

Not exactly. Brokerage commissions are completely negotiable. It is illegal for local or national brokerage firms to "fix" commission rates. That means that your negotiating skills and local competition—and *not* the managing broker of the firm you use—will determine how much commission you pay.

What is the typical commission? Generally, commissions range from 5 to 7 percent of the sales price. But some brokerage commissions are higher and some are lower. Some discount brokers will attempt to sell your home for as little as 1.5 to 2 percent of the sales price. Others have taken listings for as much as 9 or 10 percent. For example, there are brokers who will cut commissions down to nearly nothing if the seller agrees to do almost all of the work or agrees to pay for the advertising costs associated with marketing the home. In fact, some brokers have cordoned off the discount commission business and made it a successful niche. Discount brokers usually offer sellers (and buyers) a sliding scale of fees for a sliding scale of services. (For more information on discount brokers, see Question 19.)

(But you have to read between the lines. In the local MLS, a broker must offer at least half of a full commission to the buyer broker. If the average in your area is 6 percent, then the buyer broker must be offered at least half of that for bringing the buyer. If your discount broker offers to list your property for 1.5 percent commission, ask if it will be marketed on your local MLS or not. It's hard to imagine a property being listed on a local MLS for less than a 4 percent commission.)

Brokers charge a variety of fees based on a variety of services. One prominent broker in Virginia Beach, Virginia, says that this "pick-and-choose" approach to home selling allows sellers to design their own sales strategy. "Within a few miles of us, we have a company that charges only 4.5 percent [of the sales price] and another that charges 3 percent plus a $125 cash up-front advance on the commission," she notes. But self-serve real estate isn't for everyone. Ideally, we'd all want more service at a lower commission price.

Some sellers are willing to pay more than a standard commission (generally between 5 to 7 percent) for a broker with a proven track record of selling property in days rather than months. You can also use the commission to augment your marketing efforts. For example, a 10 percent commission will definitely catch a broker's eye as he or she is flipping through the multiple listing book. Offering a 10 percent commission is nearly double the typical commission, and could mean thousands of extra dollars in a broker's pocket. Or, if you don't want to offer the extra benefit equally to both your broker and the buyer's broker, consider offering a 7 percent commission where the seller broker gets 3 percent and the buyer's broker gets 4 percent.

In which circumstances might you want to raise the broker's commission?

- If you own a home that is extremely difficult to sell, either because of its location (next to a dump, a rail-

road yard, a school playground, or a highway) or its condition.
- If you need to sell very quickly because you've been transferred, or you've already bought another house, or you've had a personal tragedy such as a family illness or divorce.

How low can commissions go? Well, brokers' commissions range from 2 percent to 10 percent of the sales price, though some independent brokers may decide to market your home for a flat fee only. One real estate broker in Chicago says if she has both sides of the contract (a dual agency situation), she can negotiate a flat fee of, say, $2,000 on a $75,000 house—about half of what she would normally get—in order to make a deal happen. A full commission is usually considered to be between 5 and 7 percent of the sales price. Marta, a broker in Seattle, says: "We charge for our expertise. Our job is not only to list the property but to market the property. We offer a full range of services, [starting with] counseling homeowners on the changes that need to be made to the home before it's listed."

What most homeowners don't realize is how expensive it is to actually market a home, experts say. In addition to the broker's time, advertising can cost hundreds or thousands of dollars over the life of the listing agreement. Multiple listing services charge for each home that's listed. Then there are promotional expenses of brochures, phone calls, letters, and faxes. Finally, many listing agents will provide a brokers' open house and serve cake and coffee or lunch. In other words, seller brokers aren't pocketing your entire commission.

But even when you use a full-service brokerage firm,

commissions can be negotiated. In 1994, the C
Federation of America, a nonprofit trade organiz
leased a report that suggested that sellers should negotiate a considerably reduced commission should the seller broker act as a dual agent by bringing the buyer to the transaction. The CFA noted that part of the reason full commissions were paid was for the fiduciary duties that came along with agency. In other words, sellers pay for the work, but they also pay for the advice and counsel. If the seller broker also represents the buyer as a buyer broker, the broker becomes a dual agent, advising neither party. If advice is part of what you're paying for, and you're not getting it, the CFA suggests you shouldn't have to pay a full commission. There's some truth to this logic, recognized even by the attorney who represents the National Association of Realtors. Still, you'd have to negotiate this clause into your listing agreement up front, before you sign it. And if the listing broker agrees to reduce the commission if the same broker brings the buyer to the transaction, be sure to get it in writing.

Here are some other suggestions for negotiating the commission:

- Brokers will often ask for 5 or 6 percent on the first $100,000 of a sale and then take less than that on the rest of the sales price. Of course, the more expensive the home, the more leverage you have in negotiating commission. There's more room to maneuver and still leave the broker feeling as if he or she has earned a chunk of money. It's not uncommon to see a sales commission structured at 6 percent on the first $100,000, 5 percent on the second $100,000, and 4.5 percent on the rest of the sales price. On a $500,000 home, a straight 6 percent commission would add up to $30,000. On the lower negotiated commission, the seller would pay only $24,500 to the broker, a savings of $5,500.

- You might ask the broker to lower the commission rate by a full percentage point. If brokers often get 6 percent in your neighborhood, you might ask the broker to take 5 percent. On a $250,000 home, the 6 percent commission would be $15,000. If you pay a 5 percent commission, you'd only owe the broker $12,500, a savings of $2,500.
- Sometimes there are extenuating circumstances where sellers can renegotiate the commission rate later in the game, after the listing is signed—and even after a deal has been struck. Brokers say this is a violation of the spirit of the listing agreement you signed, and besides, it's not a nice thing to do. That may be true, but if you're deciding whether or not to renew with a brokerage company, and another company you respect offers to market your home for a smaller commission, you should go back to your original broker and ask him or her to match the offer. And consider this scenario: Your home is off the market, your listing agreement has expired, and someone wants to purchase your home. If you want your broker to help you with the deal, you can then go back and say: "Sally Smith wants to buy my house and I'd like you to represent me. But I'm willing to pay only a 3 percent commission. Do you want to help me?" (For more information on listing agreements, see Questions 21 and 22.)
- When negotiating the listing agreement, see if the broker will accept a cut in the commission if the firm

represents both sides in the transaction. If the regular commission is, say, 6 percent, and the brokerage firm also brings the buyer to the transaction, try to cut the commission to 5 percent. If your seller broker also represents the buyer, try to cut the commission to 4 percent.

Sometimes a buyer will come back to a house after the home has been taken off the market. If a buyer who saw your home when it was listed comes back within six months of the end of your listing agreement, you may owe a commission to your broker (read the terms and conditions listed in your listing agreement). On the other hand, if you explain to the broker that you and the buyer will just "wait out" the contract, you may have some leverage; after all, brokers know better than anyone that no deal means no commission. You should know, however, that this kind of renegotiation is frowned upon in the brokerage community. Brokers have a high opinion of what they do, and the best brokers do a wonderful job that's worth every penny you're going to pay them. On the other hand, a broker who did a bad job may be willing to "forgive and forget" and take a smaller commission to placate you and hopefully keep you as a client. Before you sign the listing agreement, read all the fine print. If you're still not sure what you would owe the broker in this situation, ask your real estate attorney to explain the document and the case law in your state.

If you're in a seller's market, where there are many more buyers than there are available properties, it might be possible to negotiate to lower commissions without noticing a decline in the level of service. That's because your agent might not have to work too hard to find a buyer. However, if you find yourself in a buyer's market—where there are many more houses for sale than buyers to purchase them—you may want to distinguish your home by offering a full commission plus a bonus to the agent who brings the buyer.

Successful Home Seller Tip: Brokers will often kick in a little of their commission to make a deal. If you and the buyer get within a few thousand dollars of an agreement, but for whatever reason can't (or refuse) to meet in the middle, you may be able to get your broker and the buyer's broker to kick in a piece of their commissions to make the deal happen. But brokers usually see this as a last-ditch effort to save the deal and rarely will they volunteer to give up some of their money. You'll have to suggest it to your broker and the buyer's broker, who will then attempt to do everything possible to convince you and the buyer to meet in the middle before they are forced to make up the difference.

Note: Many brokers get cranky when they have to work for less than what they consider to be a full and proper commission. That's understandable, since they are professionals. On the other hand, selling homes is business, not pleasure. And it's a business that's getting more sophisticated as the years pass. Like many other industries in this decade, real estate is experiencing a shakeout, and less able professionals are being squeezed out to make room for more efficient brokers. Although the broker will tell you it isn't nice to modify the listing agreement—and may tell you it isn't fair to ask for a reduced commission—these things go on all the time. Your job is to sell your home as quickly and as easily as possible and to net as much money as possible from the process. If that means negotiating for a somewhat reduced commission, you may have to do it.

QUESTION 15

What is the difference between a real estate agent and a real estate broker? What is the difference between a Realtor, a Realtist, and a real estate broker?

Real estate professionals go by a few different names, although the distinction shouldn't matter much to you, the seller. The only caveat here is to make certain the broker or agent you choose to work with is a licensed real estate professional. All real estate brokers and sales agents are licensed and regulated by the state. Most states have laws that require brokers and agents to post their licenses in a visible spot in their place of business. While most large firms and franchises (like RE/MAX, Coldwell Banker, Century 21, and so on) follow the law and do not hire people as brokers or real estate agents who have not passed the state licensing examination, this sort of thing apparently continues in some smaller, neighborhood firms. Working with a broker or agent who is not licensed by the state can create all sorts of problems, particularly if something goes wrong between you and the buyer. If you are not absolutely sure that your broker or agent is licensed by the state, ask to see a copy of his or her license. Or you can call the state agency that regulates real estate licenses and inquire about the status of your agent's license.

What is the difference between a real estate broker and a real estate agent? To the average home buyer or seller, there isn't too much. Before someone can take the state brokerage examination, he or she must have started out as a sales agent, completing the required number of hours and classes and passing a written examination. To become a broker, an agent must take additional classes, have a specified amount of experience in the field, and pass another exam. Both agents and brokers can assist you equally well in the purchase of property.

Having a real estate broker's license confers certain privileges, including the right to open, run, and own a real estate office and to work independently of an office. A real estate agent must work for a broker, who is legally responsible for that agent's actions.

Is it better to work with a broker than to work with a sales agent? Not necessarily. Although it makes sense to think that a broker might have more experience or be more knowledgeable than an agent, that is not always the case. Plenty of sales agents have chosen not to become brokers because they have no intention of ever running their own office. The experience and knowledge of an agent who has been working in an area for fifteen years will far surpass those of a brand-new broker. You should find the most experienced professional to work with you, regardless of whether he or she is an agent or a broker.

What is the difference between a broker who is a Realtor and a broker who is not? A Realtor is a broker or agent who belongs to the National Association of Realtors (NAR) and subscribes to that organization's code of ethics and conduct. There are around two million real estate agents and brokers in the United States, of which around 750,000 belong to the NAR. A Realtist is the designation given to an agent or a broker who is a member of the National Association of Real Estate Brokers, an organization that caters to real estate professionals who are African American.

Is it better to work with a Realtor than a broker who is not a Realtor? Not necessarily. Again, you want to find the best, most knowledgeable, and most reliable broker or agent.

Don't worry about titles, designations, and how many letters follow his or her name. Instead, worry about how respected the broker or agent is, what kind of contacts he or she has created within your local real estate community, and the track record he or she has established. These qualities are far more important to the successful sale of your home.

QUESTION 16

How do I choose the right broker? And is it better to choose a broker from a small, medium, or large firm?

Finding a broker or an agent who meets your needs and personality can be tougher than it sounds. Those buyers who have the worst experiences are often those who just walk into or call their neighborhood shop and ask for anyone at random. That is *not* how you find a good agent or broker. That is how you find a big headache.

In some ways, finding the right broker or agent is tougher for a seller than for a buyer. Both buyers and sellers should find someone with whom they feel comfortable, whose personality meshes with theirs. It's important to have someone who can listen to your concerns and can explain potential problems to you in a way you can understand.

But sellers must also hire the agent or broker who can best market their home. This may mean some compromises. For example, you might personally be more comfortable with a laid-back agent who can sit chatting with you for hours about your children, the local school system, or the price of tea leaves in China. But that kind of broker may not be as effective at selling your home as an aggressive broker with an extensive network of contacts. This is not to suggest that only aggressive brokers or agents are effective seller brokers. Laid-back brokers can be effective, too. You'll have to thoroughly interview each broker you invite into your home to determine who will be the best choice for selling your house.

When choosing the listing broker (as seller brokers and agents are often called), the first thing to do is to invite three brokers or agents into your house to do a *comparative marketing analysis* (see Question 18). A comparative marketing analysis (CMA) is a research tool brokers use to determine the value of your home. They find prices of homes that have recently sold that are similar to yours in size, condition, and location. To do a proper CMA, you should allow brokers to walk through your home and property, then give them three to seven days to find their comps (short for properties comparable to yours that have recently sold or been listed). They should then return with a brochure that includes their suggested list price for your home along with the comps that support that price. A complete CMA will include their marketing plans. Think of the CMA as a bid for your business. Generally speaking, the quality of the CMA will reflect the quality of service you can expect from that broker.

When you telephone a prospective broker, you should tell him or her that you have also contacted two other agents. It is not necessary to tell them whom you have contacted. The real estate business is a small circle no matter where you live. If you tell one broker who else you have asked to create a CMA, there is a chance the brokers will discuss their listing prices with each other.

Here are some questions you may want to ask prospective brokers:

- *Are you a broker or a sales agent?* Brokers who manage firms in addition to working with buyers and sellers may not have sufficient time to effectively market your home. But you may find broker associates (also called "associate brokers") who can assist you.
- *How long have you been in the business? Are you a full-time or part-time broker?* You want someone who is a full-time broker and relies on his or her income to pay the bills. A full-time agent will be far more available to you, both emotionally and physically, and is likely to work harder to sell your home.
- *How many homes have you listed or sold in the past year?* Ask the agent to provide you with a list of these homes and their list and sale prices. Look over the list and see how many of the homes match the profile of your property. If your home is a $250,000 four-bedroom colonial with a small garden, but most of the broker's listings are for high-rise condos priced under $150,000, you and the broker may not be the right match.
- *What homes have you shown or sold in my neighborhood in the past year?* Even if this broker has done $10 million in sales in the past year, it won't mean beans if he or she isn't intimately familiar with your particular neighborhood and the competition you'll face.
- *May I have a copy of your résumé?* Top brokers say if you're thinking about hiring someone to represent you in a transaction, it's not unreasonable to ask for a copy of his or her résumé.
- *What will you do to facilitate the sale of my property? What kinds of marketing will you do?* A multimedia strategy is best. Advertising only in the newspaper is considered

a flat marketing strategy, whereas marketing your home through newspapers, fliers, direct mail, and such interactive sales tools as twenty-four-hour computerized property descriptions are considered part of a successful multilayered marketing approach.

- *Do you use a lockbox? Or do you accompany all buyers and buyer's agents who will be going through my home?* Many listing agents like to use a lockbox (which is, quite literally, a locked box on your property that contains the key to your home, which can be accessed only by a broker-carried key card or a combination) because it relieves them of the responsibility of actually walking buyers through your home, pointing out your home's best features. But buyer brokers don't know the best features of your house, and as a result buyers who walk through homes with lockboxes may miss important features that could invigorate their interest in your property.
- *What kinds of continuing real estate education classes have you taken? Do you have any professional designations?* While brokers with professional designations are not necessarily better than brokers who don't have letters after their names, there are lots of continuing education classes required before brokers can use those letters of honor. It is important to work with a knowledgeable broker who has kept abreast of changes in the law and has made a continuing effort to improve his or her ability within the real estate community.
- *Excluding you, who are three best agents or brokers who work in my price range?* This is one way to let a broker know you are shopping for the best agent in town. But it is also an important gauge of the ethics of the

sales agent. If an agent can't compliment another agent by recommending him or her, it may be a sign of professional jealousy or ultra-competitiveness. Neither of these characteristics is desirable because real estate is a game of cooperation and deal making. If the agent provides you with names, ask what it is that he or she likes about these colleagues.

- *What is the minimum length of time you will accept for a listing?* Some brokerage firms will insist that you sign a listing agreement that lasts at least six months. Unless you are selling an extremely expensive home for your area, you shouldn't hire these brokers. If the average number of days a home is listed before selling is 40, why would you sign a listing agreement for 180 days? Instead, list your home with a brokerage firm that offers listing agreements in 90-day lengths. Agents know your home will have its maximum exposure in the first three weeks it is listed. Within a month, you'll know whether or not your home is overpriced, and a 90-day listing agreement will give you time to correct that price. If the brokerage firm you want to use insists on a six-month listing, ask for a no-cost, no-penalty cancellation clause after 90 days with two weeks' notice. Then add that clause in writing to the listing agreement.
- *How often do you stay in touch with your sellers?* Good agents will call their sellers on a weekly basis. If no sales offers have materialized during the week, the call should be about strategy and any new marketing plans the agent has in mind for your property. If no showings have occurred, the conversation might turn to lowering the listing price. On the other hand, you

should expect your agent to contact you the moment he or she receives an offer to purchase.

- *Please give me the names and telephone numbers of the last three sellers you worked with*. Recommendations are always helpful. Be sure to call these references.

Successful Home Seller Tip: Be leery of any agent who walks into your house and tosses off a suggested listing price in five minutes. While it's usually better to work with a heavily experienced agent, new agents might prove to be tireless workers in marketing your home. To make the sale, they might be willing to go the extra mile.

In addition to looking for an experienced agent, try to find someone who suits your personality. If you're an early bird, don't choose someone who is habitually late. If you're allergic to smoking, don't choose a smoker. If you're extremely organized, don't choose a broker who is constantly losing his or her keys. Over time, or on long days of multiple showings, these little personality quirks may drive you crazy.

How do you find a good broker or agent? As in choosing a doctor or an attorney, most people are referred to a broker by their friends or a family member who has recently bought or sold a home and has had a good experience. While you certainly can choose to work with a relative who is a broker or agent, you may be better served by hiring the broker who has a proven track record of selling homes quickly in your neighborhood.

Marlene, a top broker in Chicago, works in a small neighborhood called Graceland, located near the city's famous Graceland Park Cemetery. This working-class neighborhood of single-family homes and two-flats has turned into a "hot" neighborhood where broken-down homes have been bought and rehabbed, then resold to aging baby boomers who prefer living in the city to living in the suburbs. Smart brokers representing buyers who wish to live in Graceland know Marlene is the first person they should call. They know it's her turf. If she doesn't have the listing (rare), she usually knows the history of the house, its condition, and its former owners. Nearly every seller in the neighborhood lists with her or her office. Marlene, who has lived in the neighborhood for many years, sells more than $10 million worth of property there each year.

It's also important to find someone who won't push you into making a decision—or accepting the wrong offer—before you're ready. You want a broker who will tell you the facts and help you compare various offers, but you don't want someone who will scare you into taking a bad offer. On the other hand, sometimes it takes a strong broker to tell you when you've overpriced your home for the market and help you find the right listing price. If you ever feel that the broker isn't doing his or her job, or if you and your broker find that you can no longer work together successfully, contact the broker's managing broker. One of the managing broker's most important jobs is to smooth out the bumps between agents and sellers. If you look closely at your listing agreement you'll see you've contracted with the brokerage firm, not the individual real estate agent, to sell your home. The brokerage firm will want to keep your listing, so it should be happy to find you a new agent if the situation with your listing agent becomes intolerable.

Small, Large, or Franchise?

The size of the firm matters less than the people in it. But there are some basic differences between small and large real estate firms. Although you should carefully weigh many factors before choosing a real estate company to work with, size is one of the extra elements that may help you choose between two terrific brokers.

Experts say that all good real estate agents should be able to manage the basics of buying and selling property. Whether you're looking for a home or trying to sell the one you're in, good agents should stay in touch with you, give you feedback on your property or on properties you're considering buying, be able to tap into a relocation network, and help you get the best deal. Still, there are subtle differences in the services they offer.

Real estate firms generally fall into three categories: small local operations, large independent companies, and national franchise corporations.

- The mom-and-pop shops are usually one-location offices with anywhere from one to eight agents and perhaps a secretary or two. They usually are well-known within their communities but have little or no name recognition outside of them.
- Large independent firms usually have offices in various parts of a city or metro area. Such a firm has an identity and a corporate message that it tries to thread through its branches, each of which may have dozens of agents.
- Franchise operations are actually independent companies that are tied into a large national network. Some Coldwell Banker offices in the country are owned by the company. Others are franchised—that is, they're affiliated with Coldwell Banker but are independently owned and operated. Sometimes one person will own several Century 21 offices in several

neighborhoods. Other real estate companies that franchise branch offices include Electronic Realty Associates (ERA), Better Homes & Gardens, RE/MAX, and Prudential Preferred Properties.

Contacts, Contacts, Contacts

So what services can a small, a large independent, or a franchise operation offer you?

As a seller you may be best served by using the office that is most identified with the neighborhood in which you live, where the owner of that office has deep roots in the community that can be tapped for your benefit. There are several advantages to working with such a small firm. Everyone in the office is aware of each buyer's and seller's specific concerns and can help out at a moment's notice. No-frills offices are a boon to buyers and sellers, who, despite the continuing growth of the voice mail industry, usually find a real person on the telephone when they call.

Large independent firms offer other advantages. They usually have the funds to do a significant amount of advertising as well as extras like top-quality (and perhaps full-color) brochures that feature homes they have listed for sale. In a large metro area, several real estate firms may even feature their listings on weekend television shows. Large firms often give brokers bonuses for selling in-house properties, that is, selling homes listed by the firm to buyers represented by the firm. As a seller, your property will be exposed to a much larger number of prospective buyers by agents hoping to earn that extra commission.

While the names of small firms, or even some large independents, often draw a blank, most people know Century 21 and its gold-jacketed salespeople. The franchise has more than 85,000 agents in approximately six thousand offices. Coldwell Banker also has its own image, as do Better Homes & Gardens and Prudential. RE/MAX operates a little differently than the rest, which may be attractive to some sellers. Because RE/MAX agents rent their office space from the firm, they keep nearly all of their commissions, instead of splitting them with the brokerage firm. This allows RE/MAX agents a great deal of flexibility in negotiating commissions on the sale of property.

National franchise operations allow brokers in one city to receive referrals from another. So the brokerage firm that has your house listed for sale in Seattle, Washington, might receive a referral of a buyer from Boston looking for a house like yours. National relocation networks provide an additional level of service by tapping into prospective buyers who are in the process of moving from location to location.

No matter what type of firm you choose, it's important to hire one that belongs to the local multiple listing service (MLS). The MLS is the best way for you to advertise your property. Most brokers belong to the local MLS and list their properties on their computerized system. What's nice about this is that brokers tend to look up property for clients by price range, size, or location. Your home will be listed on the MLS by its price, location, size, and amenities. If a broker asks the computer to search for all properties listed for less than $100,000 in a particular neighborhood and your house meets those criteria, the computer will automatically put it into the list of prospective homes for the buyer to see. (For additional information on MLSs, see Question 24.)

Successful Home Seller Tip: Although a bit reluctant to adapt existing technology for real estate uses, the real estate industry has been playing catch-up. Today many brokers have some sort of computerized voice mail system for taking messages. Now, state-of-the-art computer systems have been bought by real estate firms, and local MLSs, in order to provide faster and better information on homes available for sale. Some firms are using a product that marries voice mail with computer data bases. This product allows buyers free access to a twenty-four-hour computer data base that plays ninety-second descriptions of any home they choose. Computer on-line services often have a local real estate bulletin board where members can list their properties for sale. No matter what size they are, real estate firms that employ advanced technologies provide additional avenues for sellers who are eager to sell. These technologies create innovative ways of getting your property noticed by prospective buyers.

QUESTION 17
What is a seller or conventional broker? What should my broker do for me?

Real estate professionals use several names, all of which can be confusing to the would-be buyer or seller. As we discussed earlier, there are real estate brokers (who have taken extra courses and passed an additional exam that allows them to own and operate a real estate firm) and real estate agents (who work for brokers). There are Realtors, who belong to the National Association of Realtors, and there are Realtists, who belong to the National Association of Real Estate Brokers. There are buyer brokers, who show buyers properties that are available for sale and who owe their loyalty to buyers rather than sellers. And there are seller brokers or agents, who list homes and represent the seller.

Seller brokers are often called "conventional" or "traditional" brokers because they used to be the only game in town. Buyer brokerage—where the broker owes his or her loyalty to the buyer rather than the seller—didn't begin to catch on nationally until the beginning of the 1990s. Prior to that, all brokers were considered seller brokers because it was the seller who paid the commission. Subagents were seller brokers who brought the buyer to the transaction. Because subagents split the commission with the listing broker—paid by the seller—the real estate industry decided they, too, owed their loyalty to the seller.

Things have changed since the introduction of buyer brokerage, and in some states subagency has been all but eliminated in favor of single agency (where brokerage firms represent only buyers or represent only sellers) or specific agency (where brokers represent the person who hires them for a specific transaction, regardless of whether it is a buyer or a seller). (For more information on buyer brokerage, see Question 20.)

The one plus to conventional brokerage is that it virtually eliminates the concept of *dual agency*. Dual agency occurs when the seller broker is the same broker who introduces the buyer to the property. The broker then becomes the middle person—some folks in the industry call them "Facilitators" or say they are "practicing nonagency"—dealing with both sides of the deal. When confronted with a dual agency situation, brokers must either choose which side they want to represent (buyer or seller) or have both buyer and seller sign a letter acknowledging the dual agency situation and granting permission for the broker to represent both sides. Dual agency has also been defined in some states as when the same brokerage firm represents the buyer and seller in a single transaction, even though different agents represent each side. This type of dual agency is stickier, simply because it's hard to know (though it's not unlikely) if the buyer's broker and the seller's broker exchanged confidential information about the deal.

Your Broker's Responsibilities

Your broker's most important job is this: to sell your home as quickly as possible for the most money possible. But this big job includes more than a dozen little jobs that will help you get organized for your sale and then successfully sell your home.

First, it's important to know what your broker probably *won't* do:

- She (or he) won't necessarily be your best friend, nor will she need to be in order to get the job done.
- She probably won't call you every twenty minutes to tell you your home hasn't sold.
- She won't hold an open house every weekend or advertise your home in the real estate section each week.
- She won't appreciate being awakened at 3:00 A.M. because you can't sleep and had a wonderful marketing idea you just had to discuss.

But there are lots of things your real estate agent or broker should do to sell your home quickly. And since you are paying a hefty commission of 5 to 7 percent of the listing price, you are entitled to expect some service. After all, that's what full-service, full-price brokers are paid for.

Here is a list of things a good broker should do for you:

- *Identify Improvements.* She should assist you in identifying improvements you can make around the house that will help it sell better. This includes: offering tips on uncluttering your home; giving you pointers on painting or other inexpensive decorating options; noticing items that need fixing, like a squeaky door or a loose doorknob; and tips on improving your home's curb appeal.
- *Comparative Marketing Analysis (CMA).* Your broker should help you decide at what price you want to list your home by pulling out "comps." The list price of your home is based on what other homes that are comparable to yours, and that are located in your neighborhood, have sold for. (For more information on CMAs, see Question 18.)
- *Marketing Strategy.* Anton, a real estate agent in Chicago, claims he doesn't sell homes, he "markets" them. If you ask him what he means by that, he'll tell you he develops a solid marketing strategy for each home he lists. Marketing is more than simply advertising your home in the local newspaper. Marketing may include open houses, fliers, computer lists, direct mail, cash or prize bonuses, a higher-than-average sales commission, mortgage buy downs, and seller financing options. Your broker should have a plan of action spelled out in writing and present it to you with the CMA.
- *Broker's Open House.* There are two kinds of open houses: the broker's open house (sometimes referred to as a "broker's open") and an open house for prospective buyers that is held on Saturday or Sunday, usually in the early afternoon. When your broker hosts a broker's open, she will issue an open invitation

to every brokerage firm in town, inviting individual brokers and agents to stop by to preview your home for their buyers. This is an excellent way to get the word out in the brokerage community about your property. If your broker is smart, she'll serve something—like cake and coffee, or even lunch—in order to attract attention. When my mother, Susanne, a veteran real estate agent in Chicago, hosts a broker's open house, she often hires a specific caterer who has an excellent reputation in the brokerage community. She knows this caterer's name alone will draw people to a broker's open. Broker's open houses usually take place during the week—often on a Tuesday or Thursday morning—and last anywhere from two to five hours. Brokers will pick up the "hot sheet" and see what new listings have come on the market (and what they're serving), then decide where to go.

- *Weekend Open House.* When your broker opens your home up on the weekend to prospective buyers, he or she will advertise the open house in the local newspaper. Some of the folks who will come through your home are curiosity seekers; many others are buyers hoping that your house will be the right house for them. Odds are, however, that an open house won't produce the buyer. But it's good exposure and you never know, maybe someone will emerge. Or an open house visitor might think your home is perfect for another buyer he or she knows. While your broker might allow you to stay at a broker's open, he or she should ask you to leave the public open house. Buyers often feel intimidated by the seller's presence and might worry about taking a really close look at the property.

- *Seller's Reality Check*. If your home isn't selling, your broker may take you on a tour of other homes in your neighborhood that are for sale. It's a good idea to keep your eye on the competition. By seeing what's available and for what price, you'll begin to understand how much homes are worth in your neighborhood.
- *Excellent Communication*. Much of the stress involved in selling your home comes from not knowing what's happening. When Beth and Mark were selling their home, their agent would occasionally touch base to let them know that people were seeing the unit but no one had made an offer. Your agent should contact you at least once a week to let you know what's going on with your home. If he or she is hosting an open house, or there has been a significant amount of activity during the week, your agent should call twice that week. Although it isn't necessarily true, you'll psychologically feel as if your agent is working harder for you if you hear from him or her more often.
- *Special Care for Vacant Homes*. If you've already moved out of your home (and perhaps out of the city or out of state), you should expect your broker to check on the house at least once or twice a week. If your curbside appeal dwindles with the growth of your landscape, your broker should let you know when it's time to pay for a gardening service to mow the lawn and trim those hedges. In winter, it is especially important that the agent check to make sure the heat is working and that no pipes have burst. Your agent should also inform you when and if you need to have your driveway and walk plowed.
- *Stay on Top of the Buyer*. Once you've negotiated the contract with the buyer, it's up to your broker to make

sure the contingencies are met and the additional earnest money checks are deposited on schedule. If you granted a financing contingency, your broker should check to make sure the buyer has been approved for his or her loan. If you granted an inspection contingency, your broker should let you know when it has been scheduled so that you or your spouse can attend. If you are unable to attend the inspection, you should feel free to ask your broker to attend. It's important for your broker to stay on top of the buyer because if the buyer defaults, and does not go through with the purchase, your house will have been off the market for several days or even several months, and you will have lost valuable marketing time.

- *The Closing.* Although it's not absolutely necessary for the broker to attend the closing, it's advisable to have him or her there, particularly if you live in a state where real estate attorneys do not normally close residential sales. Don't be surprised if your broker wants to come, however. That's where he or she can pick up the broker's commission check.

Successful Home Seller Tip: If you're selling your home on your own, you should follow many, if not all, of the broker tips listed above. After all, you're essentially representing yourself in the sale of your home. While you won't be able to host a broker's open, you can send fliers to local real estate firms announcing that your home is for sale and that you will pay a half (2.5 to 3.5 percent) sales commission to the buyer broker. For weekend open houses, make sure you have at least one other person in the house with you. That way, if you do have a big turnout, someone can watch the door and greet new prospective buyers while the other person is leading the tour. Also, it's safer to have two people. While most folks who come through an open house are legitimate (that is, they want to buy a home or they think they want to buy a home), we live in an unsafe time, and there are folks with less than honorable intentions roaming the streets. As theft is always a concern, be sure that your home is secure, with all valuables off the countertops and locked away. There is no need to tempt any visitor to your home by leaving money or valuables lying about.

QUESTION 18
What is a comparative marketing analysis (CMA)?

A comparative marketing analysis (CMA) is the most valuable tool you can use to determine the correct listing price for your home. The best CMAs compare your home to other homes for sale that are similar to yours in size, shape, condition, and location.

These comparisons are extremely specific. The CMA should identify all the variables in your home—including the number and size of rooms, number of bathrooms, amount of square footage, lot size, garage, location, and any special amenities the home may have—and compare them to what other homes in the area have. Once the comps have been identified, the CMA will match up these properties with their most current listing and selling prices.

With comps as backup, the broker will usually put a suggested listing price at the end of the CMA package. Usually this price reflects the broker's knowledge and analysis of past sales in the neighborhood mixed with a little bit of intuition. (Top brokers like to say that setting list prices is an art, not a science. You can use all the numbers you like, but each house is a unique property at that moment in time. Unless someone else owns a twin house to yours that was built at the same time and has been decorated and maintained in the same way, no two homes are going to be exactly alike.)

How does the process work? Once you've narrowed down your list of potential brokers to three, call them and ask each of them to create a CMA for your home. You should call brokers and ask for a CMA even if you've decided to try to sell your home on your own. Brokers should be happy to comply, simply because they know that most homes are sold by agents and brokers. They'll gamble that you won't be able to sell the home yourself and will think of them if and when you decide to list your property.

A properly constructed CMA is your road map to selling your home successfully. To create one, each broker should come and visit your home at least once, noting down the number and size of rooms, the number of bathrooms, the amount of square feet in the house, lot size, location, the garage size, as well as any special amenities the home may have. A good agent should also ask questions regarding property taxes (How much are they? When was your last reassessment?); recent upgrades, repairs, or improvements you've made to the property; water (municipal or well?); sewage (city sewer or a septic system?); and other costs of homeownership. Depending on your state laws regarding disclosure of defects in the house, the brokers may ask you to fill out and sign a seller disclosure form, listing any hidden material defects in the home. (If you're selling on your own, and your state requires that you give prospective buyers written seller disclosure, contact your local title company for a copy of the disclosure form. You might also want to contact a local brokerage company or check with your real estate attorney to find out what you are required to disclose.)

Armed with this knowledge, the broker will then go back to the office and search through the multiple listing service (MLS) for recently sold homes that are comparable in size and type to yours. She or he will then research at what price these homes were listed and sold, and how long they took to sell.

Once the agent has created the CMA, it is common for him or her to present the information to you in person. Agents and brokers consider the CMA to be their best selling tool, and they may dress it up with smart packaging: color photographs of your home plus photographs of the comps they used to set the list price.

If you ask three agents for CMAs, it's likely each will suggest a different listing price: One may come in on the low side, suggesting a quick sale; one may come in at about the price you'd like to get for your home; and the third may suggest you shoot for the moon.

Which agent's advice should you take? If you think they all missed the mark, or if you aren't sure which suggested listing price is the correct one to choose, don't hesitate to get a fourth opinion. Otherwise, go with the broker whose suggested listing price and marketing strategy make you feel most comfortable.

One problem sellers often have is that deep down they believe their home is worth a certain amount of money. Current market conditions don't matter, and the broker's opinion doesn't matter. Julie and Don are homeowners who decided how much their home was worth long before they listed it for sale. They bought a condo in a newly renovated brownstone in Manhattan, in a neighborhood "everyone" said was going to increase in value. Five years later, when their twin daughters were ready to be enrolled in school, they realized they wanted to move to the suburbs and purchase a single-family home with a garden. When they invited several brokers to present them with a CMA, they were astonished to discover that all three CMAs came in well below what they had expected to get for their home. What had happened? The recession of the early 1990s put the skids on redevelopment of their neighborhood. Without the constant push of developers to buy dilapidated buildings and renovate them, the neighborhood never got any better and possibly even deteriorated. But Julie and Don refused to see what the brokers were telling them. In their minds, their home was supposed to be worth a certain amount in 1995, and they weren't going to take a penny less. They eventually listed their home for about $150,000 more than the highest of the CMAs. A year later, they are still waiting, convinced that they'll get their price.

While Julie and Don have an extreme case of *Seller stubbornitis*, it isn't always easy to listen to, and follow, the advice of your broker. If you've got your mind set on a certain price, don't be surprised if you have a tough time getting the broker you like to go along with the plan. He or she will know that listing your home for that amount of money is a big waste of time. While there may be one buyer out there somewhere who is willing to pay your price, the odds of finding him or her are worse than those of finding the proverbial needle in a haystack.

QUESTION 19

What is a discount broker?

Discount brokerage seems to be an emerging trend whose success has been insured by the recent recession. Most discount brokers work with both buyers and sellers, though an emerging concept in Arizona, called Price Club Realty, is a single agent discount broker that works only with sellers.

Here is how discount brokerage works: A discount broker will list your home in the local multiple listing service (MLS), but you do much of the legwork, show your own home, negotiate your contract and counteroffers, and make your own follow-up calls. If you do all the work, then the discount broker will charge you less than a full commission.

Why should the discount broker receive anything if you're doing all the work? Good question. To begin with, the discount broker has access to the local MLS, which lists all the property for sale in the area. That's where buyers find out all the information about homes for sale, such as their size, price, and number of bedrooms and bathrooms. It's very useful for homes to be listed on the MLS, and access to it is strictly limited to member agents and brokers and their clients. By sharing the commission with the discount broker, you're essentially buying access to the local MLS. Your commission pays to have your property listed on the MLS and put on view in front of thousands of potential buyers.

Discount brokerage firms give back up to 50 percent of their share of the commission at closing. On a $100,000 property, your share might be as much as $1,500. That

$1,500 might well pay the points for your new mortgage, if you're buying another home, or cover the cost of your move. Or, if you live in the Northeast or on the West Coast, and have watched your equity vanish with the recent recession, you might need that $1,500 to pay off the lender.

Here's how the money side of discount brokerage works: The seller pays a commission to the seller broker, which is usually in the range of 5 to 7 percent. For our purposes, let's say the commission is 6 percent of the sales price. The seller broker then pays the buyer broker half of the commission, which in this case would be 3 percent. The discount broker then splits the 3 percent commission, minus any "extras," with the seller. The "extras" are where the consumer has to be careful. A discount brokerage firm puts a price tag on every service it provides for you, including every telephone call or each showing. Usually a minimum number of services are included in the deal, but if the broker does anything for you that falls outside the scope of the standard package of services, the fees for these pay-as-you-go services are deducted from your portion of the commission.

For example, there is a discount brokerage firm in Chicago that charges between 1 and 4 percent off the commission refund for each service it performs for you. So if you need the broker to place a follow-up call to the prospective buyer, the company might reduce your refund by 1 percent for each call. If the total possible refund is $1,500, each phone call would cost you $15.

Other forms of discount brokerage include conventional brokers who, for one reason or another, offer to take your listing at a flat rate, or for a flat fee. Recently, a new form of discount brokerage has emerged, and it may completely reform and standardize the practice.

Price Club Realty

Price Club Realty is pushing the envelope of discount brokerage. A division of the former The Price Club (now Price/Costco, Inc.), Price Club Realty, based in Scottsdale, Arizona, takes the warehouse principles of discount retailers and marries them to real estate. The result is a discount brokerage firm that exclusively represents sellers but has the ability to reach millions of potential buyers.

Price Club Realty started up at the end of 1993. In its first nine months, the company listed approximately 250 properties—of which it sold more than 175. The reason for the venture's popularity is that it offers sellers the opportunity to save thousands of dollars in sales commissions by charging only a flat fee.

Here's how this particular discount broker works: As we went to press, Price Club Realty charged a fee of $890 to list a property, of which the seller pays half up front (the upfront fee is nonreturnable). For that fee, the company puts the property on the local Scottsdale multiple listing service and advertises it in the local paper. It also provides its sellers with "for sale" signs, fliers with a professional photograph, and yard signs with the owner's telephone number. It also provides a comparative marketing analysis (CMA) drawn from local county residential sales records. Sellers sign a six-month listing agreement, which they may extend or cancel at any time. In addition, sellers whose advertising allotment has run out may purchase ads in local newspapers at deeply discounted rates.

Price Club Realty will list the home's availability in a Price Club flier that is distributed weekly to each of the five Price/Costco stores in the area. The flier has an estimated readership of more than 100,000. Price Club/Costco has 16 million members in the United States and Canada (anyone can become a member by paying a $25 to $50 fee), and if the program goes national, you could eventually market your home nationally for less than $1,000.

Sellers could save a significant amount of money using Price Club Realty. On a $100,000 sale, the standard 6 percent commission would be $6,000. If the seller pays a cooperating broker, his or her costs would be $3,890—the $3,000 buyer broker commission plus the $890 fee to Price Club Realty—a savings of $2,110 off the standard 6 percent commission. If the seller sells to a Price Club/Costco member, the savings could be as much as $5,110, since the total fee is $890.

How Do I Find a Good Discount Broker?

The general caveat for real estate services holds true here also: Don't necessarily use the first broker you find. Try to find more than one discount broker, then interview them at length. Compare the services they offer relative to the price they charge. Ask for references and then call those people and ask them how much time and effort they put into their home sale and how much money they received back from the broker. Remember, when you use a discount broker, you're going to be doing much—if not all—of the legwork.

QUESTION 20

What is a buyer broker? What is the difference between a buyer broker and a subagent of the seller? What is dual agency?

As we discussed earlier, a buyer broker represents the buyer, whereas a seller broker (also called the traditional or conventional or listing broker) represents the seller. Buyer brokerage emerged into mainstream real estate brokerage somewhere around 1990. In the early 1990s, the National Association of Realtors (NAR) changed its code of ethics, permitting buyer brokerage to be practiced by its 750,000 members.

If you live in a major metropolitan area, it is quite likely that the person who buys your home will be represented by a buyer broker. More and more buyers are using buyer brokers because they are troubled by these questions: How can a broker have my best interest at heart when he or she is being paid by the seller? How can a broker help me find the best property at the best price when he or she is bound legally and financially to serve the seller's best interest?

Buyer brokers function similarly to seller brokers in that they require a buyer to sign an exclusivity contract. The contract essentially says that the buyer will work with the buyer broker for a certain period of time and will pay either a flat fee, an hourly rate, or a commission based on the sales price of the home. Buyer brokers are supposed to do everything and anything (as long as it is legal) to help buyers get the best house at the best price on the best terms. That can, and should, include providing the buyer with comps, advising him or her on what price to offer for the home, uncovering the seller's motivation for selling, and helping the buyer find inspectors, lenders, and attorneys.

Subagency

Before buyer brokerage existed, buyers were represented by agents who owed their loyalty to the seller. These agents were called subagents, because while they were paid by the seller and owed their fiduciary duty to the seller, they did not work directly for the seller. The problem with subagency is that many buyers assumed that the broker with whom they were working—who shepherded them from property to property, who bought them lunch, and with whom they shared their deepest financial secrets—was actually "their" broker. Nope. "Their" broker actually worked for the seller.

Individual states are beginning to deal with the question of subagency by enacting laws that virtually eliminate it. Illinois passed such a law, that was scheduled to take effect January 1, 1995. The law basically says that agents owe their fiduciary duty to the consumer who hires them, whether that is the buyer or the seller.

Today, buyer brokerage exists in two different forms: traditional buyer brokerage and exclusive buyer brokerage. Exclusive buyer brokers are single agents; they never take listings and never do any work for sellers. Traditional buyer brokers work for a brokerage firm that represents both buyers and sellers, but not in the same transaction. Although traditional buyer brokers supposedly represent the buyer's best interest, it is possible that in the small confines of an office confidential information will be shared between the buyer's agent and the seller's agent for a single transaction. That's why brokerage firms that represent buyers and sellers are sometimes referred to as dual agents. That means they will represent either side of the transaction and, with permission from both buyer and seller, may represent both sides in the same transaction.

Dual Agency

A classic dual agency situation occurs when the broker who lists your property is the same broker who brings the buyer to the transaction. To illustrate this concept, let's say Betty is your listing agent and Max, a buyer with whom Betty has been working, takes an interest in your house. Betty can represent Max in one of two ways. If Betty is acting as a subagent of the seller—that is, she is paid by you and is representing your interests instead of Max's interests—then Betty doesn't really represent Max and there is no inherent conflict of interest if she helps him purchase your house. In this case, Betty would owe her loyalty to you, not Max. If, however, Betty and Max have signed an exclusive buyer brokerage agreement, then Betty also owes Max her fiduciary duty. This scenario presents Betty with a conflict of interest because Betty already owes you her fiduciary duty as the listing broker for your house. In other words, Betty represents both sides of the transaction and supposedly owes both parties her exclusive loyalty. If this kind of dual agency occurs, brokers will often have the buyer and the seller sign an agreement acknowledging that the broker is acting as a dual agent (or a facilitator or a nonagent)—that is, that he or she represents both sides rather than favoring one over the other.

If you buy and sell enough homes, it's likely you'll encounter some form of dual agency. My mother, Susanne, a long-time top-selling Chicago agent, had been working with a home buyer named Richard when we decided we were going to sell our home. Although we hadn't yet listed our unit, Susanne brought Richard by to see it. As luck would have it, he liked it and decided to make an offer. Although she hadn't listed our unit, Susanne was working with Richard as a buyer's agent. Susanne technically didn't represent both sides of the deal (since she was not our listing broker), but we were still concerned that there might have been a conflict of interest. Ultimately, everyone in the transaction signed a disclosure agreement.

(Dual agency can be tricky from the buyer's perspective as well. When Larry and Jane were looking for a home, the buyer broker they were working with kept showing them a property she had listed. It was a lovely house on a nice piece of property, but in addition to being a little above their price range, it had a fatal flaw: It was located across from a municipal dump. Readers of my previous book, *100 Questions Every First-Time Home Buyer Should Ask*, will recall one bit of advice: Don't buy a house across from a dump, because you never know what kind of toxic waste could leach into the ground. Larry and Jane told the agent they weren't interested in the house because of its proximity to the dump, but she kept insisting it was a good deal. "For whom?" Larry asked. Later, Larry and Jane realized that the moment their buyer broker showed them that listing she ceased to represent their best interests and was looking out primarily for the seller.)

Successful Home Seller Tip: Within the sphere of buyer brokerage, the most important issue for sellers is how the buyer broker is going to be compensated. Although the buyer promises to pay the buyer broker, what happens in the real world is that the buyer's broker and your broker are going to split the commission you pay your broker. Why should your money pay someone who owes his or her fiduciary duty and loyalty to the opposition (the buyer)? Good question. Unfortunately, there is no good answer. Buyers want buyer brokerage but they aren't willing to pay for it. Buyer brokers sometimes use the argument that all the money for the transaction comes from the buyer to begin with, so without the buyer's funds the seller wouldn't be paying his or her own broker. While you could look at it that way, you should know that the standard MLS now asks seller brokers to agree to share the commission with whatever broker brings the buyer to the transaction. Buyer brokers are supposed to inform a seller agent up front that they represent the interests of the buyer. Your listing agreement should spell out what happens to the commission if a buyer broker is involved with the sale. If you don't understand how everyone gets paid, ask the broker or consult your real estate attorney.

SIGNING THE LISTING AGREEMENT

QUESTION 21

What is the listing agreement?

The listing agreement is one of the two most important contracts you'll sign during the process of selling your home. (The other is the sales contract.) The listing agreement essentially governs the sale of your home by setting up the parameters under which a real estate brokerage firm will list and market your property.

Although the listing agreement is a valid, binding legal document, you'd be surprised at the number of sellers who sign this document without a second thought—or a second look. That's the kind of attitude that could get you into trouble down the pike. The time to make sure you really understand the listing agreement and what it says is *before* you sign on the dotted line. Before you do that is negotiable, including the length of the listing the terms under which you'll pay the broker's and how much commission you'll actually pay.

Before we go through the contract, there are some important issues to keep in mind. You want the right to:

1. *Take the property off the market.* Some listing agreements will require you to keep your property on the market for the entire span of the listing period. For example, if you sign a listing agreement for 180 days—and I can't think of an instance when you should—the agreement might include language that forces you to keep the property available for the entire 180 days. But circumstances change, and if you are trying to sell your home to move up into something bigger and better, and then you (or your spouse) are fired, you may want to stay in your smaller, more affordable home. You shouldn't be forced into selling if you've decided not to.
2. *Switch brokers and not pay a double commission.* Sometimes things don't work out with the listing broker. It can happen if you and your broker differ on a marketing strategy or the listing price, or if you have a clash of cultures. But you want to have the right to switch brokerage firms and not owe the first broker a commission on the sale of your home. Brokerage firms know that if you take away the listing, they won't get paid a commission. So they try to hang on to the milk even after the cow has left the barn. They figure: We did some work to market your property, and if someone comes back to purchase the home who saw it when it was listed with us, we should get

a commission. If you allow that kind of clause to stand, you could end up owing a double commission on the sale of your home.

3. *Pay commission only out of closing proceeds.* Brokers know that the only way they're going to get paid is if someone purchases your property. But in real estate school, agents and brokers are taught that they deserve a commission if they bring a "ready, willing, and able buyer" to your property. In other words, if the agent brings a buyer to your door who offers you a full-price contract for your home, some listing agreements will require you to pay a full commission whether or not you actually accept that offer for purchase. Strike any clause in the listing agreement that says you owe a full commission if a "ready, willing, and able" buyer is produced. While most times the "ready, willing, and able" buyer will actually close on your home, buyers and sellers do pull out of sales contracts for a plethora of reasons—including job loss, divorce, illness, death, and corporate transfer. If you don't close on your home, and you've left a "ready, willing, and able" paragraph in your listing agreement, you could end up paying a double commission: once when the first buyer is produced and again when you actually close on the home with a subsequent buyer. You should add a clause to the agreement which states that the broker will only get paid upon the closing of the sale of your home and from the proceeds from the sale.
4. *Terminate the agreement.* As we just discussed, there are several reasons you might want to cancel your listing agreement with a brokerage firm: You might have a personality conflict with your listing agent, or

you might disagree over marketing strategies, the list price, or even what is the market for your home. Or the broker may not be doing his or her job. Whatever the reason, you want to have the right to terminate your listing agreement. The best way is to terminate it on written notice, which you can deliver either personally to the brokerage firm, by fax, or through the mail. Or, if the brokerage firm balks, you can compromise by canceling the contract with notice, say after five business days or two weeks. If you terminate for cause—meaning that the broker has lied, stolen, or somehow cheated you—your contract should terminate immediately.

5. *Not pay a commission six months after termination.* Let's say you list your home in October, and a nice young couple comes to see it in February. But they don't offer enough money, and it's cold and snowy and you suddenly don't feel like moving. So you pull your house off the market and terminate your listing agreement. Three months later spring comes, and one day the young buyers knock on your door and tell you that if you're still interested in selling, they're interested in buying. They're willing to come up in price if you're willing to come down a bit. You make a deal with them on your front lawn to sell them the house. Everyone's happy until you go back and look at your listing agreement. It says you owe a commission for up to six months after termination of the listing agreement if a buyer who saw the home when it was listed comes back to purchase it. Six months is a long time, which is exactly why brokers stick that period of time into the listing agreement. Six months is supposed to be long enough to discourage you from stiffing the

broker. If the length of time was only one month, there would be little to keep you from terminating your listing agreement, calling up the buyer, and saving the 5 to 7 percent commission. On the other hand, six months seems a little long. As a compromise, offer to pay the broker a commission if within the first three months of the termination of the listing agreement you agree to sell your home to someone who first saw it when it was listed with the brokerage firm. A caveat: Many brokerage firms won't accept any terms less than six months, but it never hurts to ask.

Successful Home Seller Tip: Remember, a listing agreement is a legal document and it is perfectly within your rights to ask that you have your attorney review the agreement before you sign it. If you don't understand what a paragraph means, ask the broker to explain it. If the explanation seems clearer to you than the "legalese," don't hesitate to strike out the paragraph and write in the broker's explanation. If the broker balks at this, then perhaps he or she wasn't giving you the real explanation. As with all legal documents, it's best to have your real estate attorney, who is familiar with the law in your state, review your listing agreement and sales contract before you sign them.

The Listing Agreement, Step by Step

Now that we're through with the big issues, let's walk through an Exclusive Right to Sell agreement.

1. I agree to sell my property (together with its undivided interest in the common elements and accumulated reserves, if a condominium) commonly known as:

KAHN

MULTIPLE LISTING
EXCLUSIVE RIGHT TO SELL AGREEMENT

• TO: KAHN REALTY, INC./KAHN MANIERRE REALTY, INC. ("KAHN")

1. I agree to sell my property located at ______________________________

Included in the sale as property are the following items, if any, now on premises for which a Bill of Sale is to be given: screens, storm windows and doors; shades; Venetian blinds; drapery rods; curtain rods; radiator covers; attached TV antennas; heating, central cooling, ventilating, lighting and plumbing fixtures; attached mirrors, shelving, interior shutters, cabinets and bookcases; awnings; porch shades; planted vegetation; garage door openers and transmitters; attached fireplace screens; smoke detectors; and any additional items of personal property that seller and purchaser agree to convey. Items excluded:

CLOSING AND POSSESSION: "_______ days after contract or by mutual agreement."

2. This agreement is an Exclusive Right to Sell my property, and I agree to cooperate fully with you, refer all inquiries to you, and conduct all negotiations through you.
3. I agree to pay you a brokerage commission for the sale of the property amounting to 6% of the first $100,000 of purchase price and 5% of the balance, if the property is sold during the period of this agreement, or if it is sold directly or indirectly within one year after expiration of this agreement to a purchaser to whom it was offered during the period hereof, or if sold to a lessee who subsequently purchases. However, with respect to any sale made after the expiration of this agreement, no commission shall be due Kahn as listing broker if such sale shall have been made after we entered into a valid, written listing agreement with another licensed real estate broker.
4. The commission is due and payable on the closing date designated in an acceptable purchase contract. If property is sold on contract for deed, commission is due on the initial closing date. In the event a purchase contract is

The first item of the listing agreement is the address of the property. The listing agent can't sell your property if he or she doesn't know where it is. Then the listing agreement asks you to spell out exactly what personal property is being sold along with the property itself. Each brokerage firm has its own list of items, so each list may be slightly different. Strike out whichever items are *not* included in the sale or are not applicable. For example, if you have central air-conditioning, strike out "window air conditioners." If it is common in your area for sellers to take the refrigerator, then strike that out.

> *Included in the sale as property are the following items, if any, now on premises for which a Bill of Sale is to be given: Screens, storm windows and doors; shades, Venetian blinds; drapery rods; curtain rods; radiator covers; attached TV antennas; heating, central cooling, ventilation, lighting and plumbing fixtures; attached mirrors, shelving, interior shut-*

ters, cabinets and bookcases; awnings, porch shades; planted vegetation; garage door openers and transmitters; attached fireplace screens; smoke detectors; range(s), refrigerator(s), disposal(s), dishwasher(s), washer(s), dryer(s), window air conditioner(s); and any additional items of personal items excluded, including: [Fill in the blank]

The last item in Section 1 is "Possession." Possession is the date on which you plan to exit the home and turn over control to the buyer. Usually, possession is at closing, though it can be earlier or later. (For more information on possession, see Question 90.)

2. This agreement is an Exclusive Right to Sell my property, and I agree to cooperate fully with you, refer all inquiries to you, and conduct all negotiations through you.

There are several different types of listing agreements. The most common, and the one most preferred by brokers, is the Exclusive Right to Sell. This means that only the named brokerage firm can act as the listing broker for the period of time stated in the contract. In an open listing, any brokerage firm may act as your listing broker, and you essentially agree to pay the commission to whomever sells your property (for more information on other types of listing agreements, see Question 22).

3. I agree to pay you a brokerage commission for the sale of the property amounting to 6 percent of the purchase price, if the property is sold during the period of this agreement, or if it is sold directly or indirectly within one year after the expiration of this agreement to a purchaser to whom it was offered during the period hereof, or if sold to a lessee who subsequently purchases. However, with respect to any sale made after the expiration of this agreement, no commission shall be due Kahn as listing broker if such sale shall have been made after we entered into a valid written listing agreement with another licensed real estate broker.

Section 3 addresses several of the commission issues we touched upon before. First, this is where the broker suggests what percent commission he or she would like to receive. In the Chicago metro area, 6 percent is about average. The range for brokerage sales commissions is usually 5 to 7 percent, *but the commission is always negotiable*, even for a full-service brokerage firm. This is where you'd change the broker's commission. If you decide on a lower commission—say, 5 percent—then you'd cross out the 6 and put in a 5. If you decide on a stepped commission—say, 6 percent on the first $100,000 and 5 percent thereafter—you'd write the terms of the commission in the margin of the agreement.

The second issue addressed here is what commission is owed after the termination of the agreement and under what terms. This sample agreement says if someone sees your property when listed and you accept an offer within a year after termination of the listing agreement, you owe the broker a commission. If, however, you terminate with this broker and list your property with another brokerage firm, you would owe no commission. Tell the broker you find this clause unacceptable and try to change the yearlong period to a three-month or a six-month period.

4. The commission is due and payable on the closing date designated in an acceptable purchase contract. If property is sold on contract for deed, commission is due on the initial closing date. In the event a purchase contract is entered into and pur-

chaser defaults without fault on the Seller's part, Kahn Realty, Inc., will waive the commission, and this agreement shall be continued from the date of default through the date provided in paragraph 10.

In this section, the broker is detailing when the commission is to be paid. There is no "ready, willing, and able" clause in this particular listing agreement, though there may be on yours. If there is, be sure to change it to read that the "commission will be paid upon closing." In this agreement, the broker also agrees to waive the commission if, for some reason, the buyer backs out of the contract and the deal falls apart. That's reasonable. However, it should be clear that the broker will be paid only if the deal closes.

5. I have read Kahn Realty's policy printed on the reverse side of this sheet, and I understand that: (a) The Kahn Sales Counselor named below is designated as my sole and exclusive legal agent and representative; (b) Other Kahn Sales Counselors or employees may on occasion perform certain ministerial services for my property, such as, arranging for showings, sitting at open houses, etc., but they shall not be considered my legal agent; (c) Kahn Sales Counselors may act as either my subagents or as exclusive legal agents for potential buyers; (d) If my designated legal agent represents a potential buyer interested in my property, the dual agency situation will be resolved as described on the reverse side of this sheet; (e) Kahn Realty may share its sales commission with other brokers who may be buyers' agents, should one of their buyers purchase my property.

Let's look at this section a piece at a time. The first piece refers to the reverse side of the listing agreement. There, the contract discusses representation, buyer agency, and disclosed dual agency. When you sign this listing agreement, you've essentially said that you have read the representation section and understand it and agree to it.

Subsection (a) says you understand that while the brokerage firm is the listing broker, your designated agent is the person who signs his or her name at the bottom of the contract.

Subsection (b) says that other employees of the firm may do some of the work for your broker, including the broker's assistant, a secretary, or another agent. If you don't want anyone other than your particular listing agent to do work on your home, you can try to insert the words "only with seller's prior approval." More and more brokerage firms, however, are relying on the services of extra personnel to help brokers handle their business more efficiently.

Subsections (c), (d), and (e) deal with representation and commission. In subsection (c), you grant permission for the broker to represent buyers as a subagent for the seller. In other words, the broker still works for you. In subsection (d), you agree that a dual agency relationship will be created if your listing broker also represents the buyer as a buyer broker. In subsection (e), you agree that the broker may share his or her commission (6 percent, or whatever number you agree upon) with any buyer's agent who brings the buyer to the transaction. (See Question 20 for more information on dual agency.)

6. Should I decide to lease the property, Kahn Realty, Inc., shall be the exclusive rental agent for me for which Kahn shall, upon execution of the lease, receive from me a commission of one month's rent for the first year and 2 percent of the rent thereafter. If any lessee should purchase the property,

Kahn Realty, Inc., shall receive a sales commission in the amount stated in paragraph 3 above.

Let's say you've decided to sell your home, but you don't get any offers. So you offer it as a "Lease with an Option to Buy" or just decide to lease it. In other words, a person will rent your home for a certain amount of time and eventually purchase it. If this occurs, you agree to pay the broker a fee for renting the home. (Ask around to find out what typical leasing fees are in your neighborhood.) If the person who leases your home eventually purchases it, the broker will ask for a sales commission—in addition to the rental commission—because he or she technically introduced the buyer to the property. What isn't fair is for the broker to suggest that he or she should receive a commission if "any" renter (the lessee) purchases the property under any and all circumstances, forever into the future. If you are faced with the possibility that a prospective buyer might decide to rent your property instead of purchasing it, you should decide in advance how much rental commission would be owed to the broker if this happens. And you should also decide how much sales commission would be owed if that renter ultimately turns back into a buyer and purchases your property. However, you would be wise to set a time limit on how long you would owe the broker a commission on a renter-turned-buyer sale, or you might find yourself obligated to pay a sales commission five or even ten years after you first rented your home. All of the issues you and the broker agree to regarding commission should be attached, *in writing*, to the listing agreement. And any conflicting statements should be crossed out or otherwise made illegible. (For more information on leasing with an option to buy, see Question 99.)

7. Kahn is to list the property and diligently work to effect its sale at a price of $——, or any lesser amount that I/we agree to accept.

This is where your listing price should be entered into the contract. In some listing agreements, if the listing broker finds a buyer willing to purchase your home at this price, you may be obligated to sell it or you may owe the listing broker a commission.

8. Kahn is to take prospective purchasers through the property at convenient times, making a continued, earnest effort to sell the property, advertise the property as Kahn deems advisable, display signs, and provide information on this property to members of the local multiple listing service.

The broker is telling you what he or she will do to market your property. You may want to add that the broker will provide information on this property to "any licensed real estate broker or agent." While most brokers in your area will belong to the local MLS, there are areas of the country that do not have an MLS. It is, therefore, not in your best option to exclude anyone.

9. Kahn's sole duty is to effect a sale of the property, and they are not charged with the inspection or custody of the property, its management, maintenance, upkeep, or repair. However, nothing contained herein shall prohibit them from entering the property for the purposes of showing it to prospective purchasers.

Increasingly, brokers are worried about defending lawsuits. The most common reason a buyer sues a seller is misrepresentation: For example, when the buyer thinks the roof is new on the house and it is really fifteen years old. So brokers try to limit their liability by saying they are not responsible for inspecting the property or taking care of it. In most states, brokers must disclose to the buyer any hidden defects they know of in the home.

10. This agreement shall be effective for 180 days.

This particular listing agreement lasts for six months, or 180 days. There is no reason why you should sign a listing agreement that lasts this long. A 90-day listing agreement is long enough. (A 60-day listing agreement is even better, though most brokerage firms will not agree to it.) If your home is going to sell quickly, it will probably garner an offer sometime within the first four weeks of being on the market. If it is going to take a long time, you can easily extend the listing agreement for another 60-day or 90-day period. This is also the place to write in your termination language. You might suggest, "If I am dissatisfied with the services provided by the broker, I can cancel this agreement at no cost to me upon notice to the broker."

11. I warrant that there are no unpaid special assessments and there are no special assessment proceedings pending or confirmed relative to this property except as stated herein.

Condominium and co-op owners need to disclose to potential buyers if there is currently a special assessment (a monthly amount levied in addition to the regular assessment to pay for improvements to the common elements of the property) or if the condo board plans to levy a special assessment. You should, and in many states are required to, disclose this information to potential buyers, as it may have an impact on the price they offer to pay for your home. Your listing agreement will have at least one blank line for you to fill in any special assessments and when you believe they will cease.

12. I agree to save and hold you harmless from all claims, disputes, litigation, judgments, and costs (including reasonable attorney's fees) arising from my breach of this agreement, from any incorrect information or misrepresentations supplied by me or from any material facts, including latent defects, that are known to me that I fail to disclose.

This paragraph is an attempt by the broker to limit liability. If you lie to your broker about the true condition of your home, you are responsible for the costs of litigation if the broker gets sued. However, if you tell the broker the truth and the broker misrepresents the condition of your home, then the broker should be responsible for defending himself or herself. Real estate attorneys say you should strike this provision and any like it in the listing agreement. Provisions like this one can place a financial burden on you because they require you to pay all fees in a dispute with the broker. At the very least the listing agreement should be balanced and require the broker to do the same for you in case the broker breaches the agreement or makes any misrepresentations regarding the property.

13. I agree that should it become necessary to settle any claim relating to the property or this contract, it shall be settled by expedited arbitration in accordance with the commercial rules of the American Arbitration Association then pending.

In this paragraph, you waive your right to go to court to sue the broker or the buyer. The brokers like to use arbitration because it is less expensive than going to court. On the other hand, you may or may not get a fair shake at arbitration, or you may prefer to go to court and sue rather than arbitrate. Just because you cross off this paragraph doesn't mean you can't choose arbitration should the need arise; it merely gives you the opportunity to do either.

14. This agreement shall be binding upon and insure to the benefit of the heirs, administrators, successors, and assigns of the parties hereto. The parties to this agreement understand that it is illegal to refuse to display or to sell to any persons for reasons of race, color, religion, national origin, sex, age, sexual orientation, marital status, presence or age of children, or physical disability.

In other words, if you want to discriminate against a certain category of buyer, you cannot list your home with a broker. Although you personally have the right to refuse to sell your home to certain people, it is illegal for brokers licensed by the state to discriminate against individuals for any of the reasons listed above.

The other part of this section deals with death. If you list your home for sale and then die a week later, the broker has the right to force your heirs to continue with the contract and to pay a commission if they find a buyer for the property. In real life, brokers won't force your heirs to sell if they don't want to. Although if you die after you've agreed to sell your home but before you close, the buyer can sue your estate for specific performance and force your heirs to sell.

15. I understand that information as to the sale of my property will not be disclosed until all earnest money is collected and all contingencies are met.

Until you close on your home, you haven't sold it. And if the buyer's contract contained financing, inspection, or attorney's contingencies, you may not close until those conditions have been satisfied. Once the contingencies have been satisfied and the earnest money has been collected, you can be reasonably sure (but never 100 percent sure) that you'll sell your home to this particular buyer. Only then should your listing broker post notice in his or her office that your home has been sold. The disadvantage of posting notice that the property has sold before the contingencies are met is that someone will find out what you agreed to accept for your home. If it is less than full price, and if that information becomes public knowledge, you may have seriously compromised your ability to negotiate for the best price with the next buyer who comes along. Better to have a broker who plays this card close to the vest. (For more information on contracts and contingencies, see Questions 48 and 49.)

16. I warrant my authorization to execute this agreement and to deal with and on behalf of the said property as herein provided.

You state here that you have the authority to sell your home.

17. I am moving out of the area and would like information about my destination city and the Broker's nationwide relocation services.

The broker will offer to put you into its relocation services. Although it will not cost you anything, the broker will earn a piece of the commission for referring you to the relocation system.

18. I represent the following information to be true and correct: (a) Real Estate Tax for 19 ____ is $ _________ and reflects the following: Homeowner's Exemption (Y/N) Senior Citizen's Homestead Deduction (Y/N). My current monthly assessment is $ _________ and includes _________. My percentage of common elements is _____%. Waiver of Right of First Refusal Necessary (Y/N). Lot size is approximately _________. If condo, the approximate square footage is _________.

The listing broker will use this information to market your home. If you don't know what your current real estate tax bill is, you can contact your local tax collector's office. Only condo and co-op owners, and owners in homeowner associations, need be concerned with the assessment question. If your assessment includes your heat and hot water, that's what you should include. If your monthly assessment includes the bill for your cable television service and your electricity, be sure your broker and prospective buyers know that the assessment includes these items. The broker is interested here in your base assessment. The Right of First Refusal is the condo or co-op board's right to purchase your unit before you sell it to someone else. If the condo or co-op board declines, it will be necessary for you to secure a letter informing you that the board will not exercise its option.

At the bottom of the contract, you and the designated

broker sign the agreement. Everyone named on the deed—whether that's just you or you and your spouse and your Uncle Fred—must sign the listing agreement.

Lockboxes and Access

This particular listing agreement does not contain a provision for access to the property via a lockbox. However, lockboxes have become popular in many areas of the country because they give brokers easy access to your property. If your local MLS has a lockbox system, your listing broker will ask you to allow access that way. While it is up to you to decide whether you will or will not, lockboxes do allow greater flexibility for brokers. (See Question 25 for more information on lockboxes.)

Home Warranties and Home Protection Plans

There are two types of home warranties: the home warranty for new construction, and a home warranty for the mechanical systems and appliances in existing homes. In this book, all references to home warranties refer to those sold for existing homes.

In California, more than half of all homes are sold with a home warranty. While home warranties are not as popular in the rest of the country, they are beginning to catch on. Although the home warranty industry denies that a home warranty is insurance, it effectively functions as an insurance policy for some of the appliances and mechanical elements in your home. You pay a premium for the policy, which insures that all appliances working on the day of closing will be fixed or replaced for the period of a year after closing. The new buyer pays a service fee (a small charge of $35 to $75) each time he or she calls on the warranty.

Brokers who refer sellers to home warranty companies often receive a fee from the company. Some real estate brokers, like ERA, offer their own home protection plans. (For more information on home warranties, see Question 29.)

The Back of the Agreement

Most real estate contracts are printed on two sides. *Make sure you turn over the contract and read the reverse side BEFORE you sign the agreement.* If there is something you don't understand, ask the broker to explain it, or take it to your real estate attorney. *Never* sign a document you don't understand.

The reverse side of the listing agreement we've just discussed talks about how the brokerage firm represents you. Each state has laws that govern how real estate agents and brokers represent you in transactions. These laws are in flux, so be aware that things may have changed since the last time you sold a home. If you haven't sold a home since 1990, for example, you might not be familiar with buyer brokerage. You may still believe that all brokers work for the seller, since it is the seller who pays the commission. That is no longer true, and we may soon see a time when buyers are represented only by buyers' brokers. Some states have already virtually eliminated subagency. Buyers will now work with buyer brokers only. Sellers will work with seller brokers only. The law mimics a similar law in California, in which the buyer chooses how he or she will be represented. (For more information on agency representation and disclosure, see Question 23.)

Successful Home Seller Tip: Make sure you fully understand your listing agreement before signing it. Don't sign a listing agreement for more than ninety days, since you can easily renew it if the relationship is working out. Be sure to negotiate the commission as well as the length of the agreement before you sign the document. Also, your listing agreement should stipulate what kind of lockbox, if any, is to be used and under what circumstances the lockbox will be used. Also, don't forget to state in the contract that the broker gets paid only out of the closing proceeds from a successful sale.

Successful Home Seller Tip: If you have been trying to sell your home by yourself and then decide to list it, you can use a little-talked-about tool called exclusions. When you list your home for sale, you can exclude certain people who have already seen the home and may be interested in making an offer to purchase. If you exclude these individuals in writing on your listing agreement, and one of them comes back to purchase your home, you will not have to pay a commission to the listing broker. This happened to Mark and Amy. The market was strong for condominiums in their building, but they hadn't had any firm offers. They decided to list their condo with a local brokerage firm, but excluded two buyers who seemed to like their unit. Sure enough, one of the two buyers came back with an offer within a week after the property was listed, and Mark and Amy sold him their home. Since he was represented by a buyer broker, Mark and Amy paid him a commission of 3 percent of the purchase price for bringing the buyer to the transaction. They paid nothing to the listing broker. Be aware, most listing brokers won't allow you to have more than two or three exclusions, so choose them wisely!

QUESTION 22

What are the different types of listing agreements?

Although the most popular type of listing agreement is the Exclusive Right to Sell listing, there are other types of listings you can grant to brokers who wish to sell your property.

Exclusive Right to Sell Listing

One agent is designated within one brokerage firm as the sole agent for the property. This agent is given the sole authorization to sell your home. If you sell the home while it is listed with the brokerage firm, you owe the agent a commission, no matter who actually sells the property or who buys it from you. Brokers like this type of listing best because it virtually guarantees them a commission if they sell your home. With this type of listing, they will feel better about spending money for advertising and marketing expenses and listing your home in the local MLS.

Note: If you've been unsuccessfully trying to sell your home on your own, and decide to give your listing to a broker, you can still protect yourself should a prospective buyer who saw the property before it was listed come back to make an offer. Brokers will usually grant you a couple of *exclusions*. That is, on the listing sheet, you can name two or three buyers who previously saw the property. If one of these buyers ultimately makes you an offer, you will not owe the broker any commission. But brokers don't want to put up money for advertising and to list your home in the local MLS if they think they're not going to get paid a commission. Here's one solution: You and the broker should agree on a fixed amount which you will reimburse the broker should one of your exclusions purchase your home. The reimbursement should cover any initial costs the broker incurs to list and market your home.

Exclusive Agency Listing

With this type of listing, only one broker is designated as the exclusive listing agent. You need only pay the broker a commission if the broker, or a subagent of the broker, brings the buyer to the transaction. On the other hand, you retain the right to sell your property yourself. If you do so, under an Exclusive Agency Listing, you will not owe the broker a commission.

Open Listing.

An Open Listing—also known as a Nonexclusive Listing or a General Listing—means you have the right to enlist the services of any and all brokers to sell your home. Any broker can act as your agent in soliciting potential buyers, but you are obligated to pay a commission at closing only to the broker who brings the "ready, willing, and able" buyer to the transaction. As in the Exclusive Agency Listing, you retain the right to sell the home by yourself. An Open Listing formalizes an arrangement that many FSBOs (the acronym for "For Sale By Owner," which refers to homeowners who sell their own property without the help of a licensed real estate broker or agent) already have in place: The homeowner who sells on his or her own will often advertise that "brokers are protected," which lets buyer brokers know that the seller is willing to pay a commission. Just make sure your Open Listing agreement states that you will only pay a commission to the broker whose client successfully closes on your property.

Note: Experts agree that a listing agreement that does not specify which type of listing it is can be construed as an Open Listing, the least restrictive type of listing available.

Net Listing.

With a Net Listing the seller decides how much money he or she wants to take away from the sale of his or her property. The broker can then try to sell the property for as much money as possible, since any excess over the net amount becomes the sales commission. For example, if you tell your broker you want to net $100,000 on the sale of your home, the broker could price the home at $125,000, $150,000, or even $200,000. If the broker gets you a sales price of $130,000, then the $30,000 would become the sales commission. You're happy because you got your price, and the broker is happy because he or she got a huge commission. The problem with Net Listings is that it pits the broker's fiduciary duty to you—in which the broker promises to get you the most amount of money possible for your home—against his or her profit motive. Because greed can really mess up a real estate transaction, many states have banned Net Listings in residential sales. But while they're uncommon, they do exist, and you should be aware that they may be an option for you. (If you're unsure whether or not Net Listings are legal in your state, ask your real estate attorney or broker.)

Option Listing

The Option Listing gives the listing broker the option to purchase your home. Obviously, this type of arrangement can harm the seller because it again pits the broker's fiduciary duty to the seller against his or her profit motive. The reason brokers buy property from their sellers is that they believe they can get it at a discount and flip it quickly for a profit. For this reason, Option Listings aren't too common. There's no reason for you to use one: If your property is so well priced that your broker wants it, someone else will also want it.

Note: There are real estate companies that promise to purchase your home if it fails to sell on the open market within a specific period of time. Sound too good to be true? Be sure to read the fine print. The company may purchase your property—but well below its market price. There may also be other fees you'll have to pay and obligations you'll have to meet. Again, be sure to read—and understand—the fine print.

A Word of Caution About Brokers Who Buy Property: As we just discussed, the usual reason brokers buy property is that they think they can flip it quickly for a profit. Sometimes, unethical brokers will try to make you think that your property is worth even less than it is, simply so they can purchase the property at a discount. This happened to Geoff. Geoff is a real estate developer, but the broker who came to give him a comparative marketing analysis (CMA) of his home didn't know that. All she knew was that Geoff was divorced. She told him his place looked "too macho, too much like a bachelor pad." She also told him it wasn't in very good shape and probably wouldn't appeal to a woman. She kept denigrating his house, until he finally asked what she would list it at. She suggested a listing price that was more than $100,000 below the suggested listing prices of two other brokers who had also been through the house. As it turned out, Geoff listed the home with the broker who gave the highest suggested list price, and then asked her to list it even higher. The house sold fairly quickly at a price that was above the highest suggested list price. Later, Geoff ran into the broker who undervalued the property. He asked her why. "I thought I would buy the house myself and then flip it for a profit," said the broker. "I didn't think you knew any better."

Successful Home Seller Tip: Not every broker who suggests you lower your list price is looking to snap up your home and flip it for a profit. There are always a few bad apples in any business, and they, unfortunately, tend to give the whole industry an unpleasant smell. Your job is to know what your home is worth. If you know the market value of your home, no one will be able to take advantage of you. You'll know which agent is telling the truth and which agent is feeding you a line.

QUESTION 23
What is an agency disclosure form?

In nearly every state, the agent must disclose for whom he or she works. Usually, that disclosure is made in writing and the buyer or seller must sign it. To help brokers comply with the agency disclosure laws, some states have a statutory disclosure form written into the law. Brokerage firms can take out these paragraphs, put them on company letterhead, and present them to buyers and sellers. Brokerage firms often make their disclosure on the back of the listing agreement. It is not uncommon to see a discussion that is titled "Your Representation" followed by "Buyer Brokerage" and "Dual Agency."

Agency disclosure exists to help buyers and sellers understand who represents them in a transaction. Most buyers and sellers are confused by the jargon tossed about in the real estate business. The term "subagency" means virtually nothing to the average home buyer or seller. "Buyer broker" and "seller broker" are clearer terms, but until the agency tells you whether it is representing you as a buyer broker, a subagent of the seller, a seller broker, or a disclosed dual agency, confusion persists. Once again, here is a look at the different types of agency:

Single Agency. Single agents can represent either buyers or sellers. The Buyer's Agent, an exclusive buyer brokerage franchise, represents only buyers. Price Club Realty, the discount brokerage firm affiliated with Price Club/Costco, represents only sellers. These two companies are examples of exclusive single agency. The current working definition of "single agency," however, includes agents that represent either buyers or sellers, but not both, in a single transaction. Purists dispute the notion that a firm that represents both buyers and sellers, even if not in the same transaction, is a single agent. They believe only exclusive single agents can best protect their clients.

Subagency. A subagent is an agent who works with buyers and shows them properties but who owes his or her fiduciary duty to the seller. In several states, subagency is being phased out in favor of buyer brokerage, which more clearly informs everyone that the agent working with the buyer is working for the buyer's best interests.

Dual Agency. The most common form of dual agency occurs when the broker represents both the buyer and the seller in a single transaction. This situation requires the broker to be loyal to both parties, who most likely have opposing interests. Frankly, I can't imagine any broker who can maintain his or her fiduciary duty in this situation but rather should facilitate the transaction without giving advice to either buyer or seller. A lesser form of dual agency occurs when two different agents of a single brokerage firm represent both sides in a single transaction. Purists in the exclusive single agency corner believe that this type of dual agency has the potential to cause serious harm to unsuspecting buyers and sellers. Confidential information about deals is treated casually in many real estate offices. A seller broker may unknowingly share confidential information with a colleague who may one day bring a buyer to his or her seller's door.

Within dual agency, you have *disclosed dual agency* and *undisclosed dual agency*. With disclosed dual agency, the broker discloses to both the buyer and the seller that the broker represents both sides in the transaction. The buyer and seller must agree, and they usually sign a piece of paper stating that this is okay with them. Undisclosed dual agency occurs when a broker does not tell the buyer or the seller that he or she is representing both sides of the transaction. Some state courts have stretched the definition of "undisclosed dual agency" to include brokerage firms who do not disclose to buyers and sellers that they represent both sides of a single transaction even if there are two separate brokers involved.

If you don't understand who is representing your interests, ask your broker or your real estate attorney.

QUESTION 24

What is a multiple listing service?

Imagine a computer data base that stores all kinds of information about thousands of homes that are for sale in your area. That's the basic definition of a multiple listing service (MLS). Brokers become members of the local MLS, which allows them to list the properties they are marketing on the computer. Brokers searching for homes they can show to their buyers can tap into the system twenty-four hours a day from any member's computer.

The local MLS can be a seller's best friend. When your broker decides to hold a broker's open, he or she can enter that information and your property will pop up on the "hot sheet." When your listing first goes into the MLS, it is tagged as a brand-new property. Lots of brokers tap in regularly just to see what's come up on the market during the day, or even during the past few hours. Each week or two, the local MLS prints its computer listings, along with a recent photo, into an MLS book, which brokers can page through looking for homes for clients. As computer systems have been upgraded, color photographs have been introduced into the system. Buyers and brokers can sit side by side, electronically paging through MLS entries.

The flip side of all this technology is the fact that the MLS is a closed society of brokers. Only member brokers (most are members, however) can list properties in the MLS (and the MLS usually charges a fee for each property listed). Any broker who pays the dues can become a member. One of the best reasons to list your home with a broker who is a member of the MLS is to have your property listed on the local MLS system.

Within the MLS are rules governing the relationships between brokers. Most MLSs require that the commissions received by the seller be split equally between the listing broker and the buyer broker. Some MLSs do not allow property to be listed if the seller refuses to have the commission shared with a buyer's agent.

Brokers are required to list new property on the MLS within a short period of time after the listing agreement has been signed, usually twenty-four to seventy-two hours. In hot seller's markets, however, brokers sometimes put off entering properties until their own clientele and firm have had a chance to see the property at least once. This kind of behavior is frowned upon by the MLS community. The whole point of the MLS is to give everyone a fair shake at seeing each home.

Up until the mid-1990s, the local MLSs had a fairly strong lock on the computerized listing market. But recent advances in technology are changing that, with computers leading the way into new marketing opportunities for sellers. For example, many on-line computer systems—such as America On-Line, Prodigy, and CompuServe—now offer local real estate bulletin boards on which sellers can list property for sale. Other technological advances marry computers with voice mail technology, or put listings onto computer disks and send them around to different real estate offices.

QUESTION 25

What is a lockbox? And is it a safe way to sell a home?

Years ago, getting locked out of your house meant you might have had to reach under the front door mat or a porch flowerpot for the spare key. Today, sellers are again leaving keys. And in the most unlikely places: lockboxes.

A lockbox is a rectangular metal box that's attached to your property. It may be attached to the front or back doorknob, or nailed or glued to your sidewall, perhaps near the electricity meter. There is usually a master key—which can look like a house key, though the more sophisticated lockbox systems use electronic key cards—that any member of the local broker's board can purchase and that allows the member broker access to the box at any time. Your front door house key hangs on a hook inside the box.

Many brokers love the concept of a lockbox. Pam, a broker in Rock Hill, South Carolina, says she loves the convenience. "If you're showing four to six homes and if those homes happen to be listed with six different companies on opposite ends of town, you'll spend an amazing amount of time picking up and dropping off keys. It's especially difficult when you're lining up several showings and the buyer is trying to beat darkness or is trying to see everything on her lunch hour."

But not every broker is as keen on the concept as Pam. Troy, a broker in Zephyr Cove, Nevada, says he hates lockboxes. "I think they're fine for unfurnished homes, but I don't like anyone having keys to my homes. We deal in high-end properties. I'm not going to leave keys to $2 million properties with $100,000 vases in them lying around. Most of my clients wouldn't want me to do that."

Most brokers in Troy's area don't use lockboxes. "The convenience of them is wonderful," he says. "Brokers drive up to a house and go in. But you lose total control over who is showing the property." Troy says one way to avoid having buyer brokers drive around from brokerage firm to brokerage firm to pick up keys is for the listing broker to attend all the showings. Troy says he tries to go to every showing on his properties, and has a difficult enough time guarding against trouble without a lockbox causing more problems and aggravation.

"I've tried to train my agents to keep couples (who come to see the home) from separating. We had some thieves come into town recently, and they would go to a showing, separate, and the guy would rifle the master bedroom. When they came to one of my listings, I went and stayed with the guy and the other agent stayed with the woman, so nothing was stolen. But when the sheriff got them, they had a lot of stuff from other homes in the area," Troy recalls. If only one broker had gone to that showing, one half of the couple would have been walking around the house unattended.

Although she favors lockboxes, Pam admits lockboxes can bring about more serious problems. "If you have a shady real estate broker, anything can happen. There was a house for lease and a company in town had a lockbox on it. A real estate agent gained access to the box at four in the morning and raped and murdered the woman who was living there," she says.

Such horror stories are rare, especially in an industry that prides itself on taking good care of its listings. Pam says her company guards against problems by setting up appointments for anyone who wants to see a listing and by double-checking on agents who seem not to be quite on the level.

Her company's lockbox has a combination, instead of a key, which is given to the seller, who can remove the key at night to prevent unwelcome intrusions. Other Realtor associations have replaced the combination or key locks with computerized key cards that record which broker is seeing the property and at what times.

Increasingly, lockboxes are a fact of life for a seller. You can refuse to have a lockbox put on your home, though that may affect your ability to sell the home quickly. If your broker will attend all of the showings, you're better off not having a lockbox. In any case, listing your house for sale does carry some risks. Consider taking the following precautions:

- Put away your jewelry, guns, billfolds, and purses or lock them in a safe-deposit box.
- Never leave money or loose change lying around. If you have a change jar, put it in your dresser drawer and cover it with socks or underwear.
- Don't leave extra keys on hooks in the kitchen or by the front door. Extra sets of car keys have been known to mysteriously disappear.
- Don't leave personal calendars open on desks—or any other place they might be found. If you do have a daytimer that's visible, don't write "Start 2-week vacation today" if you're having potential buyers come through your home.
- Put some house lights on a timer, so folks canvassing the neighborhood will think you're home at odd hours.
- Consider packing away any valuables—including

paintings, crystal vases, and silver picture frames—before you start to show your home.

"I think people are basically honest," says Pam. "But you don't want to tempt anyone."

SETTING THE RIGHT PRICE

QUESTION 26

What is the difference between the list price and the sales price of my home?

Home buyers and home sellers have a few things in common. One is this: They both believe what they want to believe. Buyers believe that their dream house is located in their dream neighborhood and will cost exactly what they can afford to spend. On the other hand, sellers often believe list prices and sales prices are the same thing.

On average, the difference between the list price of a home and the sales price of a home is only about 6 percent (see Question 27). But many sellers think the list price is the price someone should pay for their home, and they often get insulted if the buyer offers anything less.

That kind of thinking can become an obstacle to a sale, especially if the seller has an overinflated view of his or her property's value. If comparable homes in the neighborhood are selling for $100,000 and the seller arbitrarily decides to list his house for $150,000, it's going to take some real magic to materialize a buyer willing to overpay by that much for the home.

Overpricing a home is also a concern if the seller has misjudged the market. Getting a buyer to pay list, or near list, price for a home is easier to do during a seller's market, where the demand for homes is greater than the number of properties available for purchase. The situation, however, is reversed in a buyer's market. In this case, sellers often lower their prices to attract the few buyers who are shopping for a home.

QUESTION 27

How do I know what kind of a market I'm in? What is the average number of listing days?

How fast will it sell? That's probably the first question you'll ask your broker. Unfortunately, the answer is a little murky, as the number of days your home may sit on the market can range from one to what feels like forever. In every major metropolitan city, there will be some units that have been for sale for as long as two years. In areas hard hit economically, some homes have been on the market for twice that long. In southern California, which in 1994 had barely begun to recover from the 1990 recession, homes had been for sale for so long that their owners have relisted them several times in order to give them a fresh appearance.

But knowing the average number of days a home in your neighborhood spends on the market is important. Numbers like these can tell you if your neighborhood is mired in a buyer's market—where there are more homes than people to purchase them, which can stagnate a market and ultimately send prices spiraling downward—or is floating along in a seller's market—where demand is so strong that homes seem to sell in days or hours rather than months, and where prices are firm or rising.

Under Thirty, and Counting

Here's a good rule of thumb: If the average number of days on the market is less than thirty, you're in a strong seller's market. That means that most homes are spending anywhere from a few days to perhaps forty-five or sixty days on the market. Since a home sees most of its activity in the first three weeks on the market, selling a home in a neighborhood with an average marketing time of thirty days means homes are selling at a fairly quick clip. Besides being overjoyed (because to be selling in a seller's market is a wonderful thing), you could respond to this type of market condition in one of two ways: You can price your home right with the market and sell it quickly, or you can price it just above the market and hope that homes are selling fast enough to justify the increase in price.

Successful Home Seller Tip: One cautious note: In a very hot seller's market, where homes are going in minutes rather than hours, there will still be some homes that sit for months without moving. The reason is simple: In a hot seller's market, buyers find themselves on a steep learning curve. Unless they luck out, they won't find a house if they're not smarter than any other buyer. Within a short time of entering a hot (or even a lukewarm) seller's market, buyers know which homes are priced fairly and which are not. They know which homes are worth the money, and those they'll jump on. The hotter the market, the more overpricing buyers will tolerate. But they won't touch the homes of greedy sellers who have greatly overpriced their property.

Forty to Seventy-Five Days

If the average days on the market is between forty and seventy-five, you've got a fairly balanced market where most homes are taking one to three months to sell. Most real estate brokers will tell you that balance is good for a market. It means there is a similar number of active buyers and sellers in the market at the same time. It means that prices may be climbing perhaps 2 to 5 percent per year, which is extremely healthy appreciation.

But a balanced market will not tolerate much overpricing. In a truly hot seller's market homes go so fast that buyers who miss seeing them can only imagine how attractive and what good buys they were. But in a balanced market, there is time for buyers to see all the homes they want to and draw their own conclusions as to the actual value being presented. If they conclude that your home is overpriced (and believe me, there is something to the herd mentality—if one buyer or broker thinks a particular home is overpriced that thought seems to sweep through the real estate community), you may not get any showings even though your neighbor is entertaining several offers.

Seventy-Five Days Plus

Once you get into an average marketing time of more than seventy-five days (two and a half months), you're teetering on the brink of a buyer's market, where there are more homes for sale than buyers to purchase them. Buyers in this type of market can take a long time to make up their minds. They might come through your home two, three, or even four times before deciding whether or not to make an offer. Sellers who do best in this kind of market do not "test the market" by overpricing their homes. Overpriced homes in strong or even mild buyer's markets get ignored, the worst fate possible for a seller. Instead, cut your price as close to the bone as possible and wait it out. If your house is priced well but is taking a long time to sell, your neighbor's home is also probably taking a long time to sell.

Successful Home Seller Tip: If your local market area regularly runs at a slower than normal pace, an average marketing time of ninety days might be perfectly normal for a balanced market. Discuss the local pulse of your neighborhood with your broker so you will know what to expect.

Another Market Indicator

Another way to test what kind of market you're in is to compare the list price and the sale price of homes. According to the National Association of Realtors, homes sell for an average of 94 percent of their list price. In other words, homes sell for 6 percent less than their owners wanted for them. If you list your home for $100,000, and you're in a typical or average market, you'll sell your home for around $94,000.

Homes that sell for more than the average—our fictional $100,000 list price home that sells for $98,000, or 98 percent of list price—are generally thought to be in a seller's market. In fact, the closer the average gets toward 100 percent, the stronger your seller's market. Once you drop below 6 percent, the barometer swings the other way, and you are thought to be in a buyer's market. So if our $100,000 home sells for $92,500, which is 92.5 percent of list price, you'd be in buyer's territory.

In any market, there will be some homes selling for more and some for less than the average, which is an inherent problem with using averages as truth. Still, these numbers can help you redirect your marketing strategy to take the best advantage possible of market conditions.

Note: Remember, these numbers compare the last list price with the final sales price. They don't take into account what the initial list price was and how many times it was reduced until it got to a point where the home sold for 6 percent less than list price. That's why the numbers can be a bit misleading out of context.

Successful Home Seller Tip: Ask your broker if the MLS keeps initial list prices for homes or if he or she can call other brokers who recently sold homes that were comparable to yours in style, size, and condition. Perhaps these brokers will be willing to divulge the initial list prices of these homes. Comparing initial list to the sales price is the best way to gauge what percent of list price the home actually sold for. You can then compare it with your situation.

QUESTION 28

How do I determine what is the competition for my home?

Sizing up the competition for your home is a little like trying to decide which athlete is going to win a race. You can look at each athlete's size and estimate his or her muscular strength, but in the end the athlete who is the fittest and the most prepared is going to take away the prize.

"Fittest" is even more difficult to quantify when it comes to homes. That's because price is the great equalizer. A fixer-upper that is priced right will usually sell as quickly as a home in mint condition that's priced right. Of course, the prices for the fixer-upper and the home in mint condition may be miles apart, but their owners might be equally happy with the results.

Let's start with some basic definitions:

The Gut Job. This is a home that needs to be stripped down to the bare walls, and sometimes the brick exterior, and essentially rebuilt from the inside out. Why not just knock it down and start again? The house may be old and have tremendous charm, or the exterior may be in excellent shape. Folks who buy a gut job usually replace all wiring and plumbing, put in new kitchens and baths, replace or refinish the floors, and replace or replaster the walls and ceiling.

Handyman's Special. When a broker refers to a home as a handyman's special, you can be fairly certain that this is a property that needs some major work done plus the usual complement of weekend projects. Sometimes the shape of a handyman's special can be closer to a gut job than a fixer-upper, but the future homeowner will have to make plenty of repairs—and possibly structural improvements—to bring the property up to the level of others in the neighborhood.

Fixer-Upper. This is a home that probably needs some tender loving care. It may have had some renovation, but usually it needs new or upgraded bathrooms, upgrading in the kitchen, and decorating. For a buyer, the best kind of fixer-upper is one that needs only cosmetic improvements, such as decorating, sanding of floors, and replacing of hardware and appliances. The worst kind is a disguised gut job or handyman's special.

Mint Condition. A house that is in mint condition has fresh neutral decorating, refinished floors, an upgraded kitchen, and either upgraded or new bathrooms. Mint condition homes are also called "move-in" homes because buyers can literally move right in without so much as painting or replacing the window treatments.

Finding the Comps

When looking for comps, you're trying to identify homes that are similar in size, shape, and amenities to yours. What do you do if all the homes in your neighborhood are fixer-uppers and yours is in mint condition? If that's the case, you then must go back and break the whole into the sum of its parts.

Let's say your house has three bedrooms, two and a half baths, an attached two-car garage, and a nice garden. The house itself has about 2,000 square feet, and you've rehabbed the bathrooms, sanded and stained the wood floors, replaced the carpet and draperies, repainted, and upgraded (new cabinet facings, new floor, and new appliances) the kitchen. Let's say all of the work you've done over the last seven years cost you $25,000. You bought the house for $150,000 and now you're hoping to sell it for something over $200,000.

There are two other houses for sale on your block, and one around the corner. The two houses on your block haven't been touched in twenty-five or thirty years. They need total upgrading. The owners are senior couples who have lived in their homes for the last twenty years or so. For the sake of explanation, let's say that one of the houses

(House A) is exactly the same size as yours, a three-bedroom, two-and-a-half-bath home, and the other (House B) is a little larger. It has four bedrooms and two and a half baths. The house around the corner (House C) is a little smaller than yours, with three bedrooms and only two baths, but the two baths have been upgraded.

How do you compare your home to these houses? By attaching a dollar figure to each home's amenities, you can then add and subtract to get a reasonable comparison to your home. Start by making a chart of all the homes in your neighborhood. Use your home as a standard, and put it at the top. The "extras" column is for amenities that your home doesn't have. You can have additional columns for the lot size, garage (attached or not, size, and condition), basement (a huge selling point in some locations), location (if the homes are not necessarily next to yours, but are scattered around the neighborhood), and school district. The more detailed you get, the more exact your comparison. In a smaller version, here's how it works:

House	*Bedrooms*	*Bathrooms*	*Extras*	*Redone?*	*Price*
Yours	3	2 ½	—	Yes	$200,000
House A	3	2 ½	FP, SL	No	$152,000
House B	4	2 ½	SP, FR	No	$225,000
House C	3	2	—	Part	$169,000

FP = fireplace (WBFP = wood-burning fireplace)
SP = swimming pool
FR = family room
SL = small lot

The standard: Your house (we're using our fictional house) has three bedrooms, two and a half brand-new baths, a formal dining room, a kitchen, a family room, an upgraded kitchen, refinished hardwood floors, a two-car attached garage, a 50-by-185-foot lot, and a basement.

Once you've got the homes that are for sale in your neighborhood plugged into the chart, you can begin to compare and contrast them with your own house. House A has a smaller lot than your house, and it hasn't been redone, but it has a fireplace. Adding a fireplace to a house is a relatively inexpensive project, costing anywhere from $2,000 to $7,000 for a preconstructed firebox. On the other hand, an inground swimming pool is fairly expensive, costing anywhere from $15,000 up. House C has many of the same amenities as your house, but it is missing the half bath, also known as the powder room. That's a feature many home buyers like to have because they have a bath on the first floor they can steer guests to without having them use the family bathrooms, which are usually upstairs.

The key to the cost comparison game is figuring out what is the cash premium for each amenity in your neighborhood. These numbers will be different from neighborhood to neighborhood and from town to town. For example, if you live in a condo in New York, and you have a terrace, that terrace will be worth a lot more to a New York City condo buyer than it would to a duplex condo buyer in Fort Wayne, Indiana. Similarly, a gorgeous view of San Francisco Bay will add significantly more to the value of a home there than a gorgeous view of Glacier National Park adds to the value of a home in Flathead Valley, Montana. If your New York condo has a terrace, it might be worth 25 to 50 percent more than an identical condo without a terrace.

Successful Home Seller Tip: Whether or not you end up using a broker to sell your home, real estate professionals are an excellent source for pinpointing how much an amenity is worth in a particular community. Real estate brokers and agents freely give out this kind of advice because it offers them an opportunity to market their services to you. Even if you're planning to sell your home on your own, they know most homes are sold with an agent's help, and selling on your own might not work out for you. They want you to think of them first when you make the decision to list.

One you've attached a value to each amenity, the rest is just mathematics. Go through each house on your list and add and subtract amenities and their values from the list price of the home. This method works even better when you use homes that have actually sold, since list prices are essentially "wish prices," whereas sale prices reflect reality.

Successful Home Seller Tip: The best way to set up your chart is to do some research. Not only should you have the broker pull the listing sheets of homes that are for sale in your neighborhood (some of this might be in your comparative marketing analysis, though brokers usually pull only the comps that support their recommended list price), you should also get out there and canvass the neighborhood. When your neighbors host open houses, you should be the first through the front door. Notice the quality of their hardware, of their kitchen appliances, of their decorating. Think about how your hardware, appliances, and decorating compares to theirs. How does your curb appeal and landscaping compare to theirs? Do they have a new roof? Do you? When you leave the house, immediately write down your perceptions on the back of the listing sheet. (For more information on listing sheets, see Question 37).

When you're done comparing and contrasting the homes in your neighborhood, you should have a good idea about value and pricing in your neighborhood. Even after you list your home for sale, it's a good idea to keep up with all market activity. Visit each new home that's for sale and keep abreast of homes that have sold. Revise those listing sheets and mark the "sold" price on them. Markets change rapidly. If sellers suddenly seem to be getting higher prices for their homes, you'll know to stand closer to your list price. If sellers are cutting their prices dramatically to make a sale, you'll know you may have to do the same. Your ability to stay fluid with the market will help insure your success as a seller.

QUESTION 29

What is a homeowner's warranty? And should I offer one?

When Pat bought her home from Mark, he promised her that all of the appliances worked on the day of closing. In case something went wrong in the first year, he offered her a warranty. Mark purchased a home warranty through his brokerage firm, an ERA office, that stated that if anything should go wrong with the appliances, plumbing, heating, or air-conditioning systems, the warranty would pick up the cost of the repair minus a small service fee.

"I'm very happy we did have it," said Pat, at the end of her first year of living in her San Diego home. "We've made several claims. We had two gas leaks, one in the hot water tank and one in a small gas stove in the basement. And then, the brand-new air-conditioning system wasn't cooling."

Pat isn't the only buyer who likes home warranties. More than half a million home warranties are purchased each year, about half of which are for homes in California. In other parts of the country, the number of sellers who purchase warranties ranges from 8 to 20 percent. But as home warranties catch on, more and more sellers are providing them as a standard sales perk.

What are home warranties? Home warranties are service contracts that cover the costs to repair or replace a broken appliance or plumbing system over and above the service fee. They do not, however, cover preexisting problems. If the appliance works on the day of closing, it's covered. Otherwise, it's not. (Don't confuse this type of home warranty with new construction home warranties for brand-new homes.)

If this talk about home warranties sounds vaguely like home insurance for appliances, you're not the only one who thinks so. Many folks confuse home warranties with insurance policies. Indeed, in many states they are regulated by the state department of insurance. Sellers pay a premium, or fee, for the one-year warranty, which is also called a service contract. Most home warranties can be extended another year, although the buyer pays the fee for the second year. The service fees are quite similar to insurance deductibles. But the home warranty industry goes to great lengths to deny any similarities to the insurance industry. That's because you have to be licensed to sell insurance. You do not have to be licensed to sell service contracts.

In California, where home warranties are heavily regulated, there is a tremendous amount of competition among home warranty companies. It is illegal for California real estate agents promoting a warranty to receive a fee from the home warranty company for recommending a seller. Because of this regulation and competition, homeowner warranties cost less there than in the rest of the country. As we went to press in early 1995, a home warranty service contract in California cost approximately $250. In the rest of the country, the same contract, with the same benefits, cost from $300 to $500.

Home warranties are usually bought by the seller, at the urging of a real estate agent, as a marketing bonus. Most policies offer the seller free additional coverage for the time that the home is on the market if the seller agrees to buy a one-year service contract that starts on the day of closing. The extra seller coverage extends for as long as your home is listed, whether that's two months or two years.

What Do Home Warranties Cover?

Home warranties don't cover everything in your home. Most important, they do not cover any structural problems, such as a crack in the basement or a leaky roof. Instead, home warranties are designed to cover those appliances that are in working condition when the home is sold. The typical policy covers the furnace, air-conditioning, kitchen appliances, water heater, trash compactor, electrical system (fuses and interior wiring), and interior plumbing. For an additional fee, the home warranty will cover things like your swimming pool.

Should You Buy a Home Warranty?

The home warranty industry's answer to that question goes something like this: In an older home, it's inevitable that some things are going to break down. Water heaters can explode. Furnaces can go out. Air conditioners can break. Without a home warranty, the buyer would probably spend $1,000 to repair a furnace or $2,500 to replace all these items. That would make the buyer unhappy, and you, the seller, don't want an unhappy—and potentially litigious—buyer, do you?

However, that doesn't really answer the question. Home warranties are a good idea if you want to reassure prospective buyers that they are covered in case something happens during the first year they own the home. But not all appliances and mechanicals are covered in every home warranty, and whoever purchases your home will still have to pay the "service fee" each time someone comes to inspect or repair an item.

If you think about home warranties as a marketing tool only, they're worth considering. A home that offers a home warranty will seem like a smarter buy than the house down the street that is similar to yours except for the warranty. Buyers like the reassurance that, if anything goes wrong, they can pick up the telephone, dial a toll-free number, and arrange for someone to come and fix the problem. Savvy sellers should consider the costs associated with such a warranty from both their and the buyers' perspectives. Although a warranty with a high service fee may be cheaper for the seller, there may be better coverage—and ultimately a happier buyer—with a service contract that has a lower service fee but a higher price.

A home warranty is also a good idea for sellers who either don't know the mechanics of their homes particularly well or who are selling a home they've never lived in. If you're not mechanically inclined, then you may not be willing to engage in hand-to-hand combat with a leaking washing machine.

John Kinker, president of Saint Louis–based Guaranteed Homes, Inc., a company that sells home warranty service contracts, and president of the National Home Warranty Association, says the best reason for sellers to buy a home warranty is that it offers peace of mind for both the buyer and seller. "The seller who purchases a warranty can put it on the listing sheet as a marketing tool to make his or her home look better than the one across the street. And it offers the buyer some guarantee that whatever is broken will be repaired," John says.

John and some real estate brokers feel that warranties also offer a measure of "legal protection" because buyers who sue sellers usually do so because they feel the condition of the home was misrepresented to them. "People sue when their appliances break down," John adds.

For more information on home warranties, contact the National Home Warranty Association (NHWA), a nonprofit industry association comprised of the leading home warranty companies. (See Appendix III, Resources for address and telephone numbers.)

QUESTION 30

What is sellers' errors and omissions insurance? Do I need it? Am I at risk of being sued?

Eight out of ten sellers believe they're going to be sued by the buyer after they sell their home, according to a study conducted in the early 1990s by HMS, a company based in Hollywood, Florida, that sells home warranties to sellers and Errors and Omission (E&O) insurance to the brokerage community. In California, 90 percent of sellers polled thought they might be sued.

In reality, the numbers are far, far less. The general counsel for the National Association of Realtors believes fewer than 1 percent of all sellers are ever sued. Still, folks appear to be worried, and in this litigious society that's not surprising.

The concept of buyer brokerage seems to be stirring the pot somewhat. Until the late 1980s, there were no buyer brokers in conventional real estate and no seller disclosure. The name of the game was *Caveat emptor* ("Buyer beware"). That phrase was meant to warn the buyer that the road ahead might be treacherous. That the house might have hidden defects. That the seller might not be telling you everything. Brokers owed their loyalty to the seller, who paid them their commission of 5 to 7 percent of the sales price.

But since the beginning of the 1990s, the tables have turned a bit on the sellers, many of whom feel they were left hanging out to dry. Buyer brokerage—where the broker owes his or her loyalty to the buyer rather than the seller—has eaten away at the seller's confidence that he or she is protected in the transaction. Unlike conventional brokers, buyer brokers are supposed to disclose everything they know about a property to the buyers, including the seller's motivations for selling. Seller disclosure has forced sellers to be painfully honest about their homes, properties, and neighborhoods.

Experts say most lawsuits are filed because buyers feel the facts of the home or property were misrepresented. Seller disclosure has made sellers worry that they forgot to disclose everything to the buyer. "The worry is you forgot to tell the buyer that the basement floods every spring," says one real estate attorney. "And unless the buyer walks through an inch of water when touring the basement, you should make a point of telling him or her."

Seller E&O insurance is similar to E&O insurance offered to real estate brokers. Broker E&O insurance protects brokers who misrepresent a property to a buyer. Seller E&O insurance is designed to protect sellers from inadvertent misrepresentations about their property. But this kind of insurance, in its earliest incarnation, appears a bit misguided. Experts say it doesn't protect sellers particularly well.

While seller E&O insurance isn't very common today, it's likely that more companies will attempt to cash in on sellers who are worried about the possibility of being sued. If anyone—and that includes your broker—offers you "free" seller's insurance, read the fine print carefully. If you don't understand it, ask your attorney for an explanation.

The best advice, experts say, is to be as honest as possible. When you are filling out your seller disclosure form, be sure to answer every question truthfully. If the buyer accuses you of misrepresenting something in your home, he or she will have to prove that you knew or should have known about the problem.

QUESTION 31

What is seller disclosure? And how does it affect me?

The advent of seller disclosure is one of the more recent phenomena of residential real estate. Essentially, seller disclosure requires you to disclose any known material latent defects in your property. That means you must disclose if your property has any hidden or unseen defects that could adversely affect the value of the property. The disclosure takes the form of a preprinted sheet filled with specific questions about the property and, sometimes, the neighborhood. Sellers must answer all of the questions honestly.

Buyers like seller disclosure because it tells them up front about the condition of the property. Some sellers like disclosing defects because it protects them from having buyers discover them during an inspection and then ask for money to fix them. These sellers would rather know up front that the roof is going to last only another year or two, or that the air-conditioning system needs a new chiller. Then they can either fix the problems themselves or adjust the purchase price. Other sellers don't like seller disclosure. They feel uncomfortable with this formal process of baring their home's soul, so to speak.

What kinds of questions do you have to answer on a seller disclosure form? In California, the Transfer Disclosure Statement is six pages long (see Appendix II, Contracts and Forms for a copy of the form.). In Illinois, sellers must respond "Yes," "No," or "Not Applicable" to each of twenty-two statements, including:

- I am aware of flooding or recurring leakage problems in the crawl space or basement.
- I am aware of material defects in the walls or floors.
- I am aware of mine subsidence, underground pits, settlement, sliding, upheaval, or other earth stability defects on the premises.
- I am aware of unsafe concentrations of radon on the premises.
- I am aware of a structural defect caused by previous infestations of termites or other wood-boring insects.
- I am aware of boundary or lot line disputes.
- I have received notice of violation of local, state, or federal laws or regulations relating to this property, which violation has not been corrected.

Here's a little bit of recent history to explain the hoopla over seller disclosure: Although it seems as though state law would already cover seller disclosure, for the most part it does not. Some state laws are silent on the issue. In effect, that means if there is a defect hidden in the house and the seller knows about it but doesn't say anything to anyone about it and the state law does not require the seller to disclose it, then the buyer is stuck with the problem. If, however, the seller tells his or her broker about the hidden defect, the broker is obligated to inform the buyer.

By 1992, only California and Maine had some sort of formal regulation requiring sellers to disclose any material latent defects (that means any defects hidden from the buyer) in the property. In 1987, California passed a law that codified the questions sellers must answer. In addition, the agent for the seller, the buyer, and the seller himself or herself must sign off that they have reasonably inspected the property and disclosed any defect. In Maine, the broker is required to ask specific questions that the state has designated. The broker is required to gather this information at the time the property is listed and provide this information in writing to the buyer prior to, or during, the preparation of an offer.

The National Association of Realtors (NAR) would like to see some form of seller disclosure mandated by every state. According to the NAR's legal counsel, one of the largest areas of controversy in the process of buying and selling homes is the failure to disclose defects in property. As we have already discussed, the majority of lawsuits after closing, where buyers are unhappy, involve the alleged failure to disclose some condition affecting value or desirability. The finger is usually pointed in the direction of the broker first, and then to the seller. Because the NAR protects the interests of brokers, its position is that sellers, rather than brokers, should shoulder the responsibility of disclosing defects in their homes. As the NAR's attorney said: "The agent has the duty to disclose factors that he can observe with a reasonably diligent inspection. The broker doesn't live there. [Seller disclosure] forces those issues to be addressed."

In 1992, Coldwell Banker, a national real estate company, announced a new policy that required all sellers listing property with the company throughout the United States to fill out and sign disclosure forms. At first, some sellers weren't thrilled with the prospect of filling out a form that asked specific questions about their house, land, and neighborhood. Not surprisingly, buyers were happy to have it and, with the media coverage surrounding the introduction of the forms, began asking sellers to provide them with a written seller disclosure form. Since Coldwell Banker initiated seller disclosure forms, other top real estate brokerage firms across the country have introduced their own versions of the seller disclosure form.

State legislatures have caught onto the idea as well. As of early 1995, more than half of all states had mandated some form of written seller disclosure, with another fifteen states considering some form of voluntary or mandatory seller disclosure. Many states require sellers to give buyers filled-out seller disclosure forms before the contract is signed. In some states, if the disclosure is given to the buyer after the contract is signed, the buyer usually has a short period of time (usually around three days) to rescind the contract if the seller disclosure form turns up a previously unknown material latent defect. Your real estate attorney or broker should be able to specifically inform you about your seller disclosure obligations.

The California Real Estate Transfer Disclosure Statement asks some of the most detailed seller disclosure questions.

DISTRIBUTED BY CALIFORNIA ASSOCIATION OF REALTORS® **FORM TDS-14**

REAL ESTATE TRANSFER DISCLOSURE STATEMENT
(CALIFORNIA CIVIL CODE 1102, ET SEQ.)
CALIFORNIA ASSOCIATION OF REALTORS® (CAR) STANDARD FORM

THIS DISCLOSURE STATEMENT CONCERNS THE REAL PROPERTY SITUATED IN THE CITY OF__________ __________, COUNTY OF__________, STATE OF CALIFORNIA, DESCRIBED AS__________.
THIS STATEMENT IS A DISCLOSURE OF THE CONDITION OF THE ABOVE DESCRIBED PROPERTY IN COMPLIANCE WITH SECTION 1102 OF THE CIVIL CODE AS OF __________, 19____. IT IS NOT A WARRANTY OF ANY KIND BY THE SELLER(S) OR ANY AGENT(S) REPRESENTING ANY PRINCIPAL(S) IN THIS TRANSACTION, AND IS NOT A SUBSTITUTE FOR ANY INSPECTIONS OR WARRANTIES THE PRINCIPAL(S) MAY WISH TO OBTAIN.

I
COORDINATION WITH OTHER DISCLOSURE FORMS

This Real Estate Transfer Disclosure Statement is made pursuant to Section 1102 of the Civil Code. Other statutes require disclosures, depending upon the details of the particular real estate transaction (for example: special study zone and purchase-money liens on residential property).

Substituted Disclosures: The following disclosures have or will be in connection with this real estate transfer, and are intended to satisfy the disclosure obligations on this form, where the subject matter is the same:__________

(LIST ALL SUBSTITUTED DISCLOSURE FORMS TO BE USED IN CONNECTION WITH THIS TRANSACTION)

II
SELLER'S INFORMATION

Here is the beginning of the form. You can find it in its entirety in Appendix II, Contracts and Forms.

QUESTION 32

What does it mean to sell my home "as is"? Does this let me off the hook for any future legal problems?

"As is" condition means the buyer takes the home as it stands, warts and all. Prior to the advent of seller disclosure, those warts could be serious defects in the home, or they could be minor decorating problems—either way, the buyer didn't know and the seller didn't say.

Today, more than half of all states require (and many others encourage) sellers to disclose hidden defects in their home. In some cases, sellers must give a written seller disclosure form to the buyer before the contract is signed. As we've discussed, you must be painfully honest when you fill out this form. If you're sued for fraud, the buyer must prove that you knew of a problem or should have known the problem existed, lawyers say.

By the year 2000, most states will require sellers to disclose problems with their home. But that doesn't mean you can't sell the house "as is." Instead, you should disclose the problems up front. You may even want to attach the seller disclosure form to the listing sheet. Then you should have your broker inform potential buyers that you, the seller, recognize there are problems with the house and that the price reflects these problems. If you are a FSBO, then you must take on the task of telling buyers that the house's price reflects its "as is" status.

Being upfront with buyers has an additional benefit. Many buyers will try to use a negative inspection report to renegotiate the sales price on the contract. By disclosing problems up front and letting everyone know that the sales price reflects the home's true condition, you should be able to avoid both the renegotiation process and a later lawsuit.

PART IV

Marketing My Home and Waiting for an Offer

QUESTION 33

What kind of seller am I—a wishful thinker, a realist, or a member of the desperate and the anxious?

Brokers say there are three kinds of sellers in the world: the wishful thinkers, the realists, and those who are desperate and anxious.

"Wishful thinkers are sellers who are kind of pie-in-the-sky [dreamers]. They perhaps don't have a good feel for what their property is worth and they overprice it," explains John, a managing broker in South Bend, Indiana. Price itself isn't the only issue for wishful thinkers. Sometimes, John says, they overestimate the value of the condition of their home.

Ken, the owner of a brokerage firm in Lake Tahoe, Nevada, says his firm once worked with a wishful thinker who had a decorating problem. "This lady has collected knickknacks from every corner of the globe. We've asked her to pack them up, but she wouldn't. Her treasures were so overwhelming that buyers only looked at them and not the home. In the meantime, she lowered the price of the home four times. She's redecorated, but instead of putting in neutral tones, she put in outdated floral carpeting," says Ken, adding: "She simply couldn't understand why her home took so long to sell."

Realists, on the other hand, are sellers who have a thorough understanding of the market. They know where their home fits in. "Realists are very tuned in to what the home is worth and what needs to be done to market it properly," says John. Consequently, sellers who are realistic usually enjoy the benefits of a fairly quick sale.

Realists are also quick to take their brokers' decorating suggestions. If the yard needs cleaning up, it's done within a few days, say brokers. If someone suggests that the porch needs repainting, it's taken care of quickly. "Realists are the sellers brokers prefer to deal with. We like them all, but realists tend to help us out the most," John notes. Bettina, a fifty-something homeowner in Phoenix, Arizona, is a realist. "I wanted to sell my condo within three months and I decided the best way to do that was to listen carefully to what the brokers were saying," she says.

When interviewing several brokers prior to listing her unit, Bettina asked them what they thought she could do to improve her chances of a quick sale. "They each suggested I repaint my orange-and-red hallway white. Two suggested I have the rugs cleaned, and another suggested I have the windows washed so that buyers could see the views from my window," Bettina says. She took all the advice, hired one of the brokers, and ended up selling her condo in six weeks.

The last group of sellers are the desperate or the anxious. These nervous Nellies are usually motivated by a financial, marital, or job transfer situation. Or they feel the need to get out in time for their children to start the semester at their new school. "Any time you have a time limitation, the sellers are going to be anxious," says John. "Selling can be a very stressful thing."

Sometimes the stress is self-inflicted. "We had some sellers who had too large a home and wanted to sell it right away. At first, we thought the price was too high, but there was interest. Still, the sellers called us every week, asking why their home hadn't sold. The wife was making herself sick keeping it clean," says Ken.

Wishful thinkers and those who are desperate to sell need to come to terms with what it takes to sell in their neighborhood, brokers say. If you hear that a home sold for a price that sounds too good to be true, it probably is. Perhaps that sales price got inflated while making the neighborhood gossip rounds. Or perhaps it included furniture. Unless you see the sales contract, you won't know.

If you're desperate to sell, the best way to motivate buyers is by lowering your price. If your property has been on the market for three months without an offer, have your broker do another market analysis to see where your home should be priced. And try to get feedback on buyers who went through your home. Ask their brokers where they eventually bought and why.

QUESTION 34

What are some good marketing tips that will help me sell my home?

When Sam and I first tried to sell our home we tried every trick in the book to encourage the hordes of buyers who came through the unit to make an offer. Our home was listed for a year and a half, and we never once received an offer. The reason was simple: The market for our type of home had collapsed. Units similar to ours that were priced $50,000 less than our unit weren't receiving offers either. When we attempted to sell the second time, we sold our home before it was even listed, for nearly the same price we had asked the first time.

The following list of marketing ideas may or may not work for you. Some will be expanded on later in the book. But this list should give you a good idea of what's available to you.

1. *Fantastic curb appeal.* Make your home look as well maintained and attractive as possible from the outside. A manicured landscape (cut your grass regularly!) is a given, but consider putting small pots of red, pink, or purple flowers on each stair up to the entrance of your home. If you have a porch, consider installing an attractive wooden porch swing. Hang baskets of brightly colored flowers from the porch ceiling (but don't overdo it). Consider putting window boxes outside the first-floor windows. If your cement front walk is badly cracked, consider ripping it up and replacing it with a brick or stone walk. Don't leave your trash cans on the curb, your kids' toys on

the front lawn, or your gardening equipment in the backyard.

2. *Stripped-down, spotless interior.* The best thing you can do for your home is to make it seem as large as possible. To do that, remove the clutter, pack away unnecessary books, store any unused furniture, take down excess wall hangings or paintings, put away toys and knickknacks, empty your counters and cupboards, and keep a clean, sparsely filled refrigerator and freezer.
3. *Give your home a finished look.* Before we sold our unit, Sam and I went to one of those bed and bath places and bought a matching comforter cover, pillow shams, sheets, towels, shower curtain, rug, and bathroom wastebasket for our master bedroom. We also bought matching towels, wastebasket, rug, and shower curtain for the guest bathroom. Although the end result was a little "too decorated" for our taste, it did help to give our home a finished look. We bought things we liked and figured we'd use in our new home. Also, touch up any cracked or peeling paint. Clean dirty walls. For areas that just look faded and unkempt, consider putting on a quick coat of fresh paint.
4. *Smells like a rose.* Brokers agree that the way a home smells has a profound impact on buyers walking through for the first time. For some buyers, the smell of sweet baked goods, whether it's cookies, brownies, or bread, smells like home. (If you decide to bake cookies, don't mess up your kitchen by whipping up a fresh batch of batter. Slice-and-bake cookies from your grocer's refrigerated case will have the same effect.) If I couldn't actually be home cooking when a

prospective buyer came through for a showing, I tried to bake something in the morning.

Freshly brewed coffee smells wonderful; consider putting a cinnamon stick in with the dry grounds. If your coffeemaker has a self-timer, consider leaving it on to brew just as the broker and buyer are getting there. Leave out two cups and two spoons, sugar and nondairy creamer (or a note that fresh milk is in the fridge). A big pot of slow-cooking soup also smells good. Potpourri accents in the right places help perk up rooms. Consider lavender for the bathrooms and rose or vanilla for the bedrooms. Just remember, a little goes a long way. You don't want your buyers to choke on conflicting smells as they walk through your home.

5. *Feed the buyer and broker.* Although they may not take anything, it's a nice gesture to leave a plate of cookies or a few slices of cake on a paper doily in the kitchen. Most buyers are polite, and unless there is a note welcoming them to help themselves, they won't try anything you leave out. Food is always a good "bribe" for overworked brokers who frequently schedule appointments during lunch. Maybe they'll remember your kindness and bring other buyers to see your home.
6. *Evening open houses.* Weekend open houses are an important way to get potential buyers to come through your home. Weekday open houses attract brokers. But consider hosting an evening open house for either brokers or prospective buyers. Advertise a weeknight open house in the real estate section the previous Saturday or Sunday, whenever your local real estate section is published. Ask your broker to list

the open house in the broker's hot sheet. Since folks will be stopping by after work (you can host it from 5:00 to 8:00 P.M.), consider having something for them to snack on. If you're selling in the spring, summer, or early autumn, you'll have the additional benefit of longer daylight hours.

7. *Buyer or broker bonuses*. In the height of the recession, it was common to see sellers offering to give the buyer a bonus for buying their home. These bonuses included cars, boats, vacations, stocks, bonds, cash, mortgage buydowns, school tuition, one year of paid real estate taxes, and one year of free parking (for condos with garages that charged a fee). Back then, giving buyers bonuses became a game, with sellers seeking to outdo their competitors rather than focus attention on the fact that their home's price was inflated. Today, most of these perks and bonuses have been eliminated. The few that remain are the most effective: increasing the broker's commission, buying down the buyer's mortgage, paying some of the buyer's closing costs, and paying any special assessments that your condo, co-op, or homeowner's association has imposed.
8. *Brochures, fliers, and listing sheets*. Successful brochures and fliers highlight the best points of your home but are detailed enough to give a prospective buyer insight into whether or not your home is right for him or her. Consider taking color photographs of the exterior and interior of your home (or hire a professional photographer). Attach reprints to each listing sheet. That goes a long way toward helping buyers remember your home more clearly than the many others they will see. Also consider attaching a color

photograph to the brochures your broker sends to other brokers. Although the local MLS will usually include a photograph of the house, a four-by-six-inch color photograph can make a striking impression.

Some of these marketing concepts will be explained further in the following questions.

THE OPEN HOUSE

QUESTION 35

What is an open house?

Socially, hosting an open house means inviting your friends, family, and acquaintances or business colleagues to drop by during an afternoon or evening. You might specify an hour range, say four to seven in the afternoon, or eleven-thirty in the morning to three in the afternoon, but there is no specific time the party starts. People come and go as their schedules permit; some stay briefly while others linger.

In real estate, an open house is the means by which you make your home available for public or broker inspection. Your home is open for a short period of time—on either a weekend, a weeknight, or a weekday—for the express purpose of having folks walk through and examine every nook and cranny.

There are two kinds of open houses. First, there is the *broker's open* (also known as the broker's open house). Brokers in your area designate one day a week (often Tuesday or

Thursday) when many of the newly listed properties are open to members of the multiple listing service. Brokers usually *caravan* (meaning, they move in groups) from property to property, staying long enough for only a quick walk-through and perhaps something to eat or drink (many of the broker's open houses serve food).

Brokers may see ten to twenty properties in a morning or afternoon. They want to see as many homes as possible, to preview them for their clients. They shop for buyers they are currently working with and to increase their store of knowledge for any potential buyers who come along. Brokers believe the broker's open is one of the best ways to market homes. It's a friendly, quite social affair, where brokers who haven't seen each other for a while catch up and trade industry gossip. They also share bits of knowledge about homes that have sold and the prices their sellers received.

The second kind of open house is a *general open* house, where you open your home to anyone who wants to take a look. Usually, general opens are held on the weekend, usually on Saturday or Sunday afternoon, for a limited amount of time—usually two or three hours. In many areas, Sunday is the preferred day for hosting open houses.

Buyers look through the weekend real estate section and plan their day of seeing open houses. Flipping open the paper, buyers may make a list of ten to twelve homes on the open house list they'd like to see. They'll write down their locations and the times the homes are open. Then they'll organize a tour of the homes that will allow them to pack as many in as possible. Usually open houses start around 11:00 A.M. and end around 5:00 P.M. Buyers like open houses because they can go to them on their own, without their broker. They allow buyers the freedom to educate themselves as to the housing stock and its value in the neighborhood.

There is another kind of open house that is slowly becoming popular in some areas—the *weeknight open* house. Brokers and sellers have begun to recognize that not everyone is available on the weekends to tour open houses. Or there may be so much competition (with too many homeowners hosting open houses at the same time), that your home might get short shrift. Weeknight open houses are often thought of as a nice marketing ploy. For working parents or spouses, stopping by an open house for a few minutes after work might be more convenient than arranging for someone to watch the family for several hours on a Saturday or Sunday. So few weeknight open houses are held that your home might just stand out from the pack.

Some brokers don't feel that hosting general open houses are worth the time and effort. They don't believe that sales contracts emerge from the stream of folks who walk through the house over a weekend. Other brokers swear by them. Judy, a broker in Seattle, Washington, says she has netted dozens of sales contracts for sellers while sitting at open houses. She has also picked up dozens of clients that way through the years—home buyers who either didn't have an agent or were unhappy with the one they were working with.

QUESTION 36

What should I do to prepare for an open house? What should I do during an open house?

The first thing you need to do for an open house is to let people know you are hosting one. The best way to do this is to advertise your open house in the weekend real estate section of your local paper. If you are working with a broker, your broker should handle all of the details, such as placing and paying for the advertisement. If you're selling on your own, you need to know what kind of advertising works, when to place it, and where to place it. The best advertising is a large "for sale" sign on your front lawn. On the day you host your open house, be sure to put an "open house today" sign outside so folks who drive by will stop in.

Place your open house notice so that it runs on the day you plan to host your open. The ad should include the following:

- *Your Address.* If you live on an obscure street, or in an obscure part of town, consider adding directions from the nearest main street or highway.
- *The Time of the Open House.* Don't say "all day" because you may have buyers stopping by at midnight. Pick either 11:00 A.M. to 3:00 P.M., or 2:00 P.M. to 4:00 P.M., or 1:00 P.M. to 5:00 P.M. When planning the time of your open house, think about possible conflicts, including possible sporting events (pro football games can seriously cut down on the number of buyers you'll see during the fall) or holidays (bad weekends include Mother's and Father's Day, the Fourth of July, Thanksgiving, Christmas, and New Year's). Your open house shouldn't be longer than four hours, otherwise you'll look desperate. Also, you're going to be exhausted by the end, so plan accordingly.
- *The Price of Your Home.* Some brokers don't like to list the price in their ads, believing it will turn off some

buyers. I think buyers want to know the price so they don't waste their time with something that's way over budget. Buyers will usually look at homes that are priced a little more than they can afford, but they don't want to spend the time on homes that are unreachable.

- *A Brief Description of the Home.* Use adjectives like "bright," "sunny," and "spacious" to give your property a unique feel. Put in the number of bedrooms and bathrooms, and any special amenities such as a fireplace, family room, library, sunroom, porch, eat-in kitchen, and lot size.

Here are some sample "For Sale" ads:

Anytown, USA—Open Sun. 1–4. New & nearly done 4 BR, 3ba, 2 frpl, lux MBR suite. 336 Beverly Dr. $325,000. 256-3220.

Anytown, USA—Fine bungalow 3 bedrooms, separate dining room, kitchen has dishwasher, frig & range. Washer/Dryer in basement, garage. $68,000. Kaine Realty 344-0890.

Anytown, USA—Open Sun 1–3 P.M. 146 Jackson Park. 3 BR brk Georgian, lrg lot. Call Reggie 747-7791.

Anytown, USA—7 rm bungalow, 4 bdr 2.5 bath, security system, fin bsmt, 2-car gar, excellent cond, double lot. $43,000. 58th and Morgan. 873-4052.

Anytown, USA—Fussy Buyer's Dream. Beautiful 4 bedroom, brick, 2 baths, dining room, newer furnace, plenty of storage, full basement. Only $64,500. Call Cathy at 596-9597.

Newspapers will require you to get your advertising to the ad department a few days before it is supposed to run. Since most papers charge by the word, or even by the letter, you'll want to use some of these common abbreviations to keep down your cost:

WBFP	Wood-burning fireplace. FP is just for fireplace, usually assumed to mean gas.
4b/2ba	This stands for "four bedrooms, two baths." Put in the numbers that correspond to your own home.
FR	Family room.
DR/LR	Dining room and living room.
GRDN	Garden.
PKG	Parking, sometimes written as "pkg incl" to indicate that parking is included.
AC	Air-conditioning.
GFA	Gas-forced air heat.
Balc	Balcony.
Prvt	Private, usually used for private laundry.
Vict'n	Victorian.
Gar	Garage.

Preparing for the Open House

Preparing for an open house is easy: Just make sure your home is spotless. "It's important that your home be as clean as possible, with everything put away," says Nancy, a broker from Tucson, Arizona. "It's also important that your home smell fresh and clean. Potpourri and the smells of something baking are nice, but if you've got rotting garbage in your kitchen can, that's going to put off a lot of buyers."

Use this checklist to prepare for showings. It will help you organize everything, room by room. Also, don't forget the exterior of your home.

Room	*Check For*	*Done?*
Kitchen	Clean countertops, garbage thrown out, sink wiped out, floor swept and washed, refrigerator/freezer cleaned, dishwasher emptied, cabinets organized.	
Dining Room	Linens folded, table cleared, floors swept, silver flatware hidden or locked up, china cabinet organized, sideboard cleaned, any exposed silver polished.	
Living Room	Tabletops cleared, sofa pillows plumped, bookshelves straightened, draperies opened, piano and photos dusted, paintings and prints straightened, plants trimmed (with dead leaves cut away), carpets/floors swept and vacuumed, toys, videotapes, and CDs put away.	
Bedrooms	Beds made, clothes hung up, closets straightened, valuables put away, money hidden, jewelry locked up, toys and books put away, curtains opened, floors/carpets swept and vacuumed, desks organized, tables straightened, wastepaper baskets emptied, clutter removed.	
Bathrooms	Dirty clothes hamper emptied, sink and toilet wiped, countertops cleared and wiped, towels neatly folded, bathtub/shower wiped down, shower curtains cleaned, soap scum wiped off, soap/hair products straightened, wastepaper baskets emptied, medicine chests organized, floor swept or washed.	

Room	*Check For*	*Done?*
Family Room	Toys put away, old newspapers and magazines thrown out, CDs and videos stored, fireplace swept out, bookshelves straightened, tabletops cleared and dusted, bar area cleared and organized, floors/carpets swept or vacuumed, window treatments opened.	
Basement	Straightened and organized, dusted and cleaned.	
Attic	Straightened and organized, dusted and cleaned.	
Exterior	Lawn mowed and edged, garage organized, toys and bicycles put away, front walk swept, flowers and flower boxes maintained.	

During the Open House

When Sam and I were looking to buy a house, we spent more Sundays than I care to count walking through dozens of open houses. We became so adept at the process that we would see perhaps fifteen or twenty houses on a single weekend. Most buyers get to a point where they can eliminate a house in a matter of minutes. That's why it's so important to make a good first impression.

Anyway, one day we went to an open house that serves as a perfect example of what *not* to do during an open house. The owners were selling the brick bungalow by themselves. The front porch and living room were clean enough, but the house had a funny smell. The owner greeted us with a baby in his arms and a small child, perhaps three or four, standing next to him. The little girl's name was Emily (we never found out the homeowner's name), and she proceeded to lead the tour, charmingly pointing out each flaw in the house to the acute embarrassment of her father.

Emily led the way into the kitchen, where the wife was feeding another baby. The house felt cluttered and small, especially with so many children running around. "We're out of room," the father admitted. We went down into the basement, which was rank and dark, lit only by a single light bulb, which the father had trouble finding. What we could see was dingy and cluttered, as if several families' lives had been stored down there.

Then we went to the second floor. As we got to the landing, we were hit with the most awful dirty diaper stench imaginable. Two more babies—identical one-year-old twins—were screaming from one dark room, its sole window blocked by a blue shade. The father went in while Emily explained that the family hadn't planned on having five children. It just happened that way. Sam and I were backing out of the room and down the stairs when the father insisted on showing us the "master bedroom." Next to the twins' tiny bedroom was a bedroom carved out under the eaves of the house, with a king-size bed sitting on the floor. The homeowner, who looked as if he was six-foot-one, could stand up only in the exact center of the room.

What did these homeowners do wrong? First, unless you're a FSBO, you should never be present at your own open house. Buyers are extremely reluctant to really examine a house if the owners are present. If you must be there, don't have your children with you; an open house is a grown-up activity, and if you can't find anyone to take your children on an outing to the park, the mall, or a movie, cancel your open house. Or you or your spouse should take the children out and have a friend help you with the open house. Do not let children run loose on the scene because it will completely disrupt the buyer's concentration. Also, too many children make a house seem too small. Buyers can't help but wonder how quickly they'll outgrow the house. Make sure all the smells are out of a house. Smells, particularly those of rotting garbage and dirty diapers, are anathema to buyers. Make sure your rooms are as bright and sunny as possible, and have every light turned on in your house.

In a buyer's market, where there are more homes to buy than people to buy them, buyers are looking for any reason to eliminate your home and move on to the next one. Your most important job is to make sure there is no reason, other than price and subjectivity, for your home to be eliminated from any buyer's list.

Successful Home Seller Tip: With crime rising, safety must be an issue at an open house. First, make sure you never do an open house alone. Always have another person with you. Since open houses are by definition open to the general public, anyone can walk in off the street and ask to see your home. Though most of the people will be your average buyers, you cannot discount the possibility that some may be more unsavory characters. With at least two people at an open house, you can keep an eye on each home buyer who comes through. Also, ask each person who comes into your house to write down his or her name, address, and telephone number, along with the name of any broker with whom he or she may be working.

Successful Home Seller Tip: If you have pets, try to keep them outside and out of the way of prospective buyers during showings. While I'm sure your pets are the best behaved of any in your neighborhood, they may frighten unsuspecting buyers and brokers—plus, there are plenty of folks who have terrible pet allergies. Unless you have a cage for your pet, keeping your pet in the basement means that the buyer may not be able to poke around down there. Consider hiring a pet sitter while your house is being shown, or take your pet with you when you leave your home.

Condos and Co-ops

While open houses are often held at condominium and co-op buildings, such buildings often have rules regulating when and how these units can be shown. The condo board may require you to have at least two people in the unit plus an additional person in the lobby directing people to the correct set of elevator banks. Or the rules may require the sign-in sheet to be at the doorman's station. Also, you may have to give advance notice of your intent to host an open house. Check with your building's management for any open house rules.

Successful Home Seller Tip: Check your local newspaper and television guide before scheduling an open house. Open house attendance usually drops on days when the home sports team is playing (football, baseball, and basketball are the biggest draws). Plan to work around the sporting event. If the big game is at 3:00 p.m., host an open house from 11:00 a.m. to 2:00 p.m. If the big game is at noon, you should plan a late afternoon open house.

QUESTION 37

What is a listing sheet? What kind of documentation should I give to prospective buyers when they tour my home?

A listing sheet is a piece of paper that contains all of the specifics about your home. It includes such things as the price, the number of bedrooms and bathrooms, the square footage of your home, the year it was built, the amount of your real estate taxes, lot size, and the like.

Listing sheets are important tools for buyers, who collect them from each home they visit and, hopefully, use them to compare and contrast homes they like. In my previous book, *100 Questions Every First-Time Home Buyer Should Ask*, I suggest that buyers take photographs of the homes they see, staple them to the listing sheets, then put the sheets in a three-ring binder. As the homes sell, the buyers can compare the listing price with the sales price to begin to understand the value of homes in a particular neighborhood.

You want to make your listing sheet as easy for buyers to read and understand as possible. It should also be as specific as possible. You should include:

- The address (with zip code).
- The square footage of the home, plus the lot size.
- The year the home was built.
- The primary exposure (toward which direction does the front door face?).
- The amount of your most recent real estate tax bill.
- The number of bedrooms (with dimensions).
- The number of bathrooms (with dimensions).
- A list of other rooms (with dimensions).

- Amenities—such as a basement, fireplace, usable attic, sun porch, enclosed porch, hardwood floors, whirlpool, swimming pool, central air, walk-in closets.
- List of mechanicals and appliances that will stay with the unit, including light fixtures and washer and dryer.
- School districts, with names of schools.
- Assessments, special assessments, and other condo/co-op amenities, including health club or workout room, swimming pool, sun deck, storage lockers, twenty-four-hour doorman or security system, live-in engineer.
- Description of parking space or garage.
- Distance to sources of transportation (train, highway, public bus system).
- Distance to parks or recreational areas.

Although I always recommend that buyers take along a Polaroid-type instant camera to showings, many don't. You'll earn the buyer's appreciation if you include a color snapshot of the exterior (and perhaps an additional one of the interior) of your home. Consider folding a piece of 8 ½-by-11-inch paper in half. Staple the exterior shot of your home to the center of the folded paper. As the buyer opens it up, you can have your listing sheet on the inside. If you like, you can staple the interior shot to the back page so the buyer will have both by which to remember your home.

Documentation

If you live in a co-op or a condo there are some other documents you might want to make available to potential buyers. For example, it's nice to have a photocopy of the floor plan of your building. You may also want to separate out your monthly assessment into individual pieces. Co-op assessment often include real estate taxes, heat, hot water, electricity, and perhaps the cable bill, if the building has contracted for a group rate. Breaking apart your assessment will allow buyers to compare each building's basic assessment and the services that are provided by that assessment. It becomes an apples-to-apples comparison. Let's say Building A is a co-op that has real estate taxes included in the assessment. Building B is a condominium where owners pay their own tax bills. By breaking down the assessment statement, it becomes easier for potential buyers to compare the monthly assessment for the two buildings:

	Building A	*Building B*
Basic Assessment	$550.00	$675.00
Special Assessment	$116.00	N/A
Real Estate Taxes	$325.00	$400/month, paid separately
Hot Water/Heating	included	$95/month, paid separately
TOTAL	$991.00	$1,170.00

If you live in Building A and a potential buyer asks to see your monthly assessment bill, he or she might be shocked by the amount when compared to Building B, where the charge may be deceptively less. In this case, a unit owner in Building B pays a smaller assessment, but when you add in the extra costs, it is more expensive to live there than in Building A. As co-op sellers, it's in your best interest to make your assessment seem as inexpensive as possible and remind buyers that the real estate taxes are included.

In addition to an easy-to-understand assessment statement, you might want to keep a copy of your condo or co-op declaration (commonly called the "condo dec"), the building's current and last year's budgets, plus the building rules and regulations on hand for buyers to page through. When you actually accept an offer for purchase, you'll provide the buyer with his or her own copy at that time.

QUESTION 38

Should I be present while my home is being shown? What about second, third, and fourth showings?

Generally speaking, buyers find it more difficult to really scrutinize a home while the seller is standing over their shoulder and breathing down their neck. Having sellers and buyers in the same room with brokers often adds tension to an already tense situation. Buyers—particularly first-time buyers—are naturally nervous when looking for a home. There may be a time pressure (they're being transferred or they need to be in a new home at the start of the school year) or they already may have lost several homes and are worried about losing another. Sellers naturally worry about who is coming through their home. If you're a seller, there is a great unasked question: Is the next buyer who comes through my house for a showing "The One"? It doesn't seem to matter if you're on your first showing or your three hundredth. You're constantly expecting the next person who walks through your front door to purchase your home.

So if you're hanging around for a showing, it's likely to make the buyer more nervous and you more anxious. It's just these kinds of emotions that can kill a deal, brokers say.

If you're working with a broker, it's best if you're not even home during the first or even second showings. If there is a third showing, ask your broker if he or she feels it would be beneficial for you to be available to answer any questions the buyers may have.

When Sam and I first tried to sell our home several years ago, we had a potential buyer and his girlfriend come through the unit a total of five times. After the third showing, we asked our broker if we could answer any questions for the prospective buyer. She asked the buyer and he said, yes, he had some questions; could we be on hand? As it turned out, we missed him at the fourth showing, but he caught both of us on the fifth showing. By that time, he was asking very specific questions about storage space, and if we could hear any noise from our upstairs neighbor. Now, our upstairs neighbor was a bachelor who usually didn't spend much time in his apartment. But as it happened, the night of the showing our neighbor had guests who were actively moving furniture across the room. That noise, just about the first we'd ever heard, effectively killed the deal.

If you're selling by yourself, you have no choice but to be present for the showing. After all, *you're* doing the showings, and buyers will expect you to be there.

How do you do a showing? The best showings are the ones where you have the time to point out all of the attributes and amenities of your property and where the buyer has the time to truly appreciate them.

Just before the appointed time of the showing, turn on every light in your house—even the ones in the closets. Open every window shade or curtain. Make sure the house is fresh and clean and as brightly lit as possible. Start your showing by greeting the buyers at the front door. Be polite.

Offer to take their coats. Show them the entryway and the hall closet. Comment on all the positives: the high ceilings, the generous entryway closet, the neutral decor. Lead the buyers into the living room, then the dining room, family room (if you have one), sunroom, and kitchen. The idea is to give the buyers a feel of the flow of your home. Point out details such as hardwood floors and the antique fireplace mantel. If there is anything you are not selling with the house, such as a light fixture you intend to take with you, be sure to tell the prospective buyers (and be sure to write it on your listing sheet).

After you've finished with the main living quarters of the home, lead the way toward the bedrooms. It's common to show the master bedroom first, since that's where the buyers will sleep, but some brokers show the smaller bedrooms first and then make their way to the biggest room. The way your home is constructed will, to a large degree, dictate the way you give your tour. Make sure that you have a steady stream of information but that you listen to the buyers' questions. Be sensitive and try to pick up on what they like and don't like about your house. Your tour should be practiced. Consider rehearsing with your children or a friend.

Buyers will want to see your attic and basement, primarily to check out the home's mechanical systems. You can expect to answer a stream of questions from the most interested buyers. In fact, the more questions they ask, the more interested they are in your home. If there is a question to which you don't know the answer, don't lie and don't fudge. Simply tell the buyer you don't know the answer but will be delighted to find out for him or her.

The best showings shouldn't take longer than twenty minutes—unless you have an unusually large or unique property. In fact, brokers often count on the fact that a showing will take less than twenty minutes, because on a busy day they will try to schedule two to three first showings per hour for their buyers. On a first showing, the buyer need only decide whether or not the house is a possibility. If the house doesn't meet the buyer's basic needs, it can be eliminated. If it does meet those needs, a second, more thorough, showing will be arranged.

As a FSBO, it is perfectly reasonable for you to call back buyers who have gone through your home. Just don't be hurt if they don't return your telephone calls. If you don't get a call back, it means they're not interested in your home. Undoubtedly, when someone is interested, he or she will call you. (Isn't that the story of life?)

Successful Home Seller Tip: When showing your own home, avoid talking too much. This is so important I'm going to say it again: *Don't talk too much when showing your own home*. And don't spend too much time discussing your decorating choices. Your taste may not be the same as the buyer's. Be aware that some (or all) of your cosmetic or structural improvements may not be to the buyer's taste. If, for example, you boarded up all the windows in one room to make a library, a prospective buyer might be wondering how easy it would be to remove what you've done and restore the room to its original use. Instead, your discussion (which is more like a running monologue) should concentrate on the construction of the home, its flow, and the mechanical elements. Be specific about which improvements you have made. If you have replaced the boiler and put on a new roof, be sure to mention it. These are things buyers want, and need, to know.

QUESTION 39

What should I do if something is missing from my home after a showing?

This is every seller's nightmare: Prospective buyers come through your home and rob you blind.

Of course, it doesn't often happen. Almost everyone who works through an agent or broker is a legitimate home buyer. But there are the exceptions that prove the rule. In Texas, there was a well-dressed couple that went from town to town posing as home buyers who were transferring to the neighborhood. They would work with the best brokers and see the best homes. While the broker was showing the husband the home, the wife would wander off and quickly rifle through the bedroom dresser drawers. At other times, the wife and broker would talk while the husband did the dirty work. Eventually they were caught. But not before nearly a dozen home sellers had lost money and jewelry.

Of more concern are the strangers who walk in off the street during a weekend or weeknight open house. That's why it's always a good idea to have at *least* two people work each open house. If the house has two levels, someone can be on each floor, guiding people from room to room.

Should you come home and find that things are missing or are misplaced after a showing, immediately contact your agent and the managing or designated broker for the real estate firm. If your home is equipped with a lockbox, the local multiple listing service can easily determine which agent went through the house. The agent should then be contacted, as should his or her buyers. If you feel the brokers aren't acting quickly enough, you can contact your local police department. You can also file a complaint with your local Realtor Association, or the National Association of

Realtors, if your broker is a member. Finally, you can lodge a complaint against the broker and brokerage firm with your state agency that regulates real estate licenses. Fortunately, the incidence of theft during home showings is relatively rare. If you take simple precautions, such as hiding your valuables and locking up jewelry and cash, you'll go a long way toward protecting yourself.

WAITING FOR AN OFFER

QUESTION 40

How long should my home sit on the market before someone makes me an offer?

While brokers are often asked how quickly a home will sell, residential experts say their best answer is only a guess. Marketing times and market conditions change as quickly as the weather. A house may be hot in one neighborhood, but in another neighborhood that same home could sit on the market for months, if not years.

But how long is long enough? How long can you expect your house to sit on the market before it's sold? And when should you know you need a change in your marketing strategy?

As we discussed in Question 27, your local MLS keeps tabs on the average number of days homes in your area stay on the market. (This number might be reported from time to time in your local newspaper, or you could ask a local broker.) That's one way to tell whether the market currently favors buyers or sellers or is relatively balanced. If the average number of marketing days is, say, thirty-five, then it's not unreasonable for you to sit tight for the first month or six weeks.

Brokers say that a house will garner its maximum attention during the first three weeks it is listed. That's when the mystery of a new listing is unveiled. All the buyers who are active in your market area when your home is first listed will see it within the first three weeks. If it clicks with one of them, you'll enjoy a reasonably quick sale and be the envy of your neighbors.

But what if it doesn't click? If your home passes through its first month or six weeks without so much as an offer, and if you're in a strong seller's market—where the number of buyers exceeds the number of homes for sale—then you may want to immediately reevaluate the price you have set for your home and the condition it is in.

Savvy sellers listen to what the market is telling them. If you want to take a flier and see if you can get someone to pay a bit more for your home, that's fine. But if no one bites, you're going to have to rethink the equation. The question turns on how quickly you want to, or have to, sell your home. (If you aren't sure of your motivations for selling, see Question 2.) If there is no pressing reason to move, and you want to keep the listing price where it is for another four to six weeks, and your broker agrees, then by all means, wait for your price. But if you need to move and there have been no offers, you should reevaluate your market position as quickly as possible.

Sellers listing their home in a buyer's market—where there are more homes for sale than there are buyers to purchase them—may need to develop some patience. Although you might want to sell quickly, it may take several months to produce an offer you'd be willing to accept. Dropping the price may or may not influence how quickly you'll receive an offer in a buyer's market simply because buyers tend to take more time in making their decisions. (Of course, if you drop your price, the buyer who was going to buy your home anyway will be delighted. But there's no way to know that, so don't spend too much time mulling it over.)

After your home has been on the market for a while, your agent will suggest to you that perhaps you should rethink your listing price. Agents and brokers believe in this real estate maxim: If you price a home at or below market value it will sell. So if your house hasn't garnered an offer within the first thirty to sixty days, your agent's first thought will be to lower the listing price. Your first thought will be that the agent should be working harder to market the property. It may also cross your mind that your home hasn't been advertised often enough.

If you're determined to keep your home listed where it is, then you and your agent need to have a marketing chat. That's where you both will sit down and discuss exactly what the agent has been doing to market your home. You should discuss weekend open houses (once about every three weeks is often enough), advertising, broker's opens, target mailings to other brokerage firms and the broker's past clients, a two-color (either black-and-white or blue-and-white) brochure with a full-color photo of the exterior of your house attached to the front, and whatever other sorts of marketing plans your broker proposed to do in the comparative marketing analysis (CMA) he or she prepared in order to get your listing.

If your listing agreement expires before you've received an offer, you'll have to decide if it's the broker's fault or your fault. If you decide it is the broker's fault, because he or she hasn't followed through on the marketing plans described in the CMA, you should consider not renewing the listing agreement. At that point, you'll have to start from scratch. Bring in three new brokers from three different firms or reconsider the other choices you previously interviewed. Ask them for CMAs and start the process all over again. If you decide your home hasn't sold simply because it's overpriced, then you need to evaluate where your home is listed and what would be a more effective list price.

Successful Home Seller Tip: Homes that are overpriced for the condition, the neighborhood, and the market may quickly get a bad reputation among brokers in the community. Brokers showing the home start chitchatting among themselves that the home is overpriced. They say it in front of their buyers, who quickly pick up that your home is not to be touched with a ten-foot pole. Suddenly, overpricing has turned into a stigma, which keeps buyers from coming to see your home, which prevents it from being sold. The longer the home sits on the market, the harder it is to sell. Folks start to wonder if there really isn't something wrong with it, even if you lower the price to the market level.

QUESTION 41

What should I do if no one makes an offer on my home?

"If your house isn't selling, then either the price isn't right or the condition isn't right," says Frank, a broker on the southwest side of Chicago. Some sellers unrealistically expect to get top dollar for a house that is in less than mint condition. That's going to be a problem for buyers who will expect to see a certain level of quality and condition for a specific price range.

If your home hasn't sold, you have two options: You can either fix up your home or lower your price. Either way, you're going to net less money from the sale of your home than you perhaps planned for.

Not getting the amount of money from your home that you expected is the toughest emotional and psychological hurdle for many sellers to cross. Many sellers often calculate their list price by starting with the profit: "I want to get $40,000 in cash out of the sale of my house, and I have a $55,000 mortgage, so I need to add around $7,000 for the broker's commission plus fees plus negotiating room. I'll list my home at, say, $120,000." That's the kind of backward thinking that can get you into trouble. And these are the sellers that will most often be disappointed by the price they receive for their home. Ultimately, real estate transactions are not dominated by individual desires and greed but by independent market forces.

Brokers say there are several options available for sellers whose homes have languished on the market:

- *Make basic cosmetic changes*. If you didn't repaint and recarpet your home in neutral tones before you listed, try doing so now. Replace your dark, worn-out carpeting with new neutral carpet, or repaint that limegreen bedroom with a coat of white paint. But remember: Every dollar you spend is a dollar that's coming directly out of your pocket. If you can paint the interior of your home yourself, do it. It is also not necessary to spend $35 per square yard on the best carpeting made. Instead, spend enough to buy decent carpet that will look good for a couple of years. For a variety of reasons, you may end up staying in your house, and you won't want to recarpet again before you sell.

- *Relist your home.* Every home listed on the MLS is assigned a number that corresponds to the date and year of listing. If your home has been on the market for more than six months, the MLS listing number may begin to look old by comparison to newer listings. If your home has been on the market past a year end, all the listings in the new year will have a newer number. You may want to consider relisting your house to give it a fresh look and a new listing number in the local multiple listing service book. While this may seem trivial, buyers' agents often scour a listing book looking specifically for old numbers, hoping that they can get a good deal on a house that has "aged" on the market. *Note:* Most MLSs won't let you just relist your home. You either have to take the property off the market, change agents or brokerage firms, raise or lower the listing price, or do something else that somehow changes the listing. Ask your broker what your local MLS requires before you can relist your home.
- *Raise your commission.* Brokers say they wouldn't force a home on a buyer simply because it had a higher than average commission. On the other hand, they wouldn't mind a bit if that home just happened to be the one that's right for their buyer. Brokers will often include a home with a higher commission in their list of showings for just that reason. Increasing the commission above normal may help garner more attention for your property. If you don't want to raise the commission, consider giving the buyer's agent a $500,

$1,000, or $2,000 bonus for bringing the buyer to the table.

- *Give the buyer a break.* Instead of, or in addition to, rewarding the buyer's agent, consider doing some special things for the person who is actually going to purchase your home. Promotions such as free lottery tickets, gift certificates, sporting event tickets, and even vacations were lures of the 1980s. In the 1990s, buyers are worried about buying a home on one salary instead of two, and are downsizing their lives. What may be more meaningful to this type of buyer is the offer of paying some or all of his or her closing costs (including lender's points or fees), paying future condo or co-op assessments, paying some of the future real estate taxes, offering a home warranty, and buying down the buyer's mortgage.
- *Lower your price.* If your home is in the best condition possible, and you've already raised the commission and offered the buyer a premium, and your broker recently relisted the home and has done an outstanding job marketing your property, you may have to accept that your home is overpriced. The good news is, while your home is overpriced, it may not be overpriced by a lot. What you need to do is determine what homes in your neighborhood are selling for, rather than what they are listed for, and then underprice your neighbors by a little bit. (For more information on how to lower your list price and when to do so, see Question 42.)

Successful Home Seller Tip: If you don't want to change the condition of your home, and you don't really want to lower your price, consider giving the buyer a "decorating" [illegible] lowance for your home. In the building I once [illegible] four-bedroom, three-bath, 2,400-square-foot [illegible] sted for $289,000. The woman who lived there hadn't redecorated in perhaps thirty years. After she died, the estate put the home on the market. The unit had wonderful space but had a dated, worn look, with velvet flocked wallpaper and peeling paint. After a few months on the market, the estate offered a $30,000 decorating allowance, which effectively lowered the selling price to $259,000. That was an excellent price for the unit, and it sold quickly. Because the value of the unit for tax purposes would be established by the sale, the estate felt it was important for the official "sales price" to be as high as possible.

(You can give allowances and credits for all sorts of things, including the roof or any broken mechanical systems. But most of these smaller credits are done at closing. Some may be a problem for your buyer's lender and you should consult with your attorney on how they should be addressed at the closing. For more information, see Question 71.)

QUESTION 42

How much should I lower my list price?

Before you figure out how much you need to lower the listing price of your home, it's important to recognize and understand how buyers purchase homes. When buyers are looking for homes, they instruct their broker to pull up homes that meet a variety of criteria. The three most important criteria are size, location, and price. If a home buyer tells the broker she wants to look at four-bedroom homes priced up to $200,000 and your home is listed at $205,000, it simply won't make the cut. (Almost all brokerage firms use computers to sort through potential properties by price, location, size, and amenity.) The buyer's broker knows that the buyer is already looking above her price range, and will believe the buyer absolutely can't afford to look above $200,000. Your home, though only $5,000 more than the buyer's upper end, won't be included on the buyer's list of potential properties.

Brokers tend to clump properties into three categories based on the price of the home: First-time buyers, move-up buyers, and high-end buyers. In high-cost, major metropolitan areas like Chicago, Boston, Philadelphia, and Washington, D.C., the upper end of the first-time buyer category is around $200,000. In San Francisco and Los Angeles, first-time buyers routinely spend up to $250,000 for a home (and may have over an hour's commute to work each way just for the privilege). In smaller cities, like Columbus, Ohio; Tampa, Florida; and Phoenix, Arizona; first-time buyers may top out at $125,000 to $150,000. In rural areas, $50,000 may be the upper end for a first-time buyer home. Move-up buyers are the middle level of home buyers. They purchase property priced roughly from $175,000 to $500,000. Except in Los Angeles and New York, high-end buyers' homes cost $500,000 and up.

Once brokers determine which category their buyers fit into, they then begin to look at the prices of property within the category. For property priced under $100,000, brokers seem to categorize homes at $5,000 to $10,000 intervals. So buyers may ask to see homes priced to $80,000 or $85,000. Once property is priced over $100,000, the intervals jump to $10,000 to $25,000 chunks. Buyers often ask to see homes priced up to $150,000 or $175,000. For homes priced over $500,000, the intervals are larger, perhaps $25,000 to

$50,000. And for homes priced over $1 million, the interval of choice is $100,000. Brokers won't even use numbers at this point. They'll often say, "I've got a house listed for one point two," meaning they've got a home listed for $1.2 million.

Part of knowing what price you should list your home at is knowing what category of buyer it appeals to. If you've got a first-time-buyer house in Fort Worth, Texas, and it's priced at $200,000, that is probably going to be too high for the targeted market. To be able to spend that kind of money, these first-time buyers will have to earn about $70,000 a year, without any debt and with a 20 percent down payment, assuming an annual interest rate of about 10 percent. There's a buyer for every house, so it's possible, not probable, that a couple of first-time buyers will walk into your home, fall in love, and make you an offer you can live with.

On the other hand, your home might have a wider draw priced at $174,000 rather than $200,000. First-time buyers in your area may not be conditioned to buy a home with a "2" on it. At $174,000 to $199,999, you'll appeal to a much larger number of home buyers.

How do you determine your new listing price? Start by asking your broker to provide you with an updated CMA. It also helps to know how quickly property is selling in your neighborhood, and for what percentage of list price. If homes are taking an average of five months to sell, but are selling within 6 percent of list price, then you are faced with an extremely slow market. Buyers will jump only for a property they feel is undervalued in the marketplace.

Your new listing price should also reflect how quickly you hope to get out of your home. If you initially had a year to sell your home and transfer to a new city, but have used up six months just seeing if you could get the price you wanted for your home, you're going to be a lot more motivated now than you were six months earlier. This is a good opportunity for you to reevaluate your motivations as a seller. How quickly do you want to sell? How quickly do you have to sell? If you need to sell quickly, consider pricing your home close to what you would actually accept for it. If you would take $185,000 for your home, consider listing it at $189,000. At $189,000, you're under $190,000, which may be an arbitrary round cut-off number used by the broker for a particular buyer.

There are two schools of thought when considering how much to lower the list price of your home. You can either cut the price to the bone in one long, painful swipe, or you can chop away at the listing price, bit by bit, until you garner an offer or your broker loses his or her patience. For example, if your original list price is $175,000 and you know similar homes in the area have been selling for $148,000, you could cut your list price either to, say, $150,000 or to $169,000. The first price demonstrates that you are a serious seller to buyers. It also shows them you know what the market is for your home. The second price brings you down into the next tier of buyers, who may think you're a little more serious (after all, the price is going in the right direction) but aren't quite there yet.

After you've made the decision to cut the price of your home, accept it. It is difficult to realize that you won't get as much money out of your home as you had hoped. Sometimes you just have to cut your losses. Los Angeles home sellers Jackie and Charlie said it was terribly painful for them when they finally realized that their house just wasn't worth what they had put into it. After a year of slowly chopping away at their list price, they finally were ready to drop the price and move out of the neighborhood. "As an investment," Charlie said, "it stunk. But it was a nice place to live."

As a seller, one of the things you have to remember is that a home is a place you live, not just a place you invest money. The days of 25 percent annual appreciation may be over in most areas. And as we've seen in some areas, that kind of instant appreciation can evaporate overnight. The best thing you can do is look honestly at your home and the neighborhood in which you live. Allow the market to dictate your price.

Successful Home Seller Tip: Brokers know that homes priced below their market value tend to be snapped up. That's one reason brokers are always looking to lower the listing price. It's easy to underprice your home. It's harder to hit the market value. Also, it's easier to lower your price than to raise it. Once you've dropped your price, brokers are on notice that you're now willing to accept that price for your property. Before you officially lower your price, make sure it's a price you can live with.

QUESTION 43

What should I do if my broker goes away on vacation?

The conventional wisdom in the real estate industry goes something like this: When brokers go on vacation, all of their listings sell. That was certainly the experience for Beth and Mark, whose condominium sat on the market for several months, until their broker took a week's vacation. A few days after she left, they received their first offer.

Even brokers need a holiday. And it's likely that your broker will take one while your home is on the market. While one vacation shouldn't impede your ability to sell your home, it's worth noting when the vacation will occur. Your home will see its greatest exposure during its first three or four weeks on the market. That's when everyone who is actively looking for a home that's your size in your price range will come through your house. Your broker should hold at least one open house, plus the broker's open, during this initial phase of the listing. Frankly, it's the time when the broker should be the most involved with your listing, drumming up support within the office and networking with other brokers she or he knows within the community.

The time to find out about vacation plans is when you are interviewing brokers. Ask if there is a special time of year the broker likes to take vacations. Ask if any are already planned (if the broker has small children, they might be). Generally speaking, brokers like to take time off at the end of the year—the week between Christmas and New Year's is typically dead, with only the most serious of buyers and sellers in the market—and usually sometime during the late summer, before the autumn market begins.

Usually, when brokers go on vacation they have another agent or broker in their office cover for them. If something happens while the substitute agent is covering the broker's turf, the broker often gives the agent a piece of his or her commission. While it's reassuring to know that someone is covering for your broker, the substitute agent generally won't be that involved with you or your property. Most cover for emergencies only. Substitute brokers will still take calls about your listing and will set up appointments with buyer brokers who want to show your home. But don't expect the substitute broker to pick up where your broker left off and begin actively marketing your property. In all but the most unusual circumstances, that just won't happen.

What you can expect is help if a contract comes in. (Sometimes, if a contract comes in on your property while your broker is away, he or she may try to negotiate it from a hotel room!) The substitute agent will call you to inform you there has been an offer and to let you know when it expires. He or she will act as your conduit to the buyer, just as your own broker would have. But you'll have to help your substitute out, since he or she won't know the ins and outs of your sale.

Successful Home Seller Tip: Before your broker leaves on an extended vacation, ask him or her to introduce you to the broker or agent who will be helping out. If you find you don't like this agent, you will have an opportunity to ask your broker to use someone else. If you initially like the substitute broker but later have a falling out, don't hesitate to approach the managing broker who runs your broker's company. Managing brokers are there to sort out problems and to keep buyers and sellers happy. If the substitute is nonresponsive, or kills a potential contract by not following through on time, you should call the managing broker immediately. On shorter trips, your broker may call in to the office at least a couple of times, and may even check in with you. If there are problems with the substitute, don't leave a message on your broker's voice mail about him or her, however, because the substitute will be picking up those messages.

QUESTION 44

What should I do if my broker and I have a personality conflict?

Finding the right broker can sometimes be a little like going on a blind date. You ask your friends if they know anyone. Some of them will, some won't. Someone will fix you up with their broker. You're not expecting too much. Maybe a little hand holding. Someone sensitive enough to understand who you are and what you are really looking for in life—and the sale of your home. So you make the phone call. You bristle every time the broker mispronounces your name. And everything goes wrong from there. The broker smokes, you're allergic. The broker is late, you're an early bird. The broker tells you your home should sell for under $200,000 and you know it's worth at least $250,000. And although some blind dates end in marriage, this one's a full-fledged disaster.

The failure rate for real estate blind dates may be a lot lower than that for real blind dates, but the personality clash can be just as traumatic. "Strangely enough, there aren't that many mismatches, because when someone refers you to a friend, they're friends because they have a similar temperament, so the fit is pretty good," says Jim, a broker in Chicago. And you want it to be, because you're probably going to sign a listing agreement for ninety days with this broker and let him or her in on the most intimate details of your lives.

Like a blind date, the relationship between a seller and a broker depends on chemistry. And though real estate agents may be reluctant to admit it, there are times when a broker and a seller just don't get along. Top brokers say the best way to prevent problems is to thoroughly interview several brokers before agreeing to work with any one specifically. Get to know the broker. Ask him or her personal questions. Get to know his or her likes and dislikes. "Brokers are professionals," says Jim. "You want them to have a clear understanding of what you want"—and what you need. The broker needs to listen to you—and you need to listen to the broker—to avoid conflict.

Often, if a personality clash is going to happen it's going to happen from the get-go, experts say. In one case, a real estate attorney who was trying to sell his own home telephoned a broker a friend was using to sell her house. "I called her for some advice and to see if she would come and look at my house. But I was immediately turned off by her self-promotion," said the attorney. "All she did was blurt out her numbers and credentials, like she was trying to sell me a used car."

The emotional upheaval involved with buying and selling property is the usual culprit behind personality clashes. There are at least a dozen ways emotions can get out of hand. Sellers often get exasperated when they find themselves stuck in a place they can't sell. Or they've gone out and bought a new house before they've sold their original home and are now frightened that they won't be able to sell. One broker recalls that a seller went stark raving mad when given a lowball first offer. He stood up and threw the documents out the window and the brokers out of the house.

Brokers usually end up in the middle, which is the trickiest place to be. The most common complaint is that the agent hasn't listened to the seller's needs and wants. "Sometimes," says Maryellen, a managing broker, "the broker doesn't pay attention to the client's needs, or is so pushy that they have the person squeezed against the wall and they're panicking."

Fixing the Problem

Sometimes, personality conflicts can be resolved by arranging a three-way meeting with the agent, the seller, and the managing broker. Managing brokers say that sellers are sometimes reluctant to approach the managing broker because they believe the broker will always take the agent's side. That's not always true. In many cases, the managing broker will try to get the broker to change his or her sales tactics.

The real estate attorney who had problems with his friend's broker says he works with dozens of brokers in his practice. "Some are wonderfully helpful and try to exert a calming influence on an emotional or tense transaction. Others are superficial and excitable, and can be set off early by any snafu or glitch. Once the contract is signed, these brokers' personalities tend to change dramatically since now they feel they have their hands around the commission, and they're not going to let go," the attorney adds.

If the problem is unfixable, ask the managing broker to reassign you to another broker. While you may think you signed your listing agreement with the agent, you actually signed it with the brokerage firm. They will want to keep you happy because they will want to keep your business. If you switch agents and find you're in another unhappy situation, find a new brokerage firm and start again.

QUESTION 45

What should I do if my broker seems to be losing interest in marketing my home?

Houses can get stale sitting on the market. And brokers can get stale marketing a property that has been on the market for a long time. How long? Some brokers get that blah, stale feeling after a few months. Some brokers remain fresh even if a property has been on the market for a year or longer. As a seller, your property will always seem fresh and exciting to you. You may just be weary from cleaning it on a daily basis for showings.

Here are some signs of a stale broker and a stale property:

- Your home has been listed for more than six or nine months without an offer.
- Your broker doesn't return your telephone calls and doesn't call you on a weekly basis.
- There are few, if any, showings at your home.
- The broker does not hold broker's opens or weekend open houses.
- Your property is rarely, if ever, advertised in the local paper.
- Your broker goes on vacation without telling you.
- You call your broker and she doesn't remember who you are.

If you find your property has become stale, or that your broker has become stale, it's probably time to make a change. Even if you've just renewed your listing agreement for another 90-day period, sit down with your agent and his or her managing broker and discuss the problem. Ask the agent what can be done to sell your home as quickly as possible. Sometimes the answer is to switch agents or brokerage firms. You might find out that the agent was hoping you'd take the listing away but was afraid to ask you to cancel the listing agreement.

Just because one agent can't sell your home doesn't mean another can't. My mother, Susanne, who has been one of the top real estate agents in Chicago for many years, likes to say this: "It's always best to be the second or third agent. By that time, the seller has tried out his or her ideal listing price and reduced the home to a realistic point, where it can be sold quickly. Or the experience with the first agent was so bad that you look like an angel."

The reason some agents work better for certain properties is that agents often sell through their network. The more people an agent knows, the more he or she can network with them to market your property. Agents will often show an agent friend's listings to their clients. They know the favor will be returned. In addition, agents have territories and, like doctors, they specialize. So if you've been trying to sell your home with a top agent who doesn't happen to specialize in your area, you might want to try hiring the agent who has sold homes in and around your neighborhood for the past ten years, even if her sales figures aren't as high. You want to be working with the agent everyone turns to to find property in your neighborhood. Once an agent develops a reputation like that, it's a little like having the golden touch.

If you feel as if your home is getting stale, and you are itchy to move on to another location, you can pull your home off the market or try to rent it out to cover your expenses. Or give your home a fresh look by storing or rearranging more furniture.

A final thought: If you like your agent, but for whatever reason (perhaps a severe economic slowdown has squelched the market in your area) your home hasn't sold, consider taking it off the market for a couple of months and putting it back on at the start of the next selling season.

QUESTION 46

I've been trying to sell my home by myself, but it hasn't sold. When should I consider hiring a broker?

There's nothing wrong with trying to sell your home by yourself. If you're in a hot neighborhood—or have a unique, coveted property—you may have more potential buyers than you know what to do with. FSBOs in this situation are incredibly lucky. Not only will you sell your home quickly, but you'll save part—or all—of the broker's commission.

But it's the savvy seller who knows when to throw in the towel. If you've tried to sell your home by yourself and you haven't received an offer, you may want to call in the experts. As was discussed earlier in the book, between 85 and 95 percent of all homes sell with the help of a broker. There's a reason for that. Real estate agents and brokers are professionals. They help people sell homes day in and day out. And if you get a good one, you can sell your home quickly and without a lot of aggravation.

When should you call in a real estate broker? That depends on how quickly you have to sell your home. Mark and Amy, who attempted to sell by themselves, called in a broker after a couple of months (though a few days after they signed the listing contract they ended up selling to a buyer who had seen their home before it was listed and whom they had excluded from the listing agreement). Some FSBOs wait six months or a year. Others call in the professionals after six weeks.

Remember, there's no need to feel ashamed for having tried unsuccessfully to sell your home by yourself. Selling a home is a complicated and demanding assignment requiring extreme flexibility, marketing ability, and luck. (Don't ever underestimate the power of luck.) Any broker worth his or her salt won't make you feel like a failure. That is, they won't say things like "Gee, I could've sold your home a month ago to my buyers; you should have called me immediately." If a broker you've called makes a remark like that, you may want to find another broker.

Also, the fact that you've called in a broker doesn't mean you can never sell on your own again. If you sign a 60- or 90-day listing agreement, and you decide you got better results on your own, you can always cancel the agreement and go back to being a FSBO.

PART V

Offers, Contracts, and Negotiations

GETTING AN OFFER

QUESTION 47

What is an offer to purchase or a contract to purchase?

At some point, a prospective buyer will walk through your front door and fall in love with your home. It's a wonderful feeling to know that someone else loves your home as much as you do. And the feeling gets better when that buyer, or another, actually makes you an offer to purchase your home.

There are three basic pieces to an offer: the address or description of the property; the consideration, or the price the buyer is prepared to pay; and the date on which the closing will take place. A valid offer can be written on anything, including a paper napkin, and can be written as simply as follows: "I, Ilyce R. Glink, offer to buy 222 Baker Street for $100,000, to close on July 13, 1996."

Although property has been bought and sold this way for centuries, making an offer today is usually a bit more complex. In some states it's common to use a "contract to purchase" form, while in others brokers have preprinted "offer for purchase" forms. The offer to purchase is usually a much simpler document than a contract to purchase. Why? Because the contract to purchase must get much more specific about the property description, fixtures, exclusions, and all the necessary legal language for property transfer, rights to sue for specific performance or damages (if the buyer or seller backs out of the contract on a whim), brokers' fees, and so forth. Every city and state will have its own real estate or Realtor (member of the National Association of Realtors) association that provides standard form contracts for the purchase and sale of real estate. (See Appendix II, Contracts and Forms, for a copy of a purchase and sale agreement.)

Although the underlying concepts of the contracts may be similar across the country, real estate law varies from state to state. Some of these contracts are written from the seller's perspective, but you should still have your real estate attorney or broker go over the contract with you and explain it to you. Do not sign any document you do not fully understand.

If you're a FSBO, the buyer's broker (or the buyer, if the buyer is acting alone) will present you with the offer for purchase. If you have your home listed with a broker, the buyer's broker will often give the contract to your broker, who will present it to you. The best presentations usually happen when the buyer's agent makes the presentation directly to you and your broker. That way, the buyer's agent can plead his or her buyer's case directly to you. (For more information on negotiation strategies, see Question 58.)

Since buyers start the process, they get to fill in the contract the way they want to. *You have the right to change any language or condition in the contract with which you do not agree.* There is no law written that says you have to accept the contract as is. In fact, the buyer most likely expects you to make a counteroffer, which will redefine the terms and conditions of the contract, as well as the price.

As a seller, it is important to remember that real estate is a very local business. Each county or municipality will have its own customs regarding who pays which fee. For example, in Florida, real estate customs can vary greatly between two counties. In some counties the seller pays for the title insurance. In others it's the buyer's responsibility. Before you use a real estate form from one county in another, check with your broker or real estate attorney to make sure you're not going to pay costs that would normally be borne by the buyer.

Since buyers usually provide at least the initial outline of the contract, you don't have to be as worried about what each line says. Your job will not be to construct the contract but to react to it. The next few questions look at some of the common terms and contingencies of today's purchase and sale agreements.

QUESTION 48
What terms should be included in the offer to purchase?

The contract spells out the agreement between you and the buyer. The terms of that agreement should cover all areas of potential dispute, including date of closing; the earnest money; the fixtures, personal property, and improvements that are being sold with the property; date of possession; prorations of taxes and utility bills; who pays for which fees and costs; the contingencies; the purchase price; and the date the offer expires. Condo and co-op contracts have a few extra issues.

Let's take a closer look:

- *Date of Closing.* This is the day that the buyer would like to take title and (normally) possession of your home. Date of closing can be, to a greater or lesser degree, a point of negotiation. There are plenty of sellers who would rather have an extra month in their home than an extra $1,000 in their pocket.
- *The Earnest Money.* This is the amount of cash the buyer is willing to put up to show that he or she is seriously interested in buying your house. The buyer should be willing to put down a significant chunk of cash, the size of which depends in large part on the custom in your area. You want the buyer to put down the largest amount possible. At the very least, you want the buyer to put down an amount high enough to compensate you for lost marketing time should the buyer walk away from the deal.
- *Fixtures, Personal Property, and Improvements.* A fixture is an item of personal property (usually a light fixture or a kitchen appliance) that has been attached to the home. Once attached, a fixture is considered to be a part of the home rather than personal property. What are some examples of fixtures? Light fixtures, plumbing, sinks, toilets, doors, door hardware, built-in bookshelves, central air-conditioning systems, the 1850s

mailbox you attached to your front door, and the wood-burning stove that you attached to the wall. The buyer will try to include each of these items in the purchase price. Make sure your broker knows ahead of time which fixtures go with the house and which fixtures you plan to take with you. (Personal property items are those items that can be removed from a house without any damage to it, like the refrigerator, your piano, and a countertop microwave.)

- *Date of Possession.* This is the day that control of the property is turned over to the buyers, the day they receive the keys and can move in. It usually takes place at the closing, where the deed is exchanged for cash, but it can take place before or after the closing, depending on whether you're willing to allow the buyers to move in before closing or whether they allow you to stay there after. If possession is going to take place after the closing, this section of the contract should stipulate the per-day fee you will have to pay for living in the home after the closing. (For more information on possession, see Questions 90 and 91.)
- *Prorations of Housing Costs.* In most states, real estate taxes are paid annually or in several installments. Utility bills are paid monthly or bimonthly. You or your attorney will determine the per-day cost of real estate taxes and utility bills and then prorate them over the time you've been in the house before closing and the time the buyer will be in the house after closing during that billing cycle. That way, both you and the buyer pay your fair share. (For more information on prorations, see Question 86.)

- *Fees and Costs.* The contract spells out which fees the buyer and seller will be responsible for, including title insurance, recording fees, transfer taxes and fees, and even the brokerage commission.
- *Contingencies.* The three most common contingencies for buyers are for a home inspection, to obtain financing, and to have an attorney review the contract. The buyer's lender may require a pest inspection, depending on where you live in the country and the type of loan being obtained. In addition, some buyers ask for additional toxic inspections for lead, radon, and contaminated soil. (For more information on contingencies and how you should respond to them, see Question 49.)
- *The Purchase Price.* Initially, the buyer puts his desired purchase price on the contract (if it is your local custom to use a contract to purchase to make the offer), and then you negotiate the price. Once you have agreed upon the price, it is inserted into the contract and initialed by all parties. Since the purchase price is one of the most important parts of the contract, it is usually located near the top of the document.
- *The Date the Contract or Offer Expires.* A married couple put a bid on a home in Los Angeles. Days went by without their hearing anything from the seller or their broker. They finally called their broker, who said, "These things take time." After a week, they finally contacted an attorney who had them withdraw the contract. Because they had never put an expiration date for the offer on the contract, the seller was under no pressure to accept or counter the offer or decline the bid quickly. Instead, he had a week to shop the

offer around. Savvy buyers will put an expiration date on the offer. You will need to be conscious of that date when structuring your counteroffer.

- *Condo Contract.* The difference between selling a condominium and selling a single-family home is slight; when you sell a condo, you are selling the airspace inside your four walls, ceiling, and floor, plus an interest in the common areas of the homeowners' association. Be aware that those homeowners' associations have special rules, such as the right of first refusal when a condo unit is sold. This allows the board to purchase the unit if it decides it is in the best interest of the condo building. In a sales contract, you will have to agree to procure the release or waiver of any option or right of first refusal and to comply with other condo rules and regulations—and even with state law requests.
- *Co-op Contract.* When you are selling a co-op, you are really selling personal property in the form of shares in the corporation that owns the building. You have been a tenant in your apartment, and your monthly maintenance assessments are considered to be rent. Not only do co-op boards have the right of first refusal (similar to a condo building), but they must usually vote a prospective buyer into the building. Co-op buyers must submit detailed financial and personal records, which are then discussed in a board meeting. After the board meets personally with your buyers, they will take a vote. You will need to provide your buyers with a list of all the documentation that they must fill out in order to make an application to the board. And the contract will need to list the informa-

tion required by the co-op board to process the buyers' application.

QUESTION 49

What are the most common contract contingencies?

A contingency allows the buyer to back out of the contract for a specific reason. There are typically three contingencies that accompany a contract or an offer to purchase: financing or mortgage, inspection, and attorney approval.

Mortgage or Financing Contingency

If the buyers ask for a mortgage contingency, it means they can back out of the contract if they cannot find a lender to give them a mortgage commitment at an agreed-upon rate by a certain date. The contingency requires the buyers to specifically state the type of mortgage and interest rate they are seeking and requires them to get mortgage approval within a limited amount of time, generally thirty to sixty days. If they can't get the mortgage, the buyers have the right to withdraw from the contract.

As a seller, you want to make sure the amount of time the buyers have to find a mortgage is limited. In some states, the contract will allow you the right to continue to show your property until the contingencies have been met. However, this isn't commonly done. If you're fairly certain that the buyer will be able to get a mortgage, you may want to stop showing your home. Of course, if the buyer can't get a mortgage, you'll have effectively taken your property out of circulation for that time period.

Inspection Contingency

This contingency gives the buyers the right to have a professional house inspector or third party examine the property within a certain period of time after the agreement to purchase has been signed. Again, the purpose of the contingency is to protect the buyer from purchasing a home that may have serious hidden structural problems or material defects. It does nothing for you, the seller, except create more anxiety ("Will my house pass inspection?"). In addition to the regular inspection contingency, the buyer may ask for the following different inspections:

- Radon.
- Asbestos.
- Lead.
- Toxic substances.
- Water.
- Structural engineer. (Increasingly common in places like southern California. The buyer may want to have a structural engineer inspect the home if he or she is uneasy about its structural integrity.)
- Soil sample for leaking underground storage facility.
- Pests, including termites, mice, rats, roaches, carpenter ants, and so forth.

Attorney Approval Rider

The buyers will want the right to have the contract approved by their attorney, who will negotiate the fine points of the contract with your attorney. It's a good idea for both you and the buyer to be advised of the legal consequences of signing the offer for purchase contracts. In some states, like California and Indiana, attornies are not commonly used for residential purchases and the broker does this job. In many other states, buyers and sellers hire real estate attorneys to help them close the purchase and sale of the home. The attorney approval rider essentially gives the buyer's attorney the right to make changes to the contract.

As a seller, you also want the right to have your attorney approve the contract. Make sure that the number of days for the attorneys to approve the contract is limited to five or ten. Under special circumstances, you might want to stretch that to two weeks. In some states, the offer for purchase is worded as follows: "This offer to purchase is subject to a contract that is agreeable to both parties." Therefore, the buyer's attorney and your attorney can agree on the form of the contract. As always, before signing a contract, be sure you completely understand it, or consult with your real estate attorney.

Other Contingencies

There are many other contingencies that might appear in a contract for purchase, including:

- Sale of the buyer's prior residence.
- Admittance to certain clubs (for example, if you live in a home near a private golf course, the buyer might try to make the purchase contingent on acceptance by the club).
- Approval by the condo or co-op board.

- Pest inspection, asbestos, radon, lead, water, electromagnetic lines (may be separate contingencies or lumped together under the inspection contingency).
- Compliance with local building code.
- Obtaining parking.
- Municipal building department approval of buyer's intended renovation of your home.
- Buyer's pet must be in compliance with homeowner association rules and regulations.
- Buyer's landing a specific job.

If you let them, the buyers will add contingency after contingency to the contract. After all, contingencies are there to protect buyers. They don't do a darn thing for sellers, except give you a reason you may have to remarket your home. As a seller, you want to see as "clean" an offer as possible; that is, one without any contingencies. The best contract is a cash offer (without the financing contingency) with no contingencies. Just because a contract comes in loaded with contingencies doesn't mean you have to accept it. If you're in a slow seller's market, you might have to. But if you're in a balanced or hot seller's market, you may not have to acquiesce. If you accept one or more of the contingencies, you may choose to continue marketing your property. If you choose to do that, be sure to include a *kick-out clause* in the contract. A kick-out clause gives you the opportunity to market your home while the buyers try to work through the contingencies. Should you receive a subsequent offer, you can give the original buyers a chance to kick out any contingencies in their contract and proceed without contingencies. (For more information on kick-out clauses, see Question 60).

QUESTION 50

What is earnest money? How much should the buyer put down? And who holds it?

The earnest money is an amount of cash the buyer puts up to show that he or she is serious about purchasing your property. The money represents the buyer's commitment to buy your home. After receiving an earnest money check, many sellers will stop showing their property and wait to see if the buyer can get a mortgage. Earnest money is important to the transaction because it shows the seller that the buyer is operating in good faith (hence the word "earnest"). The bigger the deposit, the more reassuring it is to the seller, who thinks "This buyer is serious." It also ties the buyer to the property and makes him or her think twice before looking at additional properties.

On the offer to purchase, the earnest money is also called a deposit. Usually the buyer offers from $1,000 to as much as 10 percent of the sales price of the house in cash as the earnest money. The amount should be large enough to make any buyer think twice about walking away from the house on a whim. The reason is, that cash may be forfeited to you, the seller, if the buyer breaks the contract and walks away from the deal. If, on the other hand, the buyer is unable to get financing and exercises his rights under a financing contingency clause, the earnest money is refunded to the buyer. If the buyer simply decides he doesn't like your home after all, you may have the legal right to keep the earnest money and begin marketing your property again. Your right to retain the buyer's deposit will vary from state to state and will depend on the language in the contract.

Sometimes a buyer will attach a $1,000 check to the offer to purchase to show initial good faith. The rest of the deposit, or earnest money, is due when the contract is signed by both parties, or shortly thereafter. Sometimes, especially if the house is expensive, the earnest money is paid in stages as certain conditions of the contract are met. For example, a portion of the earnest money might be due on signing, with another portion due after the inspection, and the final portion due when the buyer has obtained the mortgage.

Who holds the earnest money? The money typically goes into an escrow account held by the seller's broker, but this is largely a matter of local custom, or it can be negotiated. The buyer usually receives the interest on his or her money; however, if the deposit is forfeited to the seller, in many instances the interest is also turned over to the seller.

If the sale goes through, the earnest money is used as part of the cash down payment and is paid to the seller. If the sale does not go through for some reason covered by a contingency in the contract, the earnest money (and any interest) will be refunded to the buyer. The earnest money should also be refunded to the buyer if the sale does not go through because of a problem on the seller's side. If, however, the buyer is at fault, return of the earnest money may be in jeopardy; the contract and laws of your state would determine how the earnest money gets paid out. If your broker is holding the earnest money in an escrow account, he or she cannot release that money without first getting permission from you. If you unreasonably refuse to sign the release of escrow, the broker holding the funds may turn them over to the real estate commission for mediation or to local courts for litigation. Your broker or attorney can explain your state law and local customs regarding this matter.

Successful Home Seller Tip: Sometimes buyers and sellers will mistakenly refer to the earnest money as the down payment. That's understandable, since in a successful sale the earnest money *will* ultimately be converted into the down payment. But it is incorrect. The earnest money doesn't technically turn into the down payment until the closing, when the buyers' funds are exchanged for the deed to your home.

QUESTION 51
How do I know if the offer I've received is a good and fair offer for purchase?

Sellers want a contract that says the buyer will buy their property at a certain date for all cash. Buyers want lots of protection that the house they are going to purchase is in the best shape possible for the lowest price possible.

Walking the line between a clean and fair offer for purchase and a contract that ladles on the juice for either the buyer or the seller is a difficult matter. Sellers are often afraid to assert themselves because they worry the buyer will walk away. Buyers are nervous that sellers will be unreasonable and will reject the contract outright rather than give negotiation a chance.

Attorneys say the most fair contracts are ones in which both the buyer and the seller get some of what they want. The seller may get his or her price but have to compromise on the closing date. Or the buyer might get a lower price, but that price might not include some extras he or she had hoped for.

How do you know if you've received a good offer? Analyze the contract and see if it meets the goals and objectives you set out for yourself when you started the selling process:

- *Am I getting my price?* Wise sellers set a minimum price that they will accept for their home. You don't have to verbalize that minimum price, but keep it there, inside your head. When an offer comes in, ask yourself if you can live with the price, and remember that the initial price offered isn't necessarily the final price.
- *Can I live with the terms and conditions?* If the contract comes in with a contingency that the buyers have to sell their home before they can purchase yours, that offer may be meaningless if the buyers are unrealistic about the selling price of their own home. If you can, try to negotiate out as many terms and conditions as possible. As long as your contract has contingencies, you should negotiate the right to continue showing it and attempt to get a better deal on the open market.
- *Will the closing date work with my moving timetable?* If you want to be in your new home before the school semester starts, make sure that the closing date matches up with your schedule.

A clean and fair offer for purchase is one that makes relatively few demands and asks for only the three most common contingencies: inspection, mortgage, and attorney approval. The earnest money is up to 10 percent of the purchase price (depending on local customs), and a sizable chunk of it will be attached to the contract in the form of a check. The buyer doesn't ask for everything and the moon, too. The contract seems to be, you think, reasonable.

That's a good offer. A bad offer is one where you feel abused or taken advantage of. Where the buyer squeezes you for every last cent and is unwilling to give an inch. A transaction where the contract is lopsided is an unreasonable, unfair contract. Unless you are desperate to sell, you shouldn't consider offers that are so grossly unfair.

QUESTION 52

What is a take-it-or-leave-it offer?

Mike and Maureen spent nearly a year searching for a house. They looked at all kinds of properties, in all kinds of shapes and sizes. They finally found a house they liked, but the seller seemed inflexible on his listing price. "The seller had moved into the house only eighteen months before," says Mike. "And he had put a little bit of work into the house. He felt his house was worth what he paid, plus the work he had put in, plus a 20 percent profit on top of all the rest. He had priced himself right out of the neighborhood, which in eighteen months had barely held stable in value. We were willing to give him what he paid for the house plus the improvements, plus an additional 6 percent, which would have covered the broker's commission. But no more."

Since Mike and Maureen really liked this house, they decided to put in an offer based on the prices other comparable homes had sold for in the neighborhood. They also bid as much as they could afford to pay on any home. In fact, they sculpted what brokers call a *take-it-or-leave-it* offer.

A take-it-or-leave-it offer totally eliminates negotiation from the process of buying and selling a home. Buyers essentially say, "I'll pay this much money for your home and no more—so don't even ask." Sellers, who are conditioned into thinking that the buyer's first offer is not his or her last offer, often find themselves feeling hostile toward a take-it-or-leave-it offer. Invariably, take-it-or-leave-it offers are low offers; often, they're all the buyer can afford.

This leaves both the buyer and the seller in unfortunate positions. The seller, happy to have received an offer, is unhappy at the low price and the elimination of negotiation. The buyer, taking a stab at a house that is unaffordable, knows there is very little chance of actually purchasing this home.

Sometimes, buyers make take-it-or-leave-it offers to try to get a property for less than its market value. If buyers sense that you, the seller, are desperate, or if they know your home has been on the market for a long time, they may try to give you a one-shot offer that is a bit lower than the price you were hoping to get. These buyers can afford to pay more, but they don't want to.

What should you do if you're presented with a take-it-or-leave-it offer? If you believe the price is reasonable and the other terms and conditions of the contract—including contingencies and the closing date—are acceptable, you may want to consider accepting the offer.

If the price is unacceptable and the conditions are unacceptable, you should call the buyers or their broker and tell them you don't think the contract will work out. If they ask you why, tell them you like them very much as buyers but you simply feel your home is worth more money than they have offered. If they are truly take-it-or-leave-it buyers, they will thank you for your time and vanish from your life.

But there is another possibility. Sometimes buyers test the waters. Savvy buyers have learned that they can always go up in price but never go down. Sometimes they start with a low price, wait to see the seller's reaction, and then move up from there. What I'm suggesting is this: A take-it-or-leave-it offer might not be the end of the discussion. Don't be surprised if you reject the take-it-or-leave-it offer and a day or a week or a month later the buyer comes back with a higher offer. This new offer may be structured as another one-shot offer, but it may also be a standard contract. Either way, you should respond as if it were a standard offer and counter the offer.

Successful Home Seller Tip: Although the price on a take-it-or-leave-it offer is generally not negotiable, the terms and conditions may be. The buyer may be willing to close earlier or later, and may be willing to remove certain contingencies. If you're working with a broker, ask him or her what may be negotiable and what may work to your advantage.

Successful Home Seller Tip: Should you ever meet the buyers? That's the perennial question facing all sellers. If you're selling on your own you'll have to meet the buyers at some point, since you'll be showing your own home. If you're working with a broker, it's possible to avoid the buyers completely—you can even avoid meeting them at the closing by not going. But is this the wise move? Perhaps not. If you're working on the contract, a little face-to-face contact may help the situation. If you and your broker (if you have one) decide to invite the buyers and their broker over one evening to smooth out the details, you should serve something to eat and drink, perhaps cake and coffee. The focus should be on getting the deal done and moving the contract forward. Any goodwill you can generate should be helpful to the process. But remember, be careful about what you say and what you agree to. You might write down the buyer's point on a particular issue and say, "That sounds like it should be possible. I'll check with my attorney and get back to you on that point." The only time you should avoid the buyers is if either you or they are too emotional about the process and the contract. If there is hostility and tension between you, there's no reason to meet face-to-face. Instead, temper the hostility by using as many third-party people (attorneys and brokers) as possible.

QUESTION 53

What is the "first offer is best" theory?

Betsy and Bill owned a three-family residence in a suburb of Boston. It was rather run-down when they bought it, but they only paid around $150,000 for it. Over the years they slowly rehabbed the property, living in one unit while pouring in plenty of money and "sweat equity" to fix up the other two.

After eight years, the neighborhood had improved dramatically. So they listed the building for sale with one of the top brokers in the area and priced it at $325,000. About a week later, they received an offer to purchase the property for $285,000. Although Betsy and Bill were "completely insulted," as they put it, their broker convinced them to respond to the offer. The buyer ultimately offered them $299,000, which Betsy and Bill refused.

"At that time," says Betsy, "we felt the building was worth a minimum of $300,000. We would either get that or stay where we were. And we eventually paid for that make-it-or-break-it attitude." The building sat on the market for another year. That meant another year of paying real estate property taxes, and another year of mortgage payments, and another year of not moving on to the next project. By that time, Betsy and Bill were so desperate to sell that they lowered their asking price to $299,000 and ultimately sold the property for $275,000.

There seems to be an unwritten rule in selling real estate: Your first offer is usually your best offer. For example, if Betsy and Bill had accepted their first offer of $299,000, they would have ended up $24,000 ahead of the offer they finally accepted. And that $24,000 would have paid for their broker's commission and meant additional profit as well.

But many sellers have trouble accepting their first offer, especially if it comes within a few days or weeks after the property is listed. If the offer comes too quickly, some sellers might think they have undervalued their property and may want to hold out for an offer that is closer to the asking price.

Brokers, on the other hand, like to see quick offers. "The first three weeks after a property is listed is when it's the freshest. Brokers who are unfamiliar with the property will come by to see it and decide for themselves if they think it's worth the money or not," says Linda, a top broker in California.

A quick offer means someone has responded positively to the home on several levels, brokers say. A quick offer means the buyers believe the home is priced, if not correctly, at least within reasonable negotiation range. They believe the home is sound, in good working condition, and meets their expectations for size and space and location based on the price.

But accepting the first offer—particularly if it comes quickly—can mean a psychological readjustment for the seller. Every seller hopes that dozens of prospective buyers will jump at the chance to purchase his or her home. When the first offer comes, however, you should readjust your thinking and concentrate on making the first offer the "right" offer.

While brokers would like every first offer to be the right offer, things don't always work out that way. Beverly and Bennett were offered $250,500 for their vacation property in Lake Tahoe, Nevada. Although the dollar amount was good, the offer wasn't "clean," meaning the buyers added what Beverly and Bennett felt were onerous restrictions to the contract. For example, the buyers didn't want to put any money down and wanted to make the purchase contingent on the sale of their own vacation property.

After consulting with their broker and their attorney, Beverly and Bennett declined the offer. Several months passed, and only a few people came through for showings. Beverly and Bennett started to think they had passed on the only offer they were going to receive. Then, out of the blue, another offer came in. Although the dollar amount was only $500 less than the first offer, the contract was clean and solid.

How can you know if the first offer is the best offer? Sometimes it's a matter of trusting your instincts. If you've priced your property well and an offer comes in that's between 6 and 15 percent below your asking price, find a way to negotiate to a comfortable middle. Decide whether the offer is clean and straightforward or if it's laden with cumbersome contingencies. Decide whether or not the buyer is qualified (if he or she is willing to put down 20 percent toward the purchase price and finance no more than 80 percent, that's an excellent sign that the buyer is financially qualified. An even better sign is a letter from a lender showing the buyer has been pre-approved for his or her loan.). Decide whether or not you can live with the price, or if you'll be wishing you'd waited to see if any other buyers would bite.

Sometimes there is no way to know. Six months after listing his home for sale, a seller in Indiana received a solid offer. He accepted—and felt good about the offer until two days before the closing. Out of the blue, he received another offer for $3,000 more. Although he would have preferred to take the higher-priced offer, the buyers threatened to sue him if he backed out of their deal. So he sadly kissed that $3,000 good-bye and closed on his home.

QUESTION 54
What is seller greed? And how do I recognize it in myself?

When Sue and Bob bought their Kansas City, Missouri, house ten years ago, it was in shambles. Over the years, they put a lot of money and hard work into fixing it up and making it beautiful. When the time came to sell, they were assured of making a profit even though they were in a buyer's market and there were plenty of nice homes available. But suddenly a strange fixation overcame them. Sue calls it "the greed factor."

"Suddenly, all the time and money we spent welled up inside of us and we just wanted to make the buyer pay for it," she explains. "We just couldn't control ourselves."

But they should have. They listed the home for $300,000. Within a few days, a buyer offered $275,000. Sue and Bob refused to counter the offer. The buyer went away and the house sat on the market for another six months. Finally, after lowering the price to $275,000, they sold the house for $267,000.

Seller greed usually kicks in after the buyer has offered a number above the lowest expectations of the seller. Even though the seller had decided in advance to accept anything above a certain number, once an offer comes in higher, the seller suddenly isn't satisfied with his or her lowest expectations—he or she wants more. Unfortunately, seller greed is a common problem all over the country, and it is a byproduct of the central conflict in residential real estate: The seller wants to receive the most money possible for his or her property and the buyer wants to pay as little as possible. But when sellers get greedy, it can put the kibosh on a deal that would have otherwise been profitable.

Barb, a managing broker in Granger, Indiana, has had her share of sellers who feel compelled—even if they're going to make a huge profit on the sale of their home—to hold out for that last dollar.

"I had a situation where the sellers were going to make a lot of money anyway but wouldn't budge from a certain number. When you added in the bonus they were getting from the relocation company, it turned into greed," Barb recalls.

Barb's sellers decided to hang tough, since the relocation company had to buy them out anyway. "I told them the longer the house is on the market, the more shopworn it gets. Realistically, I said, they might end up reducing it to the price the buyer was offering." In the end, the sellers came to their senses. The house, which was listed at $249,000, sold for $243,000, which was an excellent price.

Barb says she tries to help her sellers avoid the greed trap by lowering their expectations about what kind of money they'll actually get for their home. When she takes a listing, Barb and her sellers decide on a price range for a home. She tells them what will be a good listing price, but also reiterates that the number she gives them is merely a starting point. She also helps them subtract the costs of the sale, including the brokerage commission, any transfer taxes, and closing fees. "I tell them not to expect to get it. Then I take a percentage below what I reasonably expect the house to sell for, and I tell them that's probably the bottom," she explains.

Barb says setting up realistic expectations is one way sellers can be better prepared for the ultimate price they'll pocket for their home. "It's rare that a home will sell for less than the low number we set at the beginning of the sales process, so they're less apt to be disappointed," Barb says.

Barb says that through her many years in the business she's learned to lower her sellers' usually lofty expectations. That means her sellers are less likely to overprice their homes, which means Barb doesn't have to go back to them as often to have the prices reduced.

But brokers point out that sellers don't have a monopoly on greed. Because buyers controlled many sectors of the market in the early 1990s, many still believe they can dictate the prices they will pay for homes. Also, some buyers walk through homes and see things that are not included in the sales price. Trying to have those items included and wringing every last cent out of the seller are classic symptoms of buyer greed, Barb says.

In one case, the buyers and sellers were $1,500 apart on a $200,000 home. The sellers offered to split the deal in the middle and put up another $750, plus they agreed to throw in the refrigerator. But the buyers said no and walked.

Ultimately, the problem with seller or buyer greed is that it gets in the way of making the deal happen. Greed is ugly and unproductive. It leaves people on both sides of the transaction feeling as if they've been taken for a ride. Brokers know when their sellers or buyers are being greedy—an attitude they will often call "piggy." The best brokers will gently chide their clients and remind them that money isn't everything in a deal. There's a lot to be said for accommodation and goodwill. That's because selling a home isn't just a financial transaction. It's also an emotional one.

How do you know if you're being greedy? Ask yourself if you're being reasonable. If you get an offer within 8 to 10 percent of your list price, it's not unreasonable for you to counter that offer. According to the National Association of Realtors, homes typically sell for 94 percent of their list price. That's only 6 percent less than the seller is asking. So if you've listed your home for $100,000 and get an offer for $90,000, you may not want to accept that number, but it would be considered a reasonable first offer by many industry observers. With an initial offer of $90,000, you could reasonably expect to end up the negotiations around $95,000, which would be only 5 percent less than our fictitious list price. Even if you want to get $97,000 for your home, you've got to respond to offers in order to let the buyer know where you stand. (For more information on counteroffers, see Question 57.)

Seller greed is an emotional response to a financial transaction. If you're selling your home because you and your spouse are divorcing, or your spouse has died or has lost his or her job, it may be extremely important to you to get every dollar you can out of your home. On the other hand, the longer you stay in that home, the more money you'll spend to maintain it and pay off your mortgage. Add those costs to the emotional toll of staying in a home you wish had already sold and you're paying a high price for those few extra dollars you're not sure will ever materialize.

The best antidote for seller greed is to accept the fact that your home isn't worth quite what you'd hoped it would be and move on. Wishing it were different isn't going to change the market forces that drive the residential real estate market.

QUESTION 55
What does "shopping the offer" mean?

Sometimes brokers let it be known in the brokerage community that an offer has either come in for the property or will be coming in for a property. Part of the reason brokers do this is to generate some pressure on buyers who may be dillydallying. And sometimes they do it to create a frenzied atmosphere that might result in a bidding war or multiple offers (see Question 59 for more information on bidding wars and multiple offers).

When brokers let it be known that they have an offer in hand, and either tell or hint strongly at the price on the contract, it is commonly called "shopping the offer." Basically brokers want other brokers to know specifically how much the buyer is bidding for the property to see if their clients are willing to pay more for the property.

" 'Shopping the offer' is an unattractive term and the use of that term is guaranteed to make buyers and buyer brokers climb the walls," says David, a managing broker in Chicago. "On the other hand, it is perfectly appropriate for the listing broker to let other interested parties know that an offer is coming in, or has come in, but not to divulge the confidential details of the contract."

In other words, the seller has a right to expect that his or her broker will contact those individuals who had demonstrated an interest in the property. In this instance, "interest" would mean a second showing, or a buyer broker who had specifically asked to be kept informed of the status of the property.

Divulging the details of the contract is unethical, David says, because that may not be in the seller's best interest. There are two ways to look at it. Your broker receives an offer for your home and proceeds to shop the offer by telling other brokers how much the contract is for. If your home is listed at $200,000 and the offer comes in at $150,000, your broker is hoping that other buyers will think, "Hey, the bid isn't too high. I've got a chance at buying that home." On the other hand, the other buyer might say, "Hey, that bid is a lot lower than I was going to bid for that property. Maybe the property isn't worth it and I should lower my offer." Buyers like reassurance, and in most cases they are looking for any reason *not* to buy your home.

" 'Shopping the offer' is an emotional term," David says. "The original buyer doesn't want a competing bid. But if there is another buyer or even two buyers who have continued to express interest in the home, they deserve the opportunity to make an offer. I've made that call many times in my career. Seller brokers should make it. But they should not call everyone in town prospecting for new buyers. That's not fair."

If you're selling on your own and find yourself in the fortunate situation of having two offers, you need to play fair with both buyers. If this delicate situation is not handled correctly, both buyers may walk and you'll be left with nothing. David suggests that FSBO sellers or seller brokers contact the other interested parties as soon as they know they are getting in a bid. If you or your broker calls before you actually see the offer, then you won't be able to divulge any private and confidential information.

While "shopping the offer" isn't the nicest term in real estate, it can get results. The best situation for sellers to be in is a multiple offer or bidding war situation. These concepts will be discussed in Question 59.

NEGOTIATING THE OFFER

QUESTION 56
How does the negotiation process work?

Negotiation, no matter what is being negotiated, is about give and take. The person who holds the stronger hand usually gets to give less and take more, but in a successful negotiation both sides end up compromising. In a house sale, that's really what you want. You don't want the buyer to take you for a ride, nor do you want to ride the buyer. Emotions run high anyway in something as personal as selling a home, and when negotiations get tough emotions become embittered—and the contract becomes the battle zone.

Unlike a judge's settlement, where both sides may end up profoundly unhappy with the result, a successful house negotiation can leave everyone feeling like winners. And that's the goal: You want the buyers to feel they have paid a fair price for your home. You want them to bask in the glow of having made a good deal. You want them to be excited about moving in and taking over the maintenance of your home. After all, this is a place in which you have set down roots and that you have taken care of and loved. You want to be nice to the buyers, allow them to come through with their friends and family, and extend that niceness through the closing, so that they do not make you crazy by asking for last-minute cash credits for the broken basement windowpane they somehow overlooked during other visits to your home. There is nothing worse than fighting with your buyers over items they wanted included in the contract that you always said you were taking with you. Or fighting with them over the contract. The nastiness can leave a bad taste in your mouth that may extend well beyond the closing.

So how do you negotiate fairly? How do you end up with good feelings on all sides of the table? First, enlist your broker's (or attorney's, if you choose not to work with a broker) help in keeping everyone's emotions at bay. Brokers are good at this. It's probably one of the most important parts of their job. They must present the buyer's offer as something worthwhile, not insulting. They must present it in such a way that you want to respond and make the deal happen.

In a negotiation, the buyer takes the first step by preparing the offer for purchase. Once that contract is written up, the buyer, or the buyer's broker, will make a presentation to either you and your broker or to your broker. Oftentimes, that presentation will take place over the telephone, with the buyer's broker relaying the important information to your broker. Depending on your local customs, once the buyer's broker presents the contract to your broker, your broker will either come over to your house, ask you to come over to the office, or call you on the telephone. The broker may even fax you a copy of the contract and then go over it with you line by line.

If you've already moved out of town or out of state, the broker will either make the presentation by telephone or fax you a copy of the contract. But many brokers prefer to do this important part of their job in person, especially if it's a low-priced contract, with difficult terms and conditions. Real estate is a personal business; it's the emotional connections you make to the broker and the buyer that keep the process of selling your home from feeling a bit like you've sold your soul. Once the buyer's broker leaves (if she has made the offer to you directly), you and your broker will discuss the offer. Unless it is a full-price offer that includes all of your terms and conditions, or you are extremely nervous and desperate, you will not usually accept this first offer. A first offer is, by definition, a first offer. There will usually be a second offer, and perhaps even a third and a fourth offer. Selling real estate is a little like buying a new car: Except in extreme circumstances the list price is somewhat higher than a savvy buyer will end up paying. Everyone understands that the buyer's first offer is a little bit (or quite a lot) below what he or she expects to pay for the property. The key to a successful negotiation is to remember it is a psychological game.

Here's how it works: Let's say your home is priced at $100,000. The buyer offers $90,000, which is 10 percent less than your asking price. You wouldn't be out of line to assume at this point that the buyer might be willing to compromise somewhere in the middle, say $94,000 to $96,000. Once you've made this assumption, you need to make a calculated guess: Is the buyer willing to go up to $96,000? Or will he or she stop at $94,000? Or will you meet in the middle at $95,000?

(One thing you need to remember is this: While real estate is often compared to a game, there are no hard-and-fast rules. So in this example, you can assume that if a buyer makes a first offer that is 10 percent less than your asking price he or she would be willing to meet you halfway. But that might not be the case at all. The buyer might be stretching himself or herself to the limit with that offer, and may not be able to go higher than that at all. Or the buyer may be able to afford to go higher but has decided—for whatever reason—not to. Or the buyer might be able to pay your entire list price but is trying to get the home for less.)

Once the initial offer has been made, you're in the driver's seat. The price at which you counter the offer is going to color the negotiations from this point on. You have some choices: You can instruct your broker to present a *split-the-difference* counteroffer or you can inch down, thousand by thousand, hundred by hundred. A split-the-difference counteroffer means you go back to the buyer halfway between his or her offer and your list price. In our $100,000 home scenario, your split-the-difference counteroffer would be at $95,000. The problem with the split-the-difference counteroffer is that some buyers might think if you're willing to drop down that much immediately, there's even more room to drop the price.

But let's say you think the buyer is willing to do more than split the difference. Your other option is to counter his or her offer by dropping down $1,000 or $2,000. Then the buyer will counter your counteroffer by coming up $1,000 or $2,000. Frequently, each side matches the other side's counter, which is how most deals end up in the middle.

Making the last offer is like saying "I call" in a card game. If you come down $2,500 and say that $97,500 is your final offer, take it or leave it, the buyer will have to decide if he or she wants your home at that price. Another option is the take-it-or-leave-it offer, where the buyer comes in with a flat, no-negotiation $95,000 contract. Any number of issues can turn the negotiations into a power struggle, which can get nasty. Better to keep things on a more even, if not downright friendly, pace so as to keep the negotiations moving ahead step by step. Even a take-it-or-leave-it offer can be friendly if it's communicated in the right way.

Remember, money isn't always the most important part of the transaction. If you have special timing requirements, and would like either to move immediately or to stretch out the closing for five or six months, a buyer who can accommodate that schedule may be more valuable to you than a buyer who will pay you an additional $1,000 on the contract. And selling your home to someone who will love it as much as you do can be emotionally gratifying.

Price Ceiling, Price Floor

One of the most important things you should do as a seller is decide in advance what is the least amount of money you're willing to accept for your house. It may be easier to visualize this number if you think about it as the price floor—you won't allow the price of the house to drop below the floor. Your list price, to continue the metaphor, is like the price ceiling—you may only go through the roof if you're lucky enough to have several hot prospects bidding for your property at the same time.

Knowing your bottom line—the price floor—is extremely important during the negotiations for your home. If you know what is the least amount of money you'll accept for your home, deciding whether or not to respond to an offer becomes much easier. If the initial offer is just at, or above, your price floor, then you should feel fairly comfortable that you can reach a middle ground with this buyer. For example, if your home is listed at $100,000 (the price ceiling) and the bottom number you're willing to accept is $95,500 (the price floor), if the initial offer comes in at $93,000 it's likely that you can come to a meeting of the minds. On the other hand, if your price floor is $95,500 and the buyer's first offer is $87,200 and the second offer is $89,000, you may be facing a situation where the buyer won't come close enough to your price floor to make the deal. Then you have to decide whether it's worth going lower to make the deal happen.

While it's important to know your bottom number, don't make it such a firm number that you lose a deal over $500. If your price floor is $95,500 and the final offer from the buyer is $95,000, don't turn it down unless you've got another buyer's contract for $95,500 in your pocket. That $500 may not break you, and you may be able to extract other concessions from the buyer (like selling your lawn equipment, or moving the closing to a date that suits you) to make up the shortfall. Above all, if you turn down a deal for $500 and your home sits on the market for another three months, you'll feel a little foolish—and you may not get any more for your home at that time.

How do you determine the price floor for your property? Only you can decide that—hopefully after you've given thoughtful consideration to the market conditions and the prices similar properties are fetching in your neighborhood.

The Lowball Bid

When Sam and I were making an offer for our 1880s farmhouse, the list price was quite a bit more than we could afford. Based on the neighborhood comps, it was also quite a bit more than we felt the home was worth. Our initial offer for the property was significantly less than the asking price. Our sellers were lovely people, and while it's hard to tell if they were insulted by our initial offer, they were certainly surprised.

What is the definition of a *lowball bid?* A lowball bid is one that insults the seller. It's hard to attach a cast-iron figure to the phrase, however. Depending on the seller, the price of the property, and the current market conditions, a lowball bid could be 10 percent, 15 percent, 18 percent, or 25 percent below list price. Buyers make lowball bids for two reasons: They love the house but can't afford it, or they think you are desperate and will take a below-market offer, thus insuring future profits.

Once a seller is insulted, it takes an extraordinary broker to get him or her to turn around and counter the offer, no matter how small the counter is. And lowball bids tend to give a decidedly negative cast to the negotiation process. Much of that depends on the presentation of the offer. If the buyer offers $80,000 for your $100,000 home, but offers comps that show similar homes that sold for $75,000 to $85,000, you may be more willing to counter the buyer's offer (perhaps including comps of your own) than if the $80,000 offer comes out of nowhere with no supporting comps and you are of the opinion that homes like yours are selling in the $95,000 range.

Sometimes a buyer makes a lowball offer just to test the waters. It's not a serious—nor is it a well-advised—offer. And there's room to move up. Although I think sellers should always respond to offers, even if you counter by only $1,000, it would be entirely understandable if you ignored a $50,000 offer for your $100,000 property.

QUESTION 57

What is a counteroffer? How quickly should I respond to an offer?

Let's back up a little bit. A counteroffer is what happens after the initial contract or offer is presented. The buyer makes the offer. Then you respond by making a counteroffer. Any response from you or the buyer after the initial offer presentation is, by definition, a counteroffer. When it's your turn to make a counteroffer, you're in the driver's seat. If you respond to a buyer's offer, you signal to the buyer that he or she is a serious candidate to purchase your home.

There is a fine art to making a counteroffer. Everything you put into a counteroffer, including the new, lower price you're willing to accept and the terms and conditions of the contract, signals a move in the psychological chess game. Every action has a reaction. If the buyer offers $90,000 for your home, which is listed at $100,000, you have to think about whether the buyer thinks your home is worth $95,000, or is willing to pay only $94,000, or might be willing to go as high as $97,000. If you come down to $99,000, you are signaling to the buyer that you think your home is worth "this side" of $95,000 and that you might not be willing to go that much lower. Then the buyer has a choice. He or she can match your $1,000 decrease with a $1,000 increase, which puts you on a "split-the-difference" track. Or the buyer can move up several thousand dollars, which signals that he or she might be willing to offer even more.

Of course, you can drive yourself crazy wondering what each little move means. When Sam and I received our first and only offer for our home, it was only 5 percent less than we were asking. In our heads, we had counted on an initial offer of 10 percent below asking price (remember, the typical home sells for 6 percent less than list price), so we felt we were already ahead of the game. But what did that offer mean? Would the buyer accept a "split-the-difference"? Or should we go a little further in his direction? Or was his initial offer his final offer? In the end, we were $15,000 apart. We came down $9,000, which he accepted immediately. Could we have gotten more? Perhaps another thousand or two. But we felt we had gotten a very good price for our home. And the buyer felt he had paid a fair price.

When you make a counteroffer, it is unnecessary to draw up an entirely new contract, although customs vary from state to state and from county to county. At this stage, you can simply tell your broker the new price at which you're countering the buyer's offer, and your broker can pass that information along to the buyer's broker. You can go back and forth like this until a final agreement is reached. Once you've agreed on the price and on terms and conditions, the contract can be either redrawn or simply modified, with both parties initialing the changes.

QUESTION 58

What are some negotiation tips and strategies that may help me get a better price for my home?

Negotiating the sale of your home can be either easy or difficult, like a day at the beach or like going to war. Much of this depends on the type of buyer who makes the offer. If the buyer nitpicks every detail on the contract, demands that excluded items be included in the sale, and plays good cop—bad cop games, then the negotiation is going to be that much more exhausting and complex.

It's important to negotiate from a position of strength. One way to strengthen your position is to know what your own motivations and circumstances are. Go back to Question 2 and ask yourself these questions: How quickly do I want to move? How quickly do I have to move? If you have to move quickly, you're more likely to concede more ground early on in the negotiations. If you're a "wait and see" seller, you have the time to wait out the right offer.

But part of your strength as a negotiator comes from knowing who you're up against. What kind of buyers have made you an offer?

- *The Reasonable Buyer*. These are folks who want to purchase your home at a decent price. They're not trying to stiff you. They're not trying to grind you up and leave you for mulch. They'll start their offer at perhaps 5 to 10 percent below your asking price.
- *The Nitpicker, Nonstop Negotiator*. This is the kind of buyer for whom the negotiations aren't over until after the closing. This buyer will try to wear you down by nitpicking every little detail of the contract and your home. Should the home inspector this type of buyer hires find anything wrong with your home (and the buyer will be hoping he or she does), the nitpicker will harp away, asking for cash concessions for work that "needs" to be performed. If you give in, it's unlikely this type of buyer will do the work. His or her goal is simply to get your home at the lowest price possible, and then some.
- *The Uninformed Overpayer*. Every seller hopes some-

one will come along who doesn't know the neighborhood and hasn't studied the value of the home for sale. This buyer will simply walk into your home and fall in love (not something I recommend for buyers). The buyer will make a feeble attempt to offer something less than you're asking, but is sure to come up. This happened to a friend of mine. A couple came through his home and the wife fell in love with it. Because the seller was home and the downstairs baby monitor was on, the seller heard the wife gushing about the house upstairs. When the offer came in shortly thereafter, the seller barely budged. The buyers capitulated and he got his price.

- *The Good Guy, Bad Guy*. Buyers who come in couples will often adopt the good guy—bad guy posture in order to wear you down. Not to be stereotypical, but it's usually the wife who is the good guy, heaping praise on the property. But before she can make a move, she has to check with her husband, usually the bad guy, who says, "Honey, I love it, but we just can't afford it." As they look in your eyes, they're hoping to see you're hooked emotionally and committed to selling your home to someone who loves it as much as you do. (You are, but you should also be committed to getting your price.)
- *The Overprotected, Escape Hatch Buyer*. This is the buyer who has a contingency for everything. He or she wants total protection in the deal and the right to withdraw completely for any reason. It's not that this type of buyer isn't serious—many of them are. But a good contract protects both sides reasonably. And if a buyer wants the ability to withdraw for reasons other than that the house doesn't pass inspection or he or

she can't get a mortgage, then watch out. Your answer to the escape hatch buyer: Keep showing your home until a clean contract comes in.

Now that you know who your buyer is, it's important to negotiate from a position of strength. Consider following these ten tips and strategies:

1. *Know your rock-bottom price.* It's important to know what is the least amount of money you are willing to accept for your property. This number may change, depending on how quickly you need to sell and where you are in the cycle of home selling (plenty of time, or desperate and anxious). For example, you may list your home at $175,000 and hope to get $170,000. But your rock-bottom price might be $162,500. Establishing a rock-bottom floor will help you differentiate between a bid worth accepting and one that is not worth responding to. However, it's important to remember to be flexible when it counts. You should think twice about letting a deal fall apart for $500.
2. *Find out the buyer's motivations.* Buyers and sellers are motivated by external factors including birth, death, job loss, job promotion, and marriage. Knowing your buyer's motivations can help you gain the edge in competitive negotiations. For example, if your buyer is trying to get into a house in your school district before the semester begins, he or she may be more willing to pay your price than a buyer who isn't changing school districts. Many buyer's brokers will divulge this information if asked for it. Or ask your broker to make some discreet inquiries. Know-

ing the buyer's motivations may help you negotiate around potential soft spots.

3. *Present a seller disclosure form with your listing sheet.* Often, buyers try to renegotiate the price of the home by asking for cash credits at closing to compensate for defects uncovered by their home inspector. One way to combat this is to have your home inspected *before* you list it. Then attach a copy of the home inspector's report or a completed seller disclosure form to each listing sheet you hand out. Make sure your listing sheet states that the sales price of the home reflects the age of the home and its current condition.
4. *Don't talk too much.* Silence can work wonders in a negotiation session. It effectively keeps you from talking too much, and may offer the other parties the opportunity to express their feelings on a particular problem or issue. Use this strategy when you first meet the buyers or their broker. Smile, be pleasant, but don't give away any personal details. Instruct your broker not to divulge why you're moving or when you want to—or have to—be out of your home. When the buyers' broker comes to present the offer to purchase, don't say much, and try not to show your reaction to what has been offered, even if you feel like jumping for joy.
5. *Know the effectiveness of timing.* Once buyers make an offer, they usually get very nervous while waiting for the seller's response. If you rush back with a counteroffer, the buyer might get the impression that you're desperate to sell, a feeling that may cause him or her to return to the table with a different counteroffer than he or she otherwise might. On the flip

side, your broker is going to be anxious for you to make the deal and may pressure you to move the negotiations ahead. If you wait too long, however, the buyer may think you're not seriously considering the offer. Also, excessive delays in countering the offer can give a buyer too much time to dwell on the amount of money he or she has offered for your home. Once an offer has been made, there is tremendous pressure from all sides to get the deal done. You may have to fight that pressure in order to time the negotiation to your own satisfaction, but the results could be well worth it.

6. *Play your cards close to the vest*. Typically, brokers want to know everything about their clients: How much they make, how much they can spend, and how much they want to net out of the sale of their home. Although most brokers are well intentioned, it isn't in your best interest to display your personal financial cards to anyone except your spouse. Although your broker probably won't divulge confidential information, it's always possible something will slip out one way or another (these things do happen). Your broker should be on a need-to-know basis only. Never tell him or her your rock-bottom price. If that information gets out, your rock-bottom price could effectively become your list price. It goes without saying that you should never discuss any personal or confidential information with a buyer broker.
7. *Make sure the buyer knows that other buyers are actively interested in your home*. There's nothing like competition to get a buyer's blood boiling. Even as one

buyer is circling, coming back for the second, third, or fourth time, be sure he or she knows that you are actively showing the home. Enlist your broker's support so that he or she doesn't undermine this strategy by letting it slip that there is no market for the home, showings are infrequent, or that you don't expect any other offers soon.

8. *Show your home until the contract is contingency-free.* The best contract for buyers is one that has a contingency to cover every possible problem. The best contract for sellers is one that is contingency free. Still, most contracts will include the three most common contingencies (financing, home inspection, and attorney's). But if a buyer wants the purchase contingent on the sale of his or her original home or on his or her acceptance to the local golf club, you should consider adding a rider to the contract stating that the home will be marketed until all the buyer's contingencies are satisfied or removed.
9. *Beware the 24-hour walk-through.* These days, buyers will often try to reopen the price negotiations after their final walk-through of your home. They may ask for cash credits for everything from fixing a broken window to cleaning stained carpet. If you have somehow damaged the home since the time the contract was signed, it's your responsibility to bring the home back up to that condition. And being upfront with the buyer can bring a lot of goodwill to the transaction. But if the buyer is simply looking to get a few extra bucks at your expense, you should stand firm. One thing you can do to help this final walk-through go well is to make sure your home is

"broom clean." Thoroughly clean your home after you move out. If you don't have the time or energy, consider hiring someone to do it for you.

10. *Adopt a laissez-faire attitude*. Often, negotiations seem to favor the party who seems to care the least about which way the transaction goes. In a real estate transaction, negotiations can quickly get emotional. The best way to manage a house closing is to divorce yourself from your emotions. Even if this is the only offer you think you'll receive, you must behave as if the fate of the world doesn't hinge on the outcome. Once the buyer senses you're depending on him or her to purchase your home, he or she will have you over the proverbial barrel and may begin to extract concessions in price, timing, and items to be left with the home. Be aware, however, that there is a fine line between using a "don't care" attitude to strengthen your hand and insulting your buyer. Be careful not to cross it, or you may find the buyer backing away from the deal altogether.

There is a reason the English language is filled with clichés—there's a kernel of truth in each of them. Here are a few thoughts to keep in mind when you and the buyer square off: Kill your opponent with kindness; say whatever you like as long as you say it with a smile—or, as my mother likes to put it, "You'll catch more flies with honey than with vinegar." Remember, the strongest negotiator is the one who extracts the toughest concessions while making his opponents feel as if they've gotten the greatest buy of their lifetime. If you apply some of these lessons, they should go a long way toward smoothing out your negotiations.

QUESTION 59

What is a multiple offer? What is a bidding war?

Three buyers wanted to buy one property listed at $250,000. Their brokers sat down at the bidding table holding sealed envelopes.

The first broker presented her bid: $239,500. The second broker presented her bid: $241,000. The third broker looked down at the three sealed envelopes in her bag. One was marked $235,000, the second was marked $242,000, and the third was marked $248,000. She presented the contract for $242,000. Her buyers ultimately bought the property, and she saved them $6,000 by playing the bidding war game.

Sellers typically receive one offer at a time. But some sellers find themselves in the enviable position of receiving several offers simultaneously for their property. When Sam and I were looking for our home, we made an offer on a house that had been on the market for five days. The sellers countered our offer, and we recountered. The next day, out of the blue, another offer came in. Because the seller's broker told the second buyer that we were already negotiating, the new buyers made their best offer. It was higher than the seller's initial counter to our offer, and so they withdrew from our negotiations and took the second offer. It was only a couple of thousand dollars less than the asking price. As buyers, we knew the maximum amount we were willing to pay for the home, but the seller was delighted to receive an offer significantly higher than the price he was willing to accept from us.

As a seller, you may think a bidding war is like winning the lottery. If it turns out well, a bidding war can get you more money for your property than you would have otherwise pocketed from a single offer. However, there are obstacles and pitfalls that should be avoided. How you and your broker handle each of these situations will define the type of experience you have in selling your home.

If there is more than one offer for your property, it's important to play fair with each buyer. Common sense dictates the reason: You may need those other buyers if for some unexpected reason the first buyer pulls out of the contract.

What will you do if the winning bidder cannot qualify for the mortgage or backs out of the contract for some other reason? If the buyer withdraws from the purchase of your home, you'll want to go back to the other buyers and ask them to resubmit their bids. If they feel they were unfairly treated the first time around, they may choose not to bid on your property and you could be left without any offers.

There are a couple of different ways to handle a multiple offer situation. You can consider each offer separately, as it comes in. Or you can wait until you receive all of the offers and then consider them simultaneously.

A third option is the sealed bid. If your broker knows that several buyers are interested, she or he can tell the other brokers that sealed bids will be accepted in the next seventy-two hours (or whatever time frame suits your situation). Sealed bids mean that the offers come in and are not judged until the time period is up. Then all of the bids are opened simultaneously and are compared with each other. Depending on the custom of your area, buyer brokers may present their own contracts in a sealed bid situation.

Once you've received the offers, you can decide which one you want to respond to. Your first response may be to respond to both, at the same price, and let the buyers come back with second offers. The problem with that plan is that both buyers may accept your written counteroffer and both may legally bind you. (If you counter both bids verbally, then the first offer that actually gets signed is the one you become bound to. Oral agreements are not binding in real estate transactions.)

Brokers say a better option is not to respond to the bids but to go back to the buyers and tell them there are multiple offers. Tell them how much each buyer bid so the buyers know where they stand. Ask them to submit revised offers. You might also stipulate that this will be a "best offer" situation or that you will respond only to the better offer. If both offers are similar, you may choose to respond to them in the order in which you received them. First come, first considered is judged fair play in real estate.

Experts caution sellers to be consistent. Either tell all the buyers everything or don't tell anyone anything. Otherwise, you're working against the interests of all parties, including your own. If for some reason the multiple offers don't work out, other buyers may be less willing to bid on a property whose seller has a reputation for unfairness. (It's amazing how fast word spreads among local brokers.) Once all the bids are in, it's perfectly acceptable to tell each party what the other parties bid for the property. That way, if you ask for a second round of bids, buyers will know what they're up against.

Note: Playing the bidding war game can create circumstances where multiple buyers think they each have a deal with you when they don't. If you're not sure which buyer you're obligated to legally, consult your attorney. In any event, never sign more than one contract at a time.

Successful Home Seller Tip: It's important to remember that price is only one part of the contract. If you're choosing between two or more buyers, there are other components that may be more important to you than price, including:

1. *Which buyer is best qualified financially to purchase your home?* Is there a financing contingency? Is the buyer preapproved for his or her loan or just prequalified? How much cash does the purchaser have for the down payment? What assurances have the brokers given you that the buyer can obtain a mortgage?
2. *What other contingencies or kick-out clauses are in the contract?* Does the buyer want an inspection or does he or she want to get into the local, exclusive country club?
3. *What is the closing date?* Is it the best time for you or is it the buyer's preference?
4. *How much earnest money is the buyer willing to put up?* Since the earnest money may be forfeited if the buyer walks, it's a good indication of how serious he or she is about purchasing your home.
5. *What is the timing for the contingencies?* Are they set to expire within a few working days? Or do they expire at closing? Obviously, you want the contingencies to expire as quickly as possible.
6. *What does the buyer intend to do to the house?* This issue won't apply to all sellers, but if you have two buyers interested in your home and one is going to love the house the way it is and one is going to tear it down and replace it, you may feel better about selling your home to the buyer who will keep it the way it is. But remember, just because the buyer says he or she will upgrade, rather than demolish, your home doesn't

mean he or she can't tear it down the day after closing.

QUESTION 60

What is a kick-out clause?

Let's say you receive an offer that's loaded with contingencies. The buyer wants an inspection contingency, a mortgage contingency, a sell-the-existing-home-first contingency, an attorney approval contingency, and a golf course membership contingency. You know this isn't a great contract simply because the buyer has so many outs.

Well, you have an out, too. You can keep showing your home. The contract should specify that you will continue to show and market the home until the buyer drops the contingencies. If another offer comes in, you can go back to the first buyer and say, "Hey, Buyer B has offered the same amount of money as you, but there is only a financing contingency." Your original buyer then has the right to kick out the contingencies to meet the standard of the new contract. If he or she refuses to do this, and has not met the conditions of the contract (say, he or she hasn't sold an existing home), you can cancel Buyer A's contract and sell your home to Buyer B.

Sellers don't like contingencies, but they're there to protect the buyers. Of course, buyers don't like kick-out clauses, but they do protect the sellers. Seller brokers generally like kick-out clauses because they allow the transaction to move more quickly toward closing. Kick-out clauses can differ slightly from area to area. Ask your broker or your real estate attorney what, if any, terms and conditions apply in your area.

QUESTION 61

Do I need a real estate attorney? And what should I sign without one?

Using an attorney to close residential real estate transactions differs from state to state. No state will require you to have a real estate attorney. In fact, in states like California and Indiana, attorneys are used only in difficult or complicated transactions, or where the buyer or seller specifically wants someone to read and explain the legal documents being signed. In states where the use of real estate attorneys is uncommon, brokers and closing officers advise buyers and sellers about the transaction. In many other states, however, real estate attorneys are commonly hired to assist in the purchase and sale of residential real estate.

You should hire an attorney if you are unfamiliar with the documents you are signing if attorneys are generally used in the sale of homes in your area, or if you do not have confidence in your broker. If your deal is complicated or you have a skittish, nitpicking buyer who wants to make lots of "little" changes to the contract, you may want to have an attorney review what's being done and how it affects your rights. Real estate attorneys have other functions as well. They:

- Act as another layer removing emotion from the deal.
- Can negotiate the finer points of the deal for you.
- Can protect you from getting a bad deal should the negotiation turn nasty.

- Can work with the brokers to organize and finalize the details of the closing.
- Can explain the legal consequences of the deal and any terms you may not understand.
- Are a good buy for the money, as you can usually get them to work for a fixed fee.
- May be able to get you a reduced fee from the title company for certain fees you might have to pay.
- Track all the little details of a closing, from working on the closing documents with your lender to figuring out the prorations.
- Draft and prepare all the closing documents.
- Obtain the necessary approvals, certificates, and transfer stamps for the closing.
- Provide you with a closing book that neatly organizes all the documents involved with your house closing.

You may think you're making a smart move by cutting out the real estate attorney and saving yourself the fee. But when you consider the amount of money involved ($60,000, $100,000, or $350,000, or whatever the sales price of your home is), it isn't so smart. On a $100,000 sale, your attorney's fee is minuscule, and on a bad deal that fee could save you a tremendous amount of heartache as well as money to fix whatever problems crop up. Remember, when you hire an attorney, his or her sole purpose is to be your advocate and protect your interests. The title company or escrow officer is a neutral third party who does not have your interest as a first priority. And your broker, while working on your side, has a vested interest in making sure the deal closes (sometimes at any price) so that he or she can collect the commission. Some people (not all) feel that once a seller or conventional broker has a signed contract, the broker is out to make sure the deal works even if it may not be in your best interest.

What should you sign without your real estate attorney? If you're going to use a real estate attorney, it's a good idea to get him or her involved in the deal as early as possible. Ideally, you'll know who you're going to use before you make a counteroffer. On the other hand, most sellers don't realize they need an attorney until *after* they've negotiated the terms and conditions of the contract and signed it. That's why you need your own attorney approval rider. You can sign anything you like as long as the contract gives you the right to have your attorney approve or reject the contract once you have signed it.

QUESTION 62

How do I find a real estate attorney? And how much should he or she charge me?

Not all real estate attorneys are competent, let alone good. And it's important to find one who will help, rather than hinder, the deal. Finding a good real estate attorney is like finding a good broker. First, you should ask your broker and your friends for recommendations. You want someone experienced, someone who has handled a minimum of fifty closings within the past three years. After you get several names, call them and ask them how much they charge and what they will do for that fee. You'll find a wide range of services. Don't be embarrassed to ask about fees. It's crucial that you know how much you're getting for your money.

Some attorneys (especially those in medium or large law

firms) charge by the hour. Others (especially solo practitioners) charge a flat fee. Try to find someone who will charge you a flat fee for his or her time. (Depending on the complexity of your deal, that fee can range from $250 to $1,000.) That way, if there is a problem with the closing, you won't be charged for extra work.

Looking solely at how much attorneys charge for their services is not necessarily the best way to choose your attorney. You want someone you trust, someone you feel comfortable talking to about the intimate details of your financial life. It's vital that you feel comfortable with, and perhaps even a bit close to, your attorney.

If a deal is really complicated, you will almost certainly need an attorney. Sam once worked on a house closing that seemed pretty ordinary until he found out that his buyers were purchasing a house from a seller who had ten lenders. Sam had to negotiate a separate deal with each lender until they were all satisfied. This extremely complicated closing took ten hours. Sam called it the "hour per lender" closing.

Once you hire the attorney, the general idea is to let him or her do the job. If the attorney advised you on certain points, believe him or her. If he or she tells you to do something, do it. Your attorney should know the ins and outs of real estate law much better than you do.

Note: Hiring a real estate lawyer is not the same thing as having your Uncle Harry, the tax attorney, do your real estate closing. Real estate law is specialized, and while Uncle Harry may be a whiz at writing wills, or leasing airplanes, or finding creative places to put your money, he may help you get nailed to the wall in two minutes if he truly doesn't understand the finer points of real estate law.

WHAT IS SELLER FINANCING?

QUESTION 63

What is seller financing? And when should I offer it?

Seller financing literally means that you, the seller, finance the buyer's purchase of your home. You essentially become the buyer's bank. You lend him or her the money to purchase your home, and the buyer pays you back each month by making a mortgage payment that usually consists of principal and interest.

If done correctly, seller financing can work out beautifully for both you and the buyer. The benefits to the buyer include: quick and easy loan approval; a competitive interest rate; lower (or no) fees than a bank or savings and loan; and less paperwork. Seller benefits include: The equity in your home becomes an investment on which you earn an excellent, stable rate of return compared to many other forms of investment; you have had an opportunity to interact with the borrower; and the loan is secured by an asset—your house—that you know extremely well. The detriment to seller financing is the risk; if the buyer defaults on the payments, you will need to bring legal action to get either your money or your house back.

When Janet and Steve bought their house several years ago, they didn't have enough money for a 20 percent down payment. After securing a loan from a bank for 80 percent of the home's value, they went to their seller and asked her to take back an interest-only second mortgage for five years at 8.5 percent. About a year after they were in the home, interest rates began falling. They continued to fall for another year. All of that time, the seller was earning 8.5 percent on her second mortgage while money market accounts were paying a dismal 2.5 percent. When interest rates hit 7 percent, Janet and Steve refinanced. By that time, their house had appreciated some and they had scraped together enough cash to pay off their second mortgage (the one held by the seller). While their seller received interest for only two and a half years instead of the five-year life of the loan, she still earned far more interest on her money than if she had stuck it in a money market account or even if she had bought a five-year certificate of deposit. More important, it enabled the seller to sell the home to Janet and Steve.

While many experts tout seller financing as a marvelous marketing mechanism, you should be aware that not every buyer is looking for seller financing, and it is not a popular option in every area. Also, not every seller is a good candidate for seller financing—you must have paid off, or nearly paid off, your own mortgage, and you must not need the cash for whatever move you're going to make. In other words, if you're planning to use the cash you receive from the sale of your home to purchase another home or finance a retirement lifestyle that includes second homes and world-wide travel, you're not a good candidate for seller financing. On the other hand, if you're selling this home and planning to move nearby or to retire to that vacation condo in Florida or California you've owned for ten years, and you don't need the cash for day-to-day living expenses, then you might be in the right position to offer seller financing.

Seller financing usually takes two basic forms: You can offer to finance the entire purchase price of the house minus a cash down payment; or, if your buyers can't get all the money they need to purchase your home from their primary lender (usually a bank or an S&L), you can take back a second mortgage for the difference.

Marketing Scheme

Some brokers feel that offering seller financing is one of the best marketing tools sellers have at their disposal. I'm not convinced, however, that finding a seller who will finance the purchase of their home is at the top of most buyers' agendas. Home buyers who are purchasing their second, third, or fourth home usually won't require seller financing. They will have equity built up in their homes that they can turn around and use for their new purchase. First-time buyers are the most likely candidates for seller financing; fortunately, they account for about half of all home buyers (we're talking 2 million first-timers out of approximately 4 million total buyers). Offering seller financing may pay off in neighborhoods that are targeted by first-time buyers.

If you're planning to offer seller financing, be sure to mention that in your ads. You should remember that not every buyer who wants seller financing is going to be financially qualified to purchase your home. In other words, if your buyer can't get conventional or FHA financing, he or she may not be a good credit risk. In addition to selling your home, it would be nice to have a buyer who can actually afford to make the payments on the loan you have graciously financed. Word your advertisement carefully. Rather than advertising "123 Pine Street for sale, seller will offer financing," it is better if your ad says something like this: "Seller financing available to *qualified buyers.*"

Good Seller Financing Candidates

If you're going to offer seller financing, it's important for you to distinguish between good risks and bad risks. That's what conventional lenders do: They decide whether or not to lend a prospective buyer funds to purchase your home based on the buyer's ability to pay back the loan. There's no use lending money to folks who can't pay it back. If you do, you'll end up having to evict your buyers and engage in costly and time-consuming legal battles to foreclose on your own house. At the end of it all, you'll have to put your home back on the market.

If a prospective borrower asks if you will finance his or her purchase of your home, ask the person to fill out an application form such as the one on pages 266–67. Borrowers should give you their name, address, and Social Security number; a list of their three previous addresses; their employer's name, address, and telephone number; how long they've worked in their current job; a list of their previous three jobs; a copy of their last federal and state tax returns, and a year-to-date statement showing their income (copies of their most recent pay stubs should work). You should also have the borrower sign a piece of paper agreeing to let you order a copy of his or her credit report or have the borrower furnish you with a recent copy of a credit report from one of the major credit reporting companies.

Seller Financing Application Form

Name ____
Address ______________________________________
City/State/Zip _________________________________
Applicant's Social Security Number __________________
Spouse's Social Security Number ____________________
Home Telephone, __________ Work Telephone __________
Employed As ____________________________________
Employer ______________________________________
Employer's Address ______________________________
Direct Supervisor (name and phone number) _____________
____
Spouse's Employer _______________________________
Spouse's Direct Supervisor _________________________
____
Your Annual Salary __________________
Spouse's Annual Salary __________________
Other Income (please list everything, including alimony and child support) ______________________________________
____
Total Annual Income ____________________
How long have you and your spouse worked at these jobs?
Applicant __________________ Spouse __________________
Please give the name and address of your previous employers for the last five years.

Applicant:

1. ____
2. ____
3. ____

Spouse:

1. ____
2. ____
3. ____

List previous addresses for the past three years and the names of your prior landlords or lenders.

1. ____

2. ____

3. ____

List the assets you own. ____________________________

List your current debts, including car loans, credit card debt, and other loans. ______________________________________

____

____

I hereby consent to allow ______________ (name of seller) to obtain access to my credit report for the sole purpose of using such credit report in determining my suitability for obtaining seller financing for the purchase of the property located at ______________________________________

____

____

Applicant's Signature ______________ Date __________

Applicant's Social Security Number ______________

Applicant's Birth Date ______________

Spouse's Signature ______________ Date __________

Spouse's Social Security Number ______________

Spouse's Birth Date ______________

All of this information is going to help you decide whether or not your buyer is a good credit risk. You're looking for someone who is stable, secure financially, and has a good, steady job that he or she has kept for a number of years. Look for clues to the type of borrower your buyer may be: Does he or she pay the rent on time? Is he or she late in paying off credit card debt? Is the auto loan paid on time? Ask the buyer if he or she has ever filed for bankruptcy. If he or she has filed within the past seven years, that bankruptcy case should show up on the credit report. If there is a bankruptcy, ask why your prospective borrower filed for bank ruptcy. If it was because a spouse or family member died and he or she didn't have enough money to pay for the funeral, you may consider the buyer a strong candidate despite past financial problems. If, however, there is no good explanation for a recent bankruptcy (within the last several years), you may not want to lend this person money.

The best candidate for seller financing is the buyer who has already been preapproved for a loan by a local lender and needs a little extra from you to purchase your property. "Preapproved" is different from "prequalified." Anyone can be prequalified by a local lender. This is a free service offered by every lender who wants your business. *Prequalified* means the lender has taken a quick look at your assets and liabilities, your debts and your cash, and run these numbers through a series of mathematical calculations. While being prequalified will tell a buyer which ballpark of home prices he or she should be looking in, it doesn't mean the lender is ready to hand out the money. Preapproval is a more painstaking process. The buyer may have actually paid an application fee, and has already provided a significant amount of documentation to the lender. If a buyer is *preapproved* it means that the lender is prepared to give him or her a loan for the preapproved amount today, and perhaps the only item missing is the contract for the purchase of the home and the appraisal.

If you're thinking about offering seller financing, remember this: *Lending money is never risk-free*. There are dozens of reasons why folks stop making their mortgage payments, none of them good. However, the Mortgage Bankers Association of America (MBA) reports that only 2 to 4 percent of all loans go bad. That means 96 to 98 percent of all homeowners make their payments regularly. That is an excellent number. A higher percentage of smaller loans go bad, lenders say, because many first-time buyers are on the fringe of affordability. In other words, they can afford to buy your house today, but if one spouse loses his or her job, the other may not be able to make the payments on the mortgage.

Note: Seller financing can be extremely complicated. Consult with your real estate attorney before agreeing to offer a specific buyer seller financing. Also, be sure to liberally sprinkle around phrases such as "financially qualified buyer" and "may be able to provide" when talking about seller financing. You don't want anyone to think that you're going to offer seller financing to anybody who isn't financially qualified.

QUESTION 64
What are the different types of seller financing I can offer to a prospective buyer?

If you want to offer seller financing, there are several ways to do it. Here are your options:

Purchase Money Mortgage (PMM). A PMM means that you take the place of a conventional lender and provide the buyer with all the financing he or she needs. If the buyer can afford a 20 percent down payment, then you would give him or her a loan for 80 percent of the sales price. Since your loan is the first loan, you become the primary lender. That means, if the buyer defaults on the loan you may foreclose on the house and sell it to pay yourself back first. Only a federal income tax lien—which means that the buyer also owes the government money—or a real estate lien—for unpaid real estate property taxes—takes a higher priority than the primary lender.

Articles of Agreement. Also known as an *installment purchase*, this method of seller financing means you sell your home to the buyer a little bit at a time. The buyer receives an interest in the house, but you hold title until the buyer has paid off the loan in full.

Successful Home Seller Tip: If you use a purchase money mortgage or sell your home through an articles of agreement or installment sale, you must have paid off all or most of your mortgage. To minimize your risk, you may want to require the buyer to pay a significant down payment. However, if you are still paying off a $95,000 mortgage on a $100,000 home, you should be very careful about using a PMM or articles of agreement. If your lender finds out, he or she could foreclose on your home and jeopardize your credit and the buyer's down payment. The reason? The due-on-sale clause in your mortgage that allows the lender to call your loan upon the sale of the property. For more information on due-on-sale clauses, see Question 66.

Second Mortgage. A second mortgage means that the borrower has gone to a conventional lender for the first loan and has come to you to make up the difference between the sales price of your home and the amount of the first loan.

Buydown. There is another option, but it isn't technically "financing." If you want to help out a prospective buyer, but you don't want to offer seller financing, you might offer to buy down the rate of his or her loan with a conventional lender. If the interest rate on the loan is 8.5 percent, you could buy down the rate for one, two, or three years. Here's what happens if you buy down the buyer's loan for three years: If the loan's real rate is 9.5 percent, the buyer would pay only 6.5 percent the first year, 7.5 percent the second year, and 8.5 percent the third year. Starting in the fourth year, the buyer would pay the regular 9.5 percent interest rate. When you buy down the rate, you effectively make up the difference between what the buyer pays and what the regular rate of the loan is. So, for example, in the first year, if the buyer pays 6.5 percent, you'd pay 3 percent in cash to the lender to make up the rest of the payment. You could make these payments in a lump sum, buy down the rate six months to a year, or instead of having a stepped rate (6.5 percent the first year, 7.5 percent the second year, and so on), you could simply buy down the loan a point or two for a year or two. Since you pay cash to the lender, who then readjusts the rate of the loan for the borrower, this isn't true seller financing. Why should you consider doing it? Buydowns can be extremely successful marketing techniques and very useful in helping buyers qualify for the loan necessary to buy your house.

Successful Home Seller Tip: Again, seller financing can be extremely complicated and time-consuming. Even if it isn't common to use a real estate attorney to close residential real estate transactions in your state, I urge you to work with a real estate attorney before you lend a prospective buyer any money. A good real estate attorney should be able to draw up and file loan documents (ask to see proof of the filing), and help you determine the creditworthiness of the borrower. Also, your state may have specific laws that regulate these transactions as well as the interest rates you can legally charge and your ability to foreclose on the home if your buyer defaults.

QUESTION 65

What are my financial obligations if my buyer wants to use an FHA or a VA loan?

The Federal Housing Administration (FHA) arm of the Department of Housing and Urban Development (HUD) and the Department of Veterans Affairs (still referred to as the VA, for Veterans Administration) offer loans to people who fall within certain parameters. In the case of FHA loans, anyone may apply for one, but you can borrow only a certain amount of money. Any individual who is a veteran of the armed forces may apply for a fixed-rate VA loan, which also has an upper loan limit but does not require any down payment.

Because the government wanted to give FHA and VA buyers a break, it used to prohibit these buyers from paying certain fees and costs associated with purchasing property. That meant sellers had to pick up the slack or the deal wouldn't close. In the mid-1980s, however, someone in Washington, D.C., decided that wasn't too fair to the sellers, so the rules were changed. Today, all closing costs are considered "negotiable," meaning that buyers and sellers can decide between themselves who is going to pick up what costs. But sellers are no longer required to pay any costs associated with FHA and VA loans, including pest inspection fees and lender inspection fees.

QUESTION 66

Is my mortgage assumable? What is a due-on-sale clause?

Some mortgages are *assumable*—that is, they can be assumed by someone else, who will then be responsible for making the monthly payments of principal and interest—and some mortgages are not. Strictly speaking, almost all mortgages have a *due-on-sale* clause, which means that the lender is entitled to call the loan and demand full repayment of the entire remaining balance when you sell your home or transfer title to your home to someone else. The balance of the loan is due on the sale (at the closing) of your home.

Even though most (if not all) loans carry due-on-sale language, lenders will sometimes allow a loan to be assumed by your home buyer. Home buyers like to assume loans, particularly if the loans have a lower-than-market interest rate and if they can get them cheaper than if they went into the mortgage marketplace. Sometimes, lenders will allow a home buyer to assume a loan if he or she pays a few fees and points (a point is one percent of the loan amount) in cash to the lender.

One of the big selling points of an FHA loan is that it is an assumable loan. If another buyer comes along, he or she can step into your shoes and pick up your payments. But while it's true that an FHA loan can be assumed, the home buyer must get approved by FHA just as if he or she were applying for a new loan. If your buyer's credit isn't that good, and he or she has missed some credit card payments and doesn't have quite enough income to swing the monthly payments, don't expect FHA to simply give its blessing. This process of getting the buyer approved before he or she can assume your loan is similar with many mortgage lenders. The lender will need to feel comfortable with your buyer's finances before giving the official okay.

Home buyers like assumable loans because they believe these loans offer an easier, cheaper, and faster way of getting into a house. They may be right. On the other hand, after you've lived in your home for a while, you will have paid down your mortgage. You'll have built up some cash equity. Unless you're planning to give the buyer a second mortgage for the remaining balance of the sales price, the home buyer will have to come up with enough cash to cover the amount of your home equity. Most buyers (especially first-timers) don't have that kind of cash. And those move-up buyers who do have it generally don't need to assume loans: They're qualified to get an excellent deal from a conventional lender at the prevailing interest rates.

Assuming a loan isn't as common as some people think, but you may be asked if your loan is assumable. Read your loan document carefully before answering. If you're still not sure, pick up the telephone and call your lender.

Successful Home Seller Tip: Remember, if your buyer plans to assume your loan, you must work with your lender to get your buyer approved and to get yourself released from the loan. If you don't get your lender's approval on the loan assumption, you will still be the person responsible for paying off the loan even if you no longer own the home. And if you sell your home without paying off your lender, the lender has the right to demand full repayment of the entire remaining balance of the loan or may foreclose on your house.

QUESTION 67

What is seller's remorse? What is buyer's remorse?

Buyer's remorse and seller's remorse are the emotional undertows of a residential house deal. These backlashes of feeling usually come right after the deal is struck, though they can happen at any time in the transaction, from the moment an offer is accepted to months after the closing.

Buyers and sellers basically feel the same emotion—remorse—from opposite sides. Those who experience buyer's remorse feel as though they've paid too much for a property or have taken on more debt and financial obligations than they can afford. Symptoms include staying awake all night and worrying whether or not you'll ever be able to afford to take a vacation again.

Sellers regret that they have actually sold their home—their castle—particularly if they haven't found a new home, as planned. Or a seller may find out later that he or she could have gotten more money for the property. There's nothing worse than feeling as if you've let your property go for less than its true value. Symptoms include staying awake all night, rerunning the deal over and over again in your head, wondering whether you had done this instead of that you'd have come out ahead in the end.

Seller's remorse is often more complicated than buyer's remorse. Sellers may find themselves emotionally confused or psychologically distraught at the thought of leaving their home while at the same time worrying about whether or not they've sold their home for the best price possible.

What can you do to alleviate seller's remorse? There's no quick tonic for these complicated feelings, brokers say. Instead, you have to remember why you're selling and what your home is actually worth. If you start believing your broker's marketing efforts for your house, you may start thinking that your home is worth more than it is. Also, if you haven't emotionally separated from your house—where you, as the seller, become the caretaker of the property for the next owner, rather than the proverbial "king of the castle"—it's easy to fall back into the same comfortable patterns of living and forget that you're moving.

If your bout of seller's remorse has been caused by finding out that the buyers would have actually paid $5,000 more for your house than they did, you're just going to have to live with that. In the best kind of negotiations, each side comes out feeling it got the best deal. Both sides are happy. In the second-best kind of negotiations, each side feels as if the other side got the best deal, and no one's happy. The worst kind of negotiations are when one side has all the advantages and the other side knows it, but for whatever reason can't walk away from the sale. If you end up in a position where the buyer has the stranglehold and gets you for every last penny, but you still have to sell, then just do it. Move ahead, into your new home and your new life, and don't look back.

It's a little like the case of the seller who bemoaned the fact that while the value of his home had risen 100 percent since he bought it, neighborhood prices had dropped 20 percent in the last year. "I'm selling at a loss," he said. His broker pointed out that he would still make a huge profit on his home. "Plus," the broker added, "the next home you buy [in this neighborhood] will be at a 20 percent discount."

QUESTION 68
What happens if the buyer backs out of the deal?

Martin and JoEllen thought they had sold their Dallas home. The buyers had come back three times, then made an offer. After some intense negotiations, during which Martin and JoEllen agreed to take back a 20 percent second mortgage with deferred interest, they accepted the bid. Two weeks later, the buyers backed out of the deal. They told Martin and JoEllen they couldn't qualify for a mortgage, which was one of their contract contingencies. Later, Martin and JoEllen found out the buyers simply "freaked out" about how much it would cost them to live in the home.

What can you do if the buyer backs out of a contract to purchase your home? In some cases, nothing. Buyers generally back out of contracts because they can't qualify for a mortgage or they get nervous about the expense of the home. If the home buyer has a financing contingency, an inspection contingency, and an attorney's approval contingency, and wants to back out of the purchase of your home, he or she can use the contingencies to his or her benefit (which isn't exactly ethical) and walk away.

If, however, the buyers have no legal right to terminate the contract, and the buyers walk away from your home (perhaps they realize it's a huge mistake, or one spouse is offered a fabulous job in another state or city), then you may get to keep the earnest money (see Question 50 for a more thorough discussion of earnest money). When buyers put down earnest money, they know this money may be forfeited should they back out of the contract without a just reason. (This is why you should always ask for the largest amount of earnest money possible. It keeps the buyer's eye trained on the property.) Most of the time the earnest money is held by the listing broker or another third party, and if you have a right to keep the earnest money because the buyers walked away from the deal, you will need to receive the money from the listing broker.

Successful Home Seller Tip: If you did not negotiate the listing agreement to provide that your broker gets paid only if your home sale closes, your broker may require you to pay her some of the earnest money as the brokerage commission.

If the buyers dispute your demand for the earnest money, you can go to court, or perhaps settle for less than the entire amount in the account. If the buyers walk away from a signed contract, they are breaking a written agreement to purchase your home. You can go to court and sue the buyers for your damages. You'll have to prove that you've lost money (and been "damaged") by the fact that you haven't been able to sell the house to someone else. This may be difficult to prove. To illustrate, let's say you have an offer from a buyer for $150,000 and the buyer walks away from the deal. The next buyer who comes along offers you only $125,000 for your home. In this kind of case, you may be able to prove to the court that you lost $25,000 because the first buyer broke the contract.

To recap, you have three basic options when a buyer walks away from a contract. You can return the earnest money and continue marketing your home. You can keep the earnest money (or split it with the buyer, or split it with the brokers) and continue marketing your home. Or you can take the buyer to court and sue for damages.

Note: While you may be legally entitled to the earnest money, certain circumstances may make you decide not to take it. There have been cases where a buyer has backed out of a deal only to come around again several weeks later when whatever made him or her nervous the first time has been resolved. If you have returned the earnest money to the buyer and have resolved the issues amicably, you may see that buyer again after he or she has had a change of heart. Much of your decision to keep the earnest money will depend on the deal and the circumstances surrounding your sale. As I've pointed out earlier in the book, state laws and local customs vary, so consult your real estate attorney if you decide to pursue a claim against a prospective buyer or make a claim for the earnest money.

QUESTION 69

What should I do if a family member or friend wants to purchase my house?

When their mother died, two sisters in Columbus, Ohio, inherited her house. One of the sisters' sons lived in the house for a year, keeping the house maintained in exchange for free rent. After the year was up, the son and his fiancée wanted to buy the house. The two sisters called a broker to find out how much it was worth and then began to discuss what kind of a discount they should give a family member.

Selling your house to someone you know is one of those "iffy" kinds of transactions that can test the bounds of family relationships and the most solid of friendships. While you may love your house, its quirks could drive someone else crazy. And that person might end up feeling as if he or she paid you more than the house was worth. If you're going to sell your house to a friend or relative, keep in mind the following points:

1. *Discount the sales price.* We all like to feel we've gotten a good, fair deal. If you sell your home to a friend or relative, you're going to save at least 5 to 7 percent of the sales price by not paying a brokerage commission. Consider passing all or part of that savings on to your relative or friend. To make the buyer feel even better, show him or her comps that prove that the house is actually worth more than the price you've agreed to take for it.
2. *Keep the negotiations friendly.* It's one thing to get all hard-nosed with a stranger, but it's not worth poisoning the well of friends and family by dickering over every last cent. Do your best to come to a meeting of the minds with your friend or relative. If you give up a few extra dollars, so be it. You'll still walk away with an easier deal—and probably more money, especially if a real estate broker isn't involved—than you otherwise would have had.
3. *Don't disclose your buyer's financial information.* There used to be a saying "Kiss and don't tell." That's the motto of savvy sellers, too, especially when dealing with relatives' or friends' financial information. If you're selling to a friend or relative, you're going to find out more about their finances (an incredibly per-

sonal topic) than you might otherwise ever know. The trick here is to keep your mouth shut. Don't tell Aunt Gladys how much Tom and Phyllis are making. It isn't her business, and that kind of "kiss and tell" will ultimately come back to haunt you.

4. *Keep the transaction at "arm's length."* If you decide to provide some sort of seller financing for a friend or relative who is purchasing your home, be sure to keep the transaction at "arm's length." That Internal Revenue Service (IRS) term means you must charge your friend or relative an interest rate that keeps pace with the prevailing market rate. If you show favoritism or give your relative a below-market interest rate, you could have problems with the IRS. Consult with your local real estate attorney and tax adviser to find out which rules and regulations apply to your situation.
5. *Treat your friend or relative like any other buyer.* This seems obvious, but sometimes sellers don't treat their friends or relatives as well as they would treat total strangers. If you would provide a seller disclosure form to a stranger, you should also provide it to your relative or friend. If you would give a stranger a choice of closing dates, you should do the same for a relative or friend. In fact, you should go a step further for a friend or relative because there is more at stake than simply selling a home. On the other hand, don't let that relative or friend step all over you and purchase your house for much less than it's worth.

Sometimes, a carefully-thought-out purchase and sale can result in one family member saving a tremendous amount of money. One seller I know bought his mother-in-law's home. She was in her eighties and had never taken her onetime $125,000 tax-free deduction. (Once you're over the age of fifty-five, the IRS allows you to take a onetime deduction of up to $125,000 in profits from the sale of your primary residence. For a more detailed explanation, see Question 97.) The mother-in-law's home was worth around $200,000, and after she had taken her deduction and figured out the cost basis of her home, she had very little tax to pay. Meanwhile, her son-in-law, who was sixty, also took his onetime $125,000 exemption. Since his mother-in-law's house cost about the same as his original house minus the exemption, he also deferred paying tax on his capital gain.

PART VI

Neverland: Waiting to Close

SOLVING PROBLEMS WITH TITLE, INSPECTIONS, AND THE APPRAISAL

QUESTION 70

What happens after we've agreed on the terms of sale of my home?

Real estate has a definite rhythm and order to it. After the buyers make an offer, you counter their offer. Then they counter, then you counter, and sooner or later you and the buyers compromise on the sales price, closing date, and the other terms of the contract.

Once you've agreed to the terms of the sale of your home, the buyers must work to satisfy their contingencies. For example, if they have a sixty-day financing contingency, they should immediately begin to find a mortgage to help them purchase your home. If they have ten days to have your home inspected by a professional house inspector, don't be surprised if they (or their broker) call you the next day to schedule that inspection. If you've agreed to an attorney rider, their attorney should contact you or your attorney within twenty-four to forty-eight hours to begin negotiating the finer points of the contract.

The timetable for the transaction is set by the closing date in the contract. If you and the buyers have agreed to close in thirty days, all of the contingencies will have to be satisfied quickly in order to close by the agreed-upon date. If you have ninety days until closing, everything may proceed at a more leisurely pace. A ninety-day closing will give you plenty of time to pack, close out your utility accounts, and figure out where you're going.

If there are going to be problems with the transaction, this is the period of time in which they're going to crop up. This is when the inspectors come through and the attorneys negotiate the contract. If the buyers can't qualify for a mortgage, you'll know that, too. If the sale is going to fall apart, this is when it will happen. In the rest of this section, we'll take a look at what you should do if your sale falls apart.

QUESTION 71

What should I do if the buyer's inspector finds a problem with my house? Should I fix the problem or renegotiate the sales price with the buyer?

Having your home inspected by a professional inspector is a little nerve-wracking. It's tough to have someone—a total stranger—come through your home, specifically intent on finding flaws. In fact, some professional house inspectors don't feel as if they have earned their fee unless they find something wrong with your home. (Other inspectors find little or nothing wrong, because real estate brokers—who refer business to inspectors—don't like "deal breakers." Deal breakers are inspectors who uncover too many problems with a home, unnecessarily—in the broker's view—scaring the buyers into backing out of the deal.)

Some buyers feel that a problem that emerges during an inspection is an opportunity to completely renegotiate the purchase/sales contract. Whether or not you choose to play this renegotiation game is up to you. You must also decide what you're going to do if a professional house inspector or structural engineer actually finds something wrong with your home.

What might an inspection uncover? If you had your home inspected by a professional house inspector before listing it (see Question 10 for information on seller inspections), there should be few surprises. If you have not had a seller inspection, then a home inspector may turn up anything from a leaky roof to warped floorboards. Other common problems include a boiler or furnace that needs maintenance, service, or replacement; dirty central air filters; broken windows or cracked windowpanes; damaged exterior siding; evidence of termites or other pests; asbestos; or a hot water tank that has just about reached the end of its useful life. There are literally dozens of potential problems a house inspection might uncover.

If the inspection goes well, and the inspector doesn't discover any hidden problems, you and the buyer will have nothing to dicker over. A buyer in North Carolina had the home he was purchasing inspected, and the only thing the inspector discovered was that one of the windows in a bedroom was a little difficult to open. The seller agreed to have it fixed before the closing.

On the other hand, your buyer's inspection may turn up a few new problems, even if you've had the home inspected yourself. Some of these problems may be small, and some may be large. When the buyer comes to you (as he or she most likely will) and says "What are you going to do for me?" you have three choices:

1. *Fix the problem.* The inspector may turn up minor problems in the home, quirks you've lived with for years that never bothered you but may bother the buyer. If the bathtub needs to be rodded out because it isn't draining perfectly, that may be an easy thing to fix, and it will make the buyer feel a whole lot better about the purchase. Small problems are usually easy and cheap to fix. However, to you, the seller, they may be too time-consuming to fix—finding the right person to do the repair and then having this person repair the problem can eat up gobs of packing time in addition to being a major annoyance. If that's the case, there's always Plan B . . .
2. *Give a cash credit to the buyer at closing.* If the inspector discovers that the reason you don't get real hot water is that the hot water heater is not working properly, the buyer may ask you to replace it. You may agree to pay for the entire repair, or split the cost, since the buyer isn't purchasing new construction but an older home. Since you're splitting the cost, and since the lack of hot water never really bothered you, you may not want to go ahead and replace the tank. You may, instead, opt to give the buyer a cash credit at closing

for your share of the new hot water tank. That means you'll give the buyer a check for half the repair or replacement cost either during the closing or just after. Although your buyer's lender may not officially sanction cash credits, the lender may look the other way when the funds are small and for specific purposes. *Note:* Cash credits are acceptable by local custom only. Consult with your attorney or real estate agent to find out the local customs in your area. Of course, there's always Plan C . . .

3. *Do nothing.* Just because the buyer asks for reimbursement for a problem doesn't mean you have to immediately pull out your wallet. You may say "No, I'm not going to fix those problems." Unless the problems are egregious, in most cases the buyer will still purchase your home. After all, he or she has put down earnest money and paid for a home inspection. Even if you agree to fix some problems and not others, there will come a point in time where you won't want to do any more. Just be aware that some buyers are skittish, and many first-time buyers have plugged every nickel into their purchase. They may be worried that if there is a problem looming, they won't have the cash to fix it.

Part of deciding when to say "Yes, I'll fix that" or "No, I won't" depends on how much the buyer is paying you for your home. If the buyer is paying top dollar—say, $99,500 for a home with a $100,000 list price—then you should think carefully about fixing any problems a home inspector turns up. The buyer's mentality is, "I'm paying the sellers what they think their home is worth. I want a home in perfect condition." On the other hand, if you've lowered the price of your home through the offer/counteroffer process, you may not want to do anything more for the buyer. Or you may believe you can get more from a different buyer.

Successful Home Seller Tip: There's a lot to be said for generating goodwill in an emotional transaction like selling a home. Fixing a broken window or oiling a creaky door will go a long way toward making the deal more pleasant. The idea is not to squeeze every last cent out of the buyer and broker nor to let them squeeze you. You want the buyer to feel as though he or she paid a fair price for your home. At the same time, you want to feel as though you received a good price for your home and that the buyer will love it as much as you do. These emotional intangibles can leave an indelible impression on a buyer and seller, and can elevate a financial transaction to a more satisfying level, spiritually and emotionally.

QUESTION 72
What should I do before the closing?

If you've read through this book from the beginning, or already begun the process of selling your home, you've undoubtedly realized that selling your home means you have to pay attention to detail. There may be as many as several dozen details you'll have to take care of before the closing. There are details involving the buyer that you'll want to check on, as well as details that require action on your part.

Here's a short list of details you'll want to stay on top of:

- *The Buyer.* If the buyer's contract contained contingencies (including inspections, attorney approval, and financing), you need to check to make sure that the contingencies have been satisfied or that the time limit for the buyer to exercise any contingencies has lapsed. If the buyer isn't going to get approved for a mortgage that meets the parameters stated within the contract, you need to know that as quickly as possible so you can get your property back on the market. If you're working with a broker or a real estate attorney (or both), he or she should talk to the broker or real estate attorney representing the buyer to find out where your buyer is in the process of getting that loan. If you are working alone, you'll have to make these calls yourself.
- *Municipal Inspections.* Some states, and some local municipalities, require you to have the smoke detectors in your home inspected before you close. In Massachusetts, the fire inspector comes out to do the inspection and issue the certificate. In Cicero, Illinois, the local building inspector must inspect the home and issue a certificate permitting the sale of the home. If the inspector finds building code violations, these violations will have to be corrected prior to closing. As the seller, you'll have to arrange for these inspections and obtain the certificates needed for closing. Contact your local city or village hall for more information.
- *Transfer Taxes.* Transfer taxes are fees you pay (they're usually pegged to the cost of your home) to the state, county, and/or municipality you live in to transfer ownership of your home from you to the buyer. Depending on your location and the custom in your area, you may be responsible for obtaining the transfer

stamps and paying for them. Again, contact your local city or village hall for more information.

- *Survey* (for single-family houses and town homes only). Local custom decrees who is responsible for providing an up-to-date survey for the closing, but usually it is the seller. If you recently bought the home you're selling (within the past two or three years), you may be able to simply "update" your survey and save some money. Your real estate attorney or broker can advise you further.
- *Title Insurance*. In most states, a seller can prove he has good title to the property by providing the buyer with a title insurance commitment. The commitment is issued by a title insurance company and lists all matters that affect the title to your home. In many states, the seller is responsible for obtaining and paying for the title commitment. The cost of title insurance is usually pegged to the cost of the home. If you're working with a real estate attorney, he or she will assist you in this process. Your attorney may even be able to get you a discount rate on your title insurance.
- *Pest Inspections*. Some states, municipalities, or neighborhoods (by local custom) require the seller to have his or her home inspected for pests before closing. You may have to provide the buyer with a certificate indicating that there is no evidence of pest infestation in your home.
- *Paid Assessment Letter*. If you live in a condominium or co-op, or are part of a homeowners' association, you will have to get a letter from the board of directors of the association stating that you have paid all of your assessments to the association through the closing date.

- *Waiver of Right of First Refusal.* Some condominium and co-op associations maintain a right of first refusal. That means that they have the right to purchase your home before you sell it to someone else. If you are subject to this provision, you may need a letter for the closing stating that the board has waived its right to purchase your home. Check with your association board for more details.
- *Insurance Certificate.* If you live in a condominium or a co-op, you will need to get a certificate of insurance from the company that insures your building. This certificate will name your buyer and his or her lender as insured under the policy.
- *Water Certificate.* Some municipalities require that you have a copy of your paid water bill at closing.
- *Loan Payoff Letter.* If you have a mortgage or a home equity loan, you'll need a letter from your lender(s) stating how much you owe on your loan through the closing date. (At the time you sell your home, you'll have to pay off the lenders.)
- *Utilities.* You'll need to place a telephone call to each of the utility companies that service your home and arrange to have the service cut off on the day of the closing (or the next day). If you're moving to another home within the utility's service area, you may be able to have your bills moved to your new address. If not, you may have to pay up before the closing. Be sure to call the following companies that apply: telephone, electricity, water, cable, alarm, gas, sewer, and garbage.
- *Movers.* Be sure to arrange for movers well in advance of the closing, particularly if you're closing around the first or last day of the month.

- *Mail.* It will take the post office anywhere from two weeks to a month to process your change-of-address. Don't forget to change magazine subscriptions two to six weeks in advance of your move.

Your broker or attorney should have a list of everything you need to do before you can close on your home. You should consult with one or both of them to find out what your local customs dictate in terms of who pays for what and when.

Successful Home Seller Tip: Some of the items listed above require coordination with the buyer. They will also cost money. You should wait for all of the contingencies to either expire or be satisfied before paying for a new survey, for example. On the other hand, you don't want to wait too long to order some of these things, or you may run short of time before closing. There is a delicate balance between waiting for all contingencies to be satisfied or waived and being caught unprepared for the closing. That's why it's so important to stay on top of, and in touch with, the buyer.

QUESTION 73

What is the appraisal? And what should I do if my home doesn't "appraise out"?

An appraisal is supposed to be an independent way of establishing the value of your home. When the buyer applies for a loan to purchase your home, the lender will send out an appraiser to appraise the value of the property. Ideally, the appraiser will be extremely familiar with the homes in your area and has a good idea of what value and amenities are common to the local housing stock. The appraiser then compares the sales prices of homes in your neighborhood to determine the value of your home. He or she then adds or subtracts a certain amount of money for each amenity that your home has or doesn't have as compared to homes of a similar size and price in your area.

Does all this sound familiar? It should. The appraiser looks for "comps" in much the same way your broker does when putting together the comparative marketing analysis (CMA). Like your broker, the appraiser needs to know how much homes are selling for in the neighborhood in order to establish a market value for your home.

You should think of appraisals as an inexact science, since appraisals, like CMAs, are one person's estimate of the value of your home. That means the appraisal of your property can come in higher—or lower—than the sales price. If the appraisal comes in higher, you probably won't find out about it, since this figure usually isn't made available to the seller. (The reason is that the buyer pays for the appraisal, which is done to satisfy his or her mortgage lender.) Unfortunately, if the appraisal comes in lower than the sales price, you *will* hear about it.

Since the appraisal process requires the input of other people in addition to the appraiser, there are things you can do to insure that your home "appraises out," to use the real estate jargon. Once the appraisal is ordered, the appraiser will call you (or your broker) to make an appointment to walk through your home. The appraiser may spend up to an hour examining the exterior and interior of your home, looking at everything from the number of bedrooms, bathrooms, and fireplaces to the quality and type of construction and the appliances you have in your kitchen. The appraiser may ask you questions about what you renovated or replaced in your home and when. He or she may ask, for example, how old the roof is and when you replaced the water heater. You should answer all of the appraiser's questions honestly.

In the best of all worlds, the appraiser will be familiar with your neighborhood. However, it's more likely that the appraiser will *not* be familiar with your neighborhood and won't know the value of homes. *You* (if you're a FSBO) *or your broker should provide the appraiser with the set of comps you used initially to set the listing price of your home.* A good appraiser will use your comps and come up with a few of his or her own. An average or poor appraiser will take the easy way out and use only your comps. (For more information on CMAs and comps, see Question 18.)

If your home doesn't appraise out, you'll have to deal with an irate buyer who, because he or she can't get a loan to buy your home, may have a legitimate reason for pulling out of the deal. If you accepted an offer to sell your home for $100,000 and the appraisal comes back at $95,000, the buyer's lender may provide only 80 percent of the appraised value. On $100,000, 80 percent would be $80,000. But on $95,000, 80 percent is only $76,000. If the buyer is expecting a loan for $80,000 and the lender is only willing to give a $76,000 loan, that's a $4,000 gap that must be overcome before the buyer can purchase your home.

The first person the buyer will turn to with this problem is you, the seller. In some cases, the buyer may ask you to lower the sales price so that the home appraises out. Or the buyer may ask you to take back a second mortgage to cover the gap between the sales price and the appraisal. If you choose not to help the buyer fix the appraisal problem, the buyer may have the right, under the contract, to walk away from the deal.

If you believe that your home's appraisal is way off the mark, you can call the lender and ask that another appraisal be done. Appraisals cost money, and the buyer pays for each appraisal. The buyer may not be willing to pay for another appraisal, and the lender may not permit you to pay for it (it's an obvious conflict of interest). You can hire your own appraiser, but he or she may not be approved by the bank. This is one case where a good offense is a good defense. Take the time to prepare for the appraisal (make sure your home is spotless and you have a sheaf of comps to give to the appraiser), and make sure the appraiser understands why your home is worth as much as the buyers are willing to pay for it. The more (and the better quality) information you have for the appraiser, the better off you will be.

QUESTION 74

What should I do if there is a problem with my title? What if there is a problem with the survey?

You spent months marketing your home. Finally, someone made an offer. You accepted. The buyers got their mortgage and had their inspection. You ordered title and a survey of the property. But when you read the surveyor's report, you discover that your neighbor's expensive new white picket fence is sitting four inches on your side of the property line.

Four inches. That's all it takes to create a problem with the title to your house. And for those four inches, the buyer has the right to walk away from the transaction.

Title is the evidence a homeowner has of the right to possession of land. A chain of title examines the links of ownership of a piece of property, starting with the current owner and tracing it back to the person who originally bought the land—or was granted the land—from the government.

When a seller sells property to a buyer, the buyer wants to know that he or she is purchasing the property from the true owner and that he or she is getting *clear title*. With clear title, the buyer gets ownership and exclusive use of the property. *Cloudy title* means there are other claims to ownership of your property that may interfere with your ability to use and enjoy it.

According to Jane, a title officer, there are five basic problems that can mar clear title, wreaking havoc for the seller and giving the buyer an opportunity to walk away from the deal. Each of these problems must be cleared up either before, or at, the closing. Generally, the title company will assist the seller, who may have to pay a high-risk insurance premium.

Here's a look at the five basic problems and their likely solutions:

- *Mechanic's Lien*. If you hire a contractor to perform work and there is a dispute about the payments, the contractor—or one of the subcontractors—may file a mechanic's lien against your property. Once the lien is filed, the contractor has a certain period of time to take action against you to collect payment.

  According to Jane, if the lien is still active, the title company can hold back money at the closing. The title company can surrender the money to the seller when he or she comes in with a signed waiver of lien from the contractor. If the issue is not resolved, the title company can use the money to pay off the contractor.
- *Deceased Sole Owner*. If the sole owner of a property dies after a contract is signed but before the closing,

the title company, for an extra fee, insures the buyer against possible claims against the property. But before issuing the policy, the title company looks at the death certificate, the will, and affidavits from creditors, doctors (if the individual was ill before death), and the heirs.

- *Delinquent Taxes*. If the seller hasn't paid his or her real estate taxes, the title company may hold back cash from the sale of the house. The title company can use this money to pay the delinquent tax bill, or will refund the money to the seller if the seller clears up the tax issue.
- *Encroachments and Easements*. Though sellers are worried, there are worse problems than a fence that is a few inches over the property line. Jane recalled working with a neighbor who built half his garage on a seller's land. A title company can work with the seller to issue a policy that will insure the buyer against the neighbor's removal of the garage, she said. These types of problem may show up in the surveyor's report. If you believe the surveyor's report is inaccurate, you should talk to the surveyor and title officer about having your property resurveyed. If you have documentation supporting your claim, you may need to share it with the surveyor and title company.
- *Unreleased Mortgages*. When you pay off your mortgage, or refinance your loan, the mortgage company releases you from your obligation to make monthly payments. Sometimes this release isn't recorded correctly or not at all, and an old mortgage (perhaps not yours) will turn up on the title. If an unreleased mortgage does turn up, you should contact that lender and ask for a copy of the release of mortgage. If no one can

find the release, your title company may contact the lender and deal with the issue.

Both buyers and sellers shoudl realize that title insurance doesn't clear up any problems. At best, it whitewashes their severity by providing insurance against the damages caused by an irate neighbor or a disgruntled heir. Your real estate attorney can provide you with further details.

LOOKING FOR YOUR NEW HOME

QUESTION 75

When should I start to look for my new home?

In the 1980s, when homes were selling faster than flapjacks at the corner diner, homeowners would go out and look for homes before they'd even given a moment's thought to putting theirs on the market. In fact, most folks would put an offer in on a house, play the negotiation game, and have their final counteroffer accepted before they even listed their original home. In the mid-1980s, the real estate market had been so good for so long that many homeowners simply figured they'd be able to sell their homes for outrageous amounts of money in short order to cover their bottoms—and in many cases they were right. For those unfortunate few who couldn't schedule their buy-sale perfectly, there was always a trusty bridge loan to cover the gap between the time when they purchased their new home and closed on their old home.

But the recession of 1990 (which actually started with the crash of home prices in 1989 and continued, some economists say, through 1993) changed this way of thinking. It happened in part because folks who bought new homes in 1989 and 1990 turned around and couldn't sell their original homes. Overnight, the game had changed, and a lot of people got burned. Some homeowners who had taken out bridge loans for a few weeks ended up stuck with them for a year or two, effectively paying three mortgages: their new home's mortgage, their old home's mortgage, and the bridge loan (for the down payment on the new house). You can eat up a lot of equity when you're paying three mortgages and you're not Oprah, Steven Spielberg, or billionaire Bill Gates. Today, most homeowners are cautious about even looking for a new home before theirs is sold. They know that looking means you're at risk of liking something—or worse yet, developing a passion for a particular home. They know that once you get to the "It's perfect, I've got to have it" stage, you're sunk.

On the other hand, if you wait to look for a new house until you've closed on your old house, you're going to end up making an interim move. (See Question 77 for more information on interim moves.) While this ultraconservative position means you won't be paying two or three mortgages, you will have to go through the expense and aggravation of finding two homes and planning two moves.

When should you go out and look for your new home? A large part of how you answer this question will depend on your circumstances. If you're being transferred to another city, and your company is paying for your move and will put you up temporarily in your new location until you find a home, then you should start looking immediately. (You should also immediately put your home on the market.)

If you're trading up and want to be in your new home in time for your children to start school, you should look, but realize that you may not make that self-imposed deadline. In some parts of the country, where strong seller's markets are in force, you may have no trouble selling your old home but great difficulty in finding a new one you'll be satisfied with. Sometimes you can look for a year or more and not find the right house.

Try this middle ground for size: Scout out new neighborhoods a couple of months before you list your home for sale. Visit open houses, perhaps even have your broker show you a few homes in your price range. Once you have a good idea of the general area in which you'd like to live—and the size and price of homes that are available for sale—list your home. Once it's listed, and there is some activity, you can begin your house hunt in earnest. If you can, refrain from making an offer on a new house until you have begun negotiating an offer to sell your original home. Otherwise, you should include a contingency on your purchase offer that specifically states you have to sell your original home before you can close on the new home.

If you're purchasing new construction, the builder will tell you approximately how long it will take to build and when you will be able to close. That three-to-five-month time frame allows you a perfect window of time in which to sell your home. Just remember that new homes can take a few extra weeks to complete if the builder runs into bad weather, scarcity of materials, poor workmanship, or a timing crunch. If you sell your original home too quickly and your new home isn't built yet, you may have to make an interim move or ask your buyers for extra time to stay in your original home.

If you have to put your home up for sale suddenly, with

little or no advance warning, begin your search for a new home immediately. But wait until you have some real activity—or better yet, a good offer—before making an offer on a new home. There is nothing worse than feeling as if you have no home. Homes root us and give us a sense of stability. Barbara and Max started looking for a new home and found a few neighborhoods they liked. A few months later, they put their condo on the market and sold it. It took them about a year to find their new home. Even though they leased their condo back from the new owners during the gap, it was an unsettling period of time. Once they bought their new home, they closed within thirty days and settled right in.

QUESTION 76

Should I make an offer on another home before I sell mine? What is a contingent offer?

Just as window shopping is a completely different concept from shopping the "Day After Thanksgiving" sales, looking for a home is completely different from making an offer to purchase one.

Whether or not you choose to make an offer to purchase a new home before you've sold your older home is a decision only you can make. But think about the following issues before you actually sign your name on the dotted line:

1. *Can I afford two or three mortgages?* If you make an offer to purchase before you've received an offer for your own property, you may get stuck paying two mortgages (one on the new house and one on the old

house). If you need the cash from your old house for a down payment on the new house, you'll have to take out a home equity loan or a bridge loan to cover the gap between the time you purchase the new house and when you sell your original house, taking out the equity built into your current home. A two- or three-loan situation is all right for a couple of days, or even a couple of months. But it can quickly get expensive. Work out the numbers to see what kind of a financial drain these loans would be. (For more information on bridge loans and a worksheet to help you calculate your mortgage and bridge loan expense, see Question 78.)

2. *Am I making an emotional decision or a logical one?* Falling in love with a house may not be a good enough reason to put in an offer before you've sold your original home. As a homeowner, you've probably come to realize that there are a lot of lovely homes in nice neighborhoods. You've probably realized that finding the right home means a compromise between what you want, what you need, and what you can afford to spend. If you're moving to a new city, and your company has agreed to purchase your home if you haven't sold it within a certain period of time, then you can act on your emotions and purchase a home you feel strongly about. If, however, you don't have that financial safety net, think about renting a home temporarily until you've moved closer to selling your own home. Remember, there will always be another house.
3. *Am I in a buyer's market or a seller's market?* Knowing the type of market you're facing both as a seller and as a buyer is a critical factor in deciding whether or

not to make the offer. If you're in a strong seller's market, it's likely that you'll sell your home quickly. On the other hand, other sellers will be selling quickly, too, which may mean you'll see homes you'd like to make an offer on slip right through your fingers. If you're in a strong buyer's market, buyers will, more or less, dictate the terms and timing of your sale. On the flip side, you'll be in the position to do the same once you've sold your home. Remember that homes take longer to sell when buyers control the marketplace than when sellers do.

Making a Contingent Offer

If you find a house that you can't live without, but you still want to be protected financially, consider making an offer contingent on the sale of your original home. A *prior sale contingency* is similar to a financing contingency: If you don't sell your home by a certain date, you can't close on your new home. A prior sale contingency gives you an out, so that if your buyer's contract falls through and he or she cannot purchase your house, you won't be obligated to turn around and purchase your new home.

Although a seller may negotiate a contract that carries a prior sale contingency, and may ultimately accept your offer, don't be surprised if the seller continues to show the home. If you and the seller agree that you have the right to back out of the deal if you can't sell your home, it's only fair that the seller has the right to continue showing his or her home until you satisfy the contingency (by selling your home), you withdraw the contingency, or the seller finds another buyer who makes a contingency-free offer. As a seller yourself, you, too, would want the right to continue marketing your home until all the contingencies in a contract are satisfied or removed, since a contract with contingencies isn't as solid as a contract without them. As we've discussed earlier in the book, contingencies are the weak links of a contract; they give the buyer and the seller room to wriggle out of the contract. And one of the weakest contracts is one that has a contingency for the sale of a buyer's home. It is the weakest link because the sale of that home is dependent on third parties and circumstances beyond your (and your buyer's) control.

One of the ironies of real estate is that as a seller you don't want contingencies, but as a buyer you need them.

QUESTION 77
What is an interim move? Should I consider making one?

Although home buyers are eager to purchase property and sellers are anxious to sell, beneath the surface lies the unpleasant task of actually moving from one location to another. Experts rank the stress associated with moving a houseful of furniture, kids, "stuff," and memories second only to the death of a loved one. The emotional and psychological disruption caused by packing up your belongings and changing locations can overwhelm even the sturdiest of souls.

Most buyers and sellers don't begin to think about moving until after they've begun negotiating—or have accepted—an offer. That can be a problem if you haven't thought about where you are moving to. Finding a house to purchase is going to cause a lot more stress than simply finding a temporary apartment to rent. If you've lived in a house for thirty years, packing is going to be an even more overwhelming experience than if you last moved three or four years ago. Still, the average homeowner takes a look around at the things he or she has accumulated since the last move only after the terms of the deal are set. While most homeowners dread the thought of moving, those sellers who have lived in their homes for long periods of time are hit hardest.

Because the thought of moving often strikes such an unpleasant chord, buyers and sellers try to coordinate their moves. This can be complicated and doubly stressful, since you have the stress of buying and selling at the same time. Financially conservative sellers often wait until their home starts to generate some real interest among potential home buyers before they begin to look for their next home. Many sellers hope they'll find something to purchase in the sixty to ninety days between receipt of an offer to purchase their home and the closing.

Of course, if you can schedule the closings of your purchase and your sale for the same day, or within twenty-four hours, that's great. You move only once, and funds from the sale are available for your purchase. However, the pressure to buy something—anything—within this thirty-to-ninety-day time frame overwhelms some sellers, who fail to recognize that an *interim move* is often an easier and cheaper alternative than purchasing the wrong property in a hurry.

An interim move occurs if there is time between the closing of your old home and the purchase of your new home. With any luck, the interim between your sale and your purchase will be only a few days. But, by design or circumstance, the interim between selling and buying is sometimes much longer. According to the IRS, sellers must purchase a new home within twenty-four months of selling their old one to qualify for the rollover replacement rule. That rule essentially states that if you purchase a new home that is as expensive, or more expensive, than your current residence, you can defer any tax you might owe on any profits you made on that home. (See Question 95 for more information on the rollover replacement rule.) Tax-wise, you have two years to purchase a new home, which could translate into an interim move of up to two years.

Why would anyone want to wait that long to purchase a new home? Sometimes the circumstances are out of our control. If you get transferred for a two-year assignment, it might not pay to purchase a home in your hometown, only to rent it out. Besides, you might not want to live in that neighborhood when you return. If you get transferred permanently to a new city, you might want to wait six months to a year to purchase a new home. That will give you time to explore neighborhoods and suburbs and find one that suits your needs. If you purchase quickly in a new city, you may find yourself regretting it.

Even if you know where you want to live, you might not be lucky enough to find the right home at the right price at the right time. Or the house you buy may need substantial renovations, requiring you to wait several months before moving in.

If you have to make an interim move, plan it carefully. Think about where you're going to live and how long you'll have to be there. Even if you love spending time with your parents or in-laws, moving in with them for four months might not be the right answer for you or your family. Try to find an apartment or house you can rent on a month-to-month basis. If the landlord is willing to give you a *ninety-day-out clause* (which is about the amount of time it takes to negotiate for and close on a home), you should feel free to sign a longer lease.

Although it can be emotionally and physically difficult, not to mention financially draining, to move twice, making that interim move might save you from making the wrong move. And that kind of mistake could cost you a whole lot more.

QUESTION 78

What is a bridge loan? And when might I need one?

It's always nice to receive an offer on your house. But it's especially wonderful if you took out a bridge loan to pay for a new house while you were still living in your old house—and are currently paying the equivalent of three mortgages.

Since buyers became much more cautious about buying during the recession in 1990 and 1991, sellers have become more cautious about committing to a new home until they have received an offer to purchase their original home.

But if you're sure you've found your dream house, and you are certain you don't want to lose it but don't have enough cash on hand for the down payment (you probably have most of your equity in your original home), there is a way for you to close on your home. Consider using a *bridge loan.*

A bridge loan is a short-term method of financing the purchase of a new house before you've sold your old one. Essentially, you "borrow" equity from your primary residence and use it as a down payment for the second home.

Unlike regular first or second mortgages—which can be for as long as thirty years—these loans are good for only short periods of time. Common bridge loan term lengths range from one day to six months. There are other differences. Instead of paying regular installments of principal and interest, the loan may require interest-only payments. Or, the interest on the loan and the entire principal may be due at the end of the loan period. Although the lender will usually renew the loan for a second or third period (or term), don't count on unlimited extensions if, for example, your original home doesn't sell.

Many bankers refer to bridge loans as "interim" loans because they cover the time between the sale of the first house and the purchase of the second. When used this way, a bridge loan can offer a home buyer some relatively cheap time to fix up the new property before he or she actually moves in.

There are lots of pluses to bridge loans, but what many homeowners fail to take into account is exactly how expensive bridge loans can be. Homeowners who take out a bridge loan must continue to pay the mortgage on their primary residence. They must also pay interest on the bridge loan and make mortgage payments on their new property. That's why industry professionals say taking out a bridge loan is like paying three mortgages. That's also why the number of bridge loans is dwarfed by the number of first mortgages, sometimes by as much as a hundred to one.

"Most people have a tough time qualifying for a bridge loan because they are essentially second mortgages. We secure the loan with a lien on their home," said a bank manager in New Jersey.

The costs and fees can be steep, too, with some banks charging a point or two (a point is equal to 1 percent of the loan amount). They may also charge an application fee, an appraisal fee, or a filing charge. These closing costs can add up quickly. Many banks, however, will waive some of these fees if the customer also uses the bank for the mortgage on his or her new property.

So how much does it cost to take out a bridge loan? Let's say you find a $250,000 house in a nice neighborhood. You could take out a $50,000 bridge loan (to pay the down payment) at an interest rate of 9 percent. The up-front fees may total up to $1,000. If you borrowed the money for one month, you would pay approximately $375 in interest ($50,000 × .09 ÷ 12 = $375), so your total bridge loan cost would be $1,375 for that month.

While the first month may seem doable, try paying it month after month. Bridge loans quickly get expensive. In addition to that money, you must also pay the mortgage on the new property, as well as your current mortgage. It's easy to see how bridge loan borrowers can quickly go broke if the sale of their original residence drags out.

Martin, an antiques dealer in the Los Angeles area, nearly had to file for bankruptcy because of a new house he had to have. "It took over two years for me to sell my original home. In the meantime, I had bought another beautiful home. And because of the recession, my antiques business had dried up a bit," he said. "Things were really tight for a long time. It's an unpleasant way to live."

Because bridge loans are so risky, and because the general economic climate has made many sellers and buyers nervous, there has been a general decline in the numbers of customers seeking this financing alternative. "Today, people try to get the old house sold first and then coordinate the closings for the same day," explains Rick, who is president of an Illinois mortgage company. "The reason most people need interim financing is because they closed on their new place on a Friday and won't close on their old place until the following Monday."

How to Find a Bridge Loan

If you've decided that you want or need a bridge loan, you should shop for one as if it were a first mortgage. If you have a lot of equity built up in your home, start with your lender's home equity department first. You may be able to get a *home equity loan* for less money (many lenders offer home equity loans without any points or fees) at a better interest rate than a bridge loan. If you don't have much, or enough, equity built up in your home, start talking to your local lender about bridge loans.

Shop around for a bridge loan the same way you would shop around for a regular mortgage:

- Ask your neighbors, friends, relatives, and broker for references.
- Compare interest rates and the different fees and costs that are tacked on.
- If the lender says he or she will cut the bridge loan fees if you also get the new house's loan there, check to make sure the interest rates and fees on that new loan are comparable to other lenders' loans in your area.
- Ask if the bridge loan is renewable and for how many periods.
- Ask if there are any penalties if you pay off the bridge loan early.
- Ask about the lender's reputation in the community for speed in approving and processing loans. Pay attention if you hear that someone (or several individuals) has had trouble getting his or her loan approved.

Note: A lender will decide whether or not you qualify for a bridge loan the same way as if you were applying for a regular mortgage. The lender will look at your income, assets, and liabilities, and then crunch those numbers together to see if you can afford the bridge loan. If you can't—or don't—pay off the bridge loan when it comes due, the lender can start foreclosure proceedings and force you to sell your original home (on which the lender would have a lien) at a tremendous discount.

PART VII

The Closing

QUESTION 79
What is the closing? And where is it held?

By this point in the process, your thoughts should be turning toward *the closing*. When you bought your home you had a closing, which you may remember as a bunch of folks getting together and signing a lot of papers. Since that closing might have happened ten, twenty, or thirty years ago, let's talk about what a closing is and what your responsibilities are.

Quite simply, the closing is where the buyer gathers together his or her money and hands it to you. In exchange, you give the buyer the deed to your house, the combinations to any locks you're leaving behind, and the key to the front door and, if appropriate, the mailbox.

But we're jumping ahead of ourselves. Why do we have a closing? Well, one attorney put it this way: Would you, the seller, take the buyer's personal check, fold it up and put it in your pocket, and then hand the buyer the deed to your house? Of course not. You would want some security that the check was really going to clear. On the other hand, the buyer wants some assurance that the deed is truly yours to give. The buyer's lender wants the same assurance. From the money the buyer gives you, you will want to pay off any mortgage you have on the house. The broker wants some security that you will pay the commission. And both the buyer's and the seller's attorneys want to know their fee will be paid.

In other words, everyone wants to be protected. It is from this point that today's closing evolved. *Closing a transaction* has always meant that point in time when the deal is completed. One party has paid another for certain rights, privileges, property, or other goods and services. When the passing of money or other consideration has occurred, and the goods and services have been received, a deal is deemed closed. Kaput. Finished.

According to a spokesperson at Chicago Title & Trust, about 99 percent of all residential real estate deals are closed with the help of a title company. As we discussed earlier, the title company performs several tasks during a settlement, or closing, including issuing title insurance for the buyer and his or her lender. To do this, the title company researches the chain of title to the home, often starting back when the land was first purchased from the government. The buyer's attorney will review the information furnished by the title company to make sure the buyer gets "good and marketable" title to the home when you close. Once you, the seller, have resolved any outstanding issues (that is, if they need to be resolved), the title company will then insure title in the buyer's name—with any exceptions shown on the policy—in the amount of the purchase price.

Title companies facilitate the closing by providing a forum for the free exchange of documents and releasing of funds. Generally, at the closing, the title company acts as an agent for the lender, meaning that the title company works to protect the lender's best interest (usually, for an additional fee, the title company can act as escrow agent for both buyer and seller). Depending on your local real estate customs, you, the seller, will often decide which title company will be used, particularly if you are paying for the title insurance. Who pays for, and orders, the title policy is almost always dictated by local custom. If the title company acts as an agent for the lender, the closing will generally take place at the offices of the title company or at another mutually agreed-upon location. Your attorney or closing agent will assist you in this process.

In several states, including California and New York, it's more common to have what's known as an escrow closing. In this case, the title company or escrow company acts for the benefit of both parties, using a document called an *escrow agreement*. This means that the title company will disburse money only after certain events take place. For example, in an escrow closing, the title or escrow company will send someone to the recorder's office (where deeds are recorded). Once the name on the deed has been verified as being yours, and it has been determined that there has not been an event that would impair your ability to convey title, and the transfer of title has been accomplished, the title company will allow the closing to take place. If there are any problems along the way, the title company returns the closing funds to the buyer and unwinds the transaction.

There isn't too much work for a seller to do at a closing other than, of course, sign the closing documents prepared by the attorney or escrow closing agent. The onus falls upon the buyer, who must review both the seller's documents and the loan documents, and then sign on dozens of dotted lines. After the buyer signs the loan documents, there is an exchange of documents between the buyer and seller and title company (or escrow agent). Depending on the local custom, you will have to provide certain documents for the buyer's inspection, so that he or she can verify that they are correct. These include: the deed; the bill of sale; an affidavit of title; any documentation required in the contract, including paid water bills and certificates of compliance with laws pertaining to smoke-detection equipment, lead paint, termite, or radon inspection; a copy (or the original) of the signed seller disclosure form, also known as a transfer disclosure document; condominium assessment full-payment certificate; co-op assessment full-payment certificate; condominium or co-op insurance certificate; property survey (except for condos and co-ops) or PUD (planned unit development) survey.

There are other documents you may have to sign, including:

- The RESPA (Real Estate Settlement Procedures Act) "HUD-1" statement, which outlines who provides the money and from which sources, and details how the money gets paid out.
- A disclosure statement about any construction contracts or any agreements entered into within the past three to six months for work already done or to be

done to the property. This insures that you have no outstanding obligations to contractors for work performed or to be performed that would entitle them to file a lien on the property.

- A disclosure statement about who resides at the property other than the buyer or seller if the property is leased and there are tenants involved.
- A statement about any other matters that could ultimately affect title to the property, such as lawsuits, wills, or judgments.
- Internal Revenue Service (IRS) form 1099, which relates to the sales price of the home. You will furnish the title company or escrow agent with your Social Security number, and IRS form 1099 will be sent to the IRS. It will be used to cross-check your IRS tax return with documentation signed by the title company regarding the purchase and sale of the home. (For a copy of IRS form 1099, see Appendix II.)

Many of these documents must be signed and notarized. Each state and county has its own peculiar quirks regarding documentation. For example, any document that will be recorded in Hawaii must be typed and signed in black ink only. In some parts of the country, the notary stamp must be embossed, while in others a black ink stamp has replaced the embossed stamp. Your attorney or escrow agent should advise you as to the particulars for your closing.

Once all of the documents have been signed, dated, and notarized, the title company can proceed with the review of the documents and then with the disbursement of funds. It will take the buyer's money and cut checks to the seller, the seller's lender (if applicable), the brokers, the title company, attorneys, surveyors, and other parties who must be paid at closing. Since everyone usually gets paid out of the closing proceeds, it's easy to see why the title company doesn't accept personal checks, except for amounts under, say, $50. (Title companies accept only cashier's or certified checks, or a wire transfer, because that's like accepting cash. They are not, however, set up to accept real greenbacks.)

In the next few questions, I'll dissect some of the more complicated pieces of the closing and explain why they're important.

QUESTION 80

Do I have to attend the closing? And what should I bring with me?

Buyers almost always have to attend the closing because there are loan documents to be signed, and papers to be read, and disclosures to wade through. Sellers, on the other hand, have little to do at a closing. In fact, if you sign all the documents ahead of time, your attorney or escrow agent may be able to arrange for you to skip the closing entirely.

While you can skip the closing, I don't recommend that you do, except in case of an emergency. Selling a home is a complicated, detail-riddled financial transaction. Any one of those hundreds of details could go nutty at the last moment, and fixing the problem could require you to be on hand. What happens if the buyer finds something wrong with the house on the final walk-through? If you're not there to check out the "damage," your attorney or broker will have to find you before the closing can proceed.

What should you bring to the closing? Unless you've made arrangements to stay in your house after the closing or you've already moved out, the closing will be the last time you will have anything to do with your home. These are the items you should bring with you to the closing:

- The deed to the property.
- The affidavit of title.
- The bill of sale.
- The no-lien affidavit, also known in some states as the ALTA statement. This is the statement regarding contractors that certifies that you are having no work done on the property that would cause a mechanic's lien to be filed against the title to your property.
- The affidavit certificate regarding your Social Security number, for IRS reporting purposes.
- A certificate stating you are not subject to withholding by the IRS on transactions over $300,000. (Certain foreigners or foreign entities may be subject to withholding on the transfer of property.)
- The transfer declaration, which you need in order to get your municipal transfer stamps.
- A paid receipt for real estate taxes.
- If you are representing yourself in the closing, you will need to prepare and bring to the closing all closing documents.
- House keys, all sets, for every lock in the house or on the property (including the tool shed or garage door).
- The garage door opener (this may be brought to the closing or left on the kitchen counter).
- The combination for any lock you plan to leave on the property.
- The mailbox key(s).
- The paid assessment letter. If you live in a condo or co-op, or are part of a homeowners' association, you

should bring along your paid assessment letter that indicates the condo or co-op has waived its first option rights.

- The insurance certificate from the homeowners' or co-op association that names the buyer as the new insured party with buyer's lender's information on the certificate.
- Many municipalities require sellers to provide the buyer with copies of paid water bills, building inspection forms, and certificates of compliance with building ordinances.
- A survey, if you live in a state that requires the seller, rather than the buyer, to deliver the survey of property.
- Any documents needed to clear title, including the old release of mortgage you forgot to record ten years ago.
- Transfer stamps. In many municipalities, sellers have to go to their city hall and purchase transfer stamps in advance of the closing.
- The codes for the home's alarm system.
- The home warranty, or the application for a home warranty, if you are providing one to the buyer.
- The access card or key to garage or parking areas, pool, exercise facility, or general area. Don't forget to bring the key to the main entrance of your building and any storage lockers.
- Any paperwork, including warranties or instruction manuals, may be brought to the closing or left on the kitchen counter for your buyer.
- Your favorite pen (with which to sign your name).

Successful Home Seller Tip: When you go to your local city or village hall or to the water department, you may need information regarding the property and the buyer. If you're buying transfer stamps, you may need the property identification number or the tax record number (you'll find this number on your property tax bill, or you can call your county assessor's office for this information). You may also need the names of the buyers, the exact purchase price, and the anticipated date of the closing. In addition, you may also need to tell your local government what type of deed you're using to convey title to the buyer. Among the top choices are the warranty deed, the executor's deed, and the quit-claim deed. (For more information on these deeds, see Question 83.)

Successful Home Seller Tip: It's a good idea to keep your house sale file up-to-date. Consider starting a separate file (or use a separate envelope within the file) for the documentation you'll need to bring to the closing. Use the above list as a guide, and check off items as you get them accomplished. That way you won't be caught unprepared on the actual day.

Negative Equity

If you're selling your home for less than the amount of the mortgage plus closing costs and the broker's commission, you are going to have to bring cash (in the form of a certified or cashier's check) to the closing. You will need to bring enough cash to pay off your lender, your broker, and your attorney, as well as any closing costs. Your attorney or escrow officer should be able to help you figure out what the number will be.

QUESTION 81

What is RESPA? What is the HUD-1 statement and what does it tell me?

In 1974, Congress decided that Americans were suffering from abuses in the title industry. Title companies were giving kickbacks to real estate agents and brokers who referred buyers to settlement agents. Congress decided buyers should be free to choose their own title company or settlement agency. So the Real Estate Settlement Procedures Act (RESPA) was passed to address these issues. It has since been amended and updated to better regulate changing market conditions and new technologies in the real estate industry.

The HUD-1 Settlement Statement

RESPA also requires that buyers and sellers be given a copy of the HUD-1 settlement statement (commonly called "the HUD-1"), which outlines exactly what monies come in and to whom they are paid. This is a closing document that you will have to sign. It is completed by the title company or escrow agent from all the information received from the seller, buyer, brokers, and buyer's lender. The HUD-1 is instructive for both buyers and sellers because you can see exactly where the money comes from and where it is going. The buyer's and seller's costs are also itemized side by side. It also neatly wraps up a lot of the issues we have been, and will be, talking about. (See Appendix II for a complete HUD-1 form.)

On the right side, the "Summary of Seller's Transac-

A. **Settlement Statement**

U.S. Department of Housing and Urban Development

OMB No. 2502-0265

B. Type of Loan

1. ☐ FHA 2. ☐ FmHA 3. ☐ Conv. Unins. 4. ☐ VA 5. ☐ Conv. Ins	6. File Number	7. Loan Number	8. Mortgage Insurance Case Number

C. Note: This form is furnished to give you a statement of actual settlement costs. Amounts paid to and by the settlement agent are shown. Items marked "(p.o.c.)" were paid outside the closing; they are shown here for informational purposes and are not included in the totals.

D. Name and Address of Borrower	**E. Name and Address of Seller**	**F. Name and Address of Lender**

G. Property Location	**H. Settlement Agent** / Place of Settlement	**I. Settlement Date**

J. Summary of Borrower's Transaction			**K. Summary of Seller's Transaction**		
100.	**Gross Amount Due from Borrower**		**400.**	**Gross Amount Due to Seller**	
101.	Contract sales price		401.	Contract sales price	
102.	Personal property		402.	Personal property	
103.	Settlement charges to borrower (line 1400)		403.		
104.			404.		
105.			405.		
	Adjustments for Items Paid by Seller in Advance			**Adjustments for Items Paid by Seller in Advance**	
106.	City/town taxes to		406.	City/town taxes to	
107.	County taxes to		407.	County taxes to	
108.	Assessments to		408.	Assessments to	
109.			409.		
110.			410.		
111.			411.		

tions" starts out by indicating the *contract sales price* plus the price of any *personal property* being sold to the buyer within the transaction. The next item is the *adjustments for items paid by the seller in advance*. These are items you paid for in advance and need to be reimbursed, including any city, town, or village taxes, county taxes, and condo or co-op assessments.

The next section of the HUD-1 deals with *reductions in the amount due to the seller*. These might include any excess deposit made by the buyer, any charges to the seller, and the payoff of the first and second mortgage loans. At this point, there are *adjustments for items unpaid by the seller*, including city, town, or village taxes, county taxes, and any condo or co-op assessments. (In other words, if you haven't paid these items, they will be deducted from your total proceeds.)

The left side (the buyer's side) of the first page of the HUD-1 also starts with the gross amount due from the borrower (the contract sales price plus the price of any personal property and settlement charges), the adjustments for items paid by the seller in advance, money paid by, or on behalf of, the borrower, and adjustments for items unpaid by the seller. Some of the totals from the first page are taken from an itemization on the second page. Finally, the bottom line on the first page indicates how much cash the seller will receive from the deal.

The next page looks at the charges owed by the buyer and the seller, including sales/broker's commission, survey costs, attorney's fees, title charges, and government recording and transfer charges.

A separate page, which isn't part of the HUD-1 but is given out by some title or escrow companies, looks at disbursements—who gets what money and whose name is on which check. There will be as many as ten to fifteen checks cut at the closing, including ones for title insurance, city or county stamp taxes, inspections, the real estate broker, the mortgage insurance premium, the real estate attorneys, and payments to pay off any mortgages or liens, among others. Keep in mind that in most cases your lender will release the amount held for real estate taxes and insurance (if there are any) to you within thirty to forty-five days of the closing. After all, you won't need real estate tax and insurance escrows for property you've already sold.

Some folks feel that RESPA is a waste of time. Others find the disclosures contained within the HUD-1 useful to consumers. Once you get to the closing, you can decide for yourself.

QUESTION 82

What documents will I have to sign at the closing?

Your hand is going to thank you for being a seller. As a seller, you have far fewer documents to sign than the buyer, who must sign all of his or her loan documents and disclosure statements.

You will, however, have to put your John Hancock on a few pieces of paper, including:

- The HUD-1 settlement statement.
- The closing statement (a document between buyer and seller).
- The deed.
- The affidavit of title and the bill of sale (depending on the state in which you live).
- A statement regarding liens on the property (again, the form this statement takes depends on the state).
- Declaration forms to the state, county, and municipality that state the sales price of your home and the amount of transfer tax you are paying. These forms depend on the state in which you live. In New York, for example, you must sign a form declaring your capital gains and the tax you are paying. If the sales price is over $300,000, you must sign a nonforeign affidavit (which says you are not a foreign citizen and are not subject to special withholding of proceeds by the IRS).
- The disbursement statement, depending on the state and the title company.
- A personal information affidavit, which insures that you are who you say you are (as opposed to someone

else with the same or similar name and perhaps a host of outstanding liens or lawsuits).

There may be other documents. If you are working with a title company or escrow agent, the title officer or escrow officer will prepare most of the documents you'll need to sign at the closing. If you're working with a real estate attorney, that attorney will work with the title or escrow officer to prepare the documents. If you're a FSBO and you're not using a title officer or escrow officer, you'll have to take some of the responsibility for making sure that you prepare and sign all of the documents you need to close.

QUESTION 83

How does title get transferred? What kinds of deeds are there?

Some of the papers you'll sign at the closing include the deed and a document that essentially states that you are who you say you are and that you have the right to sell your home. Once you sign these (and other) papers, and once the buyer has his or her funds together (cash and a mortgage, usually), the title company will exchange the buyer's funds for your deed and in the process transfer title from you to the buyer.

There are two types of deeds that are commonly used: the *warranty deed* and, to a lesser degree, the *quitclaim deed.* If you use a warranty deed (and most deeds are like this), it means that you guarantee that you are delivering title to the buyer. It gives the buyer recourse if, for example, you are a charlatan and are selling a legal interest in a property you do not own or if the title is not marketable.

A quitclaim deed is used to transfer any title or interest a seller may have in a property to a buyer, but this deed does not warrant (or guarantee) that the seller actually has a valid or legal interest to transfer. The famous Brooklyn Bridge scenario illustrates this nicely. Let's say you're in the market for a bridge. I come to you and say, "I own the Brooklyn Bridge. But it's for sale, for the right price." You make me an offer. I counter your offer, and we agree on a price. At the closing, I give you a quitclaim deed for the Brooklyn Bridge that transfers any legal interest I have in the bridge to you. Of course, I don't own the Brooklyn Bridge, nor do I have a legal interest in it, so essentially I've sold you nothing. If I had given you a warranty deed, you would have a claim against me for the bridge.

Quitclaim deeds came about because people didn't want to give the warranties (basic as they are) in a warranty deed or because they needed to convey any interest they might have in a property without knowing exactly what they owned or what interest they had. Again, since lenders require that buyers purchase title insurance to protect their interest in the deal, there is little difference between a warranty deed and a quitclaim deed for the average buyer and the average seller as long as the deed is reviewed by the title company and the proper insurance is obtained. However, trustees of trust accounts and executors of estates do not give warranty deeds and usually use *executor* deeds, which are similar to quitclaim deeds. Your attorney or your escrow officer will use a warranty deed unless you request a quit-claim deed.

QUESTION 84

What are my closing costs likely to be?

Closing costs are the bane of a buyer's or seller's existence. They are seemingly endless, pesky in nature, and can add up to quite a lot of money. Who remembers to subtract the $10 you'll spend to get a copy of your paid water bill when figuring out how much money you're going to net from the sale of your home?

A buyer's closing costs might typically range from 2 to 7 percent of the loan amount. If the buyer borrows $100,000 to purchase your home, he or she might end up paying an additional $2,000 to $7,000 in points, fees, taxes, and other costs.

As a seller, you may have to pay even more than that, since the typical seller's costs start with a 5 to 7 percent brokerage commission. Onto that you'll tack extra fees, taxes, and other costs. The bottom line is: Closing costs can be expensive for sellers. If you're expecting a big fat check on closing day, you don't want to be surprised by how much smaller that check actually is after your closing costs have been paid.

Real estate attorneys say a list of the usual fees and costs can include up to twenty items no matter which side of the deal you're on. And if you're selling *and* buying, you'll get hit twice. The following is a list of closing costs for sellers. Remember, not every charge will apply to your sale, and your actual fee may be higher or lower depending on your specific situation. Ask your real estate attorney, broker, or escrow agent to help you go over this list and identify how much each item might cost. At the end of the list is a worksheet that you can fill in when you get your finalized closing costs.

Closing Costs for Sellers

- *Cost of the survey*—varies by area, usually $150 to $300.
- *Title insurance*—depends on the sales price of the home, usually $150 to $500 plus.
- *Recorded release of mortgage*, which verifies that your mortgage has been completely paid off by the sale proceeds—usually $20 to $45.
- *Broker's commission*—if you're using a full-service brokerage firm, expect to pay anywhere from 5 to 7 percent of the sales price. If you're using a discount broker, or if you've sold the home yourself to a buyer represented by a buyer broker, your cost may range from a few hundred dollars to 3 percent of the sales price.
- *Local city, town, or village property transfer tax; county transfer tax; state transfer tax; state capital gains tax*—the charges that you, the seller, will pay vary from city to city and from state to state. In Illinois, for example, the seller picks up the county tax ($.50 per $1,000 of the sales price) and the state tax ($1 per $1,000 of the sales price). In Chicago, the buyer picks up the city transfer tax (a hefty $3.75 per $500 of the sales price). There may be other special taxes on high-end (expensive) property. In New York, sellers pay a state capital gains tax. And certain kinds of property, such as co-ops, may under certain circumstances be excluded from property transfer taxes. In general, property transfer taxes can range from nothing to $10 per $1,000 of the sales price or more. Or you may be assessed a flat fee of $25 or $50 per transaction.
- *Credit to the buyer of unpaid real estate taxes* for the prior

year or the current year (depending on your state)—variable.

- *Attorney's fee*—if you need an attorney, fees generally start at around $250. As we discussed earlier in the book, many excellent real estate attorneys charge only a flat fee for their services. If your deal turns out to be particularly complicated or difficult, the attorney may charge you a small amount extra. (But any extra charges that may be entailed should have been spelled out in the engagement letter your attorney sent you when you hired him or her.)
- *FHA fees and costs*—all fees are now negotiable between an FHA buyer and a seller, though the lender may not agree to close if the buyer can't afford all the fees and the seller refuses to pick them up.
- *Condo/co-op move-out fee*—a building charge that can run from nothing to more than $400.
- *Association transfer fees*—often required for condominium and town house buyers; sellers have occasionally been stuck paying these as well.
- *Paid utility bills*—in many areas, the local city or village officials will not let you close until you have proven that you are current on your utility bills. They may charge you anywhere from $10 to $25 for each copy of a paid utility bill, including water, sewer, garbage, or electricity (you will also be charged for usage through the day of closing).
- *Certificate of compliance with building codes*—your local municipality may not charge for inspecting such items as your fire extinguisher and smoke detectors, or there may be a small fee, such as $10 or more, plus the cost of correcting any items that are not in compliance.

- *Home inspections*—in some areas, local custom dictates that the seller pay for pest, radon, and other inspections, which can range from $25 to $125 each.
- *Association reserves*—in some areas, the reserves held by condominium and homeowner associations are credited to the seller on the basis of the seller's percentage of ownership in the association.

(Just so you don't think the buyer gets off scot-free, he or she will also pay a long list of closing costs, including: lender's points (a point is 1 percent of the loan amount); application fee, up to $350; lender's credit report, up to $60; lender's processing fee, up to $125; lender's document preparation fee, up to $200; lender's appraisal fee, up to $275; prepaid interest on the loan; lender's insurance escrow; lender's real estate tax escrow; lender's tax escrow service fee, up to $65; title insurance cost for the lender's policy, up to $300 or more; special endorsements to the title, up to $50 each; any outstanding home inspection fees, up to $275 each; title company closing fee, up to $400; recording fees for the deed or mortgage, up to $75; local city, town, or village property transfer tax, ranging from nothing to $10 per $1,000 of the sales price; attorney's fee; condo/co-op move-in fee; association transfer fees; and credit checks for condo and co-op buildings by the board.)

Here is a blank closing cost sheet for you to use to figure out exactly how much you'll be paying in closing costs.

Seller's Closing Cost Sheet

Name ____
Property Address ________________________________
Closing Date ___________________________________

Broker's Commission		__________
Survey		__________
Title Insurance		__________
Recorded Release of Mortgage		__________
City, Town, or Village Transfer Taxes		__________
County Transfer Tax		__________
State Transfer Tax		__________
Capital Gains Tax or Other Tax		__________
Credit to the Buyer for Unpaid Real Estate Taxes		__________
Attorney's Fee		
FHA Fees and Costs Paid for the Buyer (only if necessary)		__________
Copies of Paid Utility Bills	Water	__________
	Sewer	__________
	Garbage	__________
	Electricity	__________
Certificate of Compliance with Building Codes		__________
Condo/Co-op Move-out Fee		__________
Home Inspections		__________
First Mortgage Payoff		__________
Second Mortgage Payoff		__________
Courier Fee to Pay Off Loans		__________
Credit to Buyer for Unpaid Association Assessments		__________
Repair Credit Given to the Buyer		__________
Cost of Home Warranty Policy		__________
Other Credits Given to the Buyer		__________

Other Fees and Charges:

____________________ ________

____________________ ________

____________________ ________

____________________ ________

____________________ ________

Total Closing Costs ________

Successful Home Seller Tip: It's important to keep a list of your closing costs—as well as a copy of all your purchase and sales documents—so that you can accurately figure out your home's cost basis. The IRS requires you to keep many documents, but it's helpful to know not only your closing cost expenses but to have copies of receipts of your capital expenditures (like plumbing improvements, or a new roof). For more information on figuring out the cost basis for your home, see Question 93.

QUESTION 85

How much money will I get from the sale of my home?

Now that you've figured out how much money you'll be paying in closing costs, you're probably wondering how much cash you'll take away from the closing. It's not particularly difficult to calculate these figures (it requires only simple addition and subtraction), but it's important not to miss any categories of costs.

Let's say that you are selling your home for $250,000. You're paying a full broker's commission of 6 percent

($15,000), and other closing costs of, say, $2,500. To calculate roughly how much cash you'll take away from the closing, start with the sales price and subtract your costs:

$250,000 - $15,000 - $2,500 = $232,500

If you were selling this home, you would walk away from the closing with approximately $232,500 in cash. Of course, if you have a mortgage on the property, you'll have to subtract the mortgage balance from the sales price.

Use this spreadsheet to help you calculate your final cash on hand:

Cash from the Sale of My House

Sales Price	-	________
Closing Costs (use total from the table in Question 84)	-	________
	-	________
	-	________
Buyer's Credit to Seller for Prepaid Taxes	+	________
Buyer's Purchase of Personal Property (furniture, lawn mower, etc.)	+	________
Buyer's Credit to Seller for Prepaid Association Assessments	+	________
Buyer's Credit to Seller for Association Reserves	+	________
Buyer's Credit to Seller for Paid Water and Sewer Charges	+	________
Other Cash Paid by the Buyer to the Seller		
________________________	+	________
________________________	+	________
________________________	+	________
Net Cash		________

Figuring Out Your Profit

Figuring out how much cash you'll take away from the closing is a different ball of wax than figuring out your profit or calculating the cost basis of your home. To figure out if you've made a profit or loss on your home, start with the sales price and subtract the purchase price, the cost of purchase, the cost of sale and any improvements you made to the home. For example, let's say you paid $144,000 for your home and sold it for $220,000. Let's assume the cost of purchase was $10,000 and the cost of sale was $10,000. And let's assume you put $40,000 into capital improvements. Here's how the math would work:

$220,000	- $144,000	- $10,000	- $10,000	- $40,000	= $16,000
Sales Price	Purchase Price	Cost of Purchase	Cost of Sale	Cost of Improvements	Profit

Note: For more information on calculating your profit and calculating the cost basis of your home, see Question 94.

QUESTION 86

How do I calculate prorations?

Let's say that Wendy and Karl make an offer to purchase Steve and Judy's home. In the two months up until the closing, some bills come due that must be paid. Steve and Judy pay the water bill (which comes every six months), the second installment of real estate taxes, and a homeowners' association bill (which comes every two months). On the day of closing, Steve and Judy's attorney tells Wendy and Karl how much their share of these prorated expenses is.

Almost every closing has some prorated costs, simply because we don't pay for every housing need on a daily basis. Can you imagine trucking on down to the county clerk's office to pay your real estate taxes *every day?* What about your water bill? Homeowner association dues? Many of these costs are spread out over a long period of time. Some are billed to you directly and are cut off when you move, with a final bill going to your new address; but some are not cut off. Depending on where you live in the country, you pay your real estate taxes once or twice a year. It isn't fair for Steve and Judy to have paid an entire year's worth of property taxes if they only live in the house for nine months of that year before selling to Wendy and Karl. Likewise, if Wendy and Karl bought the house just after the second installment of property taxes was due, it wouldn't be fair for them to pay for six months of taxes when they would live in the home for only three months of that year.

So a little bit of math evens things out for everyone. How do you calculate prorations? Take the number of days covered by the bill and divide the bill by that number. That gives you a daily fee. Then multiply the daily fee by the number of days up to and including the closing. For example, let's say Steve and Judy's property taxes are $3,000, payable in two installments of $1,500 each, half due on March 15 (for the first six months of the year) and the other half due on September 15 (for the last six months of the year). The first $1,500 represents 182 days and the second $1,500 represents the second 183 days of the year:

$$\$1{,}500 \div 183 = \$8.20 \text{ per day}$$

If the closing is on September 16, Steve and Judy have already paid the real estate property taxes for the rest of the year. At closing, Wendy and Karl would have to reimburse them for the days of the year they are going to live in the house. It's 106 days from September 17 to the end of the year, including the closing date. Multiply 106 by the $8.20 daily fee:

106 days × $8.20 daily fee = $869.20

Wendy and Karl would owe Steve and Judy $869.20 at closing. It can work in reverse also. Let's say the closing is on September 14. On September 15, Wendy and Karl pay the $1,500 second installment of real estate taxes. It's 79 days from July 1 (the beginning of the second half of the year) until September 14 (including the day of closing). Multiply 79 by the $8.20 daily fee:

76 days × $8.20 daily fee = $647.80

If the closing was held on September 14, Steve and Judy would owe Wendy and Karl $647.80 for their share of property taxes.

In some states, if the next tax bill has not come out and the amount of that bill is not yet known, it's common to ask the previous owners to pay a little extra in real estate taxes above the daily fee, because in many areas (despite local politicians' promises) property taxes rise each year. So instead of asking for the daily fee multiplied by the number of days, the buyer might ask you to put up anywhere from 105 percent to 115 percent (depending on the custom in your area) of the daily fee to cover any increases. In our example, the daily fee of $8.20 would be increased anywhere from $8.61 to $9.43 to cover any increases in taxes. Your particular circumstances and the customs in your area will dictate the total increased amount.

(What happens if you pay the 110 percent of the daily fee and property taxes go down or stay the same? Your contract can stipulate that the buyer is supposed to tell you how much property taxes were. If they are lower, your contract can state that the buyer must return the excess property taxes to you. If they come in higher, there may be a provision in the contract that the buyer can come to you for your fair share above and beyond the fee you've already paid. Consult with your attorney for details regarding local custom.)

Real estate attorneys (or your broker or your escrow agent, if you live in a state where attorneys are not used for house closings) will calculate prorations for every bill that has some sort of shared time arrangement, including gas bills, water bills, assessments to homeowners associations, and real estate taxes. (In some unique situations, this may include insurance policies and other service agreements the buyer will have to pay for.)

Note: If you're delivering a homeowner's warranty to the buyers, you will have paid the premium up front as an inducement to get the buyer to purchase the home. Sometimes the buyer will ask that a homeowner's warranty be included as part of the contract. In that case, you will still have paid the premium up front. The buyer should be responsible for any service fees. (For more information on homeowner's warranties, please see Question 29).

Any bill can be prorated using basic math, but it's best to end certain services on closing day so that you don't have to prorate everything. Generally, telephone service can be shut off when an owner vacates a home, and the new owners can start their own account. The local electric company will generally change the name on the service the day of closing and begin billing the new owners. The same is true for the local gas company.

Sometimes attorneys draw up a reproration agreement that provides that the buyer and seller will recalculate the bill after the fact to reflect the actual amount paid. Here's how it works: If you thought the bill was going to be $100 and your share is 25 percent, you would have paid the buyer $25. But if the actual bill ends up being only $80, your share is only $20, so the buyer would owe you $5, which is paid whenever the recalculation is done.

Sometimes proration money is kept in escrow (by a disinterested third party), which usually happens only with substantial amounts of money. The escrow then makes payments to the buyer based on the bills that come in, and will return any extra money to the seller.

Successful Home Seller Tip: Local custom dictates much of what happens with prorations. For example, which side receives the benefit of closing day is determined by local custom rather than negotiation (though I suppose everything is technically subject to negotiation). Your attorney or your broker should be able to advise you on your local customs.

QUESTION 87

Do I have to pay off my mortgage when I close? What about my home equity loan?

When you take out a mortgage, you give a lien on your property to the lender as collateral for the loan. That means, if you default on your mortgage, the lender has the right to begin foreclosure proceedings and sell your home to pay off the loan.

Virtually all loans have a *due-on-sale clause* that states that the lender can demand payment in full of the outstanding amount of a loan upon the sale of your home. The reason lenders include a due-on-sale clause is simple: If the lender is relying on your ability to pay off the loan, he or she knows that as long as you live on the property you have an interest in making the payments.

Thus, lenders require you to pay off your loan as part of the closing. Before the closing, they will issue you a *payoff letter*, which details how much interest and principal you owe on your loan as of the date of closing and how much interest you owe per day after the closing (just in case you don't deliver payment to the lender on the day of the closing or if the closing is delayed by a couple of days). As part of the closing proceedings, the title company or escrow agent will cut a check to your lender and mail it. Remember, once you get the release of mortgage, you need to record it at your local recorder of deeds office.

Successful Home Seller Tip: Sometimes it's cheaper to spend $10 to $15 to send your payment by overnight courier to the lender than to pay the per-day charge you'd owe if you were to send the payment by regular mail.

If the buyer is assuming your mortgage, you will transfer your debt and obligations to him or her, and your property will still remain as the collateral for the loan. In this case, you're not technically paying off the loan but are transferring your obligations to repay the loan to another individual. Remember to have your lender release you from further obligations under your loan, otherwise you will still be on the hook for the loan if your buyer does not make the payments.

Home Equity Loans

Home equity loans essentially function as second home mortgages. One of the many similarities is the due-on-sale clause. Home equity loans are almost always due on the sale of the property. Your home equity loan lender has the right to foreclose on your property and sell it to repay your obligations just as your primary lender does. And home equity lenders generally do not allow these loans to be assumed by another party. So when you sell, expect the home equity loan to take a bite out of the closing proceeds.

QUESTION 88

How do I pay off my loan?

Each year, millions of homeowners pay off their mortgages. Some refinance their loans for lower rates. Most pay off their loans because they sold their home and are taking out a new loan to pay for their next house. The rest have either reached the bitter end of their loan term, or won the lottery and decided that making a monthly mortgage payment is something they no longer want to think about.

Paying off your loan isn't a terribly difficult process, but there are a few caveats about which you should be aware. If you've hired a real estate attorney, or are working with an escrow agent, you may find the process smooth as silk. However, if you are not using an attorney or are closing the transaction without a title company or escrow officer, pay strict attention to the details. It is these that can trip you up at a closing.

Starting the Process

If you're selling your home, your real estate attorney or escrow agent will start the process by asking your lender to issue something called a payoff statement—or in some states, a demand statement. If you're working alone, you'll have to call your lender and make the same request. Some lenders will ask you to send the request in writing.

The payoff statement tells the borrower how much cash is needed to pay off the loan in full. The statement shows the principal balance and the amount of daily interest due as of a certain date.

Joe, a loan officer in Northridge, California, was working to help one customer pay off his loan. The homeowner's loan balance was $156,944, with an interest rate of 7 percent. The daily interest was $30.45. If the customer decided to pay off the loan on September 5, and had already made his September 1 payment, he would have to pay $156,944 plus $152.25 in interest to cover the first five days of the month. (Of course, this assumed that the lender was nearby and could be paid in person. Otherwise, additional days of interest need to be added through the actual date the lender receives the payment.)

One of the biggest mistakes consumers make is not realizing that payoff statements are only valid for a short period of time. Rarely are payoff or demand statements good for more than a few weeks, and in some cases they're good for only a few days.

At the closing, the title or escrow officer either cuts a check to the lender in the amount listed on the payoff statement, wire transfers the funds to the lender, or sends the check by mail or overnight courier service.

While paying off your loan seems easy, there are some caveats you should be aware of:

- *Make your regular payments.* Homeowners often think that making a regular payment just before closing is like throwing away money. If you fail to make these payments, you will be in default of your loan agreement, may jeopardize your on-time payment history, and may be charged a late penalty.
- *FHA loans are different.* Homeowners who are paying off FHA loans should know that FHA accepts funds for paying off a loan only on the first of the month. If you close on the second, third, or eighteenth of the month, you'll owe interest for the whole month. The bottom line: FHA buyers should close as close to the end of the month as possible.
- *Late charges don't go away.* If you don't take care of your late charges before closing on your loan, the late charge will be added to your payoff amount.
- *Incorrect statement.* If you made extra payments on your loan that weren't credited correctly, ask your lender for a historical record of all transactions on your account for the period in question. If there is a discrepancy, says Mark, a real estate attorney in Chicago, you'll have to prove that you made the payment (a canceled check should suffice) and that it was credited incorrectly.
- *Beware of extra fees.* In some states lenders charge the

borrower a fee each time the lender issues a payoff statement. If you shop around for escrow companies and grant four different companies permission to request a payoff statement, you could be charged for four payoff statements. One lender in California charges $60 for each payoff or demand statement, the maximum currently allowed in that state. Not every state, however, allows lenders to charge this fee. Also, make sure you order your payoff statement well ahead of the closing. Lenders may charge as much as $25 to fax the statement to you.

- *Don't forget your escrow accounts.* Lenders are required to return money in impound or escrow accounts within a short period of time, mortgage experts say. A few lenders simply subtract the amount in the impound account from the principal and interest needed to pay off the loan. But if the lender just paid your real estate taxes, and the amount of the taxes was more than was in the escrow account, you will owe money to the lender. Ask the lender to indicate the date and last amount paid for real estate taxes on the statement. (For more information on getting your impound or escrow accounts refunded to you, see Question 89.)

Lenders suggest that homeowners either bring in their final payments in person, or send them via a guaranteed overnight delivery service. "For the homeowner we've been working with, every day we don't receive his check costs him an extra $30.45," says Joe. "It would certainly pay for him to overnight that check to us."

QUESTION 89

If I have a lender, when do I get my escrow or impound account money back?

If you plumb the deep recesses of your brain, and think back to the day you bought your home and closed on your loan, you may remember setting up real estate property tax and insurance escrow accounts with your lender.

These escrow accounts—which are also called "impound accounts" by some lenders in some states—are where the lender holds the cash needed to pay your real estate taxes and hazard or property insurance premiums. Each month, in addition to your mortgage, you've been paying approximately one-twelfth of your real estate taxes and insurance premiums to these accounts. Once or twice a year (depending on when you receive your property tax bill or insurance premium bill), your lender has dipped into these accounts to pay your bills. As you may recall, the reason your lender did this was to insure that your property wouldn't be sold for nonpayment of real estate taxes, and would be covered in case of a physical catastrophe such as fire or tornado.

Of course, now that you're selling your home you no longer need escrow accounts to make sure the property taxes and insurance premiums are paid; that's going to be your buyer's responsibility. What you need to be concerned with is this: When are you going to get back any excess funds that are sitting in those no-or low-interest-bearing accounts?

If it were up to most lenders, they'd keep that money for a long time. Fortunately for sellers, lenders are required to return these funds to you within forty-five days. Since you have to give the lender a large chunk of money anyway to pay off the loan (see the previous question for more details on paying off your loan), some lenders (but very few) simply subtract the amount in your escrow or impound accounts from the total needed for payoff. In other words, if you had an aggregate of $850 sitting in your escrow or impound accounts, instead of giving the lender $100,000 you might give the lender $99,150.

Unfortunately, most lenders are going to hold on to those dollars for as long as they can. That means you'll receive the residuals from your impound accounts a few weeks after the closing.

Depending on when your real estate taxes and insurance premiums are paid, and depending on when you close on your home, you may actually owe the lender some money. If you have $500 in your real estate property tax account and the bill comes in at $1,000 a few weeks before closing, the lender will pay your bill, but you will have to give the lender an additional $500 to cover the underfunded account. If this happens to you, the lender's payoff statement should include this amount. In any event, check with your lender to make sure that all funds were credited correctly.

Private Mortgage Insurance

When you bought your home, did you put down 20 percent in cash? If not, the lender will have required you to purchase *private mortgage insurance* (PMI). Lenders like to have PMI on low down payment loans because those loans are historically riskier than high down payment loans. There is a direct relationship between how much cash a homeowner has in a house and how well he or she takes care of that property.

Once you sell your home, however, you will have no need to continue paying your PMI premiums. (*Note:* If you've been in your home for a long time, and have either paid down your mortgage so that you have 20 percent equity in your home, or home values in your neighborhood have risen so that you have at least 20 percent equity in your home, you should approach your lender anyway about how to cancel your PMI payments. That's just extra money each month that you don't need to be paying.)

If you were required to put up the first year's premium in cash at closing, and then were required to start paying monthly installments of premium with your first mortgage payment, you may be entitled to receive a portion of that first year's premium back. If, however, your lender didn't charge you the upfront year's premium then there may be nothing to get back. To find out what you're owed, and under what circumstances you may be entitled to a refund, contact your lender.

QUESTION 90

What is possession? When do I have to move out?

Possession, the saying goes, is nine-tenths of the law. The concept that if you live on the land you have a right to it is an ancient principle that originates with English common law and was reaffirmed in the early- to mid-1800s, when the United States government divided millions of acres of open land into parcels called homesteads. The government gave the land to those farmers who lived on it.

Possession refers to the person or persons who are currently inhabiting a property. If you live in your house, you are said to be in possession of it. When you sell your home, you not only give the buyer a deed, you give the buyer possession of your property. Once the buyer has possession, he or she can move into the property, or rent it out.

When should you give the buyer possession? The simple answer is, what did you agree to in the contract? In almost every case, possession is dealt with when you and the buyer negotiate the finer points of the contract. After you've agreed on price. After you've agreed on the closing date. More often than not, the transfer of possession occurs on the day of closing. It may be at closing (you move out before the closing), or sometime during the day. When Sam and I moved into our first home, the sellers moved during the closing, which was held in our building. We didn't get all the keys until three that afternoon. When we sold, we moved the day before the closing (which was held in the same place). After the closing, we went with our buyer to the unit one last time and removed the final food items from what was now *his* refrigerator.

But the transfer of possession can happen either before closing or after, depending on what is negotiated. If you've already moved out of your home, and the buyer wants to get in a few days or a few weeks before closing to repaint the place, you can negotiate that into the purchase and sale agreement. If you want to stay in your home for a few days after the closing, or if you want to lease back your home from the buyer while you're looking for another place to live, you should negotiate that up front.

Some of the issues surrounding possession are dealt with by local custom. For example, in some communities it's customary to keep possession of the home for a couple of days after closing. The buyer doesn't charge the seller anything for those extra days, it's just considered de rigueur. In other areas, possession happens the moment the closing is over.

Scheduling Your Moving Day

If you and the buyer have agreed to transfer possession at closing, then you should schedule your move so that it is completed by the evening of the day before your closing or by the time the closing is scheduled to end. If you're scheduled to close on a Monday, for example, consider scheduling your move for Friday, Saturday, or Sunday. Some sellers like to play the time game. If the closing is scheduled for 4:00 P.M., they'll move out the same day, starting at seven or eight in the morning. That cuts it close on two ends: First, something may go wrong with your move. Perhaps your movers will be late, or they won't show at all, and you'll have to scramble at the last minute. Second, when you schedule your closing so late in the day, you could be in trouble if your closing runs late. Most municipal offices close at 5:00 P.M. If you or the buyer needs an additional document, your closing may be pushed over until the following morning.

If your deal has gone well, and your buyer has paid you a fair amount of money for your home, a nice thing to do is to move out in advance of the closing so that the buyer has the opportunity to take his or her final pre-closing walk-through once your home is empty. Up until now, the buyer has only seen your home filled with your furniture, rugs, and artwork. An empty house will give the buyer a chance to see that you weren't covering up anything and that he or she is actually getting the house in the shape he or she thought it was in.

Successful Home Seller Tip: Doing a final pre-closing walk-through isn't just a good idea for the buyer. It's something you should do as well. Even if you think you remembered everything, in the hubbub of moving some small items might have been left behind. After we moved out, we found a chair that had been left behind in a closet. If you live in a condo, co-op, or town house association, check all of your storerooms. If you live in a house, check the attic and basement, plus all closets. Check the medicine chest and under all sinks. If you're having your home professionally cleaned after you move but before the closing (another nice touch that the buyer will certainly appreciate), you may have left a vacuum cleaner, broom, mop, rags, and other cleaning supplies. If you're leaving the refrigerator for the buyer, make sure you've emptied it of all the condiments, beer cans, and ice cream containers. Defrost the freezer—and don't forget to leave any ice cube trays that came with the unit. Remember, once you leave the house and hand over the keys at closing, you've given the buyer possession of your home. And if the buyer doesn't want to, he or she doesn't have to let you in again.

QUESTION 91

Can the buyer charge me for staying in the home after closing? How much will I be charged?

The easy, though unfortunate, answer to this question is yes. The buyer has the right to charge you for staying in your home once possession has been transferred and he or she owns the home.

If you move out early and the buyer takes possession before closing, you can charge the buyer a daily or flat fee. Of course, whether or not you charge the buyer or the buyer charges you will depend somewhat on local custom. If it is customary in your area for buyers to allow sellers a couple of extra days gratis after closing to move out of their home, then you could invoke "local custom" and the buyer might encounter opposition from his or her broker if he or she tries to charge you. On the other hand, if it is customary to allow the buyer into the home before closing, gratis, you might face the same situation. As a general rule, it is best to avoid giving early possession to a buyer. If a problem arises at the closing and the buyer can't purchase your home, you may become an unwilling landlord.

If you are going to be charged, you should be aware of how these fees are set. Again, some of this is done by local custom. To understand why daily fees are set where they are, it's helpful to understand a bit of buyer psychology: The buyer wants you out of his or her home as quickly as possible, unless you are leasing back the property for an extended period of time. Believe it or not, there are sellers who refuse to vacate the property after closing, and just continue to live in the home. And while you won't be one of those sellers, many buyers get nervous when sellers talk about staying in the home after the closing.

In order to get you out as quickly as possible, buyers like to set a daily rate high enough to compensate them for their costs. If you stay beyond the date on which you agreed to deliver possession, the buyer may hike the daily fee so much that it will be cheaper for you to move and go to a hotel than it will be to stay in the home. While buyers may want to charge an extremely high daily rate from the get-go, smart brokers will try to hold down the initial cost to something reasonable. Buyers and brokers will often prorate the cost of the mortgage (principal and interest), insurance, utilities, assessments (if applicable), and add a couple of dollars on top of that number or base it on what properties in your general area rent for. That's fair. After all, the buyer shouldn't lose money while you live in his or her home.

Here's how it works. Let's say the buyer is purchasing your home for $125,000. A $100,000, thirty-year mortgage at 9 percent interest will cost the buyer $804 per month. That breaks down to $26.80 per day. Let's say utilities are another $100 per month. That breaks down to $3.33 per day. If real estate taxes are $2,500 per year, that breaks down to $6.85 per day. If it costs $500 to insure the house for a year, that would be $1.37 per day.

Cost	*Per-Day Charge*
Mortgage	$26.80
Utilities	3.33
Real Estate Taxes	6.85
Insurance	1.37
TOTAL	$38.35

If you multiply $38.35 times 30 (the average number of days in a month), you'll realize that the buyer is charging you a daily rate equal to $1,150.50 a month in rent. After the date agreed to for the seller to give up possession, this amount could climb to $100 to $150 per day, a sum so large that it would be cheaper for you to move than to stay.

By the same token, what you charge the buyer if he or she wishes to move in early will be determined by your costs or the cost of similar rentals in your neighborhood. Above all, you want to be sure that the buyer doesn't wreck your home a couple of days before closing. Most likely this won't happen, but you can't be too sure. You can charge the buyer a daily fee, or not. But ask the buyer to do his or her final walk-through with you before moving in, and ask for a written statement that the condition of the property is satisfactory to the buyer. That way, both you and the buyer know what condition the home was in before the buyer moved in was acceptable to the buyer. Later, just before closing, you'll have some recourse if the buyer tries to say that certain things were wrong with the home or that your movers damaged something while moving you out.

Successful Home Seller Tip: If you decide to allow the buyer to move in early, always obtain a written document from the buyer outlining the arrangement you have agreed to. And consult with your attorney to make sure you are protected.

In the best of situations, when you move out and when the buyer moves in won't matter so much. In a friendly closing—which all closings should strive to be—there is a fair amount of trust and respect for what each side is trying to do. But when house deals go bad, and conversation turns to accusations, you should think carefully before allowing the buyer to take possession before closing. One San Diego seller said her house deal went sour just after she let the buyer in early to do some painting. The buyer refused to allow her access to her own home, and at the closing, accused her movers of damaging the stairway. Needless to say, that closing wasn't over within an hour.

QUESTION 92

What if something goes wrong at the closing?

Sometimes a closing is like a mirage in the desert: Just as you feel like you're getting there, it appears to move farther away. Or, it disappears altogether. You solve one problem and another crops up. And another. And another.

When problems occur in a closing, it often comes from the buyer's side. Either the loan documents are incorrect, or the funds which were wired didn't arrive as scheduled. One seller couldn't find his mailbox key. During the final walk-through, one buyer discovered that the seller's beautiful oriental carpet in the entryway covered a terrible cat urine stain.

There are at least ten reasons why a closing doesn't happen, or is delayed for a few days, or is stretched out by several hours:

1. *Money problems.* Money problems are one of the most frequent reasons why home sales may not close on time. For example, if the buyer is transferring funds by wire, there's always the possibility that the money will get tied up or that there will be a delay in the processing of the wire transfer. Sometimes the numbers don't add up and a buyer will find that he or she is short of funds. Since lenders and title companies usually don't take personal checks for more than $25 or $50, the buyer may have to run across town to get that personal check converted into a certified or cashier's check. That can add an hour or more to the closing.
2. *Missing loan package.* If the lender's documents aren't there, you and the buyer aren't closing. If the loan package has to come from out of state, and it's shipped via overnight delivery, it's always possible that the package will be lost or delayed. If the loan package is missing documents, they may have to be

sent by messenger or faxed over to the closing. Even after the documents are delivered, the closing may be extended if the lender and buyer wrangle over who will actually pay for the messenger service or fax.

3. *Disagreement over documents.* If the buyer discovers that there are errors in the documents, the closing may be delayed or extended while the lender and buyer discuss and correct the documents.
4. *Incorrect loan documents.* Nothing can create problems like incorrect information on loan documents. If the lender has to send back to his or her office for replacement documents, think about grabbing a cup of coffee or a doughnut. You and your attorney (to whom you are hopefully paying a flat fee rather than by-the-hour charges) may be waiting a while.
5. *Last-minute requests.* Sometimes the lender will make a last-minute request for documentation at the closing. A request for a canceled deposit check can send the unprepared buyer back home and you back to the coffee shop.
6. *Walk-through problems.* Buyers often ask sellers for the right to do a final walk-through of the property. The best time for buyers to do this is after you've moved out of the house, within twenty-four hours of the closing. If the buyers find a problem, then they, or their attorney, will bring it up at the closing and attempt to negotiate a resolution. In other words, how much money will you give them to make the problem go away? If they find a lot of things wrong with your home, this nickel-and-diming can really drag out the closing.

7. *Title problems.* Sometimes last-minute title problems creep up. A long-lost relative of yours turns up to claim part ownership of your property. Or the title company discovers a mortgage lien that's ten years old. Or a contractor you hired to do a little painting around the place before you put it on the market has filed a mechanic's lien. The buyer will insist that you resolve these liens before the closing, but occasionally, you'll have to deal with one the day of closing.
8. *Someone dies.* It doesn't happen too often, but you should know what can happen if either you or the buyer dies after the contract is signed and before closing. If you die, your estate must go through with the sale. However, it may be difficult for the closing to occur on schedule, especially if you die intestate (without a will), and your estate has to go through probate court. If the buyer dies, you may be able to force the buyer's estate to go through with the purchase, but in the real world, sellers rarely force the sale. Some or all of the earnest money may be given to the seller, particularly if the next buyer doesn't offer as much as the buyer who died. Check with an attorney for further details about your rights in your state.
9. *Catastrophe strikes.* Almost every home buyer worries that the property he or she is purchasing will be destroyed before closing by flood, fire, earthquake, lightning, or mud slide. But buyers, unlike sellers, won't actually be living in the home should a catastrophe strike. And they won't have to clean up your mess. A catastrophe can certainly put the kibosh on a sale. The buyer has the option, in most cases, of

walking away from the deal. If the buyer elects to stay, he or she can request that you use the insurance proceeds to repair the home to the level where it was when the contract was signed. Or the buyer may purchase the house "as is"—either for a reduced price or for the same price plus your hazard insurance proceeds. Either way, your closing may be delayed, if not postponed. If the buyer took possession of the property before closing and before the disaster struck, he or she may lose the right to withdraw from the deal. Check with your attorney for details on your state and local laws regarding your rights in this type of situation.

10. *Your deal falls through*. If you're like most sellers, you'll take the cash from the sale of your home and apply it toward the purchase of another home. If the seller of your new home has a change of heart, however, you may want to go back to the buyer and ask to postpone the closing for a few days or a few weeks so you have time to either find another house or find a rental apartment to move into as an interim move. Another option is to ask the buyer if he or she will rent the home back to you for a specified period of time after closing. But don't be surprised if the buyer turns you down. The buyer may be counting on moving into your home because the home he or she is moving from is being occupied by someone else.

How long should the closing last? Many closings take less than an hour. One attorney estimates that 10 percent of his closings take less than half an hour. An additional 50 percent take about an hour. Another 30 percent take less than an hour and a half, and an additional 10 percent take less than two hours. So 90 percent of all closings happen in less than two hours. And the final 10 percent? Well, they could take ten hours, or ten days, or never happen at all. But most closings happen. And when the last fire has been put out, and yours is over, you'll have sold your home. Congratulations!

PART VIII

The Tax Consequences of Selling Your Home

QUESTION 93

Do I have to pay taxes on the profit I earn from selling my home?

During the 1996 presidential election campaign, Bob Dole made a startling announcement. If elected, he proposed to eliminate, for most Americans, any taxes that would be owed on the sale of their home.

He suggested that any American could take up to the first $250,000 in capital gains tax-free. If you were married when you sold your home, you and your spouse could take up to $500,000 in profits tax-free. Any profits above and beyond this would be paid at the long-term capital gains rate. Better yet, you could do this as long as you lived in your house for two of the past five years.

Dole was trying to appeal to the wallets of aging baby boomers, many of whom had lived in their homes for twenty or thirty years and had, at that time, reaped huge gains during the 1970s and 1980s. He wanted their votes and was willing to cut homeowners a big break in order to secure his election.

But what happened was sort of interesting. As the vast majority of homeowners collectively cried, "Finally!" President Clinton proposed virtually the same program.

And so it became clear that whichever candidate was elected, homeowners would receive the best present ever.

How We Used to Pay Taxes

In true IRS fashion, the old way of calculating the amount of taxes owed was complicated, inefficient, and difficult to track. You had to determine the "cost basis" of each home you ever owned by keeping track of all the costs of buying and selling these homes, plus keeping track of the costs of any capital improvements (think structural improvements rather than cosmetic improvements).

If you were lucky, you'd end up with a reasonably accurate "cost basis" for your home, from which you could determine your taxable profit, if any.

Once you had determined your taxable profit, the government allowed you to delay paying taxes on the profit as long as you bought a replacement home within 24 months of selling your prior home. This was called the 24-month rollover replacement rule.

Once you were 55, the government allowed you to pay no tax on the first $125,000 of profit from the sale of your home. This was referred to as the over-55, $125,000 one-time tax-free exclusion. Married couples could take only a single $125,000 tax-free exclusion, while single homeowners each got their own $125,000 exclusion (another so-called marriage penalty).

Once you'd taken your one-time tax-free exclusion, you could never take it again. So if you had gains above and beyond your $125,000, you paid tax on the gain at the current capital gains tax rate. And if you only used part of it—say, your profits totaled only $60,000—and you used your one-time exclusion, you lost the remainder of the exclusion forever.

Here's How It Works Today

The Taxpayer Relief Act of 1997 changed the way sellers compute their profits and how much tax they have to pay. The act eliminated the one-time, $125,000 tax-free exclusion available to those individuals over the age of 55. In addition, the act eliminated the 24-month rollover replacement rule.

According to current tax law, homeowners may now take up to $250,000 in profits (up to $500,000 if you're married) tax free when they sell their home. To qualify, you must have lived in your home two out of the last five years. If you have to move sooner than that (for a new job fifty miles away or for health reasons), you may take a portion of your profits tax free. Finally, you may take your $250,000 (or $500,000 if you're married) in profits tax free once every 24 months.

Any gain in excess of these amounts is taxed at your capital gains tax rate, which is currently 20 percent (if your marginal tax bracket is 28 percent or above), or 10 percent (if your marginal tax rate is 15 percent or below). But in years to come, these numbers may change again. Check with your accountant or tax preparer for details.

The Plan in Action

Here's an example of how the new tax law might work. Let's say Sallie and Jessie, a married couple, buy a house. They paint it, fix it up, replace the carpet and window treatments, and upgrade the kitchen. They paid $150,000 for the house, put in $50,000 and sell it two years later for $300,000. They have a profit of $100,000 on the property.

Under the old rules, they'd have to pay tax on the $100,000 profit unless they bought a replacement house within 24 months for the same or more money. Under the new rules, the $100,000 profit is tax-free, even if they never buy another home.

Now they buy another home, and do the same thing. As long as they live in the second house for another 24 months, they will pay no tax on any profits (up to $500,000 for married couples) when they sell.

Home Seller Tip: Although it seems too good to be true, the Tax Reform Act of 1997 has given homeowners tremendous flexibility when making housing choices. Home sellers can trade down without necessarily triggering a tax on their profit or they can renovate homes every few years and pocket the profit.

QUESTION 94

Do I have to tell the IRS if I've sold my house?

Under the old tax reporting system, there was a complicated tax form that home sellers needed to complete and file with their federal income tax return.

Under the Tax Reform Act of 1997, much of that paperwork has been eliminated. Today, you only need file certain tax forms if your profit on the sale of your home exceeds $250,000 for individuals or $500,000 for married taxpayers. If that's the case, congratulations! And, check with your tax advisor for details.

QUESTION 95

How do the tax laws affect the sale of second homes or other properties?

As baby boomers age and grow more wealthy (thanks in no small part to the booming stock market of the 1990s), one of the things they are spending their money on is a little place in the country, where they can get away from it all. So it's no great surprise that the purchase and sale of second homes is on the rise.

Studies have shown that people often purchase a second home with the thought that they'll eventually retire there. Typically, second homes are located just 150 miles from the homeowner's primary residence, in a beautiful community that features plenty of recreational opportunities.

One of the very nice things about the Tax Reform Act of 1997 is that it throws a bone to the increasing numbers of homeowners who also own second homes.

In the previous version of the tax law, you were allowed to delay paying capital gains tax only on your primary residence. So if you bought and sold several second homes, and made money each time, you'd have paid capital gains tax at the current rate on the profit earned with each sale. Or if you sold your current home and moved into your second home, it would never have qualified as your primary residence for tax purposes. You'd have ended up paying capital gains tax on any profits earned once the 24-month rollover replacement rule period expired.

With the Tax Reform Act of 1997, you are now permitted to turn your second home into your primary residence, and as long as you've made that your primary residence for two of the past five years, you can keep any profits earned on the sale of your second home tax free.

So you can sell your primary residence, pocket the $250,000 (or $500,000 if you're married) in profits, move into your second home, sell that home, and pocket an additional $250,000 (up to $500,000 if you're married) in profits. All within a five-year period.

But if you buy and sell your second home while you still maintain a primary residence, you will have to pay capital gains taxes at the current tax rate on any profits you receive.

QUESTION 96

If I lose money on the sale of my home, can I deduct the loss?

If you own stock, and the value of that stock doubles, you'll pay capital gains tax on your profit when you sell. But let's say you own another company, and the value of that company drops. If you sell, you will have incurred a loss on the investment.

Current tax law permits you to offset that loss against another capital gain. So if you sell the stock at a loss at the same time you sell a stock that has a gain, and the loss and the gain are about the same, you will end up paying little or no taxes on your profits.

Since a home is, for most folks, their single largest asset or investment, it would make sense that if you incurred a loss when you sold your home, you'd be able to use that loss to offset another capital gain, right?

That's what many folks in southern California and the Northeast were hoping.

Plenty of folks bought in those areas in 1988, at the height of the last real estate boom. By 1990, we were in the midst of the Gulf War, and prices of many homes had been slashed by 50 percent. By 2000, some of those home valuations had climbed back to where they were a decade earlier. Some more than exceeded their former valuation.

But plenty of folks were left holding the bag, particularly those who had to sell out before the market recovered. Short sales, when a home is sold for less than the current mortgage amount, became common. And lenders would often take the sales price of the home and write off that extra part of the mortgage, if the homeowners were completely tapped out. Talk about pouring salt into a wound, the IRS treated the written-off part of the mortgage as income and went to the sellers to collect income tax on this phantom income!

For those sellers, and for those today who for whatever reason find themselves facing a loss when they sell their home, it would be nice to be able to write off the loss as you would any other kind of investment loss on your federal income taxes.

Unfortunately, you can't. You may not offset a loss incurred on the sale of your home against another capital gain. Nor can you carry the loss forward to offset future gains.

As we went to press, there was talk on Capitol Hill of changing the law to allow you to use a loss incurred from the sale of your home to offset other investment gains. But that's all it is for the moment—talk.

QUESTION 97
Are moving expenses deductible?

As Congress and the president look for more ways to trim the budget, they are going to continue chipping away at income tax deductions that were formerly allowed.

The changes in the moving expense deductions are a good example. Prior to the 1993 tax year, individuals who were moving could deduct the cost of moving their household goods and themselves, but they could also deduct the cost of traveling to find a new home, premoving expenses, temporary living expenses, meals, the cost of getting out of a lease early, and qualified real estate expenses. At one point, almost everything could be deducted. Then, as limits were imposed, there was a maximum amount that could be deducted.

Starting with the 1993 tax year, moving expense deductions were severely curtailed. Here is a brief sketch of some of the rewritten code. Remember, laws may change, and these codes may be rewritten again—perhaps each year. Check with your tax preparer before filing your tax return.

- Under the old rules, you could deduct your moving expenses if your new office was thirty-five miles from your old home. Under the new rules, the spread has been increased to fifty miles. In other words, your new office must be fifty miles or more from your old residence.
- Under the rewritten code, your deductible moving expenses are limited to household goods, your personal effects, and the transportation costs of getting to your new home. You are also entitled to deduct lodging costs and meals during the actual move from your old home to your new home.
- When companies pay to transfer you from one city to another, they normally reimburse you, which shows up on your W-2 form. Under the new tax law, however, you can't deduct all of the expenses you previously were entitled to. The IRS sees the reimbursement as a benefit, and you must pay tax on it. For example, if it costs you $20,000 to move and the company gives you $20,000, you may think you're even. But the new IRS rules require you to pay tax on the entire amount you're reimbursed (the IRS sees it as income).

Again, before you file your taxes, ask your accountant or tax preparer to fully explain the benefits and deductions you may be entitled to.

PART IX

If I Decide Not to Sell, What Options Do I Have?

There may come a time in the home-selling process when you sit down and realize that the situation has changed: Either you cannot sell your home at a price you'd be willing to accept or you have decided not to sell. If you still need to get some cash out of your home (either because you need the money for daily living expenses or because you've already bought another home and moved), here are some options that might help get you through this period.

QUESTION 98

What is a home equity loan? What is a reverse mortgage?

Peter, a vice president for a major bank, has heard some out-of-the-ordinary reasons for taking out a home equity loan. But the strangest yet was to buy a racehorse. "The borrower could definitely afford it, even if the horse lost," Peter says.

A home equity loan is a loan that you secure by pledging the equity that you've built up in your home. *Equity* is the cash stake you have in your home at any one time. For example, if your home cost $100,000 and you put down $15,000 in cash, that would be your equity stake. As property values rise, your stake will increase. Your equity stake will also increase as you pay off your mortgage.

Let's say you live in your home for five years and the value of your home rises to $125,000. You now have home equity of $25,000 (the difference in price between what you paid for your home and what it is now worth) plus the $15,000 you put down in cash, plus another $1,000 or so from paying down your mortgage for five years. All told, you will probably have more than $41,000 in equity built up in your home.

Once you have equity built up, you can borrow against it. There are two ways to do this: You can either get a home equity loan or establish a home equity line of credit. A home equity loan is like a traditional second mortgage in that you get the cash in a big lump sum. An equity line of credit allows you to draw out the money you need a little bit at a time, repay it in a large chunk, and then re-borrow.

While *home equity lines of credit* are often lumped together with home equity loans, they are really a different animal.

With a home equity line of credit, you are given a fixed amount of credit against which you can draw funds by writing on special checks. With this type of loan, you pay interest only for the duration of the loan term, usually five to seven years, and then pay off the loan with one balloon payment. (Lenders might refer to this loan as an "interest-only" loan.) Or, as you reach the end of the loan term, some lenders will allow you to refinance the amount for another term.

Home equity loans, however, are similar to the more familiar second mortgage. These loans are usually longer in length (like a first mortgage) and require regular monthly payments of principal and interest.

Whatever form your loan takes, it is important to remember that it is secured by your home: If you fail to meet your minimum monthly obligation, you could lose your property.

Home equity loans are relative newcomers to the wide world of finance. Financial institutions began offering them in 1984, when the federal government started to allow tax deductions for interest paid on home equity loans of up to $100,000. (Currently, mortgage interest is deductible for mortgages of up to $1 million for first or second homes.)

Home equity loans began to gain strength and market share with the passage of the 1986 Tax Reform Act, which phased out personal interest deductions over five years. Personal interest, including interest on credit card debt and car loans, is no longer deductible. Interest on home equity loans, however, remains fully deductible, although that, too, could change. Congress has considered limiting the deductions on home loan interest as part of its deficit-cutting strategy, although no firm proposals have been made at this time.

Although they don't all buy horses, plenty of Americans are making use of home equity loans. A government survey done in the early part of the 1990s found that American homeowners had accumulated nearly $4.5 trillion in home equity through repayment of their mortgages and appreciation of property values. Today, homeowners are borrowing billions in home equity credit to repay credit card debt, pay their taxes, pay off their car loans, and send their children to college.

Instead of selling their home and moving to a larger one, many homeowners take out a line of home equity credit and finance renovation work on their homes. Judy, a homeowner in Newton, Massachusetts, borrowed $40,000 in home equity to make repairs on the home she has lived in for more than twenty-five years. These repairs included rebricking her front steps and the garden retaining wall, and painting the exterior of the house. And at the same time that many homeowners refinanced their primary mortgages as interest rates hit 7 percent in late 1993 and early 1994, would-be sellers began to take out home equity loans to enlarge their homes and give them some of the amenities they might find in a nicer home or neighborhood. Many sellers then decided to stay in their larger homes.

If you need cash and think that a home equity loan sounds like a good idea, you should know that there are limits on the amount of money your lending institution will allow you to borrow. According to one consumer loan officer, banks generally lend up to 75 percent of your home equity minus any debt, such as a car loan or credit card bills. How does that work? Let's say you have $40,000 in equity built up in your property, and let's assume that you've paid off your car and have no credit card debt. Going by the 75 percent rule, a lender should be willing to float a home equity loan of $30,000. Here's how the math works:

$40,000 (your home equity) - $0 (your personal debt) × .75 = $30,000

But lenders also look at your ability to repay the loan. In other words, banks want to know if you have the income to support this extra debt. So the lender will look at your debt-to-income ratio. That computation takes the total amount of debt you have accumulated, including car loans and first and second mortgages, and compares it to your salary. Lenders generally operate on the principle that your house debt (mortgage and home equity loan) cannot exceed 28 percent of your gross income, and that your total debt (which includes everything) cannot exceed 33 percent of your income. Looking at the debt-to-income ratio helps loan officers determine if a home equity loan is just what the doctor ordered or if it will be an overwhelming addition to the homeowner's monthly expenses.

Shopping for a Home Equity Loan

Shop around for a home equity loan the way you would shop around for a primary loan. Consider following these steps:

- *Familiarize yourself with today's rates.* Look through the weekend real estate or business section of your local paper and see what various lenders in your marketplace are offering in terms of rates and points (a point is 1 percent of the loan amount).
- *Get referrals.* Friends, relatives, and co-workers should

be excellent, and endless, sources of referrals to different lenders around town. Find out who had a good or bad experience. Find out about any problems they've had closing on their loan.

- *Interview at least three lenders.* Once you've narrowed down the cheapest loans with the best packages from the better lenders, it's time to call and ask for specifics. Ask what costs and fees are involved. Don't be afraid to press the point if you feel you're getting the runaround.
- *Choose a lender with a track record.* It's not always the best idea to pick the lender offering the cheapest rates. Instead, consider reliability, customer referrals, and quality service that emphasizes doing things right the first time.
- *Think before you borrow.* Before you run out to your local home equity lender, think about why you want the money and what you're going to use it for. You don't want to fritter it away on nonessentials—it's going to cost you too much money for that. Instead, know ahead of time how much you need for that room addition or roof replacement, and then go searching for lenders. If you plan to stay in your home for only another year, you may prefer an interest-only loan to an amortized loan. Be honest with the lender when you discuss your needs. Perhaps he or she will have a uncommon mortgage product that will fit the bill.

Reverse Mortgages

Have you decided you don't want to sell your home? Are you a little strapped for cash? Are you living in a house that's fully paid for while struggling to make ends meet on your retirement benefits? If you are, then you may be a perfect candidate for a reverse mortgage.

A *reverse mortgage* is a loan against your home that gives you a lump sum or monthly installments of cash and requires no repayments until you die or sell your home. Available exclusively to seniors, who are often house-rich and cash-poor, the reverse mortgage allows homeowners to use their home's equity as a bank from which they receive regular monthly payments—or a lump sum cash advance at closing—to help with living expenses. There is no repayment of the loan due while the owner owns the home, though all money borrowed must be repaid with interest when it is sold or the homeowner has permanently moved.

The concept of reverse mortgages developed slowly. In the early 1980s, only a handful of reverse mortgage programs could be accessed, and most were sponsored by non-profit or governmental agencies. There were other problems as well: There was no flexibility to the way payments were made, and homeowners were forced to pay steep costs and fees associated with making the loan. Today, the loans have been made more flexible, though there have been reports of extraordinary fees and costs.

As reverse mortgages have become better known, and as the Department of Housing and Urban Development (HUD) and FHA stepped in to guarantee some of these loans, more lenders became willing to write up this business. Today, nearly every state has at least one private mortgage company willing to issue a government-backed reverse mortgage. And this number is likely to grow. Other state-sponsored programs help senior homeowners with property tax deferral programs (which lend money for paying property taxes), deferred payment loans (for repairing or improving homes), and state housing finance loans.

Mortgage companies in several states have begun offering privately insured reverse mortgages, which offer greater loan advances than the FHA program, and uninsured reverse mortgages, which provide monthly cash advances for a fixed term and must be repaid in full when the loan advances stop. As these loans become better known, other types will be developed that suit the needs of more senior homeowners. There are organizations that provide free information on reverse mortgages. See Appendix III, Resources, for more details.

Note: Before you sign a reverse mortgage note, have the document thoroughly checked by an attorney. Some finance magazines have reported that numerous seniors are being taken advantage of by unscrupulous lenders who give them reverse mortgages but take whopping fees and charge exorbitant interest rates. Not all reverse mortgages are like this, however. Learn all you can about the loan and the lender, and then consult with your attorney and tax preparer.

QUESTION 99

What is a lease with an option to buy? And can I simply rent my home?

Indiana residents, Laurie and Bob are your typical first-time buyers. They know they can afford to pay the mortgage on a nice two-bedroom older home in their town, but they've had trouble putting aside the cash for the down payment. One way they can painlessly save for their down payment is to rent a house with an option to buy it later. Commonly called "lease with an option to buy," this method of purchasing a house has a lot of pluses for those buyers who wouldn't otherwise be able to purchase a home.

It also has a lot of pluses for some sellers. Sellers who lease their homes with options on them talk about how quickly they get responses from buyers who might not otherwise be willing to take a second look at their home. They also talk about how ads that say "$5,000 moves you in" garner a lot of telephone calls and drive-bys.

But we're getting a little ahead of ourselves. Let's start at the top. How does it work? The buyer purchases a one-year (or two-year) option on the house with a nonrefundable option fee, which is usually a small percentage of the price of the house. In addition to that, the buyer pays rent each month, a portion of which may be credited back to the buyer as the down payment for the home.

For example, if the buyer pays $1,000 per month in rent, and 33 percent of the rent is credited toward the down payment, the buyer accumulates $333 each month, or nearly $4,000 per year, toward a down payment for the home. In addition, the option fee is generally credited toward the down payment.

You and the buyer will have to negotiate how much of the rent should be credited toward the down payment. The buyer will want most or all of the rent credited toward the down payment, while you, the seller, naturally want as little rent as possible credited toward the down payment. It's not uncommon to see rent credits of 33 percent, though some credits may be more or less. While the buyer is looking for a strong incentive, you don't want to lose money on your home. It's important that you cover your cash flow, particularly if you're still paying a mortgage on the property.

Even before you negotiate the rent credit, however, you and the buyer should negotiate the sales price of the home.

Lease with an option to buy is treated legally as if the home were being sold outright. Once it is determined, the price of the home never varies, even if the house appreciates in value.

But while you've sold the buyer an option to purchase your property at a later date for a specific amount of money, you remain the sole owner until the buyer exercises his or her option and closes on the home. That means you also retain the tax benefits of home ownership.

What happens if the buyer doesn't exercise his or her option? Nothing. The buyer will want to have the right to renew his or her option to purchase until time ends. Sometimes buyers are so nervous about buying that they're happy just having the option to purchase something. Your buyer may continue to renew the option each year, or may one day decide to pay his last month's rent and walk away from your home altogether. Sometimes, if the buyer renews his or her option, a seller will ask for another nonrefundable option fee. Sometimes, but not always, the seller will renew the option gratis. Buyers have more to lose by walking away from a lease with an option to buy than sellers. If buyers walk away from the house, they lose the nonrefundable option fee plus all the rent they have been paying over the years. On the other hand, if the buyer does walk, you'll have to fix up your home and put it on the market again.

At a home buyers' and sellers' fair in California several years ago, one home investor said she had been renewing her option on a particular house for twenty-three years.

Advantages and Disadvantages

Buyers like leasing with an option to buy because it allows them to painlessly build up a sizable down payment. It also allows them to test out a home and its neighborhood, finding its good points and bad points. They can also see if home prices are going up or down. Finally, leasing a home allows buyers the ultimate financial flexibility: They can buy your home or just walk away at the end of the lease term.

Unless you are looking to get into the property management business, there are fewer pluses for a seller in a lease/option situation than for a buyer. If you're stuck, and can't sell your home, leasing the home might quickly bring offers. On the plus side, you may get your cash flow covered, but on the other hand, you won't get your money out of the house until the buyer exercises the option. If the buyer doesn't exercise the option, you can pocket the option money. But when you wake up the morning after the lease term ends, you will still have to start the sales process all over again. One of the biggest disadvantages is becoming a landlord and taking on all the responsibilities that position entails.

Paying the Broker

How does the broker get paid on a lease with an option to buy? Many brokers don't really like getting involved with lease options because they know they won't receive their sales commission until the buyer actually closes on the home. In the case of the woman who has renewed her option for twenty-three years, the broker is still waiting.

Often, brokers who find rentals for people are paid a fee by the owner. In the case of a lease/option, the seller may decide to pay the broker a rental fee for the first year or two of the lease, and then pay the commission when the house is actually sold. Your listing agreement may cover this issue.

A lease with an option to buy is a complicated legal transaction since it involves both the sale and the rental of a home. You should consult with your real estate attorney about your legal rights and responsibilities before signing any documents.

Renting Your Home

When all else fails, and you can't sell your home, and you're not old enough to qualify for a reverse mortgage, and you have already moved to another home, one last option is to try to rent your home.

A lot of homeowners don't like to rent their homes because they believe it entails a tremendous amount of work (it can) while providing relatively few financial benefits (sometimes true). On the other hand, if you're hemorrhaging money by paying your original mortgage, a new mortgage, and a bridge loan, renting your primary home should at least help you recover some funds while continuing to market your home.

You've got to place carefully written ads (that don't discriminate against anyone based on race, religion, sex, or disability), and you've got to carefully screen your tenants. You're not only looking for quality individuals, but quality people who can pay their bills and who will maintain your home in its current condition. I once went to inspect a rental home that had a brand-new kitchen. "We had to put it in because our tenants liked to cook Asian food over high flames and there were grease stains on the ceilings and floors we couldn't get out," said the owner.

Renting your home has its drawbacks: You must maintain the home and make sure your tenant is happy. On the plus side, good tenants will provide a steady stream of rental income.

Why would you rent your home but not offer a lease with

an option to sell? As you may recall, once you set the option price, you're stuck with it. So if you set the option at, say, $100,000, and prices rise 15 percent in your neighborhood within a year, you're going to miss out on that appreciation because of your fixed option price. If you're in a slow market, where prices are depressed because of the local economy, or because developers built too many new homes this year, consider renting for a year rather than selling immediately. If you wait until prices have bottomed out, you may be able to recover some of your home's lost value.

QUESTION 100

What if someone accuses me or my broker of fraud or misrepresentation in the sale of my home?

With sellers now required in more than half of all states to disclose all material defects in their home to prospective buyers, and with our society as litigious as it has become so late in the twentieth century, it isn't unthinkable that some disgruntled buyer may accuse you of pulling the wool over his or her eyes with regard to your home.

The problem with answering a question like this in print is that there are so many variables. If a buyer sees ten houses in an afternoon, and seven of the sellers say they've put on a new roof, will the buyer remember that you said your roof was "newer but not new"? If this buyer purchases your house, he could well come back down the road and say that you told him there was a new roof when, in fact, you didn't.

For most buyers to prove there was fraud, they have to

prove (in many states) that you knew about the problem (or should have known) and lied about it. All of this is subjective, unless the buyer can prove definitively that you lied or covered up something. Fraud is telling the buyer that you've never had water in the basement when you know full well your entire neighborhood floated away during the Great Iowa Flood of 1993.

Sometimes buyers forget that they're buying an existing house. I firmly believe that if you're buying brand-new construction, straight from the developer, you're entitled to have everything work perfectly for at least a year. But when buyers purchase existing homes, they forget that these homes were built twenty, thirty, forty, or even a hundred years ago. In an older—or old—house, things go wrong. You'd be smart to frequently remind prospective buyers of the age of your home. And have your broker remind them and their broker.

If you lied about something in your house, then you have only yourself to blame. Lying in this sense can be considered fraud, and there are steep penalties for your actions. If, however, you did not lie, but there has been a misunderstanding, hire the best real estate attorney you can find and try to negotiate a settlement with your buyers. Try to have a little empathy for them. After all, they're the ones who have to live with your house now.

Finally, the Fair Housing Act prohibits discrimination against anyone because of religion, race, creed, sex, disability, marital status, or because they have young children. While you have the right to sell your home to anyone you please, you may give up that right if you list your home with a broker or on a multiple listing service. Also, any advertisement you place in a newspaper, in a magazine, or on radio or television must be nondiscriminatory. As we discussed early on in the book, the seller who advertised for a "Christian handyman" to rent out her spare bedroom, paid a large fine for her violation of fair housing laws.

And while we're on the subject, it's a crime to discriminate against anyone with a disability, including anyone who has AIDS—or HIV, the virus that causes AIDS. AIDS is considered to be a disability in many states. Remember the seller's motto: It doesn't matter what color the buyers are (or what disabilities they have) as long as the color of their money is green.

Again, if someone accuses you of lying or of fraud, do not try to negotiate a settlement by yourself. You may negotiate yourself into a deep hole. And if your broker is also accused of misrepresentation (usually, everyone involved with the deal will be sued in the hope that someone will have a "deep pocket"), do not use his or her attorney. Find your own, and make sure he or she is a good one.

APPENDIX I

Top Thirteen Mistakes Home Sellers Make

Selling a home is tougher than it sounds. There's more to it than simply putting up a sign in your front yard and cashing a check at the closing. No matter how carefully you prepare for your sale, almost everyone stumbles occasionally. Brokers call these slipups "mistakes," and while they're not egregious errors, they can trip up your deal.

It's tough to recognize your own mistakes, particularly while you're making them. So I've put together this list of thirteen common mistakes home sellers make with the hope that if you know what mistakes commonly creep up in the process, it will make them easier to avoid.

While you may not see yourself making every mistake on this list, brokers agree that the average home seller makes at least one of the following mistakes:

1. Mistaking Motivation. Are you selling because you want to or because you have to? The honest answer to this question will directly affect every part of your home sale: when you list your home, how you price it, and even which broker, if any, you choose. Sometimes a couple will be split on whether or not to actually sell the home. This can lead to mixed messages during the pricing and negotiation phases of selling, which can confuse the brokers and potential buyers. Are you simply trying to test the waters? Sellers who have overvalued their homes and refuse to lower the price may be wasting everyone's time.

2. *Not Preparing Your Home for Sale*. Yes, you can sell a home that is in less-than-perfect condition. However, don't expect anyone except the bargain hunters to get excited about your chipped paint and peeling wallpaper. If your house needs work, and you're selling it in the condition it is in, you may have to price your home under what similar homes in better condition are selling for in your neighborhood. Otherwise, you may wait a long time for a buyer who recognizes the potential and is willing to pay for it. A better idea is to spend some time to thoroughly clean—and clean out—your home. Invest in a couple of cans of white paint. Improve your curb appeal. Make your home look as good as possible both inside and out.

3. Choosing the Wrong Broker or No Broker. Most homeowners who think they can do a better job selling their home without a professional's help find out later that they're wrong. By that time, unfortunately, they may have wasted a lot of time, money, and energy. But choosing the wrong broker can be just as bad a mistake. Not only do you want someone whose personality complements yours, you should pick the broker who can get you the results you need in the time frame you've outlined.

4. Overpricing Your Home. Price and your home's condition are the two factors you control during the process of selling. While price can be your greatest tool to lure in buyers, too many sellers decide their home is worth a certain amount and refuse to lower the price even when faced with evidence to the contrary. While picking the right price can be difficult, asking brokers to provide you with a comparative marketing analysis and investigating the sales price of homes comparable to yours in your area can help you make the right decision.

5. *Hanging Around During the Showings.* There's nothing worse than having the seller breathe down your neck while you're trying to look around his or her house. Buyers are easily distracted during showings. Having you around might make them nervous, and nervous buyers won't ever feel comfortable in your home. A tangential mistake is that sellers often talk too much around buyers and buyer brokers. If you're not at the showing, you can't "accidentally" tell the buyer how much you'd be willing to accept for your home. If the home is "for sale by owner," be sure to show the home quickly and professionally, and then let the buyers have some time at the end to walk through the home on their own, without your tagging along.

6. *Smelly Pets and Odors.* Pet lovers beware: The people who purchase your home may not love pets as much as you do. In fact, they may be allergic. To avoid having your buyers develop a sneezing attack in your foyer, keep your pets away from buyers. The best choices are to keep them outside during showings, or place them in a locked cage. Buyers are also turned off by noxious odors, including the remnants of cigar or cigarette smoke, hospital-like smells, and an overdose of perfume or potpourri.

7. *Limiting Access to Your Home.* When a buyer wants to see your home, you'd better be prepared to open the door. That means weekdays, evenings, weekends, and holidays. If a

buyer wants to see ten houses on a particular day and yours isn't available, the buyer may choose one of the other nine. Sellers who limit access to their homes may also be sending out an subconscious message that selling isn't a top priority.

8. Letting Your House or Your Broker Go Stale. In a buyer's market—where there are more homes than buyers to purchase them—a house can sit on the market a long time without an offer. If a house is on the market for too long, it can become "stale" in the eyes of brokers and active buyers who comb through the papers and listing sheets each week. To some brokers, a stale home means it can be bought at a discount. Others may perceive that there is something wrong with the house (rather than the market). Rather than letting your home grow stale, consider taking it off the market for a few months, then relisting it at a lower price. If your broker has grown bored, use the off-list period to interview and hire a new broker to market your property.

9. Timing Problems. When sellers buy a new home before they have sold their original home, they create a pressurized situation that may force them to accept less for their home than it is worth. In addition, these sellers may need to take out a bridge loan to cover the gap between the sale of their old home and their new home purchase. Instead of jumping the gun, consider waiting until you have received an offer to purchase or there is strong interest in your home before shopping for a new one. In the worst-case scenario, you'll sell before you buy and end up making an interim move. While that may be a difficult, it could save you from making an even costlier mistake.

10. Failing to Recognize a Good Offer. Brokers like to say that a seller's "first offer is best." Many times that's true. But some sellers have trouble recognizing a good offer when they see it. A good offer consists of a financially solid buyer (a buyer who is preapproved for his or her loan is even better), who is willing to pay a price above your minimum acceptable price, and who will close within a reasonable amount of time. A good offer from a reasonable buyer is a workable offer. You should take this type of offer—and buyer—seriously, and try to make this deal work.

11. Getting Greedy. Sellers should remember that the difference between the list and sales price is the difference between a dream and reality. But some sellers believe any offer below the list price is an insult. When sellers allow greed to drive the negotiations rather than market forces, it will almost certainly spoil the deal, if not kill it entirely.

12. Not Making Your Last Mortgage Payment Before Closing. Some sellers don't realize that they must still make every mortgage payment on time even if they have signed a contract to sell their home. When the escrow officer or your attorney draws up the closing documents, all of the numbers are calculated based on the payments that have been received by the lender. If you haven't made any payments during the four months prior to closing, your lender will calculate the payoff letter based on the last amount you paid and add in the interest and any penalties you owe. For more details, check with your attorney, escrow, or title company officer.

13. Incorrectly Calculating Your Cost Basis. When you sell your home, the federal government will want to know how much profit you made on your home. You should know that there is more to calculating the cost basis of your home than simply the difference between the price you paid for it and the price you sold it for. To the purchase price, you should add the costs of purchase (that you haven't already deducted), the costs of sales, and any capital improvements that you may have made while you lived there. A capital improvement is anything that essentially stays with the home, like a new roof or hot water heater, decorating excepted. The IRS offers a free publication (form 2119, see Appendix II) that explains how to calculate your cost basis.

APPENDIX II

Contracts and Forms

Since the business of real estate is chockful of long documents with teeny-tiny writing, I thought it would be helpful to have a copy of some of the most common contracts and forms used. I've included copies of an offer to purchase contract and a listing agreement that were discussed in earlier chapters, along with the California transfer disclosure statement, which is, to borrow a phrase, the "mother" of all seller disclosure forms. There is also a copy of the HUD-1 settlement statement, which you will use at your own closing. Though you may want to use these contracts and forms as a guide, they may not include the exact language that will protect you in your state. Have your real estate attorney, broker, or escrow officer provide you with the correct forms for your state.

MULTIPLE LISTING
EXCLUSIVE RIGHT TO SELL AGREEMENT

● TO: KAHN REALTY, INC./KAHN MANIERRE REALTY, INC. ("KAHN")

1. I agree to sell my property located at ______________________________

____

Included in the sale as property are the following items, if any, now on premises for which a Bill of Sale is to be given: screens, storm windows and doors; shades; Venetian blinds; drapery rods; curtain rods; radiator covers; attached TV antennas; heating, central cooling, ventilating, lighting and plumbing fixtures; attached mirrors, shelving, interior shutters, cabinets and bookcases; awnings; porch shades; planted vegetation; garage door openers and transmitters; attached fireplace screens; smoke detectors; and any additional items of personal property that seller and purchaser agree to convey. Items excluded:

CLOSING AND POSSESSION: "__________ days after contract or by mutual agreement."

2. This agreement is an Exclusive Right to Sell my property, and I agree to cooperate fully with you, refer all inquiries to you, and conduct all negotiations through you.

3. I agree to pay you a brokerage commission for the sale of the property amounting to 6% of the first $100,000 of purchase price and 5% of the balance, if the property is sold during the period of this agreement, or if it is sold directly or indirectly within one year after expiration of this agreement to a purchaser to whom it was offered during the period hereof, or if sold to a lessee who subsequently purchases. However, with respect to any sale made after the expiration of this agreement, no commission shall be due Kahn as listing broker if such sale shall have been made after we entered into a valid, written listing agreement with another licensed real estate broker.

4. The commission is due and payable on the closing date designated in an acceptable purchase contract. If property is sold on contract for deed, commission is due on the initial closing date. In the event a purchase contract is entered into and purchaser defaults without fault on the Seller's part, Kahn will waive the commission, and this agreement shall be continued from the date of default through the date provided in paragraph 10.

5. I have read Kahn's policy printed on the reverse side of this sheet, and I understand that: (a) The Kahn Sales Counselor named below is designated as my sole and exclusive legal agent and representative; (b) Other Kahn Sales Counselors or employees may on occasion perform certain ministerial services for my property, such as arranging for showings, sitting at open houses, etc., but they shall not be considered my legal agent; (c) Kahn Sales Counselors may act either as my subagents or as exclusive legal agents for potential buyers; (d) If my designated legal agent represents a potential buyer interested in my property, the dual agency situation will be resolved as described on the reverse side of this sheet; and (e) Kahn may share its sales commission with other brokers who may be buyers' agents, should one of their buyers purchase my property.

6. Should I decide to lease the property, Kahn shall be the exclusive rental agent for me for which Kahn shall, upon execution of the lease, receive from me a commission of 7% of the first year's rent and 2% thereafter. If any lessee should purchase the property, Kahn shall receive a sales commission in the amount stated in paragraph 3 above.

7. Kahn is to list the property and diligently work to effect its sale at a price of $____________________, or any lesser amount that I agree to accept.

8. Kahn is to take prospective purchasers through the property at convenient times, make a continued, earnest effort to sell the property, advertise the property as Kahn deems advisable, display signs, and provide information on this property to members of the local multiple listing service.

9. Kahn's sole duty is to effect a sale of the property, and they are not charged with the inspection or custody of the property, its management, maintenance, upkeep or repair. However, nothing contained herein shall prohibit them from entering the property for the purpose of showing it to prospective purchasers.

10. This agreement shall be effective for 180 days after acceptance by Kahn.

11. I warrant that there are no unpaid special assessments and there are no special assessment proceedings pending or confirmed relative to this property except as stated herein. ______________________________
____

12. I agree to save and hold you harmless from all claims, disputes, litigation, judgments, and costs (including reasonable attorney's fees) arising from my breach of this agreement, from any incorrect information or misrepresentations supplied by me or from any material facts, including latent defects, that are known to me that I fail to disclose.

13. I agree that should it become necessary to settle any claim relating to the property or this contract, it shall be settled by expedited arbitration in accordance with the commercial rules of the American Arbitration Association then pending.

14. This agreement shall be binding upon and inure to the benefit of the heirs, administrators, successors, and assigns of the parties hereto. The parties to this agreement understand that it is illegal to refuse to display or to sell to any person for reasons of race, color, religion, national origin, sex, age, sexual orientation, marital status, presence or age of children, or physical disability.

15. I understand that information as to the sale of my property will not be disclosed until all earnest money is collected and all contingencies are met.

16. I warrant my authorization to execute this agreement and to deal with and on behalf of the said property as herein provided.

17. **I am moving out of the area and would like information about my destination city and Kahn's nationwide relocation services.** ☐ **Yes** ☐ **No**

Telephone: (H) ______________________ (O) ______________________

Sales Counselor and Designated Exclusive Legal Agent ______________________

● Accepted by: KAHN REALTY, INC./KAHN MANIERRE REALTY, INC.

Realtor® ______________________ Seller ______________________

Date of Acceptance ______________________ Seller ______________________

MLSA White — Kahn File Copy Canary — Seller's Copy after acceptance by Kahn Form No. KR-KM-101-S

(over) Rev. 10/93

DISTRIBUTED BY CALIFORNIA ASSOCIATION OF REALTORS®

FORM DLF-14

CALIFORNIA ASSOCIATION OF REALTORS

☐

REAL ESTATE PURCHASE CONTRACT AND RECEIPT FOR DEPOSIT

THIS IS MORE THAN A RECEIPT FOR MONEY. IT IS INTENDED TO BE A LEGALLY BINDING CONTRACT. READ IT CAREFULLY.
CALIFORNIA ASSOCIATION OF REALTORS® (CAR) STANDARD FORM

DATE: ______________________, 19_____ AT ______________________, California,

RECEIVED FROM ______________________ ("Buyer")

THE SUM OF ______________________ Dollars $__________

as a deposit to be applied toward the

PURCHASE PRICE OF ______________________ Dollars $__________

FOR PURCHASE OF PROPERTY SITUATED IN ______________, COUNTY OF ______________, California,

DESCRIBED AS ______________________ ("Property").

1. **FINANCING: THE OBTAINING OF THE LOAN(S) BELOW IS A CONTINGENCY OF THIS AGREEMENT. Buyer shall act diligently and in good faith to obtain all applicable financing.**

   A. FINANCING CONTINGENCY shall remain in effect until (Check ONLY ONE of the following):

   1. ☐ (If checked). The designated loan(s) is/are funded and/or the assumption of existing financing is approved by Lender.

   OR 2. ☐ (If checked). ______ calendar days after acceptance of the offer. Buyer shall remove the financing contingency in writing within this time. If Buyer fails to do so, then Seller may cancel this agreement by giving written notice of cancellation to Buyer.

   B. OBTAINING OF DEPOSIT AND DOWN PAYMENT by the Buyer is NOT a contingency, unless otherwise agreed in writing.

   C. DEPOSIT to be deposited ☐ with Escrow Holder, ☐ into Broker's trust account, or ☐ ______________ $ __________

   BY ☐ Personal check, ☐ Cashier's check, ☐ Cash, or ☐ ______________,

   PAYABLE TO ______________________

   TO BE HELD UNCASHED UNTIL the next business day after acceptance of the offer, or ☐ ______________.

   D. INCREASED DEPOSIT, within ______ calendar days after acceptance of the offer, to be deposited ☐ with Escrow Holder, ☐ into Broker's trust account, or ☐ ______________ . . . . $ __________

   E. BALANCE OF DOWN PAYMENT to be deposited with Escrow Holder on demand of Escrow Holder . . . . $ __________

F. FIRST LOAN IN THE AMOUNT OF . . . . $ ____________

☐ NEW First Deed of Trust in favor of ☐ LENDER, ☐ SELLER; or

☐ ASSUMPTION of existing First Deed of Trust; or ☐ ________________________________;

encumbering the Property, securing a note payable at approximately $____________ per month (☐ or more), to include ☐ principal and interest, ☐ interest only, at maximum interest of _____% ☐ fixed rate, ☐ initial adjustable rate, with a maximum lifetime interest rate increase of _____% over the initial rate, balance due in _______ years. Buyer shall pay loan fees/points not to exceed ______________.

G. SECOND LOAN IN THE AMOUNT OF . . . . $ ____________

☐ NEW Second Deed of Trust in favor of ☐ LENDER, ☐ SELLER; or

☐ ASSUMPTION of Existing Second Deed of Trust; or ☐ ________________________________;

encumbering the Property, securing a note payable at approximately $____________ per month (☐ or more), to include ☐ principal and interest, ☐ interest only, at maximum interest of _____% ☐ fixed rate, ☐ initial adjustable rate, with a maximum lifetime interest rate increase of _____% over the initial rate, balance due in _______ years. Buyer shall pay loan fees/points not to exceed ______________.

H. TOTAL PURCHASE PRICE, not including costs of obtaining loans and other closing costs . . . . $ ____________

I. LOAN APPLICATIONS: Buyer shall, within the time specified in paragraph 26B(1), submit to lender(s) (or to Seller for applicable Seller financing), a completed loan or assumption application(s), and provide to Seller written acknowledgment of Buyer's compliance. For Seller financing: (1) Buyer shall submit a completed loan application on FNMA Form 1003; (2) Buyer authorizes Seller and/or Broker(s) to obtain, at Buyer's expense, a copy of Buyer's credit report; and (3) Seller may cancel this purchase and sale agreement upon disapproval of either the application or the credit report, by providing to Buyer written notice within 7 (or ☐ _____) calendar days after receipt of those documents.

J. EXISTING LOANS: For existing loans to be taken over by Buyer, Seller shall promptly request and upon receipt provide to Buyer copies of all applicable notes and deeds of trust, loan balances, and current interest rates. Buyer may give Seller written notice of disapproval within the time specified in paragraph 26B(5). Differences between estimated and actual loan balance(s) shall be adjusted at close of escrow by:

☐ Cash downpayment, or ☐ ________________________________.

Impound account(s), if any, shall be: ☐ Charged to Buyer and credited to Seller, or ☐ ____________________.

K. LOAN FEATURES: LOANS/DOCUMENTS CONTAIN A NUMBER OF IMPORTANT FEATURES AFFECTING THE RIGHTS OF THE BORROWER AND LENDER. READ ALL LOAN DOCUMENTS CAREFULLY.

L. ADDITIONAL SELLER FINANCING TERMS: The following terms apply ONLY to financing extended by Seller under this agreement. The rate specified as the maximum interest rate in F or G above, as applicable, shall be the actual fixed interest rate for seller financing. Any promissory note and/or deed of trust given by Buyer to Seller shall contain, but not be limited to, the following additional terms:

1. REQUEST FOR NOTICE OF DEFAULT on senior loans.
2. Buyer shall execute and pay for a REQUEST FOR NOTICE OF DELINQUENCY in escrow and at any future time if requested by Seller.
3. Acceleration clause making the loan due, when permitted by law, at Seller's option, upon the sale or transfer of the Property or any interest in it.
4. A late charge of 6.0% of the installment due, or $5.00, whichever is greater, if the installment is not received within 10 days of the date it is due.
5. Title insurance coverage in the form of a joint protection policy shall be provided insuring Seller's deed of trust interest in the Property.
6. Tax Service shall be obtained and paid for by Buyer to notify Seller if property taxes have not been paid.
7. Buyer shall provide fire and extended coverage insurance during the period of the seller financing, in an amount sufficient to replace all improvements on the Property, or the total encumbrances against the Property, whichever is less, with a loss payable endorsement in favor of Seller.
8. The addition, deletion, or substitution of any person or entity under this agreement, or to title prior to close of escrow, shall require Seller's written consent. Seller may grant or withhold consent in Seller's sole discretion. Any additional or substituted person or entity shall, if requested by Seller, submit to Seller the same documentation as required for the original named Buyer. Seller and/or Broker(s) may obtain a credit report on any such person or entity.
9. If the Property contains 1 to 4 dwelling units, Buyer and Seller shall execute a Seller Financing Disclosure Statement (CAR FORM SFD-14) (Civil Code §§2956-2967), if applicable, as provided by arranger of credit, as soon as practicable prior to execution of security documents.

M. ADDITIONAL FINANCING TERMS: ______________________________

____

____

Buyer and Seller acknowledge receipt of copy of this page, which constitutes Page 1 of ______ Pages.

Buyer's Initials (________) (________) Seller's Initials (________) (________)

THIS STANDARDIZED DOCUMENT FOR USE IN SIMPLE TRANSACTIONS HAS BEEN APPROVED BY THE CALIFORNIA ASSOCIATION OF REALTORS® IN FORM ONLY. NO REPRESENTATION IS MADE AS TO THE APPROVAL OF THE FORM OF ANY SUPPLEMENTS NOT CURRENTLY PUBLISHED BY THE CALIFORNIA ASSOCIATION OF REALTORS® OR THE LEGAL VALIDITY OR ADEQUACY OF ANY PROVISION IN ANY SPECIFIC TRANSACTION. IT SHOULD NOT BE USED IN COMPLEX TRANSACTIONS OR WITH EXTENSIVE RIDERS OR ADDITIONS.

A REAL ESTATE BROKER IS THE PERSON QUALIFIED TO ADVISE ON REAL ESTATE TRANSACTIONS. IF YOU DESIRE LEGAL OR TAX ADVICE, CONSULT AN APPROPRIATE PROFESSIONAL.

REVISED 1/94

OFFICE USE ONLY

Reviewed by Broker or Designee ________

Date ________

EQUAL HOUSING OPPORTUNITY

M-R-Jan-94

☐

Property Address: ______________________________ ____________, 19____

2. **ATTACHED SUPPLEMENTS:** The following ATTACHED supplements are incorporated in this agreement:
☐ ______________________ ☐ ______________________
☐ ______________________ ☐ ______________________

3. **ESCROW:** Escrow instructions shall be signed by Buyer and Seller and delivered to ______________________, the designated Escrow Holder, within ______ calendar days after acceptance of the offer (or ☐ at least ______ calendar days before close of escrow). Buyer and Seller hereby jointly instruct Escrow Holder and Broker(s) that Buyer's deposit(s) placed into escrow or into Broker's trust account will be held as a good faith deposit toward the completion of this transaction. Release of Buyer's funds will require mutual, signed release instructions from both Buyer and Seller, judicial decision, or arbitration award. Escrow shall close ☐ on ______________, 19____, or ☐ within ______ calendar days after acceptance of the offer. Escrow fee to be paid as follows: ______________________.

4. **OCCUPANCY:** Buyer ☐ does, ☐ does not intend to occupy Property as Buyer's primary residence.

5. **POSSESSION AND KEYS:** Seller shall deliver possession and occupancy of the Property to Buyer ☐ on the date of recordation of the deed at ________ AM/PM, or ☐ no later than ____ calendar days after date of recordation at ________ AM/PM, or ☐ ______________. Property shall be vacant unless otherwise agreed in writing. If applicable, Seller and Buyer shall execute Interim Occupancy Agreement (CAR FORM IOA-14) or Residential Lease Agreement After Sale (CAR FORM RLAS-11). Seller shall provide keys and/or means to operate all Property locks, mailboxes, security systems, alarms, garage door openers, and Homeowners' Association facilities.

6. **TITLE AND VESTING:** Buyer shall be provided a current preliminary (title) report at ______________ expense. Buyer shall, within the time specified in paragraph 26B(5), provide written notice to Seller of any items reasonably disapproved. (A preliminary report is only an offer by the title insurer to issue a policy of title insurance and may not contain every item affecting title.) At close of escrow: (a) Title shall be transferred by grant deed; (b) title shall be free of liens, except as provided in this agreement; (c) title shall be free of other encumbrances, easements, restrictions, rights, and conditions of record or known to Seller, except for: (1) all matters shown in the preliminary (title) report which are not disapproved in writing by Buyer as above, and (2) ______________; (d) Buyer shall receive a California Land Title Association (CLTA) policy issued by ______________________ Company, at ______________ expense. (An ALTA-R policy may provide greater protection for Buyer and may be available at the same or slightly higher cost than a CLTA policy. The designated title company can provide information, at Buyer's request, about availability and desirability of other types of title insurance.) For Seller financing, paragraph 1L(5) provides for a joint protection policy. Title shall vest as designated in Buyer's escrow instructions. **(THE MANNER OF TAKING TITLE MAY HAVE SIGNIFICANT LEGAL AND TAX CONSEQUENCES; THEREFORE, BUYER SHOULD GIVE THIS MATTER SERIOUS CONSIDERATION.)**

PRORATIONS:

A. Real property taxes and assessments, interest, rents, Homeowners' Association regular dues and regular assessments, premiums on insurance assume by Buyer, payments on bonds and assessments assumed by Buyer, and ____________________ shall be paid current and prorate between Buyer and Seller, unless otherwise shown in paragraph 7B or 7C, as of: ☐ date of recordation of the deed, or ☐ __________

B. Mello-Roos and other Special Assessment District bonds and assessments which are now a lien shall be:
☐ paid current by Seller as of the date shown in paragraph 7A (payments that are not yet due shall be assumed by Buyer without credit toward th purchase price); or ☐ ____________________

C. Homeowners' Association special assessments, which are now a lien, shall be: ☐ paid current by Seller as of the date shown in paragraph 7A (paymen that are not yet due shall be assumed by Buyer without credit toward the purchase price); or ☐ ____________________

D. County transfer tax or transfer fee shall be paid by ____________________. City transfer tax or transfer fee shall be paid b ____________________. Homeowners' Association transfer fee shall be paid by __________

E. THE PROPERTY WILL BE REASSESSED UPON CHANGE OF OWNERSHIP. THIS WILL AFFECT THE TAXES TO BE PAID. Any supplemental tax bil shall be paid as follows: (1) for periods **after close** of escrow, by Buyer (or by final acquiring party, if part of an exchange), and (2) for periods prior to clos of escrow, by Seller. TAX BILLS ISSUED **AFTER** CLOSE OF ESCROW SHALL BE HANDLED DIRECTLY BETWEEN BUYER AND SELLER.

CONDOMINIUM/P.D.: If the Property is in a condominium/planned development: (a) the Property has ______ assigned parking space(s); (b) the current regul Homeowners' Association dues/assessments are $________________ ☐ monthly, or ☐ ____________________ (c) Seller shall promptly disclose in writing to Buyer any known pending special assessments, claims, or litigation; and (d) Seller shall promptly request, and, upo receipt, provide to Buyer copies of covenants, conditions, and restrictions; articles of incorporation; by-laws; other governing documents; most current financi statement distributed (Civil Code §1365); statement regarding limited enforceability of age restrictions, if applicable; current Homeowners' Association stateme showing any unpaid assessments (Civil Code §1368); any other documents required by law; most recent six months Homeowners' Association minutes, if availabl and ____. Buyer shall, within the time specified in paragraph 26B(5), provide writte notice to Seller of any items disapproved. READ PARAGRAPH 7 FOR PRORATIONS AND TRANSFER FEES.

BUYER'S INVESTIGATION OF PROPERTY CONDITION: Buyer shall have the right to conduct inspections, investigations, tests, surveys, and other studie ("Inspections") at Buyer's expense. Buyer shall, within the times specified in paragraphs 26B(2) and (3), complete these Inspections and shall notify Selle in writing of any item(s) disapproved. Buyer is strongly advised to exercise this right and to make Buyer's own selection of professionals with appropriate qualification to conduct Inspections of the entire Property. If Buyer does not exercise this right to conduct Inspections, Buyer is acting against the advice of Broker(s). I any event, Buyer is relying upon Inspections made or obtained by Buyer. **BUYER AND SELLER ARE AWARE THAT THE BROKER(S) DO(ES) NOT GUARANTE AND IN NO WAY ASSUME(S) RESPONSIBILITY FOR, THE CONDITION OF THE PROPERTY. BUYER IS ALSO AWARE OF BUYER'S AFFIRMATIVE DUTY T EXERCISE REASONABLE CARE TO PROTECT HIMSELF OR HERSELF, INCLUDING THOSE FACTS WHICH ARE KNOWN TO OR WITHIN THE DILIGENT ATTENTIO AND OBSERVATION OF THE BUYER (Civil Code §2079.5).**

Seller shall make the Property available for all Inspections. Buyer shall keep the Property free and clear of liens; shall indemnify and hold Seller harmless from all liability, claims, demands, damages, and costs; and shall repair all damages arising from the Inspections.

No Inspections may be made by any building or zoning inspector or government employee without the prior written consent of Seller. Buyer shall provide to Seller, at no cost, upon request of Seller, complete copies of all Inspection reports obtained by Buyer concerning the Property.

BUYER IS STRONGLY ADVISED TO INVESTIGATE THE CONDITION AND SUITABILITY OF ALL ASPECTS OF THE PROPERTY AND ALL MATTERS AFFECTING THE VALUE OR DESIRABILITY OF THE PROPERTY, INCLUDING, BUT NOT LIMITED TO, THE FOLLOWING:

A. Built-in appliances, structural, foundation, roof, plumbing, heating, air conditioning, electrical, mechanical, security, pool/spa systems and components, and any personal property included in the sale.

B. Square footage, room dimensions, lot size, and age of Property improvements. (Any numerical statements regarding these items are APPROXIMATIONS ONLY and should not be relied upon.)

C. Property lines and boundaries. (Fences, hedges, walls, and other natural or constructed barriers or markers do not necessarily identify true Property boundaries. Property lines may be verified by survey.)

D. Sewer, septic, and well systems and components. (Property may not be connected to sewer, and applicable fees may not have been paid. Septic tank may need to be pumped and leach field may need to be inspected.)

E. Limitations, restrictions, and requirements regarding Property use, future development, zoning, building, size, governmental permits, and inspections.

F. Water and utility availability and use restrictions.

G. Potential environmental hazards including asbestos, formaldehyde, radon gas, lead-based paint, other lead contamination, fuel or chemical storage tanks, contaminated soil or water, hazardous waste, electromagnetic fields, nuclear sources, and other substances, materials, products, or conditions.

H. Geologic/seismic conditions, soil and terrain stability, suitability, and drainage.

I. Neighborhood or Property conditions including schools, proximity and adequacy of law enforcement, proximity to commercial, industrial, or agricultural activities, crime statistics, fire protection, other governmental services, existing and proposed transportation, construction and development, airport noise, noise or odor from any source, other nuisances, hazards, or circumstances, and any conditions or influences of significance to certain cultures and/or religions.

J. Buyer is advised to make further inquiries and to consult government agencies, lenders, insurance agents, architects, and other appropriate persons and entities concerning the use of the Property under applicable building, zoning, fire, health, and safety codes, and for evaluation of potential hazards.

K. Other: ______________________________

____

Buyer and Seller acknowledge receipt of copy of this page, which constitutes Page 2 of ______ Pages.

Buyer's Initials (________) (________) Seller's Initials (________) (________)

OFFICE USE ONLY

Reviewed by Broker or Designee ________

Date ________

EQUAL HOUSING OPPORTUNITY

M-R-Jan-94

☐

Property Address: ______________________________ ______________, 19____

10. CONDITION OF PROPERTY: (Initial ONLY paragraph A or B; DO NOT initial both.)

Buyer's Initials ____/____ Seller's Initials ____/____

A. SELLER WARRANTY: (If A is initialled, DO NOT initial B.) Seller warrants that on the date possession is made available to Buyer: (1) Roof shall be free of KNOWN leaks; (2) built-in appliances (including free-standing oven and range, if included in sale), plumbing, heating, air conditioning, electrical, water, sewer/septic, and pool/spa systems, if any, shall be operative; (3) plumbing systems, shower pan(s), and shower enclosure(s) shall be free of leaks; (4) all broken or cracked glass shall be replaced; (5) Property, including pool/spa, landscaping, and grounds, shall be maintained in substantially the same condition as on the date of acceptance of the offer; (6) all debris and all personal property not included in the sale shall be removed; (7) ______________________________.

NOTE TO BUYER: This warranty is limited to items specified in this paragraph A. Items discovered in Buyer's Inspections which are not covered by this paragraph shall be governed by the procedure in paragraphs 9 and 26.

NOTE TO SELLER: Disclosures in the Real Estate Transfer Disclosure Statement (CAR FORM TDS-14), and items discovered in Buyer's Inspections, do NOT eliminate Seller's obligations under this warranty unless specifically agreed in writing.

OR

Buyer's Initials ____/____ Seller's Initials ____/____

B. "AS-IS" CONDITION: (If B is initialled, DO NOT initial A.) Property is sold "AS-IS," in its present condition, without warranty. Seller shall not be responsible for making corrections or repairs of any nature except: (1) Structural pest control repairs, if applicable under paragraph 19, and (2) ______________________________.

Buyer retains the right to disapprove the condition of the Property based upon items discovered in Buyer's Inspections under paragraph 9. **SELLER REMAINS OBLIGATED TO DISCLOSE ADVERSE MATERIAL FACTS WHICH ARE KNOWN TO SELLER AND TO MAKE OTHER DISCLOSURES REQUIRED BY LAW.**

11. TRANSFER DISCLOSURE STATEMENT: Unless exempt, a Real Estate Transfer Disclosure Statement ("TDS") (CAR FORM TDS-14) shall be completed by Seller and delivered to Buyer (Civil Code §§1102-1102.15). Buyer shall sign and return a copy of the TDS to Seller or Seller's agent: (a) ☐ Buyer has received a TDS prior to execution of the offer, **OR** (b) ☐ Buyer shall be provided a TDS within ______ calendar days after acceptance of the offer. If the TDS is delivered to Buyer after the offer is executed, Buyer shall have the right to terminate this agreement within three (3) days after delivery in person, or five (5) days after delivery by deposit in the mail by giving written notice of termination to Seller or Seller's agent. DISCLOSURES IN THE TDS DO NOT ELIMINATE SELLER'S OBLIGATIONS, IF ANY, UNDER PARAGRAPH 10.

12. PROPERTY DISCLOSURES: When applicable to the Property and required by law, Seller shall provide to Buyer, at Seller's expense, the following disclosures and information. Buyer shall then, within the time specified in paragraph 26B(5) and (6), investigate the disclosures and information and provide written notice to Seller of any item disapproved pursuant to A-C and E1(b) below.

A. GEOLOGIC/SEISMIC HAZARD ZONES DISCLOSURE: If the Property is located in a Special Studies Zone (SSZ) (Public Resources Code §§2621-2625), Seismic Hazard Zone (SHZ) (Public Resources Code §§2690-2699.6), or in a locally designated geological, seismic, or other hazard zone(s) or area(s) where disclosure is required by law, Seller shall, within the time specified in paragraph 26B(7), disclose in writing to Buyer this fact(s) and any other information required by law. (GEOLOGIC, SEISMIC AND FLOOD HAZARD DISCLOSURE (CAR FORM GFD-14) SHALL SATISFY THIS REQUIREMENT.) Construction or development of any structure may be restricted. Disclosure of SSZs and SHZs is required only where the maps, or information contained in the maps, are "reasonably available" as defined in Public Resources Code §§2621.9(c)(1) and 2694(c)(1).

B. SPECIAL FLOOD HAZARD AREAS: If the Property is located in a Special Flood Hazard Area designated by the Federal Emergency Management Agency (FEMA), Seller shall, within the time specified in paragraph 26B(7), disclose this fact in writing to Buyer. (GEOLOGIC, SEISMIC AND FLOOD HAZARD DISCLOSURE (CAR FORM GFD-14) SHALL SATISFY THIS REQUIREMENT.) Government regulations may impose building restrictions and requirements which may substantially impact and limit construction and remodeling of improvements. Flood insurance may be required by lender.

C. STATE FIRE RESPONSIBILITY AREAS: If the Property is located in a State Fire Responsibility Area, Seller shall, within the time specified in paragraph 26B(7), disclose this fact in writing to Buyer (Public Resources Code §4136). Disclosure may be made in the Real Estate Transfer Disclosure Statement (CAR FORM TDS-14). Government regulations may impose building restrictions and requirements which may substantially impact and limit construction and remodeling of improvements. Disclosure of these areas is required only if the Seller has actual knowledge that the Property is located in such an area or if maps of such areas have been provided to the county assessor's office.

D. MELLO-ROOS: Seller shall make a good faith effort to obtain a disclosure notice from any local agencies which levy on the Property a special tax pursuant to the Mello-Roos Community Facilities Act, and shall deliver to Buyer any such notice made available by those agencies.

E. EARTHQUAKE SAFETY:

1. PRE-1960 PROPERTIES: If the Property was built prior to 1960, and contains ONE-TO-FOUR DWELLING UNITS of conventional light frame construction, Seller shall, unless exempt, within the time specified in paragraph 26B(7), provide to Buyer: (a) a copy of "The Homeowner's Guide to Earthquake Safety," and (b) written disclosure of known seismic deficiencies (Government Code §§8897-8897.5).
2. PRE-1975 PROPERTIES: If the Property was built prior to 1975, and contains RESIDENTIAL, COMMERCIAL, OR OTHER STRUCTURES constructed of masonry or precast concrete, with wood frame floors or roofs, Seller shall, unless exempt, within the time specified in paragraph 26B(7), provide to Buyer a copy of "The Commercial Property Owner's Guide to Earthquake Safety" (Government Code §§8893-8893.5).
3. ALL PROPERTIES: If the booklets described in paragraphs E1 and E2 are not required, Buyer is advised that they are available and contain important information that may be useful for ALL TYPES OF PROPERTY (Civil Code §§2079.8 and 2079.9).

F. SMOKE DETECTOR(S): State law requires that residences be equipped with operable smoke detector(s). Local ordinances may have additional requirements. Unless exempt, Seller shall, prior to close of escrow, provide to Buyer a written statement of compliance and any other documents required, in accordance with applicable state and local law. (SMOKE DETECTOR STATEMENT OF COMPLIANCE (CAR FORM SDC-11) SHALL SATISFY THE STATE PORTION OF THIS REQUIREMENT.) Additional smoke detector(s), if required, shall be installed by Seller at Seller's expense prior to close of escrow.

G. ENVIRONMENTAL HAZARDS BOOKLET: The booklet, "Environmental Hazards: Guide for Homeowners and Buyers," is published by the California Department of Real Estate, and contains information that may be useful for ALL TYPES OF PROPERTY (Civil Code §2079.7).

H. LEAD BASED PAINT: Buyers obtaining new FHA-insured financing on residential properties constructed prior to 1978 are required to sign a lead paint disclosure form. (NOTICE TO PURCHASERS OF HOUSING CONSTRUCTED BEFORE 1978 (CAR FORM LPD-14) SHALL SATISFY THIS REQUIREMENT.)

I. OTHER: ______________________________.

GOVERNMENTAL COMPLIANCE: Seller shall promptly disclose to Buyer any improvements, additions, alterations, or repairs ("Improvements") made by Seller or known to Seller to have been made without required governmental permits, final inspections, and approvals. In addition, Seller represents that Seller has no knowledge of any notice of violations of City, County, State, or Federal building, zoning, fire, or health laws, codes, statutes, ordinances, regulations, or rules filed or issued against the Property. If Seller receives notice or is made aware of any of the above violations prior to close of escrow, Seller shall immediately notify Buyer in writing. Buyer shall, within the time specified in paragraph 26B(5), provide written notice to Seller of any items disapproved.

RETROFIT: Compliance with any minimum mandatory government retrofit standards, including but not limited to energy and utility efficiency requirements and proof of compliance, shall be paid for by ☐ Buyer, ☐ Seller.

15. **FIXTURES:** All existing fixtures and fittings that are attached to the Property or for which special openings have been made are INCLUDED IN THE PURCHASE PRICE (unless excluded below) and are to be transferred free of liens. These include, but are not limited to, electrical, lighting, plumbing and heating fixtures, fireplace inserts, solar systems, built-in appliances, screens, awnings, shutters, window coverings, attached floor coverings, television antennas/satellite dishes and related equipment, private integrated telephone systems, air coolers/conditioners, pool/spa equipment, water softeners (if owned by Seller), security systems/alarms (if owned by Seller), garage door openers/remote controls, attached fireplace equipment, mailbox, in-ground landscaping including trees/shrubs, and ______________________________.

ITEMS EXCLUDED: ______________________________.

16. **PERSONAL PROPERTY:** The following items of personal property, free of liens and without warranty of condition (unless provided in paragraph 10A) or fitness for use, are included: ______________________________

____

______________________________.

17. **HOME WARRANTY PLANS:** Buyer and Seller are informed that home warranty plans are available. These plans may provide additional protection and benefit to Buyer and Seller. Broker(s) do not endorse, approve, or recommend any particular company or program. Buyer and Seller elect (Check ONLY ONE):

☐ To purchase a home warranty plan with the following optional coverage ______________________________, at a cost not to exceed $__________, to be paid by ____________________, and to be issued by ______________________________ Company,

OR

☐ Buyer and Seller elect NOT to purchase a home warranty plan.

18. **SEPTIC SYSTEM: (If initialled by all parties.)**

Buyer's Initials _____/_____ **Seller's Initials** _____/_____

☐ Buyer, ☐ Seller shall pay to have septic system pumped and certified. Evidence of compliance shall be provided to the other party before close of escrow.

☐ Buyer, ☐ Seller to pay for sewer connection if required by local ordinance.

Buyer and Seller acknowledge receipt of copy of this page, which constitutes Page 3 of ________ Pages.

Buyer's Initials (__________) (__________) Seller's Initials (__________) (__________)

OFFICE USE ONLY

Reviewed by Broker or Designee __________

Date __________

EQUAL HOUSING OPPORTUNITY

M-R-Jan-94

Property Address: ______________________________ ______________, 19____

19. PEST CONTROL: (If initialled by all parties.)

Buyer's Initials ____/____ **Seller's Initials** ____/____

A. Seller shall, within the time specified in paragraph 26B(8), provide to Buyer a current written Wood Destroying Pests and Organisms Inspection Report. Report shall be at the expense of ☐ Buyer, ☐ Seller, to be performed by ______________________________, a registered Structural Pest Control Company, covering the main building and **(If checked):**
☐ detached garage(s) or carport(s); ☐ the following other structures on the Property: ______________________________.

B. If requested by Buyer or Seller, the report shall separately identify each recommendation for corrective work as follows:
"Section 1": Infestation or infection which is evident.
"Section 2": Conditions that are present which are deemed likely to lead to infestation or infection.

C. If no infestation or infection by wood destroying pests or organisms is found, the report shall include a written Certification that on the inspection date no evidence of active infestation was found (Business and Professions Code §8519(a).)

D. Work recommended to correct conditions described in "Section 1" shall be at the expense of ☐ Buyer, ☐ Seller.

E. Work recommended to correct conditions described in "Section 2," **if requested by Buyer**, shall be at the expense of ☐ Buyer, ☐ Seller.

F. Work to be performed at Seller's expense may be performed by Seller or through others, provided that: (a) all required permits and final inspections are obtained, and (b) upon completion of repairs a written Certification is issued by a registered Structural Pest Control Company showing that the inspected property "is now free of evidence of active infestation or infection." (Business and Professions Code §8519(b).)

G. If inspection of inaccessible areas is recommended in the report, Buyer has the option to accept and approve the report, or request in writing within 5 (or ☐ ______) calendar days of receipt of the report that further inspection be made. BUYER'S FAILURE TO NOTIFY SELLER IN WRITING OF SUCH REQUEST SHALL CONCLUSIVELY BE CONSIDERED APPROVAL OF THE REPORT. If further inspection recommends "Section 1" and/or "Section 2" corrective work, such work, and the inspection, entry, and closing of the inaccessible areas, shall be at the expense of the respective party designated in paragraphs (A), (D) and/or (E). If no infestation or infection is found, the inspection, entry, and closing of the inaccessible areas shall be at the expense of Buyer.

H. Inspections, corrective work, and certification under this paragraph shall not include roof coverings. Read paragraph 9A concerning inspection of roof coverings.

I. Work shall be performed in a skillful manner with materials of comparable quality, and shall include repair of leaking shower stalls and pans and replacement of tiles and other materials removed for repair. It is understood that exact restoration of appearance or cosmetic items following all such work is not included.

J. Funds for work agreed in writing to be performed after close of escrow shall be held in escrow and disbursed upon receipt of a written Certification that the inspected property "is now free of evidence of active infestation or infection." (Business and Professions Code §8519(b).)

K. Other: ______________________________.

20. SALE OF BUYER'S PROPERTY: (If initialled by all parties.)

Buyer's Initials ____/____ **Seller's Initials** ____/____

This agreement is contingent upon the close of escrow of Buyer's property described as ______________________________ situated in ______________________________. Buyer's property is: ☐ Listed with ______________________________ Company, ☐ In escrow No. __________ with ______________________________ Company, scheduled to close escrow on ______________, 19____.

A. (Check ONE:) ☐ Seller shall have the right to continue to offer the Property for sale, ☐ Seller shall NOT have the right to continue to offer the Property for sale (other than for back-up offers), ☐ Seller shall NOT have the right to continue to offer the Property for sale (other than for back-up offers) until ______ calendar days after acceptance of the offer.

B. If Seller has the right to continue to offer the Property for sale (other than for back-up offers) and Seller accepts another offer, Seller shall give Buyer written notice to (1) remove this contingency in writing and (2) comply with the following additional requirements ______________________________

____.

If Buyer fails to complete those actions within ______ hours or ______ calendar days after receipt of such Notice from Seller, then this agreement and any escrow shall terminate and the deposit (less costs incurred) shall be returned to Buyer.

C. If Seller does not give the Notice above and Buyer's property does not close escrow by the date specified in paragraph 3 for close of escrow of this Property, then either Seller or Buyer may cancel this agreement and any escrow by giving the other party written notice of cancellation, and the Buyer's deposit (less costs incurred) shall be returned to Buyer.

21. CANCELLATION OF PRIOR SALE/BACK-UP OFFER: (If initialled by all parties.)

Buyer's Initials ______/______ **Seller's Initials** ______/______

Buyer understands that Seller has entered into one or more contracts to sell the Property to a different buyer(s). The parties to any prior sale may mutually agree to modify or amend the terms of that sale(s). This agreement is contingent upon the written cancellation of the previous purchase and sale agreement(s) and any related escrow(s).

(Check ONLY ONE of the following.)

☐ CANCELLATION OF PRIOR SALE: If written cancellation of the previous agreement(s) is not received on or before ______________________, 19____, then either Buyer or Seller may cancel this agreement and any escrow by giving the other party to this agreement written notice of cancellation. Buyer's deposit, less costs incurred, shall then be returned to Buyer.

☐ BACK-UP OFFER: This is a back-up offer in back-up position No. ________. BUYER'S DEPOSIT CHECK SHALL BE HELD UNCASHED until a copy of the written cancellation(s) signed by all parties to the prior sale(s) is provided to Buyer. Until Buyer receives a copy of such cancellation(s), Buyer may cancel this agreement by providing written notice to Seller. Buyer's deposit shall then be returned to Buyer. AS RELATES TO A BACK-UP OFFER, TIME PERIODS IN THIS AGREEMENT WHICH ARE STATED AS A NUMBER OF DAYS SHALL BEGIN ON THE DATE SELLER GIVES TO BUYER WRITTEN NOTICE THAT ANY PRIOR CONTRACT(S) HAS BEEN CANCELLED. IF CLOSE OF ESCROW OR ANY OTHER EVENT IS SHOWN AS A SPECIFIC DATE, THAT DATE SHALL NOT BE EXTENDED UNLESS BUYER AND SELLER SPECIFICALLY AGREE IN WRITING.

22. COURT CONFIRMATION: (If initialled by all parties.)

Buyer's Initials ______/______ **Seller's Initials** ______/______

This agreement is contingent upon court confirmation on or before ______________________, 19____. The court may allow open, competitive bidding, resulting in the Property being sold to the highest bidder. Buyer has been advised to be in court when the offer is considered for confirmation. Court confirmation may be required in a probate, conservatorship, guardianship, receivership, bankruptcy, or other proceeding. Buyer understands that the Property may continue to be marketed by Broker(s) and others, and that Broker(s) and others may represent other competitive bidders prior to and at the court confirmation. If court confirmation is not obtained by date shown above, Buyer may cancel this agreement by giving written notice of cancellation to Seller.

23. **NOTICES:** Notices given pursuant to this agreement shall, unless otherwise required by law, be deemed delivered to Buyer when personally received by Buyer or ______________________________, who is authorized to receive it for Buyer, or to Seller when personally received by Seller or ______________________________, who is authorized to receive it for Seller. Delivery may be in person, by mail, or facsimile.

24. **TAX WITHHOLDING:**

A. Under the Foreign Investment in Real Property Tax Act (FIRPTA), IRC §1445, every Buyer must, unless an exemption applies, deduct and withhold 10% of the gross sales price from Seller's proceeds and send it to the Internal Revenue Service, if the Seller is a "foreign person" under that statute.

B. In addition, under California Revenue and Taxation Code §§18805 and 26131, every Buyer must, unless an exemption applies, deduct and withhold 3-1/3% of the gross sales price from Seller's proceeds and send it to the Franchise Tax Board if the Seller has a last known address outside of California or if the Seller's proceeds will be paid to a financial intermediary of the Seller.

C. Penalties may be imposed on a responsible party for non-compliance with the requirements of these statutes and related regulations. Seller and Buyer agree to execute and deliver any instrument, affidavit, statement, or instruction reasonably necessary to carry out these requirements, and to withholding of tax under those statutes if required. (SELLER'S AFFIDAVIT OF NON-FOREIGN STATUS AND/OR CALIFORNIA RESIDENCY (CAR FORM AS-14), OR BUYER'S AFFIDAVIT (CAR FORM AB-11), IF APPLICABLE, SHALL SATISFY THESE REQUIREMENTS.)

25. **RISK OF LOSS:** Except as otherwise provided in this agreement, all risk of loss to the Property which occurs after the offer is accepted shall be borne by Seller until either the title has been transferred, or possession has been given to Buyer, whichever occurs first. Any damage totalling 1.0 (one) % or less of the purchase price shall be repaired by Seller in accordance with paragraph 10, if applicable. If the land or improvements to the Property are destroyed or materially damaged prior to transfer of title in an amount exceeding 1.0 (one) % of the purchase price, then Buyer shall have the option to either terminate this agreement and recover the full deposit or purchase the Property in its then present condition. Any expenses paid by Buyer or Seller for credit reports, appraisals, title examination, or Inspections of any kind shall remain that party's responsibility. If Buyer elects to purchase the Property and the loss is covered by insurance, Seller-shall assign to Buyer all insurance proceeds covering the loss. If transfer of title and possession do not occur at the same time, BUYER AND SELLER ARE ADVISED TO SEEK ADVICE OF THEIR INSURANCE ADVISORS as to the insurance consequences thereof.

Buyer and Seller acknowledge receipt of copy of this page, which constitutes Page 4 of ______ Pages.

Buyer's Initials (________) (________) Seller's Initials (________) (________)

OFFICE USE ONLY
Reviewed by Broker or Designee ________
Date ________________

EQUAL HOUSING OPPORTUNITY

M-R-Jan-94

☐

Property Address: ______________________________ ______________, 19____

26. CONTINGENCIES/COVENANTS: METHODS OF SATISFACTION/REMOVAL, TIME FRAMES, DISAPPROVAL/APPROVAL:

A. METHOD OF SATISFYING/REMOVING CONTINGENCIES: Contingencies are to be satisfied or removed by one of the following methods:

(1) **PASSIVE METHOD:** IF BUYER FAILS TO GIVE WRITTEN NOTICE OF DISAPPROVAL OF ITEMS OR OF CANCELLATION OF THIS AGREEMENT WITHIN THE STRICT TIME PERIODS SPECIFIED IN THIS AGREEMENT (except financing contingency, if paragraph 1A(2) is checked), THEN BUYER SHALL CONCLUSIVELY BE DEEMED TO HAVE COMPLETED ALL INSPECTIONS AND REVIEW OF APPLICABLE DOCUMENTS AND DISCLOSURES AND TO HAVE MADE AN ELECTION TO PROCEED WITH THE TRANSACTION WITHOUT CORRECTION OF ANY ITEMS WHICH THE SELLER HAS NOT OTHERWISE AGREED TO CORRECT. **OR**

(2) **ACTIVE METHOD:** IF BUYER AND SELLER INITIAL THIS PARAGRAPH, THEN PARAGRAPH A(1) SHALL NOT APPLY.

Buyer's Initials **Seller's Initials**

_____ / _____ _____ / _____ BUYER'S DISAPPROVAL OF ITEMS OR REMOVAL OF CONTINGENCIES SHALL BE IN WRITING (except financing contingency, if paragraph 1A(1) is checked). IF BUYER FAILS TO REMOVE OR WAIVE ALL CONTINGENCIES IN WRITING WITHIN THE STRICT TIME PERIODS SPECIFIED IN THIS AGREEMENT, THEN SELLER MAY CANCEL THIS AGREEMENT BY GIVING WRITTEN NOTICE OF CANCELLATION TO BUYER.

B. TIME FRAMES: Buyer and Seller agree to be bound by the following time periods:

BUYER has the following number of calendar days to take the action specified, BEGINNING ON THE DATE OF ACCEPTANCE OF THE OFFER:

1. ____ Loan Application(s) (submit to lender(s) for new loan(s) and assumption(s), submit to Seller for seller financing), submit written acknowledgment to Seller (Para 1I)
2. ____ Buyer Inspections of Property (complete inspections, except GEOLOGIC, and give notice of disapproval) (Para 9)
3. ____ Buyer Inspections of Property (complete GEOLOGIC inspections and give notice of disapproval) (Para 9)
4. ____ ______________________________

BUYER has the following number of calendar days to DISAPPROVE the items listed below, BEGINNING ON THE DATE OF BUYER'S RECEIPT OF EACH ITEM:

5. ____ Existing Loan Documents (Para 1J),
Preliminary (Title) Report (Para 6),
Condominium/Planned Development Documents (Para 8),
Geologic/Seismic/Flood/State Fire Zones/Areas (Para 12A-C),
Governmental Notices Disclosure (Para 13)
6. ____ ______________________________

SELLER has the following number of calendar days to PROVIDE to Buyer, as applicable, the information listed below, BEGINNING ON THE DATE OF ACCEPTANCE OF THE OFFER:

7. ____ Geologic/Seismic/Flood/State Fire Zones/Areas Disclosures, if applicable (Para 12A-C), Homeowner's Guide to Earthquake Safety and/or Commercial Property Owner's Guide to Earthquake Safety (Para 12E)
8. ____ Pest Control Report (Para 19)
9. ____ ______________________________

The items listed below, as applicable, shall promptly be requested and upon receipt provided to Buyer:

10. Existing Loan Documents (Para 1J),
Preliminary (Title) Report (Para 6),
Condominium/Planned Development Documents (Para 8),
Mello-Roos Disclosure (Para 12D)
11. ______________________________

C. DISAPPROVAL/APPROVAL OF ITEMS:

(1) If, within the time specified, Buyer provides written reasonable disapproval to Seller of any item for which Buyer has a disapproval right, Seller shall respond in writing within ______ calendar days after receipt of Buyer's notice. If Seller is unwilling or unable to correct the items disapproved by Buyer, then Buyer may cancel this agreement by giving written notice of cancellation to Seller within ______ calendar days (after receipt of Seller's response, or after expiration of the time for Seller's response, whichever occurs first), in which case Buyer's deposit shall be returned to Buyer. If paragraph A2 is initialled, then Buyer shall provide Seller with a written notice of either cancellation or election to proceed. If Buyer elects to proceed with the transaction without Seller's correction of items, Buyer shall assume all liability, responsibility, and expense for repairs or corrections, including the expense of compliance with governmental agency requirements. This does not, however, relieve the Seller of any contractual obligations to repair or correct items otherwise agreed upon.

(2) If a MELLO-ROOS DISCLOSURE notice under paragraph 12D is delivered to Buyer after the offer is executed, Buyer shall have three (3) days after delivery in person or five (5) days after delivery by deposit in the mail to give written notice of termination to Seller.

D. FOR ALL TIME PERIODS:

1. Buyer and Seller understand that time periods can be changed only by mutual written agreement.
2. If this is a back-up offer (paragraph 21), time periods which are shown as a number of days beginning on the date of acceptance of the offer shall instead begin on the date Seller gives to Buyer written notice that any prior contract(s) has been cancelled.

27. FINAL VERIFICATION OF CONDITION: Buyer shall have the right to make a final inspection of the Property approximately 5 (or ☐ ______) calendar days prior to close of escrow, NOT AS A CONTINGENCY OF THE SALE, but solely to confirm that: (a) Seller has completed alterations, repairs, replacements, or modifications ("Repairs") as agreed in writing by Buyer and Seller, and has complied with warranty obligations, if any, in paragraph 10, and (b) the Property is otherwise in substantially the same condition as on the date of acceptance of the offer. Repairs under this agreement shall be completed prior to close of escrow unless otherwise agreed in writing, and shall comply with applicable building code and permit requirements. Materials used shall be of comparable quality to existing materials.

28. MEDIATION OF DISPUTES: BUYER AND SELLER AGREE TO MEDIATE ANY DISPUTE OR CLAIM BETWEEN THEM ARISING OUT OF THIS CONTRACT OR ANY RESULTING TRANSACTION BEFORE RESORTING TO ARBITRATION OR COURT ACTION. Mediation is a process in which parties attempt to resolve a dispute by submitting it to an impartial, neutral mediator who is authorized to facilitate the resolution of the dispute but who is not empowered to impose a settlement on the parties. Mediation fee, if any, shall be divided equally among the parties involved. Before the mediation begins, the parties agree to sign a document limiting the admissibility in arbitration or any civil action of anything said, any admission made, and any documents prepared, in the course of the mediation, consistent with Evidence Code §1152.5. In addition, if paragraph 30 is initialled by Broker(s), Buyer and Seller agree to mediate disputes or claims involving an initialling Broker, as defined by that paragraph, consistent with this provision. The election by Broker(s) to initial or not initial paragraph 30 shall not affect the applicability of this mediation provision between Buyer and Seller and shall not result in the Broker(s) being deemed parties to the purchase and sale agreement. IF ANY PARTY COMMENCES AN ARBITRATION OR COURT ACTION BASED ON A DISPUTE OR CLAIM TO WHICH THIS PARGRAPH APPLIES WITHOUT FIRST ATTEMPTING TO RESOLVE THE MATTER THROUGH MEDIATION, THEN IN THE DISCRETION OF THE ARBITRATOR(S) OR JUDGE, THAT PARTY SHALL NOT BE ENTITLED TO RECOVER ATTORNEY'S FEES EVEN IF THEY WOULD OTHERWISE BE AVAILABLE TO THAT PARTY IN ANY SUCH ARBITRATION OR COURT ACTION. However, the filing of a judicial action to enable the recording of a notice of pending action, for order of attachment, receivership, injunction, or other provisional remedies, shall not in itself constitute a loss of the right to recover attorney's fees under this provision. The following matters are excluded from the requirement of mediation hereunder: (a) a judicial or non-judicial foreclosure or other action or proceeding to enforce a deed of trust, mortgage, or installment land sale contract as defined in Civil Code §2985, (b) an unlawful detainer action, (c) the filing or enforcement of a mechanic's lien, and (d) any matter which is within the jurisdiction of a probate court.

29. **ARBITRATION OF DISPUTES:** Any dispute or claim in law or equity between Buyer and Seller arising out of this contract or any resulting transaction which is not settled through mediation shall be decided by neutral, binding arbitration and not by court action, except as provided by California law for judicial review of arbitration proceedings. In addition, if paragraph 30 is initialled by Broker(s), Buyer and Seller agree to arbitrate disputes or claims involving an initialling Broker, as defined by that paragraph, consistent with this provision. The election by Broker(s) to initial or not initial paragraph 30 shall not affect the applicability of the arbitration provision between Buyer and Seller, and shall not result in the Broker(s) being deemed parties to the purchase and sale agreement.

The arbitration shall be conducted in accordance with the rules of either the American Arbitration Association (AAA) or Judicial Arbitration and Mediation Services, Inc. (JAMS). The selection between AAA and JAMS rules shall be made by the claimant first filing for the arbitration. The parties to an arbitration may agree in writing to use different rules and/or arbitrator(s). In all other respects, the arbitration shall be conducted in accordance with Part III, Title 9 of the California Code of Civil Procedure. Judgment upon the award rendered by the arbitrator(s) may be entered in any court having jurisdiction thereof. The parties shall have the right to discovery in accordance with Code of Civil Procedure §1283.05. The following matters are excluded from arbitration hereunder: (a) a judicial or non-judicial foreclosure or other action or proceeding to enforce a deed of trust, mortgage, or installment land sale contract as defined in Civil Code §2985, (b) an unlawful detainer action, (c) the filing or enforcement of a mechanic's lien, (d) any matter which is within the jurisdiction of a probate or small claims court, and (e) an action for bodily injury or wrongful death, or for latent or patent defects, to which Code of Civil Procedure §337.1 or §337.15 applies. The filing of a judicial action to enable the recording of a notice of pending action, for order of attachment, receivership, injunction, or other provisional remedies, shall not constitute a waiver of the right to arbitrate under this provision.

"NOTICE: BY INITIALLING IN THE SPACE BELOW YOU ARE AGREEING TO HAVE ANY DISPUTE ARISING OUT OF THE MATTERS INCLUDED IN THE 'ARBITRATION OF DISPUTES' PROVISION DECIDED BY NEUTRAL ARBITRATION AS PROVIDED BY CALIFORNIA LAW AND YOU ARE GIVING UP ANY RIGHTS YOU MIGHT POSSESS TO HAVE THE DISPUTE LITIGATED IN A COURT OR JURY TRIAL. BY INITIALLING IN THE SPACE BELOW YOU ARE GIVING UP YOUR JUDICIAL RIGHTS TO DISCOVERY AND APPEAL, UNLESS THOSE RIGHTS ARE SPECIFICALLY INCLUDED IN THE 'ARBITRATION OF DISPUTES' PROVISION. IF YOU REFUSE TO SUBMIT TO ARBITRATION AFTER AGREEING TO THIS PROVISION, YOU MAY BE COMPELLED TO ARBITRATE UNDER THE AUTHORITY OF THE CALIFORNIA CODE OF CIVIL PROCEDURE. YOUR AGREEMENT TO THIS ARBITRATION PROVISION IS VOLUNTARY."

"WE HAVE READ AND UNDERSTAND THE FOREGOING AND AGREE TO SUBMIT DISPUTES ARISING OUT OF THE MATTERS INCLUDED IN THE 'ARBITRATION OF DISPUTES' PROVISION TO NEUTRAL ARBITRATION."

Buyer's Initials ______/______ Seller's Initials ______/______

Buyer and Seller acknowledge receipt of copy of this page, which constitutes Page 5 of ______ Pages.

Buyer's Initials (______) (______) Seller's Initials (______) (______)

OFFICE USE ONLY

Reviewed by Broker or Designee ______

Date ______

EQUAL HOUSING OPPORTUNITY

M-R-Jan-94

☐

Property Address: ______________________________ ______________, 19____

30. **BROKERS: (If initialled.) Any Broker who initials below agrees to (a) mediate any dispute or claim with Buyer, Seller, or other initialling Broker, arising out of this contract or any resulting transaction, consistent with paragraph 28, and (b) arbitrate any dispute or claim with Buyer, Seller, or other initialling Broker arising out of this contract or any resulting transaction, consistent with paragraph 29. However, if the dispute is solely between the Brokers, it shall instead be submitted for mediation and arbitration in accordance with the Board/Association of REALTORS® or MLS rules. If those entities decline to handle the matter, it shall be submitted pursuant to paragraphs 28 and 29. The initialling of this paragraph shall not result in any Broker being deemed a party to the purchase and sale agreement. As used in this paragraph, "Broker" means a brokerage firm and any licensed persons affiliated with that brokerage firm.**

Selling Broker
By:

Listing Broker
By:

________________ (Initials) ________________ (Initials)

31. **LIQUIDATED DAMAGES:** **(If initialled by all parties.)**

Buyer's Initials ____/____ **Seller's Initials** ____/____ **Buyer and Seller agree that if Buyer fails to complete this purchase by reason of any default of Buyer:**

A. Seller shall be released from obligation to sell the Property to Buyer.

B. Seller shall retain, as liquidated damages for breach of contract, the deposit actually paid. Buyer and Seller shall execute RECEIPT FOR INCREASED DEPOSIT/LIQUIDATED DAMAGES (CAR FORM RID-11) for any increased deposits. However, the amount retained shall be no more than 3% of the purchase price if Property is a dwelling with no more than four units, one of which Buyer intends to occupy as Buyer's residence. Any excess shall be promptly returned to Buyer.

C. Seller retains the right to proceed against Buyer for specific performance or any other claim or remedy Seller may have in law or equity, other than breach of contract damages.

D. In the event of a dispute, Funds deposited in trust accounts or escrow are not released automatically and require mutual, signed release instructions from both Buyer and Seller, judicial decision, or arbitration award.

32. **ATTORNEY'S FEES:** In any action, proceeding, or arbitration between Buyer and Seller arising out of this agreement, the prevailing party shall be entitled to reasonable attorney's fees and costs, except as provided in paragraph 28.

33. **MULTIPLE LISTING SERVICE:** If Broker is a Participant of a multiple listing service (MLS), Broker is authorized to report the sale, price, terms, and financing for publication, dissemination, information, and use of the MLS, its parent entity, authorized members, participants, and subscribers.

34. **OTHER TERMS AND CONDITIONS:** ____

____

____

____.

35. **TIME OF ESSENCE; ENTIRE CONTRACT; CHANGES:** Time is of the essence. All prior agreements between the parties are incorporated in this agreement, which constitutes the entire contract. Its terms are intended by the parties as a final, complete and exclusive expression of their agreement with respect to its subject matter and may not be contradicted by evidence of any prior agreement or contemporaneous oral agreement. The captions in this agreement are for convenience of reference only and are not intended as part of this agreement. **This agreement may not be extended, amended, modified, altered, or changed in any respect whatsoever except by a further agreement in writing signed by Buyer and Seller.**

36. **AGENCY CONFIRMATION:** The following agency relationship(s) are hereby confirmed for this transaction:

Listing Agent: ______________________________ is the agent of (check one):
(Print Firm Name)

☐ the Seller exclusively; or ☐ both the Buyer and Seller.

Selling Agent: ______________________________ (if not same as Listing Agent) is the agent of (check one):
(Print Firm Name)

☐ the Buyer exclusively; or ☐ the Seller exclusively; or ☐ both the Buyer and Seller.

(IF THE PROPERTY CONTAINS 1-4 RESIDENTIAL DWELLING UNITS, BUYER AND SELLER MUST ALSO BE GIVEN ONE OR MORE DISCLOSURE REGARDING REAL ESTATE AGENCY RELATIONSHIPS FORMS (CAR FORM AD-11).)

37. **OFFER:** This is an offer to purchase the Property. **All paragraphs with spaces for initials by Buyer and Seller are incorporated in this agreement only if initialled by both parties. If only one party initials, a Counter Offer is required until agreement is reached.** Unless acceptance is signed by Seller and a signed copy delivered in person, by mail, or facsimile, and **personally received** by Buyer or by ______________________________, who is authorized to receive it, by ____________________, 19____ at ________ AM/PM, the offer shall be deemed revoked and the deposit shall be returned. Buyer and Seller acknowledge that Broker(s) is/are not a party(ies) to the purchase and sale agreement. Buyer has read and acknowledges receipt of a copy of the offer and agrees to the above confirmation of agency relationships. This agreement and any supplement, addendum, or modification, including any photocopy or facsimile, may be executed in two or more counterparts, all of which shall constitute one and the same writing.

Receipt for deposit is acknowledged:

BROKER ______________________________

By ______________________________

BUYER ______________________________

BUYER ______________________________

Address ______________________________

____

Telephone ____________________ Fax ____________________

ACCEPTANCE

The undersigned Seller accepts the above and agrees to sell the Property on the above terms and conditions and agrees to the above confirmation of agency relationships (☐ subject to attached counter offer). Seller agrees to pay compensation for services as follows:

____________________ to ____________________, Broker, and

____________________ to ____________________, Broker,

payable: (a) on recordation of the deed or other evidence of title, or (b) if completion of sale is prevented by default of Seller, upon Seller's default, or (c) if completion of sale is prevented by default of Buyer, only if and when Seller collects damages from Buyer, by suit or otherwise, and then in an amount equal to one-half of the damages recovered, but not to exceed the above compensation, after first deducting title and escrow expenses and the expenses of collection, if any. Seller hereby irrevocably assigns to Broker(s) such compensation from Seller's proceeds in escrow. In any action, proceeding, or arbitration relating to the payment of such compensation, the prevailing party shall be entitled to reasonable attorney's fees and costs, except as provided in paragraph 28. The undersigned Seller has read, acknowledges receipt of a copy of this agreement, and authorizes Broker(s) to deliver a signed copy to Buyer.

Date __________ Telephone __________ Fax __________ SELLER ____________________

Address ____________________

____________________ SELLER ____________________

Real Estate Broker(s) confirm(s) agency relationship(s) as above. (Real Estate Brokers are not parties to the purchase and sale agreement between Buyer and Seller.):

Real Estate Broker (Selling) ____________________ By ____________________ Date __________

Address ____________________ Telephone ____________________ Fax __________

Real Estate Broker (Listing) ____________________ By ____________________ Date __________

Address ____________________ Telephone ____________________ Fax __________

Page 6 of __________ Pages.

OFFICE USE ONLY

Reviewed by Broker or Designee __________

Date __________

EQUAL HOUSING OPPORTUNITY

M-R-Jan-94

DISTRIBUTED BY CALIFORNIA ASSOCIATION OF REALTORS®

FORM TDS-14

REAL ESTATE TRANSFER DISCLOSURE STATEMENT

(CALIFORNIA CIVIL CODE 1102, ET SEQ.)

CALIFORNIA ASSOCIATION OF REALTORS® (CAR) STANDARD FORM

☐

THIS DISCLOSURE STATEMENT CONCERNS THE REAL PROPERTY SITUATED IN THE CITY OF ____________________, COUNTY OF ____________________, STATE OF CALIFORNIA, DESCRIBED AS ____________________.

THIS STATEMENT IS A DISCLOSURE OF THE CONDITION OF THE ABOVE DESCRIBED PROPERTY IN COMPLIANCE WITH SECTION 1102 OF THE CIVIL CODE AS OF ________________, 19____. IT IS NOT A WARRANTY OF ANY KIND BY THE SELLER(S) OR ANY AGENT(S) REPRESENTING ANY PRINCIPAL(S) IN THIS TRANSACTION, AND IS NOT A SUBSTITUTE FOR ANY INSPECTIONS OR WARRANTIES THE PRINCIPAL(S) MAY WISH TO OBTAIN.

I
COORDINATION WITH OTHER DISCLOSURE FORMS

This Real Estate Transfer Disclosure Statement is made pursuant to Section 1102 of the Civil Code. Other statutes require disclosures, depending upon the details of the particular real estate transaction (for example: special study zone and purchase-money liens on residential property).

Substituted Disclosures: The following disclosures have or will be in connection with this real estate transfer, and are intended to satisfy the disclosure obligations on this form, where the subject matter is the same: ____________________

____

____

____

(LIST ALL SUBSTITUTED DISCLOSURE FORMS TO BE USED IN CONNECTION WITH THIS TRANSACTION)

II

SELLER'S INFORMATION

The Seller discloses the following information with the knowledge that even though this is not a warranty, prospective Buyers may rely on this information in deciding whether and on what terms to purchase the subject property. Seller hereby authorizes any agent(s) representing any principal(s) in this transaction to provide a copy of this statement to any person or entity in connection with any actual or anticipated sale of the property.

THE FOLLOWING ARE REPRESENTATIONS MADE BY THE SELLER(S) AND ARE NOT THE REPRESENTATIONS OF THE AGENT(S), IF ANY. THIS INFORMATION IS A DISCLOSURE AND IS NOT INTENDED TO BE PART OF ANY CONTRACT BETWEEN THE BUYER AND SELLER.

Seller ☐ is ☐ is not occupying the property.

A. The subject property has the items checked below (read across):

☐ Range	☐ Oven	☐ Microwave
☐ Dishwasher	☐ Trash Compactor	☐ Garbage Disposal
☐ Washer/Dryer Hookups	☐ Window Screens	☐ Rain Gutters
☐ Burglar Alarms	☐ Smoke Detector(s)	☐ Fire Alarm
☐ T.V. Antenna	☐ Satellite Dish	☐ Intercom
☐ Central Heating	☐ Central Air Conditioning	☐ Evaporator Cooler(s)
☐ Wall/Window Air Conditioning	☐ Sprinklers	☐ Public Sewer System
☐ Septic Tank	☐ Sump Pump	☐ Water Softener
☐ Patio/Decking	☐ Built-in Barbeque	☐ Gazebo
☐ Sauna	☐ Pool	☐ Spa ☐ Hot Tub
☐ Security Gate(s)	☐ Automatic Garage Door Opener(s)*	☐ Number of Remote Controls ________
Garage: ☐ Attached	☐ Not Attached	☐ Carport
Pool/Spa Heater: ☐ Gas	☐ Solar	☐ Electric
Water Heater: ☐ Gas	☐ Solar	☐ Electric
Water Supply: ☐ City	☐ Well	☐ Private Utility ☐ Other ________
Gas Supply: ☐ Utility	☐ Bottled	

Exhaust Fan(s) in ________________ 220 Volt Wiring in ________________

Fireplace(s) in ____________ ☐ Gas Starter

☐ Roof(s): Type: ____________ Age: ____________ (approx.)

☐ Other: ____________

Are there, to the best of your (Seller's) knowledge, any of the above that are not in operating condition? ☐ Yes ☐ No If yes, then describe. (Attach additional sheets if necessary.): ____________

B. Are you (Seller) aware of any significant defects/malfunctions in any of the following? ☐ Yes ☐ No If yes, check appropriate space(s) below.

☐ Interior Walls ☐ Ceilings ☐ Floors ☐ Exterior Walls ☐ Insulation ☐ Roof(s) ☐ Windows ☐ Doors ☐ Foundation ☐ Slab(s)
☐ Driveways ☐ Sidewalks ☐ Walls/Fences ☐ Electrical Systems ☐ Plumbing/Sewers/Septics ☐ Other Structural Components

(Describe: ____________)

If any of the above is checked, explain. (Attach additional sheets if necessary): ____________

*This garage door opener may not be in compliance with the safety standards relating to automatic reversing devices as set forth in Chapter 12.5 (commencing with Section 19890) of Part 3 of Division 13 of the Health and Safety Code.

Buyer and Seller acknowledge receipt of copy of this page, which constitutes Page 1 of 2 Pages.

Buyer's Initials (______) (______) Seller's Initials (______) (______)

OFFICE USE ONLY
Reviewed by Broker or Designee ______
Date ______

IN COMPLIANCE WITH CIVIL CODE SECTION 1102.6 / EFFECTIVE JULY 1, 1991.

EQUAL HOUSING OPPORTUNITY

M-PM-5/94

☐

Subject Property Address: ______________________________ ______________, 19 ____

C. Are you (Seller) aware of any of the following:

1. Substances, materials, or products which may be an environmental hazard such as, but not limited to, asbestos, formaldehyde, radon gas, lead-based paint, fuel or chemical storage tanks, and contaminated soil or water on the subject property. ☐ Yes ☐ No
2. Features of the property shared in common with adjoining landowners, such as walls, fences, and driveways, whose use or responsibility for maintenance may have an effect on the subject property. ☐ Yes ☐ No
3. Any encroachments, easements or similar matters that may affect your interest in the subject property. ☐ Yes ☐ No
4. Room additions, structural modifications, or other alterations or repairs made without necessary permits. ☐ Yes ☐ No
5. Room additions, structural modifications, or other alterations or repairs not in compliance with building codes. ☐ Yes ☐ No
6. Landfill (compacted or otherwise) on the property or any portion thereof. ☐ Yes ☐ No
7. Any settling from any cause, or slippage, sliding, or other soil problems. ☐ Yes ☐ No
8. Flooding, drainage or grading problems. ☐ Yes ☐ No
9. Major damage to the property or any of the structures from fire, earthquake, floods, or landslides. ☐ Yes ☐ No
10. Any zoning violations, nonconforming uses, violations of "setback" requirements. ☐ Yes ☐ No
11. Neighborhood noise problems or other nuisances. ☐ Yes ☐ No
12. CC&R's or other deed restrictions or obligations. ☐ Yes ☐ No
13. Homeowners' Association which has any authority over the subject property. ☐ Yes ☐ No
14. Any "common area" (facilities such as pools, tennis courts, walkways, or other areas co-owned in undivided interest with others). ☐ Yes ☐ No
15. Any notices of abatement or citations against the property. ☐ Yes ☐ No
16. Any lawsuits against the seller threatening to or affecting this real property. ☐ Yes ☐ No

If the answer to any of these is yes, explain. (Attach additional sheets if necessary.): ______________________

____

____

____

Seller certifies that the information herein is true and correct to the best of the Seller's knowledge as of the date signed by the Seller.

Seller____ Date____________________

Seller____ Date____________________

III
AGENT'S INSPECTION DISCLOSURE

(To be completed only if the seller is represented by an agent in this transaction.)

THE UNDERSIGNED, BASED ON THE ABOVE INQUIRY OF THE SELLER(S) AS TO THE CONDITION OF THE PROPERTY AND BASED ON A REASONABLY COMPETENT AND DILIGENT VISUAL INSPECTION OF THE ACCESSIBLE AREAS OF THE PROPERTY IN CONJUNCTION WITH THAT INQUIRY, STATES THE FOLLOWING:

____

____

____

Agent (Broker
Representing Seller)______________________ By__________________________ Date______________
(PLEASE PRINT) (ASSOCIATE LICENSEE OR BROKER-SIGNATURE)

IV
AGENT'S INSPECTION DISCLOSURE

(To be completed only if the agent who has obtained the offer is other than the agent above.)

THE UNDERSIGNED, BASED ON A REASONABLY COMPETENT AND DILIGENT VISUAL INSPECTION OF THE ACCESSIBLE AREAS OF THE PROPERTY, STATES THE FOLLOWING:

____

____

____

Agent (Broker
obtaining the Offer)______________________ By__________________________ Date______________
(PLEASE PRINT) (ASSOCIATE LICENSEE OR BROKER-SIGNATURE)

V

BUYER(S) AND SELLER(S) MAY WISH TO OBTAIN PROFESSIONAL ADVICE AND/OR INSPECTIONS OF THE PROPERTY AND TO PROVIDE FOR APPROPRIATE PROVISIONS IN A CONTRACT BETWEEN BUYER AND SELLER(S) WITH RESPECT TO ANY ADVICE/INSPECTIONS/DEFECTS.

I/WE ACKNOWLEDGE RECEIPT OF A COPY OF THIS STATEMENT.

Seller ____________________ Date __________ Buyer ____________________ Date __________

Seller ____________________ Date __________ Buyer ____________________ Date __________

Agent (Broker
Representing Seller) ____________________ By ____________________ Date __________
(PLEASE PRINT) (ASSOCIATE LICENSEE OR BROKER-SIGNATURE)

Agent (Broker
obtaining the Offer) ____________________ By ____________________ Date __________
(PLEASE PRINT) (ASSOCIATE LICENSEE OR BROKER-SIGNATURE)

A REAL ESTATE BROKER IS QUALIFIED TO ADVISE ON REAL ESTATE. IF YOU DESIRE LEGAL ADVICE, CONSULT YOUR ATTORNEY.

OFFICE USE ONLY
Reviewed by Broker or Designee ________
Date ________

EQUAL HOUSING OPPORTUNITY

M-PM-5/94

REAL ESTATE TRANSFER DISCLOSURE STATEMENT (TDS-14 PAGE 2 OF 2)

A. Settlement Statement

U.S.Department of Housing and Urban Development

OMB No. 2502-0265

B. Type of Loan			
1. ☐ FHA 2. ☐ FmHA 3. ☐ Conv. Unins. 4. ☐ VA 5. ☐ Conv. Ins	6. File Number	7. Loan Number	8. Mortgage Insurance Case Number

C. Note: This form is furnished to give you a statement of actual settlement costs. Amounts paid to and by the settlement agent are shown. Items marked "(p.o.c.)" were paid outside the closing; they are shown here for informational purposes and are not included in the totals.

D. Name and Address of Borrower	**E. Name and Address of Seller**	**F. Name and Address of Lender**

G. Property Location	**H. Settlement Agent** Place of Settlement	**I. Settlement Date**

J. Summary of Borrower's Transaction			**K. Summary of Seller's Transaction**		
100.	**Gross Amount Due from Borrower**		**400.**	**Gross Amount Due to Seller**	
101.	Contract sales price		401.	Contract sales price	
102.	Personal property		402.	Personal property	
103.	Settlement charges to borrower (line 1400)		403.		
104.			404.		
105.			405.		
	Adjustments for Items Paid by Seller in Advance			**Adjustments for Items Paid by Seller in Advance**	
106.	City/town taxes to		406.	City/town taxes to	
107.	County taxes to		407.	County taxes to	
108.	Assessments to		408.	Assessments to	
109.			409.		
110.			410.		
111.			411.		
112.			412.		
120.	**Gross Amount Due from Borrower**		**420.**	**Gross Amount Due to Seller**	

No.	Description		Amount	No.	Description		Amount
200.	**Amounts Paid by or in Behalf of Borrower**			**500.**	**Reductions in Amount Due to Seller**		
201.	Deposit or earnest money			501.	Excess deposit (see instructions)		
202.	Principal amount of new loan(s)			502.	Settlement charges to seller (line 1400)		
203.	Existing loan(s) taken subject to			503.	Existing loan(s) taken subject to		
204.				504.	Payoff of first mortgage loan		
205.				505.	Payoff of second mortgage loan		
206.				506.			
207.				507.			
208.				508.			
209.				509.			
	Adjustments for Items Unpaid by Seller				**Adjustments for Items Unpaid by Seller**		
210.	City/town taxes	to		510.	City/town taxes	to	
211.	County taxes	to		511.	County taxes	to	
212.	Assessments	to		512.	Assessments	to	
213.				513.			
214.				514.			
215.				515.			
216.				516.			
217.				517.			
218.				518.			
219.				519.			
220.	**Total Paid by/for Borrower**			**520.**	**Total Reduction Amount Due Seller**		
300.	**Cash at Settlement from/to Borrower**			**600.**	**Cash at Settlement to/from Seller**		
301.	Gross Amount due from borrower (line 120)			601.	Gross amount due to seller (line 420)		
302.	Less amounts paid by/for borrower (line 220)		( )	602.	Less reductions in amt. due seller (line 520)		( )
303.	**Cash** ☐ **From**	☐ **To Borrower**		**603.**	**Cash** ☐ **To**	☐ **From Seller**	

L. Settlement Charges					
700.	**Total Sales/Broker's Commission Based on Price $**		**@ %** =	Paid From Borrower's Funds at Settlement	Paid From Seller's Funds at Settlement
	Division of Commission (line 700) as follows:				
701.	$	to			
702.	$	to			
703.	Commission paid at settlement				
704.					
800.	**Items Payable in Connection with Loan**				
801.	Loan origination fee	%			
802.	Loan discount	%			
803.	Appraisal fee	to			
804.	Credit report	to			
805.	Lender's inspection fee				
806.	Mortgage insurance application fee	to			
807.	Assumption fee				
808.					
809.					
810.					
811.					
900.	**Items Required by Lender to be Paid in Advance**				
901.	Interest from to	@ $	/day		
902.	Mortgage insurance premium for		months to		
903.	Hazard insurance premium for		years to		
904.			years to		
905.					
1000.	**Reserves Deposited with Lender**				
1001.	Hazard insurance	months @ $	per month		
1002.	Mortgage insurance	months @ $	per month		
1003.	City property taxes	months @ $	per month		
1004.	County property taxes	months @ $	per month		
1005.	Annual assessments	months @ $	per month		
1006.		months @ $	per month		

1007.		months @ $	per month		
1008.		months @ $	per month		
1100. Title Charges					
1101.	Settlement or closing fee	to			
1102.	Abstract or title search	to			
1103.	Title examination	to			
1104.	Title insurance binder	to			
1105.	Document preparation	to			
1106.	Notary fees	to			
1107.	Attorney's fees	to			
	(includes above items numbers:		)		
1108.	Title insurance	to			
	(includes above items numbers:		)		
1109.	Lender's coverage	$			
1110.	Owner's coverage	$			
1111.					
1112.					
1113.					
1200. Government Recording and Transfer Charges					
1201.	Recording fees: Deed $	; Mortgage $	; Releases $		
1202.	City/county tax/stamps: Deed $	; Mortgage $			
1203.	State tax/stamps: Deed $	; Mortgage $			
1204.					
1205.					
1300. Additional Settlement Charges					
1301.	Survey	to			
1302.	Pest inspection	to			
1303.					
1304.					
1305.					
1400. Total Settlement Charges (enter on lines 103, Section J and 502, Section K)					

Form **2119**

Department of the Treasury
Internal Revenue Service

Sale of Your Home

▶ Attach to Form 1040 for year of sale.

▶ See separate instructions. ▶ Please print or type.

OMB No. 1545-0072

1994

Attachment Sequence No. **20**

Your first name and initial. If a joint return, also give spouse's name and initial. Last name	Your social security number
Fill in Your Address Only If You Are Filing This Form by Itself and Not With Your Tax Return — Present address (no., street, and apt. no., rural route, or P.O. box no. if mail is not delivered to street address)	Spouse's social security number
City, town or post office, state, and ZIP code	

Part I Gain on Sale

1 Date your former main home was sold (month, day, year) . . . . . ▶ **1** / /

2 Have you bought or built a new main home? . . . . . ☐ Yes ☐ No

3 If any part of either main home was ever rented out or used for business, check here ▶ ☐ and see instructions.

4 Selling price of home. Do not include personal property items you sold with your home . . **4**

5 Expense of sale (see instructions) **5**

6 Subtract line 5 from line 4 . . . . . **6**

7 Adjusted basis of home sold (see instructions) **7**

8 **Gain on sale.** Subtract line 7 from line 6 . . . . . **8**

Is line 8 more than zero?

- **Yes** ▶ If line 2 is "Yes," you **must** go to Part II or Part III, whichever applies. If line 2 is "No," go to line 9.
- **No** ▶ **Stop** and attach this form to your return.

9 If you haven't replaced your home, do you plan to do so within the **replacement period** (see instructions)? ☐ Yes ☐ No

- If line 9 is "Yes," stop here, attach this form to your return, and see **Additional Filing Requirements** in the instructions.
- If line 9 is "No," you **must** go to Part II or Part III, whichever applies.

Part II One-Time Exclusion of Gain for People Age 55 or Older—By completing this part, you are electing to take the one-time exclusion (see instructions). If you are not electing to take the exclusion, go to Part III now.

10 Who was age 55 or older on the date of sale? . . . . . ☐ You ☐ Your spouse ☐ Both of you

11 Did the person who was age 55 or older own and use the property as his or her main home for a total of at least 3 years (except for short absences) of the 5-year period before the sale? If "No," go to Part III now . . ☐ Yes ☐ No

12 At the time of sale, who owned the home? . . . . ☐ You ☐ Your spouse ☐ Both of you

13 Social security number of spouse at the time of sale if you had a different spouse from the one above. If you were not married at the time of sale, enter "None" . . . . ▶ **13** ____ : ____ : ____

14 **Exclusion.** Enter the **smaller** of line 8 or $125,000 ($62,500 if married filing separate return). Then, go to line 15 . . . . **14**

Part III Adjusted Sales Price, Taxable Gain, and Adjusted Basis of New Home

15 If line 14 is blank, enter the amount from line 8. Otherwise, subtract line 14 from line 8 . . . **15**

- If line 15 is zero, stop and attach this form to your return.
- If line 15 is more than zero and line 2 is "Yes," go to line 16 now.
- If you are reporting this sale on the installment method, stop and see the instructions.
- All others, stop and **enter the amount from line 15 on Schedule D, col. (g), line 4 or line 12.**

16 Fixing-up expenses (see instructions for time limits) **16**

17 If line 14 is blank, enter amount from line 16. Otherwise, add lines 14 and 16 . . . . . . **17**

18 **Adjusted sales price.** Subtract line 17 from line 6 . . . . **18**

19a Date you moved into new home ▶ ____ / ____ / ____ **b** Cost of new home (see instructions) **19b**

20 Subtract line 19b from line 18. If zero or less, enter -0- **20**

21 **Taxable gain.** Enter the **smaller** of line 15 or line 20 . . . . **21**

- If line 21 is zero, go to line 22 and attach this form to your return.
- If you are reporting this sale on the installment method, see the line 15 instructions and go to line 22.
- All others, **enter the amount from line 21 on Schedule D, col. (g), line 4 or line 12,** and go to line 22.

22 Postponed gain. Subtract line 21 from line 15 . . . . **22**

23 **Adjusted basis of new home.** Subtract line 22 from line 19b **23**

Sign Here Only If You Are Filing This Form by Itself and Not With Your Tax Return

Under penalties of perjury, I declare that I have examined this form, including attachments, and to the best of my knowledge and belief, it is true, correct, and complete.

Your signature	Date	Spouse's signature	Date
▶		▶	

If a joint return, both must sign.

☆ U.S. GPO:1994-375-330

Printed on recycled paper

Form **3903**

Department of the Treasury
Internal Revenue Service

Moving Expenses

▶ **Attach to Form 1040.**

▶ **See separate instructions.**

OMB No. 1545-0062

1994

Attachment
Sequence No. **62**

Name(s) shown on Form 1040 | **Your social security number**

Part I **Moving Expenses Incurred in 1994**

Caution: *If you are a member of the armed forces, see the instructions before completing this part.*

1	Enter the number of miles from your **old home** to your **new workplace** .	1	miles
2	Enter the number of miles from your **old home** to your **old workplace** . .	2	miles
3	Subtract line 2 from line 1. Enter the result but not less than zero . . .	3	miles

Is line 3 at least 50 miles?

Yes ▶ Go to line 4. Also, see **Time Test** in the instructions.

No ▶ You **cannot** deduct your moving expenses incurred in 1994. Do not complete the rest of this part. See the **Note** below if you also incurred moving expenses before 1994.

4	Transportation and storage of household goods and personal effects	4	
5	Travel and lodging expenses of moving from your old home to your new home. **Do not** include meals	5	

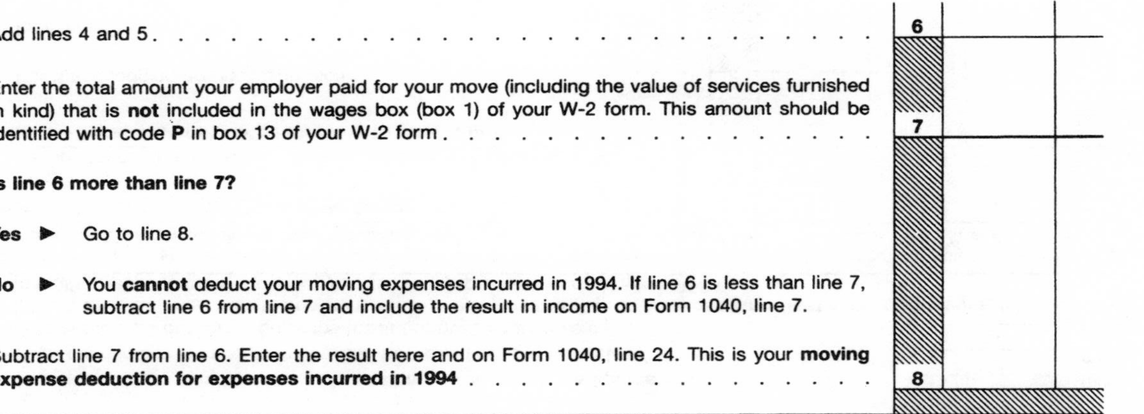

6	Add lines 4 and 5	**6**	
7	Enter the total amount your employer paid for your move (including the value of services furnished in kind) that is **not** included in the wages box (box 1) of your W-2 form. This amount should be identified with code **P** in box 13 of your W-2 form	**7**	
	Is line 6 more than line 7?		
	Yes ▶ Go to line 8.		
	No ▶ You **cannot** deduct your moving expenses incurred in 1994. If line 6 is less than line 7, subtract line 6 from line 7 and include the result in income on Form 1040, line 7.		
8	Subtract line 7 from line 6. Enter the result here and on Form 1040, line 24. This is your **moving expense deduction for expenses incurred in 1994**	**8**	

Note: *If you incurred moving expenses* ***before 1994*** *and you did not deduct those expenses on a prior year's tax return, complete Parts II and III on the back to figure the amount, if any, you may deduct on* **Schedule A,** *Itemized Deductions.*

Name(s) shown on Form 1040. Do not enter name and social security number if shown on other side. | **Your social security number**

Caution: *If you are a member of the armed forces, see the instructions before completing Parts II and III.*

Part II Moving Expenses Incurred Before 1994

1 Enter the number of miles from your **old home** to your **new workplace** . . . . | 1 | miles

2 Enter the number of miles from your **old home** to your **old workplace** . . . . | 2 | miles

3 Subtract line 2 from line 1. Enter the result but not less than zero . . . . ▶ | 3 | miles

If line 3 is 35 or more miles, complete the rest of this part and Part III. Also, see **Time Test** in the instructions. If line 3 is less than 35 miles, you **cannot** deduct your moving expenses incurred before 1994.

Note: *Any payments your employer made for your moving expenses incurred before 1994 (including the value of any services furnished in kind) should be included as wages on your W-2 form. Report that amount on* ***Form 1040, line 7.***

Section A—Transportation of Household Goods

4 Transportation and storage of household goods and personal effects. . . . . | 4 |

Section B—Expenses of Moving From Old To New Home

5 Travel and lodging **not** including meals . . . . | 5 |

6 Total meals . . . . | 6 |

7 Multiply line 6 by 80% (.80) . . . . | 7 |

8 Add lines 5 and 7 . . . . | 8 |

Section C—Pre-move Househunting Expenses and Temporary Quarters
(for any 30 days in a row after getting your job)

9	Pre-move travel and lodging **not** including meals	9	
10	Temporary quarters expenses **not** including meals	10	
11	Total meal expenses for both pre-move househunting and temporary quarters — 11		
12	Multiply line 11 by 80% (.80)	12	
13	Add lines 9, 10, and 12	13	

Section D—Qualified Real Estate Expenses

14	Expenses of (check one) **a** ☐ selling or exchanging your old home, or **b** ☐ if renting, settling an unexpired lease.	14	
15	Expenses of (check one) **a** ☐ buying your new home, or **b** ☐ if renting, getting a new lease.	15	

Part III **Dollar Limits and Moving Expense Deduction For Expenses Incurred Before 1994**

Note: *If you and your spouse moved to separate homes, see the instructions.*

16	Enter the **smaller** of: • The amount on line 13, or • $1,500 ($750 for certain married individuals filing a separate return—see instructions).	16	
17	Add lines 14, 15, and 16	17	
18	Enter the **smaller** of: • The amount on line 17, or • $3,000 ($1,500 for certain married individuals filing a separate return—see instructions).	18	
19	Add lines 4, 8, and 18. Enter the total here and on Schedule A, line 27. This is your **moving expense deduction for expenses incurred before 1994** ▶	19	

Printed on recycled paper

☆ U.S. GPO:1994-375-361

You should receive a completed copy of this form from the closing agent following the sale of your home.

☐ CORRECTED (if checked)

FILER'S name, street address, city, state, and ZIP code		1 Date of closing	OMB No. 1545-0997 **1994**	**Proceeds From Real Estate Transactions**
		2 Gross proceeds $		
FILER'S Federal identification number	TRANSFEROR'S identification number	3 Address or legal description		**Copy B** **For Transferor** This is important tax information and is being furnished to the Internal Revenue Service. If you are required to file a return, a negligence penalty or other sanction may be imposed on you if this item is required to be reported and the IRS determines that it has not been reported.
TRANSFEROR'S name Street address (including apt. no.) City, state, and ZIP code		4 Transferor received or will receive property or services as part of the consideration (if checked) . . . ▶ ☐		
Account number (optional)		5 Buyer's part of real estate tax (See **Box 5** on back.) $		

Form **1099-S** (Keep for your records.) Department of the Treasury - Internal Revenue Service

APPENDIX III

Resources

Reverse Mortgages

To find out more about reverse mortgages, you may contact the following organizations:

American Association of Retired Persons

Headquarters:
AARP Home Equity Information Center
601 E Street, NW
Washington, DC 20049

You can request the free 47-page booklet, *Homemade Money*, by mailing a postcard with your return address on it.

Federal National Mortgage Association (Fannie Mae)

Fannie Mae has a reverse mortgage program that offers a free information packet to anyone who requests it. They can also tell you more about federally insured reverse mortgage lenders in your area.

Call (800) 732-6643 and ask for the reverse mortgage program.

National Center for Home Equity Conversion

Headquarters:
7373 147th Street West
Apple Valley, MN 55124
(612) 953-4474

Ken Scholen is the director for the National Center for Home Equity Conversion and the author of a book about reverse mortgages. For more information about reverse mortgages, or to purchase a copy of his book, you can call or write the center.

Home Inspectors and Structural Engineers

To find a qualified home inspector or structural engineer to perform a prelisting inspection on your home, you should try one of these sources. Both should be able to refer you to a qualified home inspector or structural engineer in your area.

American Society of Home Inspectors (ASHI)

Headquarters:
85 West Algonquin Road
Suite 360

Arlington Heights, IL 60005-4423
(708) 290-1920

Criterium Engineers

Headquarters:
650 Brighton Avenue
Portland, ME 04102
(207) 828-1969

Criterium Engineers is a nationwide network of professional engineers specializing in home and building inspections. The company publishes a free pamphlet called *Your Home*, which you may find useful.

Consumer Publications

For a list of consumer publications that may be useful to you as a seller, write to Consumer Publications, Pueblo, Colorado, 81003.

Consumer Federation of America (CFA)

Headquarters:
1424 16th Street NW, Suite 604
Washington, DC 20036
(202) 387-6121

The Consumer Federation of America has 240 pro-consumer organizations with an aggregate of 50 million individual members. It is a lobbying group that represents consumer interests on Capitol Hill. It publishes *CFANews* eight times each year. Occasionally, it will copublish a booklet on residential real estate with a related organization.

Council of Better Business Bureaus

Headquarters:
4200 Wilson Boulevard, Suite 800
Arlington, CA 22203
(703) 276-0100

This organization is dedicated to consumers and attempts to be an effective national self-regulation force for business. The headquarters can help you find the bureau nearest you.

National Home Warranty Association

Corporate Headquarters:
National Home Warranty Association
20 Ellerman Road
Lake Saint Louis, MO 63367
(800) 325-8144

The NHWA is the nonprofit trade group representing national companies that write more than 90 percent of the nation's home warranty contracts for pre-existing homes. For more information about home warranties, contact the corporate headquarters.

United Homeowners Association (UHA)

Headquarters:
United Homeowners Association
1511 K Street, NW
Washington, DC 20005
(202) 408-8842

This is the only lobbying group in Washington dedicated to advancing the cause, and protecting the rights, of homeowners. For membership information, write or call the UHA.

Glossary of Real Estate Terms

Abstract (of Title) A summary of the public records affecting the title to a particular piece of land. An attorney or title insurance company officer creates the abstract of title by examining all recorded instruments (documents) relating to a specific piece of property, such as easements, liens, mortages, etc.

Acceleration Clause A provision in a loan agreement that allows the lender to require the balance of the loan to become due immediately if mortgage payments are not made or there is a breach in your obligation under your mortgage or note.

Addendum Any addition to, or modification of, a contract. Also called an amendment or rider.

Adjustable-Rate Mortgage (ARM) A type of loan whose prevailing interest rate is tied to an economic index (like one-year Treasury Bills), which fluctuates with the market. There are three types of ARMs, including one-year ARMs, which adjust every year; three-year ARMs, which adjust every three years; and five-year ARMs, which adjust every five years. When the loan adjusts, the lender tacks a margin onto the economic index rate to come up with your loan's new rate. ARMs are considered far riskier than fixed-rate mortgages, but their starting interest rates are extremely low, and in the past five to ten years, people have done very well with them.

Agency A term used to describe the relationship between a seller and a broker, or a buyer and a broker.

Agency Closing The lender's use of a title company or other party to act on the lender's behalf for the purposes of closing on the purchase of a home or refinancing of a loan.

Agent An individual who represents a buyer or a seller in the purchase or sale of a home. Licensed by the state, an agent must work for a broker or a brokerage firm.

Agreement of Sale This document is also known as the contract of purchase, purchase agreement, or sales agreement. It is the agreement by which the seller agrees to sell you his or her property if you pay a certain price. It contains all the provisions and conditions for the purchase, must be written, and is signed by both parties.

Amortization A payment plan which enables the borrower to reduce his debt gradually through monthly payments of principal and interest. Amortization tables allow you to see exactly how much you would pay each month in interest and how much you repay in principal, depending on the amount of money borrowed at a specific interest rate.

Annual Percentage Rate (APR) The total cost of your loan, expressed as a percentage rate of interest, which includes not only the loan's interest rate, but factors in all the costs associated with making that loan, including closing costs and fees. The costs are then amortized over the life of the loan. Banks are required by the federal Truth-in-Lending statutes to disclose the APR of a loan, which allows borrowers a common ground for comparing various loans from different lenders.

Application A series of documents you must fill out when you apply for a loan.

Application Fee A one-time fee charged by the mortgage company for processing your application for a loan. Sometimes the application fee is applied toward certain costs, including the appraisal and credit report.

Appraisal The opinion of an appraiser, who estimates the value of a home at a specific point in time.

Articles-of-Agreement Mortgage A type of seller financing which allows the buyer to purchase the home in installments over a specified period of time. The seller keeps legal title to the home until the loan is paid off. The buyer receives an interest in the property—called equitable title—but does not own it. However, because the buyer is paying the real estate taxes and paying interest to the seller, it is the buyer who receives the tax benefits of home ownership.
Assumption of Mortgage If you assume a mortgage when you purchase a home, you undertake to fulfill the obligations of the existing loan agreement the seller made with the lender. The obligations are similar to those that you would incur if you took out a new mortgage. When assuming a mortgage, you become personally liable for the payment of principal and interest. The seller, or original mortgagor, is released from the liability, and should get that release in writing. Otherwise, he or she could be liable if you don't make the monthly payments.

Balloon Mortgage A type of mortgage which is generally short in length, but is amortized over twenty-five or thirty years so that the borrower pays a combination of interest and principal each month. At the end of the loan term, the entire balance of the loan must be repaid at once.
Broker An individual who acts as the agent of the seller or buyer. A real estate broker must be licensed by the state.
Building Line or Setback The distance from the front, back, or side of a lot beyond which construction or improvements may not extend without permission by the proper governmental authority. The building line may be established by a filed plat of subdivision, by restrictive covenants in deeds, by building codes, or by zoning ordinances.
Buy Down An incentive offered by a developer or seller that allows the buyer to lower his or her initial interest rate by putting up a certain amount of money. A buy down also refers to the process of paying extra points upfront at the closing of your loan in order to have a lower interest rate over the life of the loan.
Buyer Broker A buyer broker is a real estate broker who specializes

in representing buyers. Unlike a seller broker or conventional broker, the buyer broker has a fiduciary duty to the buyer, because the buyer accepts the legal obligation of paying the broker. The buyer broker is obligated to find the best property for a client, and then negotiate the best possible purchase price and terms. Buyer brokerage has gained a significant amount of respect in recent years, since the National Association of Realtors has changed its code of ethics to accept this designation.

Buyer's Market Market conditions that favor the buyer. A buyer's market is usually expressed when there are too many homes for sale, and a home can be bought for less money.

Certificate of Title A document or instrument issued by a local government agency to a homeowner, naming the homeowner as the owner of a specific piece of property. At the sale of the property, the certificate of title is transferred to the buyer. The agency then issues a new certificate of title to the buyer.

Chain of Title The lineage of ownership of a particular property.

Closing The day when buyers and sellers sign the papers and actually swap money for title to the new home. The closing finalizes the agreements reached in the sales agreement.

Closing Costs This phrase can refer to a lender's costs for closing on a loan, or it can mean all the costs associated with closing on a piece of property. Considering all closing costs, it's easy to see that closing can be expensive for both buyers and sellers. A home buyer's closing costs might include: lender's points, loan origination or loan service fees; loan application fee; lender's credit report; lender's processing fee; lender's document preparation fee; lender's appraisal fee; prepaid interest on the loan; lender's insurance escrow; lender's real estate tax escrow; lender's tax escrow service fee; cost for the lender's title policy; special endorsements to the lender's title policy; house inspection fees; title company closing fee; deed or mortgage recording fees; local municipal, county, and state taxes; and the attorney's fee. A seller's closing costs might include: survey (which in some parts of the country is paid for by the buyer); title insurance; recorded release of mortgage; broker's commission; state, county, and local municipality transfer taxes; credit to the buyer for unpaid real estate taxes and other bills; attorney's fees; FHA fees and costs.

Cloud (on title) An outstanding claim or encumbrance that adversely affects the marketability of a property.

Commission The amount of money paid to the broker by the seller (or, in some cases, the buyer), as compensation for selling the home. Usually, the commission is a percentage of the sales price of the home, and generally hovers in the 5 to 7 percent range. There is no "set" commission rate. It is always and entirely negotiable.

Condemnation The government holds the right to "condemn" land for public use, even against the will of the owner. The government, however, must pay fair market price for the land. Condemnation may also mean that the government has decided a particular piece of land, or a dwelling, is unsafe for human habitation.

Condominium A dwelling of two or more units in which you individually own the interior space of your unit and jointly own common areas such as the lobby, roof, parking, plumbing, and recreational areas.

Contingency A provision in a contract that sets forth one or more conditions that must be met prior to the closing. If the contingency is not met, usually the party who is benefitting from the contingency can terminate the contract. Some common contingencies include financing, inspection, attorney approval, and toxic substances.

Contract To Purchase Another name for Agreement of Sale.

Contractor In the building industry, the contractor is the individual who contracts to build the property. He or she erects the structure and manages the subcontracting (to the electrician, plumber, etc.) until the project is finished.

Conventional Mortgage A conventional mortgage means that the loan is underwritten by banks, savings and loans, or other types of mortgage companies. There are also certain limitations imposed on conventional mortgages that allow them to be sold to private institutional investors (like pension funds) on the secondary market. For example, as of 1993, the loan must be less than $203,500, otherwise it is considered a "jumbo" loan. Also, if you are buying a condominium, conventional financing decrees that the condo building be more than 70 percent owner-occupied.

Co-op Cooperative housing refers to a building, or a group of buildings, that is owned by a corporation. The shareholders of the corporation are the people who live in the building. They own shares—which gives them the right to lease a specific unit within the building—in the corporation that owns their building and pay "rent" or monthly maintenance assessments for the expenses associated with living in the building. Co-ops are relatively unknown outside of New York, Chicago, and a few other cities. Since the 1970s, condominiums have become much more popular.

Counteroffer When the seller or buyer responds to a bid. If you decide to offer $100,000 for a home listed at $150,000, the seller might counter your offer and propose that you purchase the home for $140,000. That new proposal, and any subsequent offer, is called a counteroffer.

Covenant Assurances or promises set out in the deed or a legally binding contract, or implied in the law. For example, when you obtain title to a property by warranty, there is the Covenant of Quiet Enjoyment, which gives you the right to enjoy your property without disturbances.

Credit Report A lender will decide whether or not to give you a loan based on your credit history. A credit report lists all of your credit accounts (such as charge cards), and any debts or late payments that have been reported to the credit company.

Cul de Sac A street that ends in a U-shape, leading the driver or pedestrian back to the beginning. The cul de sac has become exceptionally popular with modern subdivision developers, who use the design technique to create quiet streets and give the development a nonlinear feel.

Custom Builder A home builder who builds houses for individual owners to the owners' specification. The home builder may either own a piece of property or build a home on someone else's land.

Debt Service The total amount of debt (credit cards, mortgage, car loan) that an individual is carrying at any one time.

Declaration of Restrictions Developers of condominiums (or any other type of housing unit that functions as a condo) are required to file a condominium declaration, which sets out the rules and restrictions for the property, the division of ownership, and the rights and privileges of the owners. The "condo dec" or "home owner's dec," as it is commonly called, reflects the developer's original intent, and may only be changed by unit-owner vote. There are other types of declarations, including homeowners' association and town house association. Co-op dwellers are governed by a similar type of document.

Deed The document used to transfer ownership in a property from seller to buyer.

Deed of Trust A deed of trust or trust deed is an instrument similar to a mortgage that gives the lender the right to foreclose on the property if there is a default under the trust deed or note by the borrower.

Deposit Money given by the buyer to the seller with a signed contract to purchase or offer to purchase, as a show of good faith. Also called the earnest money.

Down Payment The cash put into a purchase by the borrower. Lenders like to see the borrower put at least 20 percent down in cash, because lenders generally believe that if you have a higher cash down payment, it is less likely the home will go into foreclosure. In recent years, however, lenders have become more flexible about cash down payments; recently, lenders have begun accepting cash down payments of as little as 5 percent.

Dual Agency When a real estate broker represents both the buyer and the seller in a single transaction it creates a situation known as dual agency. In most states, brokers must disclose to the buyer and to the seller whom they are representing. Even with disclosure, dual agency presents a conflict of interest for the broker in the transaction. If the broker is acting as the seller broker and the subagent for the seller (by bringing the buyer), then anything the buyer tells the broker must by law be brought to the seller's attention. If the broker represents the seller as a seller broker and the buyer as a buyer broker in the same transaction, the broker will receive money from both the buyer and the seller, an obvious conflict of interest.

Due on Sale Clause Nearly every mortgage has this clause, which states that the mortgage must be paid off in full upon the sale of the home.

Earnest Money The money the buyer gives the seller up front as a show of good faith. It can be as much as 10 percent of the purchase price. Earnest money is sometimes called a deposit.

Easement A right given by a landowner to a third party to make use of the land in a specific way. There may be several easements on your property, including for passage of utility lines or poles, sewer or water mains, and even a driveway. Once the right is given, it continues indefinitely, or until released by the party who received it.

Eminent Domain The right of the government to condemn private land for public use. The government must, however, pay full market value for the property.

Encroachment When your neighbor builds a garage or a fence, and it occupies your land, it is said to "encroach on" your property.

Encumbrance A claim or lien or interest in a property by another party. An encumbrance hinders the seller's ability to pass good, marketable, and unencumbered title to you.

Escrow Closing A third party, usually a title company, acts as the neutral party for the receipt of documents for the exchange of the deed by the sellers for the buyer's money. The final exchange is completed when the third party determines that certain preset requirements have been satisfied.

Escrow (for Earnest Money) The document that creates the arrangement whereby a third party or broker holds the earnest money for the benefit of the buyer and seller.

Escrow (for Real Estate Taxes and Insurance) An account in which monthly installments for real estate taxes and property insurance are held—usually in the name of the home buyer's lender.

Fee Simple The most basic type of ownership, under which the owner has the right to use and dispose of the property at will.

Fiduciary Duty A relationship of trust between a broker and a seller or a buyer broker and a buyer, or an attorney and a client.
First Mortgage A mortgage that takes priority over all other voluntary liens.
Fixture Personal property, such as a built-in bookcase, furnace, hot water heater, and recessed lights, that becomes "affixed" because it has been permanently attached to the home.
Foreclosure The legal action taken to extinguish a home owner's right and interest in a property, so that the property can be sold in a foreclosure sale to satisfy a debt.

Gift Letter A letter to the lender indicating that a gift of cash has been made to the buyer and that it is not expected to be repaid. The letter must detail the amount of the gift, and the name of the giver.
Good Faith Estimate (GFE) Under RESPA, lenders are required to give potential borrowers a written Good Faith Estimate of closing costs within three days of an application submission.
Grace Period The period of time after a loan payment due date in which a mortgage payment may be made and not be considered delinquent.
Graduated Payment Mortgage A mortgage in which the payments increase over the life of the mortgage, allowing the borrower to make very low payments at the beginning of the loan.

Hazard Insurance Insurance that covers the property from damages that might materially affect its value. Also known as homeowner's insurance.
Holdback An amount of money held back at closing by the lender or the escrow agent until a particular condition has been met. If the problem is a repair, the money is kept until the repair is made. If the repair is not made, the lender or escrow agent uses the money to make the repair. Buyers and sellers may also have holdbacks between them, to ensure that specific conditions of the sale are met.
Homeowner's Association A group of home owners in a particular

subdivision or area who band together to take care of common property and common interests.

Homeowner's Insurance Coverage that includes hazard insurance, as well as personal liability and theft.

Home Warranty A service contract that covers appliances (with exclusions) in working condition in the home for a certain period of time, usually one year. Home owners are responsible for a per-call service fee. There is a home owner's warranty for new construction. Some developers will purchase a warranty from a company specializing in new construction for the homes they sell. A home owner's warranty will warrant the good working order of the appliances and workmanship of a new home for between one and ten years; for example, appliances might be covered for one year while the roof may be covered for several years.

Housing and Urban Development, Department of Also known as HUD, this is the federal department responsible for the nation's housing programs. It also regulates RESPA, the Real Estate Settlement Procedures Act, which governs how lenders must deal with their customers.

Inspection The service an inspector performs when he or she is hired to scrutinize the home for any possible structural defects. May also be done in order to check for the presence of toxic substances, such as leaded paint or water, asbestos, radon, or pests, including termites.

Installment Contract The purchase of property in installments. Title to the property is given to the purchaser when all installments are made.

Institutional Investors or Lenders Private or public companies, corporations, or funds (such as pension funds) that purchase loans on the secondary market from commercial lenders such as banks and savings and loans. Or, they are sources of funds for mortgages through mortgage brokers.

Interest Money charged for the use of borrowed funds. Usually expressed as an interest rate, it is the percentage of the total loan charged annually for the use of the funds.

Interest-Only Mortgage A loan in which only the interest is paid on

a regular basis (usually monthly), and the principal is owed in full at the end of the loan term.
Interest Rate Cap The total number of percentage points that an adjustable-rate mortgage (ARM) might rise over the life of the loan.

Joint Tenancy An equal, undivided ownership in a property taken by two or more owners. Under joint tenancy there are rights of survivorship, which means that if one of the owners dies, the surviving owner rather than the heirs of the estate inherits the other's total interest in the property.

Landscape The trees, flowers, plantings, lawn, and shrubbery that surround the exterior of a dwelling.
Late Charge A penalty applied to a mortgage payment that arrives after the grace period (usually the 10th or 15th of a month).
Lease with an Option to Buy When the renter or lessee of a piece of property has the right to purchase the property for a specific period of time at a specific price. Usually, a lease with an option to buy allows a first-time buyer to accumulate a down payment by applying a portion of the monthly rent toward the down payment.
Lender A person, company, corporation, or entity that lends money for the purchase of real estate.
Letter of Intent A formal statement, usually in letter form, from the buyer to the seller stating that the buyer intends to purchase a specific piece of property for a specific price on a specific date.
Leverage Using a small amount of cash, say a 10 or 20 percent down payment, to purchase a piece of property.
Lien An encumbrance against property, which may be voluntary or involuntary. There are many different kinds of liens, including a tax lien (for unpaid federal, state, or real estate taxes), a judgment lien (for monetary judgments by a court of law), a mortgage lien (when you take out a mortgage), and a mechanic's lien (for work done by a contractor on the property that has not been paid for). For a lien to be attached to the property's title, it must be filed or recorded with local county government.

Listing A property that a broker agrees to list for sale in return for a commission.

Loan An amount of money that is lent to a borrower, who agrees to repay it plus interest.

Loan Commitment A written document that states that a mortgage company has agreed to lend a buyer a certain amount of money at a certain rate of interest for a specific period of time, which may contain sets of conditions and a date by which the loan must close.

Loan Origination Fee A one-time fee charged by the mortgage company to arrange the financing for the loan.

Loan-to-Value Ratio The ratio of the amount of money you wish to borrow compared to the value of the property you wish to purchase. Institutional investors (who buy loans on the secondary market from your mortgage company) set up certain ratios that guide lending practices. For example, the mortgage company might only lend you 80 percent of a property's value.

Location Where property is geographically situated. "Location, location, location" is a broker's maxim that states that where the property is located is its most important feature, because you can change everything about a house, except its location.

Lock-In When a borrower signals to a mortgage company that he or she has decided to lock in, or take, a particular interest rate for a specific amount of time. The mechanism by which a borrower locks in the interest rate that will be charged on a particular loan. Usually, the lock lasts for a certain time period, such as thirty, forty-five, or sixty days. On a new construction, the lock may be much longer.

Maintenance Fee The monthly or annual fee charged to condo, coop, or town house owners, and paid to the homeowners' association, for the maintenance of common property. Also called an assessment.

Mortgage A document granting a lien on a home in exchange for financing granted by a lender. The mortgage is the means by which the lender secures the loan and has the ability to foreclose on the home.

Mortgage Banker A company or a corporation, like a bank, that lends its own funds to borrowers in addition to bringing together lenders and borrowers. A mortgage banker may also service the loan (i.e., collect the monthly payments).

Mortgage Broker A company or individual that brings together lenders and borrowers and processes mortgage applications.

Mortgagee A legal term for the lender.

Mortgagor A legal term for the borrower.

Multiple Listing Service (MLS) A computerized listing of all properties offered for sale by member brokers. Buyers may only gain access to the MLS by working with a member broker.

Negative Amortization A condition created when the monthly mortgage payment is less than the amount necessary to pay off the loan over the period of time set forth in the note. Because you're paying less than the amount necessary, the actual loan amount increases over time. That's how you end up with negative equity. To pay off the loan, a lump-sum payment must be made.

Option When a buyer pays for the right or option to purchase property for a given length of time, without having the obligation to actually purchase the property.

Origination Fee A fee charged by the lender for allowing you to borrow money to purchase property. The fee—which is also referred to as points—is usually expressed as a percentage of the total loan amount.

Ownership The absolute right to use, enjoy, and dispose of property. You own it!

Package Mortgage A mortgage that uses both real and personal property to secure a loan.

Paper Slang usage that refers to the mortgage, trust deed, installment, or land contract.

Personal Property Moveable property, such as appliances, furniture, clothing, and artwork.

PITI An acronym for Principal-Interest-Taxes-and-Insurance. These are usually the four parts of your monthly mortgage payment.

Pledged Account Borrowers who do not want to have a real estate tax or insurance escrow administered by the mortgage servicer can, in some circumstances, pledge a savings account into which enough money to cover real estate taxes and the insurance premium must be deposited. You must then make the payments for your real estate taxes and insurance premiums from a separate account. If you fail to pay your taxes or premiums, the lender is allowed to use the funds in the pledged account to make those payments.

Point A point is one percent of the loan amount.

Possession Being in control of a piece of property, and having the right to use it to the exclusion of all others.

Power of Attorney The legal authorization given to an individual to act on behalf of another individual.

Prepaid Interest Interest paid at closing for the number of days left in the month after closing. For example, if you close on the 15th, you would prepay the interest for the 16th through the end of the month.

Prepayment Penalty A fine imposed when a loan is paid off before it comes due. Many states now have laws against prepayment penalties, although banks with federal charters are exempt from state laws. If possible, do not use a mortgage that has a prepayment penalty, or you will be charged a fine if you sell your property before your mortgage has been paid off.

Prequalifying for a Loan When a mortgage company tells a buyer in advance of the formal application approximately how much money the buyer can afford to borrow.

Principal The amount of money you borrow.

Private Mortgage Insurance (PMI) Special insurance that specifically protects the top 20 percent of a loan, allowing the lender to lend more than 80 percent of the value of the property. PMI is paid in monthly installments by the borrower.

Property Tax A tax levied by a county or local authority on the value of real estate.

Proration The proportional division of certain costs of home ownership. Usually used at closing to figure out how much the buyer and seller each owe for certain expenditures, including real estate taxes, assessments, and water bills.

Purchase Agreement An agreement between the buyer and seller for the purchase of property.

Purchase Money Mortgage An instrument used in seller financing, a purchase money mortgage is signed by a buyer and given to the seller in exchange for a portion of the purchase price.

Quitclaim Deed A deed that operates to release any interest in a property that a person may have, *without a representation that he or she actually has a right in that property*. For example, Sally may use a quitclaim deed to grant Bill her interest in the White House, in Washington, D.C., although she may not actually own, or have any rights to, that particular house.

Real Estate Land, and anything permanently attached to it, such as buildings and improvements.

Real Estate Agent An individual licensed by the state, who acts on behalf of the seller or buyer. For his or her services, the agent receives a commission, which is usually expressed as a percentage of the sales price of a home and is split with his or her real estate firm. A real estate agent must either be a real estate broker or work for one.

Real Estate Attorney An attorney who specializes in the purchase and sale of real estate.

Real Estate Broker An individual who is licensed by the state to act as an agent on behalf of the seller or buyer. For his or her services, the broker receives a commission, which is usually expressed as a percentage of the sales price of a home.

Real Estate Settlement Procedures Act (RESPA) This federal statute was originally passed in 1974, and contains provisions that govern the way companies involved with a real estate closing must treat each other and the consumer. For example, one section of RESPA requires lenders to give consumers a written Good Faith Estimate within three days of making an application for a loan. Another section of RESPA prohibits title companies from giving referral fees to brokers for steering business to them.

Realtist A designation given to an agent or broker who is a member of the National Association of Real Estate Brokers.

Realtor A designation given to a real estate agent or broker who is a member of the National Association of Realtors.

Recording The process of filing documents at a specific government office. Upon such recording, the documents becomes part of the public record.

Redlining The slang term used to describe an illegal practice of discrimination against a particular racial group by real estate lenders. Redlining occurs when lenders decide certain areas of a community are too high risk and refuse to lend to buyers who want to purchase property in those areas, regardless of their qualifications or credit-worthiness.

Regulation Z Also known as the Truth in Lending Act. Congress determined that lenders must provide a written good faith estimate of closing costs to all borrowers and provide them with other written information about the loan.

Reserve The amount of money set aside by a condo, co-op, or homeowners' association for future capital improvements.

Sale-Leaseback A transaction in which the seller sells property to a buyer, who then leases the property back to the seller. This is accomplished within the same transaction.

Sales Contract The document by which a buyer contracts to purchase property. Also known as the purchase contract or a Contract to Purchase.

Second Mortgage A mortgage that is obtained after the primary mortgage, and whose rights for repayment are secondary to the first mortgage.

Seller Broker A broker who has a fiduciary responsibility to the seller. Most brokers are seller brokers, although an increasing number are buyer brokers, who have a fiduciary responsibility to the buyer.

Settlement Statement A statement that details the monies paid out and received by the buyer and seller at closing.

Shared Appreciation Mortgage A relatively new mortgage used to help first-time buyers who might not qualify for conventional financing. In a shared appreciation mortgage, the lender offers a below-market interest rate in return for a portion of the profits made by the home owner when the property is sold. Before entering into a shared appreciation mortgage, be sure to have your real estate attorney review the documentation.

Special Assessment An additional charge levied by a condo or co-op board in order to pay for capital improvements, or other unforeseen expenses.

Subagent A broker who brings the buyer to the property. Although subagents would appear to be working for the buyer (a subagent usually ferries around the buyer, showing him or her properties), they are paid by the seller and have a fiduciary responsibility to the seller. Sub-agency is often confusing to first-time buyers, who think that because the subagent shows them property, the subagent is "their" agent, rather than the seller's.

Subdivision The division of a large piece of property into several smaller pieces. Usually a developer or a group of developers will build single family or duplex homes of a similar design and cost within one subdivision.

Tax Lien A lien that is attached to property if the owner does not pay his or her real estate taxes or federal income taxes. If overdue property taxes are not paid, the owner's property might be sold at auction for the amount owed in back taxes.

Tenancy by the Entirety A type of ownership whereby both the husband and wife each own the complete property. Each spouse has an ownership interest in the property as their marital residence and, as a result, creditors cannot force the sale of the home to pay back the debts of one spouse without the other spouse's consent. There are rights of survivorship whereby upon the death of one spouse, the other spouse would immediately inherit the entire property.

Tenants in Common A type of ownership in which two or more parties have an undivided interest in the property. The owners may or may not have equal shares of ownership, and there are no rights of survivorship. However, each owner retains the right to sell his or her share in the property as he or she sees fit.

Title Refers to the ownership of a particular piece of property.

Title Company The corporation or company that insures the status of title (title insurance) through the closing, and may handle other aspects of the closing.

Title Insurance Insurance that protects the lender and the property owner against losses arising from defects or problems with the title to property.

Torrens Title A system of recording the chain of ownership for property, which takes its name from the man who created it in Australia in 1858, Sir Robert Torrens. While that system was popular in the nineteenth century, most cities have converted to other, less cumbersome, systems of recording.

Trust Account An account used by brokers and escrow agents, in which funds for another individual are held separately, and not commingled with other funds.

Underwriter One who underwrites a loan for another. Your lender will have an investor underwrite your loan.

Variable Interest Rate An interest rate that rises and falls according to a particular economic indicator, such as Treasury Bills.

Void A contract or document that is not enforceable.

Voluntary Lien A lien, such as a mortgage, that a homeowner elects to grant to a lender.

Waiver The surrender or relinquishment of a particular right, claim, or privilege.

Warranty A legally binding promise given to the buyer at closing by the seller, generally regarding the condition of the home, property, or other matter.

Zoning The right of the local municipal government to decide how different areas of the municipality will be used. Zoning ordinances are the laws that govern the use of the land.

Acknowledgments

I have been fortunate in my career as an author and a journalist to have come across real estate professionals who were willing to share their anecdotes, advice, and wisdom about the way homes are bought and sold. I am deeply grateful to the dozens of talented agents, brokers, experts, and observers who have allowed me to share these insights with home buyers and sellers through my books and weekly syndicated column, including: Jo Ann Allen, Dickson Realty; Priscilla Ball, RE/MAX South Suburban; Kristine Blomkvest; Nancy Bohlen, Prudential Preview Properties; John Brady, Coldwell Banker Anchor Real Estate; Jane Byers, Chicago Title & Trust; Tom Corbitt, Tomacor; Joe Duncan, Great Western Financial Corp.; Wayne Falcone, Accurate Home and Building Inspection Service; Ginny Furst, Prudential Preferred Properties; Tom Hathaway, The Buyer's Agent; Dorcas Helfant; Charles Hendrickson, RE/MAX Christina; Robert Herrick, Professional Home Inspectors; Ken Harthausen, PHH US Mortgage Corp.; Susan Bodnar Jeros, Coldwell Banker First American; Ken

Kjer, Century 21 Ken Kjer Realty; John Kinker, Guaranteed Homes, Inc.; Jim Kinney, Rubloff; Burt Klein, Airoom, Inc.; Art Layton, The Hessel Group; Mark Litner, Much Shelist Freed Denenberg & Ament; Pam Morell, People's First Realty; Richard Nash, North Shore Mortgage and Financial Services; Marble Owen, Rubloff; Sam Palormo, Jr., Palormo Realty; Phil Ravid, Ravid & Bernstein; Scott Riegel, RE/MAX Realty Ltd.; Carol Stevens, Century 21 Prime Realty; Barb Tharp, RE/MAX Connection; John Tuccillo, National Association of Realtors; Geoff Ward, Price Club Realty; and Wallis Weinper, La Thomas & Co.

Special thanks to the brokers of Kahn Realty, in Chicago, including David Robins, Elaine Waxman, Rick Druker, and David Hall, from whom I have learned much about buying and selling homes over the past eight years; and to Liz Duncan, of the National Association of Realtors, Kevin Hawkins, of Federal National Mortgage Association, and Roger Cruzan, of Fleishman/Hillard, who never fail to field the fly ball.

I could not have brought this project to life without the guidance, support, and vision of several friends, including my attorney, Ralph Martire, and my agent, Alice Martell, who regaled me with stories of her own sale when my spirits were low. The folks at Times Books have been kind and generous; I am particularly grateful to my publisher, Peter Osnos, associate publisher, Carie Freimuth, Mary Beth Roche, Malka Margolies, Diane Henry, and my editor, Geoff Shandler, for their publishing expertise and endless enthusiasm for this and other projects.

On a personal level, I am grateful for the many friends who put up with the charming idiosyncrasies of my chosen profession, and who have graciously allowed me to dissect their buying and selling experiences in print. Sincere thanks to John Koten, Patrick Clinton, and Steve Rynkiewicz, who continue to push my writing in new directions, and to Wayne Faulkner, Sallie Gaines, and Janet Franz, who have shaped it in the past; to Thea Flaum, who has given me so much time and attention through the years; and to Ann Hagedorn, Henry Ferris, Beth and Mark Kurensky, Brad and Debby Saul, Leo and Genna Galperin, Gerhard Plaschka and Emanuele Trouillot, Judy and Steve Schraiber, Susan Shatkin,

Geoff Kalish, Ellyn Rosen, Karen Egolf, Ellen Shubart, and the members of The Tuesday Night Screenwriter's Group, for their advice and astute suggestions.

My family provides me with ongoing love and encouragement despite unending deadlines, early starts, late nights, missed dinners, and tardy arrivals. I'd like to thank my in-laws, Linda and Simon, Mitch and Alice, Brad and Maru, Judy, and Stanley, and my mother-in-law, Marilyn, for her well-timed phone calls. I'd especially like to thank my sisters, Phyllis and Shona, and my brother-in-law, Jonathan, for understanding when I didn't want to talk shop. My mother, Susanne Glink, still one of the best real estate agents in Chicago, has contributed excellent insights and suggestions over the years, many of which I hope will prove invaluable to the readers of this book. Finally, I would never have finished this book without the unstinting help of my husband and best friend, Samuel J. Tamkin, the world's best real estate attorney, who continues to believe all my wildest dreams will come true.

Index

ABOUT THE AUTHOR

ILYCE R. GLINK is an award-winning nationally syndicated journalist who writes about real estate, business, television, and film. Her work has been published by *Worth* magazine, the *Chicago Sun-Times*, *Chicago Tribune*, *Washington Post*, *Los Angeles Times*, *Working Woman* magazine, *Chicago* magazine, *Electronic Media*, *Crain's New York Business*, *Crain's Chicago Business*, *Interactive Age*, and other publications. Her weekly column, "Real Estate Matters," is read by millions of readers in newspapers published from coast to coast. Her best-selling first book, *100 Questions Every First-Time Home Buyer Should Ask*, was named Best Consumer Reference Book of 1994 by Chicago Women in Publishing. In 1992, Glink was named Best Consumer Reporter by the National Association of Real Estate Editors, and in 1990, she was honored by the National Association of Real Estate Editors for an article on Chicago's building boom of the 1980s. She is currently writing a workbook and computer software for home buyers.